Capitalism in the Web of Life

Jason W. Moore is an environmental historian and political economist in the Department of Sociology at Binghamton University and coordinator of the World-Ecology Research Network.

Capitalism in the Web of Life

Ecology and the Accumulation of Capital

Jason W. Moore

VERSO

London • New York

First published by Verso 2015
© Jason W. Moore

3 5 7 9 10 8 6 4

Verso
UK: 6 Meard Street, London W1F 0EG
US: 20 Jay Street, Suite 1010, Brooklyn, NY 11201
www.versobooks.com

Verso is the imprint of New Left Books

ISBN-13: 978-1-78168-902-8 (PB)
ISBN-13: 978-1-78168-901-1 (HC)
eISBN-13: 978-1-78168-904-2 (US)
eISBN-13: 978-1-78168-903-5 (UK)

British Library Cataloguing in Publication Data
A catalogue record for this book is available from the British Library

Library of Congress Cataloging-in-Publication Data

Moore, Jason W.
Capitalism in the web of life : ecology and the accumulation of capital / Jason W. Moore. — 1st Edition.
pages cm
ISBN 978-1-78168-902-8 (paperback) — ISBN 978-1-78168-901-1 (hardcover) — ISBN 978-1-78168-904-2 (ebook : US) — ISBN 978-1-78168-904-2 (ebook : UK)
1. Economic development—Environmental aspects. 2. Economic policy—Environmental aspects. 3. Environmental policy. I. Title.
HD75.6.M66 2015
333.7—dc23
2015013430

Typeset in Minion Pro by Hewer Text UK Ltd, Edinburgh, Scotland
Printed in the US by Maple Press

For Malcolm,
Who inspired this book.

And for his generation,
may they may find the inspiration they need to see
themselves and the world as One,
and to change it accordingly.

And for Diana,
Who made it all possible.

CONTENTS

ACKNOWLEDGMENTS   ix

INTRODUCTION: The Double Internality: History as if Nature Matters   1

PART I: FROM DUALISM TO DIALECTICS: CAPITALISM AS WORLD-ECOLOGY

1. From Object to *Oikeios*: Environment-Making in the Capitalist
World-Ecology   33
2. Value in the Web of Life   51
3. Towards a Singular Metabolism: From Dualism
to Dialectics in the Capitalist World-Ecology   75

PART II: HISTORICAL CAPITALISM, HISTORICAL NATURE

4. The Tendency of the Ecological Surplus to Fall   91
5. The Capitalization of Nature, or, The Limits
of Historical Nature   111
6: World-Ecological Revolutions: From Revolution to Regime   141

PART III: HISTORICAL NATURE AND THE ORIGINS OF CAPITAL

7. Anthropocene or Capitalocene?: On the Nature and
Origins of Our Ecological Crisis   169
8. Abstract Social Nature and the Limits to Capital   193

PART IV: THE RISE AND DEMISE OF CHEAP NATURE

9. Cheap Labor?: Time, Capital, and the Reproduction of
Human Nature   221
10. The Long Green Revolution: The Life and Times
of Cheap Food in the Long Twentieth Century   241

CONCLUSION: The End of Cheap Nature?   291

INDEX   307

Acknowledgments

This book is an invitation. It is offered as an opening to conversation, and an incitement to serious debate, over humanity's place in nature, and how our thinking about this place in nature shapes our view of history, our analysis of the present crisis, and the politics of liberation for *all* life.

Capitalism in the Web of Life is, perhaps more than most, the product of an extended and sustained global conversation. There are many fingerprints on this book. Some are more obvious than others. Observations and reflections from a great many colleagues—many encountered through gracious invitations to give talks at universities in North America, Europe, and China—have made their way into the book. Audiences forced me to think in new ways; even when we have not agreed, their questions and critiques sharpened this book's clarity in unexpected, and deeply appreciated, ways. So too the extraordinary contributions of the intellectual fields on which I build: environmental and economic history, world history and world-systems analysis, political ecology and critical human geography, Marxist feminism, global political economy, agro-food and critical development studies, and many, many more. It is with great respect and admiration for a half-century of radical scholarship that I have sought to build out and synthesize the dialectical implications of these fields (and not just these) for the study of humanity-*in*-nature.

Capitalism in the Web of Life reflects two decades of reflection and study at the nexus of two great concerns: the history of capitalism and environmental history. It has been a long, productive, exciting, and often tumultuous, journey. This book's ideas were formulated on both coasts of North America, on both sides of the Atlantic, at eight universities. Diana C. Gildea, my wife, best friend, and co-conspirator, has been with me for all of it. You would not be reading these words—or any of those that follow—without Diana's affirmation that world-ecology, and this book in particular, was a project worth pursuing, and her insistence that the project be pursued with intellectual creativity and rigor.

This journey towards a "unified" theory of historical capitalism and historical nature first took shape out of conversations with John Bellamy Foster two decades ago. Although many of this book's formulations are at odds with John's arguments today, my debt to him as a teacher and colleague is incalculable. From Edumund (Terry) Burke III and Giovanni Arrighi, I learned the strange arts of world history. Terry saved me from taking theory as a substitute for history; Giovanni helped me to see that world history is indispensable to our analysis of the present crisis. Richard Walker—known affectionately as DW to his friends—finally convinced me that geography matters. (I mean: *Geography. Really. Matters.*) And, equally, that the "endless accumulation" could not simply be invoked; a *theory* of capital accumulation had to be central to thinking capitalism's world histories. More than that, DW's rare combination of rigorous scholarship, elemental kindness, and academic good sense has contributed mightily not only to the book's intellectual clarity, but to the conditions under which the book was written. Henry Bernstein encouraged me to do the book with Verso, and his sustained critique—and encouragement—allowed me to sharpen my arguments well beyond what I thought possible.

Numerous colleagues read and commented upon various incarnations of my argument in this book. I am especially grateful to Sharae Deckard, Michael Niblett, Stephen Shapiro, and their wonderful colleagues in the "Warwick diaspora" of world literary studies. They have been a constant source of inspiration and encouragement. In addition to those already mentioned, thanks also to Benjamin D. Brewer, Holly Jean Buck, Jay Bolthouse, Alvin Camba, Christopher Cox, MacKenzie K.L. Moore, Phil McMichael, Mindi Schneider, and Christian Parenti, for comments on these arguments in draft.

I am deeply thankful for an extended family of scholars who have been a party to, though not always in agreement with, the world-ecology argument: Haroon Akram-Losdhi, Elmar Altvater, Farshad Araghi, Marco Armiero, Árni Daníel Júlíusson, Stefania Barca, Jun Borras, Neil Brenner, Sandy Brown, Bram Büscher, Liam Campling, Jennifer Casolo, Eric Clark, Carol Crumley, Barbara Epstein, Samuel Day Fassbinder, Paul Gellert, Kyle Gibson, Pernille Gooch, Alf Hornborg, Erik Jönsson, Shiloh Krupar, Ashok Kumbamu, Rebecca Lave, Richard E. Lee, Larry Lohmann, Birgit Mahnkopf, Andreas Malm, Jessica C. Marx, Daniel Münster, Carl Nordlund, Denis O'Hearn, Kerstin Oloff, Beverly J. Silver, Eric Vanhaute, Michael Watts, Tony Weis, Anna Zalik, and (especially!) Harriet Friedmann, Immanuel Wallerstein, and Dale Tomich. Xiurong Zhao and Gennaro Avallone, both brilliant scholars in their own right, deserve special thanks for book-length translations of my essays, forcing me along the way to clarify fuzzy arguments and murky formulations. (Now *that's* commitment!) My graduate students in the Department of Sociology at Binghamton University also deserve credit: Kushariyaningsih (Wiwit) Boediono, Alvin Camba, Joshua Eichen, Benjamin Marley, Cory Martin, Roberto J. Ortiz, Andy Pragacz, Shehryar Qazi, and Manuel Francisco Varo. Finally, my thanks to Binghamton University and the Department of Sociology, which under William G. Martin's chairmanship offered exceptionally favorable conditions for completing this book. (Thanks, Bill!)

Very special thanks also to my editor, Sebastian Budgen, who put up with all sorts of delays, and who supported this project from the beginning.

Finally, my great thanks to Mike and Mary Anne Hofmann, for raising me in a home where ideas mattered; to Barbara Rose, for being the world's coolest mother-in-law; to Marge Thomas, whose friendship and wisdom sustained this book to completion; and to my father, John W. Moore, who did not live to see this book but I'm sure has been charting its progress all along, and would be very pleased indeed to see a little philosophy mixed in with hard-headed political economy.

Above all, *Capitalism in the Web of Life* has always been my son Malcolm's book, even before his arrival in 2010. I am not certain which—if any—of this book's formulations will stand the test of time. I *am* certain that it is a contribution to the kind of thinking, and the kinds of conversations, necessary if we are to rebuild a world that is not only habitable but just. I dedicate this book to Malcolm and to his generation—and to young people of every age across the world—for their willingness to see the web of life in its mosaic of connectivity and creativity. It is in a new vision and with a new generation, that humanity's extraordinary capacity for creativity and cooperation will find new life, and the rest of the planet with it.

Vestal, New York
December 2014

The Double Internality: History as if Nature Matters

We must recognize in materialism the enthusiastic effort to transcend the dualism which postulates two different worlds as equally substantial and true, [and] to nullify this tearing asunder of what is originally One. (Hegel, 1971)

The human prospect in the twenty-first century is not an altogether happy one. From the outset, our future can be specified at two levels of abstraction. The first is humanity-in-nature. Human engagement with the rest of nature has, over the past decade, reached the point "where abrupt global environmental change can no longer be excluded."[1] The second is capitalism-in-nature. The unfolding crisis of neoliberal capitalism—now in between the *signal* crisis of 2008 and the unpredictable but inevitable onset of terminal crisis—suggests we may be seeing something very different from the familiar pattern. That pattern is one in which new technologies and new organizations of power and production emerged after great systemic crises, and resolved the older crises by putting nature to work in powerful new ways. The neoliberal revolution after the 1970s is only the most recent example. Today, however, it is increasingly difficult to get nature—including human nature—to yield its "free gifts" on the cheap. This indicates we may be experiencing not merely a transition from one phase of capitalism to another, but something more epochal: the breakdown of the strategies and relations that have sustained capital accumulation over the past five centuries. *Capitalism in the Web of Life* is about how the mosaic of relations that we call capitalism work *through* nature; and how nature works *through* that more limited zone, capitalism. This double movement—of capitalism through nature, of nature through capitalism—is what I call the "Double Internality."

Since 2008, the flood of instability and change manifest in the allegedly separate domains of "Nature" and "Society" has become impossible to ignore. This poses problems—often unrecognized—of conceptual language, with the proliferation of crisis language (energy, finance, employment, austerity, climate, food, etc.) creating more, rather than less, uncertainty about the present historical moment. For critical scholars, the rush of world events has overwhelmed many. No new synthesis—*yet*—has emerged. Instead, a broad consensus has taken

---

1   J. Rockström et al., "Planetary Boundaries," *Ecology and Society* 14, no. 2 (2009).

shape. The turbulence of the twenty-first century derives from "converging crises."[2] This convergence's most salient expression is the "triple crisis" of food, energy, and finance.[3] While many prefer a different, or longer, list of crisis categories—surely climate must be included!—the import of environmental factors, conditions, and relations has registered in critical political economy as never before. This is an advance over the crisis discourse of the 1970s, when political ecology and political economy rarely overlapped. The converging crises argument is the highest stage of "Green Arithmetic": political economy plus Nature equals converging crises.

Or does it? My sense of Green Arithmetic is that it appears to work because we assume Society plus Nature add up. But does this assumption hold up under closer examination? *Capitalism in the Web of Life* opens an alternative path. I argue that "Society" and "Nature" are part of the problem, intellectually and politically; the binary Nature/Society is directly implicated in the colossal violence, inequality, and oppression of the modern world; and that the view of Nature as external is a fundamental condition of capital accumulation. Efforts to transcend capitalism in any egalitarian and broadly sustainable fashion will be stymied so long as the political imagination is captive to capitalism's either/or organization of reality. And relatedly, efforts to discern the limits of capitalism today—such discernment is crucial to any anti-systemic strategy—cannot advance much further by encasing reality in dualisms that are immanent to capitalist development.

Green Arithmetic and its language of converging crises does more than misrecognize nature and capitalism. It is unable to grasp the specific working-out of the present turning point. "*The* economy" and "*the* environment" are not independent of each other. Capitalism is not an economic system; it is not a social system; it is *a way of organizing nature*.

We can begin with a guiding distinction about this phrase: "a way of organizing nature." Capitalism's governing conceit is that it may do with Nature as it pleases, that Nature is external and may be coded, quantified, and rationalized to serve economic growth, social development, or some other higher good. This is capitalism *as a project*. The reality—the *historical process*—is radically different. While the manifold projects of capital, empire, and science are busy making Nature with a capital 'N'—external, controllable, reducible—the web of life is busy shuffling about the biological and geological conditions

2   Cf. S. George, "Converging Crises," *Globalizations* 7, no. 1–2 (2010): 17–22; J.B. Foster, "Marx and the Rift in the Universal Metabolism of Nature," *Monthly Review* 65, no. 7 (2013): 1–19.

3   P. McMichael, "The Land Grab and Corporate Food Regime Restructuring," *Journal of Peasant Studies* 39, nos. 3–4 (2012): 681–701.

of capitalism's process. The "web of life" is nature as a whole: *nature* with an emphatically lowercase *n*. This is nature as us, as inside us, as around us. It is nature as a flow of flows. Put simply, humans make environments and environments make humans—and human organization.

There is no widely accepted term for the process through which civilizations, themselves forces of nature, are caught up in the co-production of life. And so Green thinkers, even those who pioneered new ways of seeing and thinking humanity's place in nature, have tended to default to an older vocabulary: Society with a capital 'S'.[4] This is observation more than critique: we are products of our times. And those times are today different, different even from two decades ago. A new paradigm is now possible—it is breaking out all over, especially among younger scholars. I will call that new paradigm *world-ecology*. This book is a contribution to it, though far from an encompassing definition. World-ecology— or whatever name we end up attaching to this paradigm—is not only intellectually, but politically, necessary if we are to meet the challenges of the twenty-first century.

World-ecology makes one old argument, and one new one. On the one hand, the new paradigm unfolds from a rich mosaic of relational thinking about capitalism, nature, power, and history. On the other hand, world-ecology says that the relationality of nature implies a new method that grasps humanity-in-nature as a world-historical process. In this respect, Capra's insistence that the world's crises—debt, biodiversity, poverty, climate—are unified through a "crisis of perception" is correct.[5] But we can take this insistence further. Modernity's structures of knowledge, its dominant relations of power, re/production, and wealth, its patterns of environment-making: these form an organic whole. Power, production, and perception entwine; they cannot be disentangled because they are unified, albeit unevenly and in evolving fashion. World-ecology asks us to put our post-Cartesian worldview to work on the crucible of world-historical transformation—understood not as history from above but as the fundamental co-production of earth-moving, idea-making, and power-creating across the geographical layers of human experience. Our task is to see how these moments fit together, and how their combinations change, quantitatively and qualitatively. From this perspective, I ask the reader to consider capitalism as a *world-ecology*, joining the accumulation of capital, the pursuit of power, and the co-production of nature in dialectical unity. Far from asserting the unfettered

---

4   Cf. D. Harvey, "The Nature of Environment," in *Socialist Register 1993*, (1993), 1–51; F. Capra, *The Turning Point* (New York: Bantam, 1982); C. Merchant, *The Death of Nature* (New York: Harper & Row, 1980).

5   F. Capra, *The Web of Life* (New York: Anchor, 1996), 4.

primacy of capitalism's capacity to remake planetary natures, capitalism as world-ecology opens up a way of understanding capitalism as already co-produced by manifold species, extending even to our planet's geo-biological shifts, relations, and cycles.

The crisis today is therefore not multiple but singular and manifold. It is a not a crisis of capitalism *and* nature but of modernity-*in*-nature. That modernity is a capitalist world-ecology. Rather than collapse distinctions—the danger of Green holism—this perspective allows for the multiplication of questions that turn on the *oikeios*: the creative, generative, and multi-layered relation of species and environment. The *oikeios* names the relation through which humans act—and are acted upon by the whole of nature—in our environment-making. Through the *oikeios*, premised on the dialectic of life-making, we may open new pathways for investigating how capitalism's historical geographies—past and present—are premised on specific configurations of humanity-in-nature. Such a perspective allows us to move beyond the "What?" and the "Why?" of today's crises and towards a deeper understanding of *how* the crisis is likely to unfold in coming decades.

Key to realizing such a deeper understanding is developing a language, a method, and a narrative strategy that puts the *oikeios* at the center. Although the challenge cannot be reduced to conceptual language, neither can we make headway without confronting the problem of language. We must "name the system," to borrow a phrase from the generation of Sixties radicals. If naming can be a first step to seeing, it is also more than a discursive act. In the circumstances of civilizational crisis, as the old structures of knowledge come unraveled without yet being interred, the imperative and the power of fresh conceptual language can become a "material force," as Marx might say.[6] Radicals have been good at this for a long time. The languages of gendered and racial domination have been significantly discredited, if as yet inadequately transcended. But I think the violence of the Nature/Society dualism has been given a pass. By this I mean something different from the Green critique of capitalism's "war on the earth."[7] Rather, I am arguing that the dualism of Nature/Society—with a capital 'N' and a capital 'S'—is complicit in the violence of modernity at its core. Just as we have been learning to move beyond the dualisms of race, gender, sexuality, and Eurocentrism over the past four decades, it is now time to deal with the source of them all: the Nature/Society binary. For this dualism drips with blood and dirt, from its sixteenth-century origins to capitalism in its twilight, every bit as much as the others. Perhaps even more.

---

6 K. Marx, *Critique of Hegel's 'Philosophy of Right'* (Cambridge, UK: Cambridge University Press, 1970 [1843]), 137.

7 J.B. Foster, B. Clark, and R. York, *The Ecological Rift* (New York: Monthly Review Press, 2010).

If the politics of the present conjuncture demand a new vocabulary, the problems run much deeper. The old language—Nature/Society—has become obsolete. Reality has overwhelmed the binary's capacity to help us track the real changes unfolding, accelerating, amplifying before our eyes. And yet, a new language—one that comprehends the irreducibly dialectical relation between human and extra-human natures in the web of life—has yet to emerge. Not for want of trying, I know: cyborgs, assemblages, networks, hybrids, and many more have been offered as a way forward. They *have* pointed the way forward. They have not, however, directly challenged the dualist framing of world history. For those concerned about the earth, its people, and the web of life, the great patterns and processes of modern world history have remained firmly encaged within the prison house of the Cartesian binary. No theoretical critique will open the cage. Such opening requires that we build an alternative to the logic of dualism, and this requires new methodological procedures, narrative strategies, and conceptual language *all at the same time*.

The Cartesian narrative unfolds like this. Capitalism—or if one prefers, modernity or industrial civilization—emerged *out of* Nature. It drew wealth *from* Nature. It disrupted, degraded, or defiled *Nature*. And now, or sometime very soon, Nature will exact its revenge. Catastrophe is coming. Collapse is on the horizon.

How we tell stories of our past, and how we respond to the challenges of the present, are intimately connected. For many environmentalists and Green scholars, the separation of humanity and nature has encouraged a way of thinking about history that privileges what humanity *does to* nature. This way of thinking lends itself quite readily to the catastrophist and collapse narratives that have gained such traction in Green Thought, and among wider scholarly and popular audiences.[8] An alternative begins neither with "humans" nor with "nature" but with the *relations* that co-produce manifold configurations of humanity-in-nature, organisms and environments, life and land, water and air. "History," in this sense, is the history of a "double internality": humanity-in-nature/nature-in-humanity. (And yes, there is a longer history of earth and all the rest that precedes humans.) In this double internality, everything that humans do is *already* joined with extra-human nature *and* the web of life: nature as a whole that includes humans.

This argument is—and at the same time is not—a commonplace. *Capitalism in the Web of Life* builds on the groundbreaking contributions of what I will call Green Thought (an imprudent but necessary generalization). Green Thought, broadly conceived, is that diverse tradition in the humanities and

---

8   Cf. J. Diamond, *Collapse* (New York: Viking, 2004).

social sciences concerned with environmental change, past and present. It comprises some elements of the physical sciences, especially those scholars concerned with planetary change.[9] This book highlights three of Green Thought's defining features: the reduction of humanity to a unified actor; the reduction of market, production, political, and cultural relations to "social" relations; and the conceptualization of Nature as independent of humans, even when the evidence suggests the contrary.

Today, more than forty years after the first Earth Day, there is broad agreement among many environmentally oriented scholars, and most environmentalists, that humans are a part of nature. This is the perspective of humanity-in-nature. What to do with this awareness has been a vexing problem. It is one thing to say that humans are natural forces, and quite another to say that human organizations— families, empires, corporations, markets, and all the rest—are natural forces. Green Thought has embraced the former and resisted the latter. To say that humans are a part of nature feels good. To say that human organization is a part of nature feels wrong to most environmentalists, inside and outside the universities. For critical scholars—Red, Green, and many blends in between—the consensus is clear: capitalism acts upon a nature that operates independently of humanity. (And vice versa.) For a broader public concerned about climate and sustainability, a cognate consensus now reigns: humanity makes a "footprint" on the earth, which must be reduced.

Is the image of nature as passive mud and dirt—a place where one leaves a footprint—really the best metaphor to capture the vitality of the web of life? I think we can do better. This book tries to show that the hardened dualism of Nature/Society is not the only possible distinction. It is not even the best. To say that humans are a part of nature is to highlight the *specificity* of humanity within the web of life—its specific forms of *sociality*,[10] its capacities for collective memory and symbolic production, and much more.

It has been a rocky road indeed to travel from humanity-in-nature to capital-ism-*in*-nature. Does not such a journey deprive us of our ability to distinguish between "good" and "bad" human interactions with the rest of nature? Does it not leave us powerless to explain the specifically human, and the specifically natural, in the contemporary plunge into global crisis?

---

9   Cf. W. Steffen, P.J. Crutzen and J.R. McNeill, "The Anthropocene: Are Humans Now Overwhelming the Great Forces of Nature?" *Ambio* 36, no. 8 (2007): 614–21.

10   We may "distinguish between 'sociality' and 'society'. The latter, as contrasted with the 'sensuous' (sensible) immediateness of the particular individuals, is an abstraction: to grasp it one must transcend this immediateness of the individuals. 'Sociality', however, is actually inherent in every single individual. This is why a society may never be justifiably called 'natural', whereas sociality is rightly defined as man's second nature.' (I. Mészáros, *Marx's Theory of Alienation* [London: Merlin Press, 1970], 175).

I do not think so. This book is an effort to explain why. And it is an attempt to show that a view of humanity as natural force allows us to see new connections between human nature, global power and production, and the web of life. In an era of tightly linked transformations of energy, climate, food and agriculture, labor markets, urbanization, financialization, and resource extraction, the imperative is to grasp the inner connections that conduct flows of power, capital, and energy through the grid of capital accumulation—and in so doing, to shed new light on the limits of that very grid.

So the question bears repeating: If not Nature/Society, then *what*? The alternative, long outlined by Green Thought but rarely (*rarely*) practiced, inverts the Cartesian privileging of substances over relations. Instead of a contemporary world produced by two discrete, interacting, substances—Society and Nature—we might instead look at the history of modernity as co-produced, *all the way down and through*. One substance, Humanity, does not co-produce historical change with another substance, Nature. Rather, the species-specificity of humans is already co-produced within the web of life. Everything that humans do is a flow of flows, in which the rest of nature is always moving through us. The forms of sociality that we evolve reflect a species-specificity that is unusually plastic. In this, "consciousness" is not outside but inside. Consciousness itself is a "state of matter."[11] The stories of human organization are co-produced by *bundles* of human and extra-human nature. Humans build empires on their own as much as beavers build dams on their own. Both are "ecosystem engineers."[12] Neither exists in a vacuum.

To "bundle," however, does not carry us nearly far enough. Even this metaphor inadequately grasps the intimacy, porosity, and permeability of humans and human organizations within the web of life. Absent a conceptual vocabulary that names the relations—rather than the end-points of Nature/Society—we will tend to default to a binary that reasserts the independence of human and extra-human natures. We must have a way of naming—and building the conversation through—the relation of life-making. In this relation, species make environments, and environments make species. It is a relation open to inorganic phenomena as well: plate tectonics, orbital variation, meteors, and much more "make" environments too. So we begin with an open conception of life-making, one that views the boundaries of the organic and inorganic as ever-shifting.[13] It is a multi-layered relation

---

11   M. Tegmark, "Consciousness as a State of Matter," *arXiv* 1401, no. 1219v2 (2014).

12   J. Wright and C. Jones, "The Concept of Organisms as Ecosystem Engineers Ten Years On," *BioScience* 56, no. 3 (2006): 203–9.

13   C. Birch, and J.B. Cobb, *The Liberation of Life* (Cambridge: Cambridge University Press, 1981).

through which there are no basic units, only webs within webs of relations: "worlds within worlds."[14]

THE *OIKEIOS*: TOWARDS ENVIRONMENT-MAKING

Capitalism in the Web of Life takes flight by naming this relation of life-making: the *oikeios*. From this relation—as much methodological orientation as ontological claim—we can see manifold species-environment configurations emerge, evolve, and ultimately become something else entirely. In what follows, ecology, nature, and all manner of cognate phrases derive from the *oikeios*. To be clear, the *oikeios* is a relation that includes humans, and one through which human organization evolves, adapts, and transforms. Human organization is at once product and producer of the *oikeios*: it is the shifting configuration of this relation that merits our attention. In this spirit I understand "capital" and "capitalism" as producers and products of the *oikeios*. Capitalism as *world-ecology* is therefore not the ecology of the world, but a patterned history of power, capital, and nature, dialectically joined.[15]

As we see in Chapter One, the concept of the *oikeios* goes back to Theophrastus. My usage extends the concept, drawing on trailblazing insights, from scholars

---

14   R.E. Ley et al., "Worlds within Worlds: Evolution of the Vertebrate Gut Microbiota," *Nature Reviews Microbiology* 6, no.10 (2008): 776–88.

15   The original formulation of capitalism as world-ecology dates back more than a decade (Moore, "Capitalism as World-Ecology," 2003), but the present argument is possible only because the world-ecology perspective has taken on a life of its own. The contributions of this book have been facilitated by a community of world-ecology scholars whose distinctive elaborations, powerful insights, and comradely encouragements have given this book a richness that would have been otherwise impossible: G. Avallone, "Tra finanziarizzazione e processi ecologici," *Sociologia Urbana e Rurale*, no. 101 (2013): 85–99; S. Deckard, "Mapping the World-Ecology," *Ecologies Technics and Civilizations*, (forthcoming); M. Niblett, "World-Economy, World-Ecology, World Literature," *Green Letters*, 16, no. 1 (2012): 15–30; C.R. Cox, *Synthesizing the Vertical and the Horizontal: A World-Ecological Analysis of 'the' Industrial Revolution* (M.Sc. thesis, Portland State University, 2014); A.G. Jakes, *State of the Field: Agrarian Transformation, Colonial Rule, and the Politics of Material Wealth in Egypt, 1882–1914* (PhD Diss., New York University, 2015); B. Marley, "The Coal Crisis in Appalachia: Agrarian Transformation, Commodity Frontiers, and the Geographies of Capital," *Journal of Agrarian Change* (2015, early view); Roberto José Ortiz, "Latin American Agro-Industrialization, Petrodollar Recycling, and the Transformation of World Capitalism in the Long 1970s," *Critical Sociology* (2014) online first; C. Parenti, "Environment Making State," *Antipode* (early view); Tony Weis, *The Ecological Hoofprint: The Global Burden of Industrial Livestock* (London: Zed, 2013).

across the Two Cultures, on dialectical method.[16] Naming the relation through which the mosaic of species-environment configurations form and re-form—above all those swirling around (and within) humanity—is indispensable. To go forward without naming the relation is to end up where we began: re-labeling Society and Nature as human and extra-human nature.

The *oikeios* lets us ask two important questions from the beginning. Both invert Green Thought's most basic questions: How did humanity become separated from nature? And how do humans disrupt nature, causing environmental degradation? (And eventually, crisis?) From the perspective of the *oikeios*, we are led to very different questions. First, how is humanity *unified* with the rest of nature within the web of life? Second, how is human history a *co-produced* history, through which humans have put nature to work—including other humans—in accumulating wealth and power?

The first question—how is humanity *unified* with and within nature?—encourages us to ask how specific human organizations are premised on internal variation realized through the web of life. There is a widespread conviction among critical scholars that Nature/Society is the best way to highlight the specificity of "social" relations. Holism seems to obscure this. But holism only obscures specificity when severed from a dialectical method. Dualism is a blunt instrument for discerning specificity. The most elementary forms of differentiation—let us say, class, race, and gender, although this hardly exhausts matters—unfold as bundles of human and extra-human natures, interweaving biophysical and symbolic natures at every scale. The relations of class, race, and gender unfold through the *oikeios*; they are irreducible to the aggregation of their so-called social and ecological dimensions. And if I have framed the point through the *oikeios*—which permits an alternate way of seeing differentiation—the elements of the argument have been with us for a long time. Modern class relations emerge through early capitalism's primitive accumulation—an audacious movement of environment-making if there ever was one. Modern gender relations were forged through this same process of capitalist agrarian transformation—on both sides of the Atlantic—and symbolically encoded, not least through the era's successive scientific revolutions.[17] Modern racism was born of the transatlantic slave trade, the human pivot of the sugar commodity frontier: among the era's decisive motors of capital accumulation and greatest commodity-centered force for landscape transformation that humanity had ever seen.[18]

---

16   Cf. B. Ollman, *Alienation* (Cambridge: Cambridge University Press, 1971); R. Levins and R. Lewontin, *The Dialectical Biologist* (Cambridge, MA: Harvard University Press, 1985).

17   Cf. Merchant, *The Death of Nature* (1980).

18   Moore, "Ecology and the Rise of Capitalism," Ph.D. dissertation (Department of Geography, University of California, Berkeley, 2007).

I write these words because some may be tempted to read this argument as another case of *big history* and *big theory*. In my view, there is no such thing as big history or big theory, only history and theory that informs our knowledge of historical-geographical patterns. These may be patterns that obtain over large and small space, long or short *durées*. Patterns of class, race, and gender—and of course, others—can be made more sensible through a method that seeks to pinpoint the rules and patterns of reproducing power and wealth, production and reproduction, in specific historical systems ... and specific historical natures. (Such systems are, to be sure, multi-layered and uneven.) And if these rules have often been called structural, I prefer a different metaphor: civilizations as "coral reefs of human existence," but not only of human existence.[19] Their physical structures, ways of seeing, and methods of producing are born of trillions of creatures reproducing daily and intergenerational life.

My focus in this book is trained upon capitalist civilization—a co-produced world-ecology of capital, power, and nature. And if the capitalist world-ecology "as a whole" is more than the sum of its parts, it is also surely less. One cannot do everything at once. Whatever insights I have gained stem from a world-ecology perspective—pivoting the *oikeios*—that has allowed me to grapple with the problem of capital accumulation and the transformation of the earth in new ways.

The *oikeios* enables—but on its own does not accomplish—a theory of capital accumulation in the web of life. For me, the *oikeios* is compelling because it allows me to name the relational process implicit in two of the most frequently quoted passages in geographical thought since the 1970s. The first is that capital incessantly drives towards the "annihilation of space by time."[20] Capital seeks to create a world in which the speed of capital flows—its turnover time—constantly accelerates. The privileging of time over space in capital's project is not passive but active: every effort to accelerate turnover time implies a simultaneous restructuring of space. The second is Lefebvre's powerful observation that capital not only occupies, but also *produces*, space.[21] Space is not incidental; the accumulation of capital *is* the production of space. Accumulation crises do not only produce spatial restructuring after the fact; they are, *in themselves*, products and producers of spatial configurations whose contradictions have reached a boiling point. From these two observations, the signal contribution of nearly a half-century of radical geographical thought goes something like this: all social relations

19   I. Wallerstein, *The Modern World-System I* (New York: Academic Press, 1974), 3.

20   K. Marx, *Grundrisse: Introduction to the Critique of Political Economy*, trans. M. Nicolaus (New York: Vintage, 1973), 424.

21   H. Lefebvre, *The Production of Space*, trans. D. Nicholson-Smith (Oxford: Blackwell, 1991).

are spatial relations; social relations develop through, and actively co-produce, space; spatial configurations are always in motion, but are also "fixed" for definite periods of time. Space is, then, not simply "out there" but joins in specific complexes of social relations and "built environments" that shape the possibilities for contingency, but not infinitely so.[22]

When geographers say *space*, may we not also say *nature*? All social relations are spatial relations, relations within the web of life. Socio-spatial relations develop through nature. All species "build" environments—they are "ecosystem engineers." But some engineers are more powerful than others. Humans have been especially powerful. This is not simply because of thought and language—which are of course central—but also because hominid evolution favored distinctive extroversions: a smaller digestive system and the use of fire as an external stomach; a narrower birth canal and community as external womb; less hair and the production of clothing and shelter as external fur. That list could be extended. The point is to highlight the ways in which evolutionary processes were powerfully co-produced: humanity is a species-environment relation.

It is, clearly, also historical. Capitalism's dynamism owes much to a specific, and absurd, way of dealing with this relation: by severing it symbolically, and then acting accordingly. (Thus, what was "natural" became a crucible of legitimation.) This specific and absurd mode of environment-making is revealed in today's biocidal wreckage. For five centuries it has served to liberate, then fetter, then restructure and renew capital accumulation. The attendant accumulation crises have been cyclical—making possible contingent outcomes through crisis—but also cumulative. Importantly, the cumulative trend shapes the possibilities for the cyclical resolution of accumulation crises: a point underscored by contemporary resource depletion and the accumulation of greenhouse gases in the atmosphere.

Like many readers, I suspect, I have little patience with grand theory. No one theory can answer the questions I pose in this book. Only a relational method and made of theorizing will suffice. My intention is to elaborate a method that carries the core insights of Marxism and environmental historiography into a new synthesis. This synthesis says that environment-making is much more than a story of environmental consequences. It is a story of how power and re/production in its quotidian, civilizational, and commercial forms are, *already*, environmental history. Power and production—and so much more—*are* "environmental." This allows us to move from environmental histories *of* modernity

---

22   D. Harvey, *The Limits to Capital* (Chicago: University of Chicago Press, 1982); M. Storper and R. Walker, *The Capitalist Imperative* (New York: Basil Blackwell, 1989); N. Smith, *Uneven Development* (Oxford: Basil Blackwell, 1984); E. Soja, *Postmodern Geographies* (London: Verso, 1989).

to modernity's projects and processes *as* environmental history—as environment-making processes. My point of departure therefore privileges the patterned and the specific. Specificities emerge within world-historical patterns, what I call *historical natures*[23]—even and especially when the topic seems removed from these concerns (e.g. labor, financialization).

Dualism does not allow for greater specificity in our understanding of "social" relations for a very good reason: it takes human differentiation as forming outside the *oikeios*. This comprises not only the accumulation of capital but also enduring patterns of class, gender, race, and nation. Are these not better understood as products and producers of the *oikeios*? From here we may ask, How do humans *fit* into the web of life, understood as a totality of distinctive and interpenetrating evolutionary trajectories? And how are the cycles and trends of human organization subjected to recurrent moments of chaos and restabilization? For me, the implications of privileging the differentiated unities of humanity-in-nature/nature-in-humanity have made it impossible to go back to the dualist view. Rather than separate humans from nature, capitalist civilization has enmeshed individual life-activity into a web of life whose interconnections are much denser, more geographically expansive, and more intimate than ever before. And far from being a recent development, the processes that have turned our breakfasts, our cars, and our working days into world-historical activity find their origins in the "long" sixteenth century (1451–1648).

The unity of humans with the rest of nature gets us part of the way towards a world-ecological reading of human history. And yet, this kind of philosophical statement—humans are a part of nature, and so on—has been around for a long time. The *oikeios* is offered as a bridge between philosophical claim and historical method. The bridge works by inverting the premise of most environmental thought in the humanities and social sciences. Rather than presume humanity's separation, in the recent or distant past, the *oikeios* presumes that humanity has always been unified with the rest of nature in a flow of flows. What changes are the ways in which specific aspects of humanity, such as civilizations, "fit" within nature.

In this book, nature assumes three major forms: human organization; extra-human flows, relations, and substances; and the web of life. These are not independent; rather, they are interpenetrating, and their boundaries and configurations shift in successive historical-geographical eras. This last is pivotal: nature is not "just there." It is *historical*. This way of seeing leads us to a second major inversion. Instead of asking what capitalism *does to* nature, we may begin to ask how nature *works for* capitalism? If the former question implies

---

23   Following Marx and Engels; *The German Ideology* (New York: International Publishers, 1970), 41.

separation, the latter implicates unification: capitalism-in-nature/nature-in-capitalism. It allows us to grapple with a new set of relations, hitherto obscured by the dualism of Nature/Society.

How is nature's work/energy transformed into value? This is the crux of the problem faced by capitalism today. The question shifts our thinking away from too much of one thing (humans, or capitalism) and too little of another thing (Nature), and towards the *longue durée* relations and strategies that have allowed capitalism-in-nature to survive. And capitalism has survived not by destroying nature (whatever this might mean), but through projects that compel nature-as-*oikeios* to work harder and harder—for free, or at a very low cost. Today, it is becoming increasingly difficult to get nature—of any kind—to work harder. Inverting the problem of degradation shifts our initial premise from working *on* to working *through* nature. (And, in turn, to being worked *through* by the web of life.) This opens a new set of questions about how this limit—the limit of putting nature to work—may be a fundamental barrier to capital accumulation in the twenty-first century.

These inversions—of humanity-in-nature, of nature working for capitalism—are dialectical, not mechanical. Hence, the double internality. Capitalism does, of course, impose real and violent transformations on planetary life. But the unilateral model—doing *to* rather than acting *through*—cannot get us where we need to go. It cannot move us towards a deeper, *and more practical*, understanding of capitalism's manifold crisis today. These two inversions open a new vista through which we can explore and reconstruct how capitalism produces new conditions for its recurrent booms, and through which the contradictions that follow have been resolved. By situating these dynamics within the *longue durée* of historical capitalism, we can throw into sharp relief the relation between cyclical movements (phases of capitalism) and the accumulation of socio-ecological contradictions in life, capital, and power over the past five centuries.

Taking the double internality of human organization as our guiding thread, we can begin to reconstruct narratives of two *simultaneous* movements. the first is capitalism's internalization of planetary life and processes, through which new life activity is continually brought into the orbit of capital and capitalist power. The second is the biosphere's internalization of capitalism, through which human-initiated projects and processes influence and shape the web of life. This guiding thread—framed as a double internality—allows us to move beyond a kind of "soft" dualism that re-presents the dialectic of human and extra-human natures as an alternative to Nature/Society.

My focus in this book is capitalism as project and process: the logic of capital and the history of capitalism. This capitalism is not, as we have seen, a narrow set of economic or social relations, since these categories are part of the problem. Capitalism is, rather, best understood as a *world-ecology* of capital, power, and re/production in the web of life. The point of view of capitalism as a whole—and the decisive conditions and contradictions of the accumulation process—is but one possible vantage point. Without a world-historical reconstruction, however, the critique of Nature/Society dualism will remain theoretical when it needs to be methodological and *historical*. My central thesis is that capitalism is historically coherent—if "vast but weak"—from the long sixteenth century; co-produced by human and extra-human natures in the web of life; and cohered by a "law of value" that is a "law" of Cheap Nature. At the core of this law is the ongoing, radically expansive, and relentlessly innovative quest to turn the work/energy of the biosphere into capital (value-in-motion).

The concept of work/energy looms large in this argument. It allows us to pierce the Cartesian fog that surrounds the unity of human and extra-human work.[24] Marx's observation that large-scale industry is a mechanism for turning "blood into capital" was no mere polemic. It was a means of highlighting the ways that the capital-relation transforms the work/energy of *all* natures into a frankly weird crystallization of wealth and power: value (Chapter Two).

Work/energy helps us to rethink capitalism as a set of relations through which the "capacity to do work"—by human and extra-human natures—is transformed into value, understood as socially necessary labor-time (abstract social labor). "Work/energy" (or *potential* work/energy) may be capitalized—as in commodified labor-power via the cash nexus—or it may be appropriated via non-economic means, as in the work of a river, waterfall, forest, or some forms of social reproduction. My conceptualization follows White's view of

> energy as the capacity to do work. Work, in turn, is the product of a force acting on a body and the distance the body is moved in the direction of that force. Push a large rock and you are expending energy and doing work; the amount of each depends on how large the rock and how far you push it. The weight and flow of water produce the energy that allows rivers to do the work

---

24   The origins of this concept and its typography—work/energy—come from Caffentzis, who situates the "energy" and "work" crises of the 1970s within a unified field. Caffentzis' insight was to link "capital's control over work across the planet . . . [to] how energy commodities were . . . used to impose once again the control that capital once had over the work process" (G. Caffentzis, *In Letters of Blood and Fire* [Oakland: PM Press, 2013], 2–3). This points strongly in the right direction. My use of work/energy extends it to capitalism's unified logic of appropriating human and extra-human "work" that is transformed into value.

of moving rock and soil: the greater the volume of water in the river and the steeper the gradient of its bed, the greater its potential energy.[25]

White's sketch is focused on the geophysical work/energy implied in the historical geography of a river (the Columbia, in this instance). But work/energy is also about organic life: from photosynthesis to hunting prey to bearing children. What bears emphasis is *how* the work/energy of the web of life is incorporated into the relations of power and re/production. Food—in capitalism as for all civilizations—is a crucial nexus of all these (see Chapter Ten). The work/energy concept allows us to transcend the metabolic fetish of Green materialism, in which living flows are narrowly biophysical, can be disrupted, and can be subsequently repaired to some Edenic, pristine state. The work/energy alternative sees metabolism through the double internality: flows of power and capital in nature, flows of nature in capital and power. In this, the issue is not "metabolic rift" but *metabolic shift* (Chapter Three).

To this conception of work/energy we may add an outline of labor productivity. Labor productivity is understood in terms of the rate of exploitation and the production of surplus value. The usual Marxist model turns on the relation of machinery and labor-power: more powerful machines allow the average worker to produce more average commodities. Many wrinkles have been added to the model: organizational innovation, labor process rationalization, the impact of transportation, information, and communications technologies. Within this model, the rate of exploitation (surplus value production) increases when the average worker produces a rising mass of value (often, a rising physical volume of commodities), so long as wages increase more slowly than productivity. Alternatively, exploitation may advance when the worker produces a static mass of value, so long as wages decrease. Thus, accumulation may advance on the basis of rising wages and rapidly advancing productivity, as during Fordism, or on the basis of falling (or static) wages and very slow productivity growth, as during the neoliberal era. Part of this dynamic is captured in the classic distinction between relative and absolute surplus value. In this, a twentieth century auto plant would embody relative surplus value (rising labor productivity per hour) whereas textile production in the sixteenth century typifies absolute surplus value, in which the production of surplus value was determined by the number of hours worked, not by rising output per hour.

I worry that this distinction between absolute and relative surplus value has too often been hardened into categorical difference. For one, the usual Marxist thinking on the subject presumes early capitalism as static, certainly not a system characterized by the production of relative surplus value. The great advances of

---

25   R. White, *The Organic Machine* (New York: Hill & Wang), 6.

the nineteenth century obscured the *equally* significant advance in labor productivity after 1450 (see Chapters Seven and Eight). My point, however, extends beyond the historical observation. The reason both Reds and Greens see "real" capitalism emerging after 1800 turns on a reluctance to look at how capital, science, and empire appropriated nature—including the unpaid work/energy of humans—in service to surplus value production. In metals and mining, shipbuilding, agriculture, textiles, and many other strategic sectors of early capitalism, labor productivity advanced dramatically through new techniques and procedures of harnessing nature's bounty. Early capitalism mobilized technical innovation, systemic violence, and symbolic innovation to lengthen the working day *as well as* to produce and appropriate Cheap Nature so as to reduce *de facto* unit labor costs. In such situations—here I think of Norwegian forests or Polish grain or even African slaves—the appropriation of "natural fertility" (Marx) may act like an increase in relative surplus value. Appropriated nature becomes a productive force. If one includes the conquest of the Americas, the direct and indirect implications for labor productivity growth were gigantic. The appropriation of global natures and the accumulation of capital are closely joined through the production of surplus value. From this perspective, we may reasonably ask: Does the ongoing closure of frontiers today signal an exhaustion of capitalism's Cheap Nature strategy, with its prodigious history of appropriating uncommodified nature as a way to advance labor productivity?

These questions suggest a rethinking of value. Value operates through a dialectic of exploitation and appropriation that illuminates capitalism's peculiar relation with, and within, nature. The relations of exploitation produce abstract social labor. The relations of appropriation, producing abstract social nature, enabled the expanded accumulation of abstract social labor. On the one hand, the system turns on a weird coding of what is valuable, installing human work within the commodity system as the decisive metric of wealth. This work is usually conceptualized as wage-labor: a term that I will treat expansively, and not limited to the ideo-typical figure of the proletarian.[26] In this domain, the exploitation of labor-power is the pivot upon which all else turns. On the other hand, the exploitation of wage-labor works only to the degree that its reproduction costs can be checked. The mistake is to see capitalism as defined by wage-labor, any more than it is defined by the world market. Rather, the crucial question turns on the historical-geographical connections between wage-work and its necessary conditions of expanded reproduction. These conditions depend on massive contributions of unpaid work, outside the commodity

---

26   We are justifiably cautious in defining the proletarian relation too narrowly. Modern slavery, for instance, was a form that entwined relations of exploitation and appropriation (S. Mintz, "Was the Plantation Slave a Proletarian?" *Review* 2, no. 1 [1978]: 81–98).

system but necessary to its generalization. Sometimes this is called the domain of social reproduction,[27] although the adjective "social" here seems especially unsuitable—where does the "social" moment of raising children end, and the "biological" moment begin? Clearly, we are dealing with a zone of reproduction that transcends any neat and tidy separation of sociality and biology, which are better viewed as internal to each other. Neither is this zone of reproduction—the domain where unpaid work is produced for capital—a narrowly human affair. For unpaid work not only makes possible the production of potential—or the reproduction of actual—labor-power as "cheap" labor; it also involves the unpaid work of extra-human natures. In this domain of reproduction, the *appropriation* of unpaid work is central (Chapters Two and Nine).

My use of *appropriation* therefore differs from that of Marx, who deployed the term more or less interchangeably with the exploitation of wage-labor. Appropriation, in what follows, names those extra-economic processes that identify, secure, and channel unpaid work outside the commodity system into the circuit of capital. Scientific, cartographic, and botanical revolutions, broadly conceived, are good examples, themes we explore in Chapter Eight. Movements of appropriation, in this sense, are distinct from movements of the exploitation of wage-labor, whose tendential generalization is premised on the generalization of appropriative practices. So important is the appropriation of unpaid work that the rising rate of exploitation depends upon the fruits of appropriation derived from Cheap Natures, understood primarily as the "Four Cheaps" of labor-power, food, energy, and raw materials.

This Cheap Nature project—appropriating uncapitalized nature as the pedestal of labor productivity— cannot be understood as a narrowly economic process. At the heart of modernity's co-productions is the incessant reworking of the boundaries between the human and the extra-human. Yes, the distinction between humans and the rest of nature is longstanding. Never before, however, had a civilization organized around a *praxis* of external nature: a world-praxis in which representations, rationality, and empirical investigation found common cause with capital accumulation in creating Nature as external. The boundary setting between what was, and what was not, "natural" was intellectually arbitrary—and often deeply racist and patriarchal. It was not, however, *historically* arbitrary, but patterned strongly on capital's law of value as a law of Cheap Nature. Consider the tightly bound connection between science and gender across the early modern era;[28] the early sixteenth-century debates between Las Casas and Sepúlveda over

---

27   Cf. I. Bakker and S. Gill, eds., *Power, Production, and Social Reproduction* (New York: Palgrave Macmillan, 2003).

28   Merchant, *The Death of Nature* (1980).

"natural slaves";[29] or the colonial designation of indigenous peoples in the later sixteenth-century Andes and elsewhere as *naturales*.[30] Of course, early capitalism's boundary-setting procedures were more than representational and ideological; they were also bound up with new modes of knowledge production. Bookended by Copernicus and Newton (c. 1470s-1720s) we see "irreversible and fundamental changes . . . [in] Western regimes for the *discovery, development and diffusion of such knowledge . . . radically transformed in scope and scale.*"[31]

But there was more to this than the accelerating "comprehension of the natural world."[32] Such comprehension unfolded within a historical project that aimed at rendering nature external—Nature with a capital 'N'—the better that it could be subordinated and rationalized, its bounty extracted, in service to capital and empire.

As capitalism evolves and restructures, so do the terms of the double internality. Every phase of capitalism has woven together new *and* old strands of the *oikeios*: thus do new historical capitalisms and new historical natures flow together. These historical natures take shape out of modernity's manifold revolutions—scientific, industrial, bourgeois, agricultural, financial, demographic, and all the rest. They unfold through, while creating anew, the *oikeios*.

HISTORICAL NATURE AND THE CARTESIAN REVOLUTION

The *oikeios* points us towards an alternative. Capitalism makes nature. Nature makes capitalism. Both are true, provided we take these as interpenetrated realities in which "capitalism" is co-produced. This is not—emphatically not—the co-production of two separate entities: Humanity and Nature. Capitalism is a co-produced history of human-initiated projects and processes bundled with (and within) specific natures. Historical-geographical specificity is called for at every step. The web of life itself evolves historically. In this, "nature" (and its cognates) is a way of conceptualizing not merely the objects of capitalist activity. For the web of life is more than "taps" and "sinks." It is the field upon which capitalism unfolds. And we can go still further. Nature is no static field,

---

29   B. Tierney, *The Idea of Natural Rights* (Atlanta: Scholars Press, 1997).

30   Stavig, "Ambiguous Visions," *Hispanic American Historical Review* 80, no. 1 (2000): 77–111.

31   P. O'Brien, "Historical Foundations for a Global Perspective on the Emergence of a Western European Regime for the Discovery, Development and Diffusion of Useful and Reliable Knowledge," *Journal of Global History* 8, no. 1 (2013): 15. Emphasis added.

32   Ibid.

but is itself renewing and evolving in cyclical and cumulative fashion. Nature is, above all, *historical.*

This means two things. First, capitalism does not "produce" nature in a linear fashion, but is an evolving whole that joins the accumulation of capital, the pursuit of power, and the co-production of nature. Second, capitalism is not a structurally invariant, monolithic Society, acting upon a structurally invariant, external Nature. Rather, the history of capitalism is one of successive *historical natures,* which are both producers *and* products of capitalist development. The point is elementary but underappreciated. At a time when no serious critical scholar would undertake a study of neoliberal capitalism by using "production in general,"[33] much of Green Thought continues to embrace a notion of "nature in general." This point may seem far removed from contemporary political questions. I wish to suggest that it is anything but. For the concept of "nature in general" has made it easy for many scholars and activists to embrace the apocalyptic imaginaries of catastrophe and collapse. Absent the specification of historical natures that encompass humanity, nature-in-general has driven Green politics into an "either/or" position: sustainability or collapse.[34]

Although the distinction between humans and the rest of nature has a long history that predates capitalism, the construct of Nature/Society is thoroughly modern. The notion that social relations (humans without nature) can be analyzed separately from ecological relations (nature without humans) is the ontological counterpoint to the real and concrete separation of the direct producers from the means of production. From this perspective, revolutions in ideas of nature and their allied scientific practices are closely bound to great waves of primitive accumulation, from early modernity's Scientific Revolution to neoliberalism's genomic revolutions (Chapter Eight, "Abstract Social Nature").

I have called this Nature/Society dualism Cartesian. The term *Cartesian* derives from René Descartes' famous argument about the separation of mind and body. I use it to name philosophical and analytical worldviews—and modes of enquiry—that conceptualize society and nature as ontologically discrete. These worldviews emerged during an era of "scientific revolution." We might also call it a Cartesian revolution. This revolution did three major things. It "imposed an ontological status upon entities (substance) as opposed to relationships (that is to say energy, matter, people, ideas and so on became things)." Second, "it imposed . . . a line in which a logic of either/or (rather than both/

---

33   Marx, *Grundrisse* (1973), 85.
34   Cf. R. Costanza et al, "Sustainability or Collapse," *Ambio* 36, no. 7 (2007): 522–7.

and) predominated.[35] And finally, it strongly favored the "idea of a purposive control over nature through applied science."[36]

Descartes hardly stands alone; he represents a broader historical movement towards the dualisms at the core of bourgeois thought. The emergence of Nature—*the* environment—was a symbolic-material process that began at least a century before Descartes, and continues to this day. One can quibble about names, but Descartes' biography is instructive: he wrote most of his major works between 1629 and 1649 while living in the Dutch Republic, the "model capitalist nation of the seventeenth century," and the epicenter of a world-ecological revolution that stretched from Southeast Asia to the north Atlantic.[37]

The relation between Descartes and Dutch capitalism is worth emphasizing, since new ideas of nature and the material transformations of capitalism are closely joined. The example of Descartes illustrates how different phases of capitalism—*as* environmental history—entail not only massive deforestation, pollution, food insecurity, and resource exhaustion, but also implicate new ways of seeing the world. Viewed in this light, the systematizing thrust of Descartes' intellectual endeavors—his concern for the "systematic rationality of the universe"[38]—can be viewed as both symptomatic of, and contributing to, the seventeenth century's massive reorganization of power, capital, and nature. If the accumulation of capital is the proletarianization of labor,[39] it is also the production of knowledges aimed at controlling, mapping, and quantifying the worlds of commodification and appropriation. For early modern materialism, the point was not only to interpret the world but to control it: "to make ourselves as it were the masters and possessors of nature."[40] In the history of capitalism, the "material" and the "symbolic" form an organic whole.

Cartesian dualism is a peculiar creature. These abstractions of Nature/Society separate symbolically what is unified practically in the history of capitalism: the life activity of the human species in the web of life. On the one hand, the binary is clearly falsifying and confused. It presumes an ontological separation that animates

---

35   M.J. Watts, "Nature: Culture," in *Spaces of Geographical Thought*, eds. P. Cloke and R. Johnston (London, Sage, 2005), 150–1.

36   C. Glacken, *Traces on the Rhodian Shore* (Berkeley: University of California Press, 1967), 427.

37   Marx, *Capital*, Vol. I, trans. B. Fowkes (New York: Vintage, 1977), 916; J. W. Moore, "'Amsterdam Is Standing on Norway' Part II: The Global North Atlantic in the Ecological Revolution of the Long Seventeenth Century," *Journal of Agrarian Change* 10, no. 2 (2010).

38   W.J. Bouwsma, *A Usable Past* (Berkeley: University of California Press, 1990), 123.

39   Marx, *Capital*, Vol. I (1977), 763–4.

40   R. Descartes, *A Discourse on the Method of Correctly Conducting One's Reason and Seeking Truth in the Sciences* (Oxford: Oxford University Press, 2006 [1637 orig.]), 51.

historical narratives in which relations between human ("social" relations) are theoretically independent of relations between humans and the rest of nature. The binary, moreover, confuses particular natures that are objects of capitalist development with nature as the matrix within which capitalism develops. Nature/Society forms a binary of violent abstractions in Sayer's sense of the term[41]—removing constitutive relations from the historical phenomena under investigation. One can no more extract "nature" from the constitution of capitalism than one could remove law, class struggle, the modern state, science, or culture.

On the other hand, a binary that is empirically falsifying does not deprive it of real historical force. Here the Cartesian binary is an "abstraction not as a mere mask, fantasy, or diversion, but as a force operative in the world."[42] The Cartesian binary is a curious sort of real abstraction, created out of the dialectic of value formation as abstract social labor and abstract social nature. It is an abstraction born of—and immanent to—capitalist development, with deep roots in early modern materialist and scientific revolutions, even as the "household concepts" of society, economy, and ecology assumed familiar form only after the nineteenth-century triumph of British capitalism.[43] Thus, an unorthodox value-relational approach regards the modernist cognition of the world—which I shorthand as the Cartesian binary—as constitutive of the bizarre disciplines and environment-making patterns inherent in regimes of abstract social labor. Cognition, too, must be grasped as a "material force" under conditions of bourgeois hegemony. Such a value approach does not dissolve the differences between symbolic and material, human and extra-human re/production—nor between the "economic" moment of abstract social labor and the "symbolic" moment of abstract social nature. Instead, I take such cohered differences as my starting point, without however collapsing the tension between the abstract and the concrete in human environment-making.

WORLD-ECOLOGY: *WHAT'S IN A NAME?*

If, as Marx proposes, humans are themselves "natural forces" and "natural beings"; if humans linked to nature as "nature is linked to itself"; if humans, in our life-activity, transform "external nature" through work, in so doing

---

41   D. Sayer, *The Violence of Abstraction* (Oxford: Blackwell, 1987).

42   A. Toscano, "The Open Secret of Real Abstraction," *Rethinking Marxism* 20, no. 2 (2008): 274.

43   Cf. E. Wolf, "Inventing Society," *American Ethnologist* 15, no. 4 (1988): 752–761; T. Mitchell, *Rule of Experts* (Berkeley: University of California Press, 2002); J.B. Foster and B. Clark, "The Sociology of Ecology," *Organization and Environment* 21, no.3 (2008): 311–352.

transform our "own nature" . . . If all these hold, *philosophically*, then they ought to hold theoretically and methodologically. If they are plausible, the relations of humanity-in-nature ought to be fundamental to the stories we tell about our past, and about our possible futures. To follow through on Marx's philosophy of internal relations is to grasp historical change as co-produced by humans and the rest of nature—but not as two interacting boxes, or even overlapping circles in the well-worn style of a Venn Diagram. The dialectical thrust of Marx's philosophy is to see humanity/nature as a flow of flows: as humans internalizing the whole of nature, and the whole of nature internalizing humanity's mosaic of difference and coherence.

This is a challenge to the conceit of Cartesian dualism.

This conceit does not hold up well under close examination. Do a Google search. Get on an airplane. Shop for groceries. Pick up your child from school. Everything humans do, in our everyday lives, and in the major political, economic, and cultural events of our times, is bound up with the earth. Everything that we "do" is bound up with our ideas of this relation. "Nature" and "Society" were useful, for a time, in producing a rough-and-ready picture of global nature and humanity's place within it. We may be One with nature, but the web of life is also extraordinarily diverse, and diversifying. Distinctions are clearly necessary.

If new distinctions are needed—and they clearly are—they cannot be made in the old ways. *A new mode of distinguishing* is necessary. And this is not easy, because etched in our socio-cultural DNA is a pre-conceptualization of what is and what is not Nature; what is and what is not Society. Worse, Cartesian dualism as a mode of distinguishing confuses the difference between ontological dualism and analytical distinction within evolving wholes. Our scholarly vocabularies, even after four decades of Green Thought, are still contained within—and constrained by—an essentially Cartesian notion of nature-society interaction. Nature goes into one box; Society goes into another. The two interact and shape each other, but the messily bundled and interpenetrating relations of manifold human and extra-human natures are abstracted from the movements of the parts, and the constitution of the Whole. The dualist construction of Nature and Society—Green Arithmetic—poses a question it cannot answer: the question of the Whole. Why? Because Nature plus Society does not add up. Something is missing.

Just what that *something* is can be summed up in two words: vocabulary and method. It is on this basis that I ask the reader to evaluate *Capitalism in the Web of Life*. The origins of this book can be located in two series of discussions that bookended the first decade of the twenty-first century. In one, at the turn of the new millennium, my fellow graduate students in the Department of Geography at UC Berkeley made our way towards a powerful conclusion: "physical" and "social" geography were in fact one, and ought to be brought together in a new synthesis.[44] A second series of conversations took shape with a wonderful group of graduate students at Lund University in 2009. In these conversations, we posed a question that was hardly new, but seemed to assume a new urgency after the near-meltdown of the world-economy in 2008. To what degree do we need, and to what degree is it possible, to construct a unified vocabulary that joins humanity-in-nature and nature-in-humanity? The call for such a unified vocabulary had been sounded many times before. Birch and Cobb had done so in their magnificent *Liberation of Life*.[45] Harvey did the same in his seminal essay on "The Nature of Environment."[46] But to no avail. Such calls found some resonance in theory, and even here the most famous metaphors—Haraway's cyborgs, Actor-Network Theory's hybrids—found little resonance in the theory of historical change.

New conceptual languages cannot be invented; they can only emerge. Such emergence, in turn, can only be facilitated or obstructed. It has been one thing to call for a conceptual vocabulary that unifies the apparently independent ontological domains of the natural and the social. It is quite a different task to collaboratively develop such a conceptual language in a way that can be, first, legible, and second, readily put to work.

The barrier, it turned out, was methodological: not in terms of accumulating data, but in the ways that we go about bounding, or configuring, human and extra-human natures. The objects Nature/Society were so useful because they were pre-fabricated, legible, and fit easily with a popular imagination of Nature as "out there." The bounding of time, space, and nature was already done. Sophisticated analyses taking shape out of political ecology and critical geography problematized this, but almost without exception they did so on a regional-scale. In so doing, they reproduced another dualism: of regional change as "real" and global change as "theoretical."[47] A method that unfolded the world-historical implications of both political ecology and critical geography awaited, one that would comprehend social relations as spatial relations as relations within the web of life.

To make this argument "work"—to practice what one preaches—is disorienting. Why? Because we are asked to give up the sacred distinction of Nature/Society, and to reconstruct historical objects—such as neoliberalism or Fordism or capitalism—as co-produced by human and extra-human natures. This

44   See especially R. Lave, et al., "Intervention: Critical Physical Geography," *The Canadian Geographer* 58, no. 1 (2014): 1–10.

45   Birch and Cobb, *The Liberation of Life* (1981).

46   Harvey, "The Nature of Environment.".

47   R. Peet, et al., eds., *Global Political Ecology* (London: Routledge, 2011).

challenge is all the more vexing because it entails new narrative strategies that go beyond the commonplace invocation of local-global connections and the theoretical assertion of capitalist dynamics in general. Such narrative strategies must transcend regionalism *and* globalism in order to see that capitalism, too, is a real *place*—every bit as much as Paris or the American Midwest or the Punjab. And it requires an approach that is willing to "tack" back and forth in an ongoing way—between the apparently "social" and the apparently "ecological" in search of the durable relations that co-produce wealth, power, and re/production across successive historical natures.[48]

Forging a new synthesis that crystallizes our two levels of abstraction—humanity-in-nature, capitalism-in-nature—has so far eluded critical scholars. But the elements of such a synthesis are not lacking. Since the 1970s, we have frequently glimpsed the outlines of a unified theory of capital accumulation in its double internality: as capital's internalization of nature, and as nature's internalization of capital. Its philosophical basis is found in the relational holism implicit—however unevenly practiced—in both Red and Green Thought.[49] By the 1980s, the philosophical perspective joined—again, unevenly and implicitly—with a conceptualization of capitalism as *already* a relation of humans with the rest of nature.[50]

However frequently we have glimpsed the possibilities, there has been too little movement in translating the philosophical position (humanity-in-nature) into historical method (capitalism-in-nature). There are many good—and some bad—reasons for the slow pace of transition from philosophy to method. Chief among the good reasons is this: it was, practically speaking, impossible to construct methods and narratives of historical change as co-produced when most nature was invisible—as was the case in world social science until the 1990s. In other words, the accumulation of knowledge about humanity *and* nature had to reach critical mass. Until it did—and it *has*—it was impractical to develop modes of analysis that pivoted, ontologically *and* methodologically, on the *oikeios*. For this reason, philosophy and meta-theory were ahead of their times. These contributions, especially those unfolding across the long 1970s,

---

48　Geographical scale as co-produced by human and extra-human natures is provocatively explored by N. Sayre in "Ecological and Geographical Scale," *Progress in Human Geography* 29, no. 3 (2005): 276–90.

49　Cf. B. Ollmann, *Alienation* (1971); R. Williams, "Ideas of Nature," in *Ecology*, ed. J. Benthall (1972); D. Harvey, "Population, Resources, and the Ideology of Science," *Economic Geography* 50, no. 3 (1974); A. Naess, "The shallow and the deep, long-range ecology movement," *Inquiry* 16, no. 1 (1973): 95–100.

50　N. Smith, *Uneven Development* (1984); J. O'Connor, *Natural Causes* (New York: Guilford Press, 1998); J.B. Foster, *Marx's Ecology* (New York: Monthly Review Press, 2000); P. Burkett, *Marx and Nature* (New York: St. Martin's Press, 1999).

were deeply prefigurative, and often celebrated.[51] But they were rarely embraced in the study of historical change. Historical change remained *social* change. Environmental consequences were added. Green Arithmetic thrived.

We have now reached a different moment. The proposition that historical change can be contained with the containers of "Nature" and "Society" is no longer tenable. The accumulation of knowledge about humanity and nature has reached critical mass. Our planetary knowledge continues to grow, and rapidly. At the same time, the growth of our understanding of how humans are made by the rest of nature, and of how nature is made by humanity has stalled. Nowhere is this clearer than in the popularity and influence of the dominant Anthropocene argument.[52] In this framework, humans constitute a set of vectors—propelling the "Great Acceleration"[53]—which threaten planetary crisis. Humans are placed in one category, Nature in another, and the feedbacks between them identified. The evidence amassed by the scholars working in the Anthropocene and cognate perspectives is indispensable. Such evidence helps us outline the problem, and descriptively answer the first key question, "What is occurring?" But such perspectives pose a deeper question they cannot answer: *How do humans co-produce patterns and relations of power and production within nature?* The question cannot be answered in a dualist frame. And this dualist frame constrains our vision of the possible contours and deepening contradictions of the century ahead. For key to understanding the unfolding systemic crisis of the twenty-first century is a historical method—which implies a new radical *praxis*—in which human and extra-human natures co-produce historical change.

In the pursuit of such a method, Marx's philosophy of internal relations[54] guides us towards unifying humanity and nature not only epistemically, but ontologically; unified (if non-equivalent) on the terrain of modern world history. Here too, we find important prefigurative arguments that, like Green Thought, date from the 1970s. The translation of dialectics into historical method has always been fraught—everything is connected to everything, but always unevenly, always in motion, always with new points of fracture and new levers of change. It has been easier to assert a dialectical method than to practice it. The world-historical tradition learned this in the 1970s and '80s. The relationality of historical capitalism was celebrated, but developing world-historical narratives

---

51   Cf. Smith, *Uneven Development* (1984).

52   Cf. W. Steffen et al., "The Anthropocene: Are Humans Now Overwhelming the Great Forces of Nature?" (2007); "The Anthropocene: Conceptual and Historical Perspectives," (2011); "The Anthropocene: From Global Change to Planetary Stewardship," (2011).

53   Costanza et al., "Sustainability or Collapse" (2007).

54   Ollman, *Alienation* (1971); K. Kosík, *Dialectics of the Concrete* (Boston: D. Reidel Publishing, 1976).

that revealed this relationality turned out to be exceedingly arduous.[55] In this, world-historical scholars discovered that it was one thing to pursue regional history imbricated in "world process"[56] and another thing entirely to relationally construct world-historical process as the object of investigation.

To treat the history of capitalism in and through a double internality that sees the ceaseless transformation of the earth in the endless accumulation of capital—and vice versa—was more vexing still. This was the project of integrating world accumulation with everyday life that Wallerstein and Arrighi[57] suggested, in distinct registers. Such a synthesis involves an ongoing movement between bodies and environment, production and reproduction, on the "ground floor" of everyday life and the dynamics of world accumulation, world power, and world knowledge. This means that capital and power do not act *upon* nature but develop *through* the web of life. They operate across geographical scales and they move in relation to the whole. That whole is neither world-scale process nor the aggregation of regional units but a dynamic totality with properties distinct from its scalar moments.

I have done my best to pursue this synthesis from the standpoint of work and the worker, though more expansively than conventional renderings of these terms. The transition from capitalism *and* nature to capitalism-*in*-nature asks us to place human bodies as sites of environmental history, as bodies engaged in producing "real" commodities and reproducing the "false" commodity, labor-power. From here, we can reconceptualize capitalism: as a system whose chief contradictions turn on the antagonism and interdependence of commodity-relations and the totality of the conditions of reproduction. The human body, in this frame, becomes a crucial site of the contradictions of world accumulation. Marx's great observation that capitalism "simultaneously undermine[s] . . . the soil and the worker" applies well beyond the era of large-scale industry . . . and well beyond the wage-worker.[58] The exploitation of labor-power and the appropriation of nature are interwoven in the system's drive towards endless commodification. From here, it follows that *all* relations between humans are always—already—relations at once "*of* nature" and "*to* the rest of nature." (There is a deep Cartesian bias to our conceptual language, such that we speak of

---

55   See T. Hopkins, "World-Systems Analysis," in *World-Systems Analysis,* ed. T.K. Hopkins, et al. (Beverly Hills: Sage, 1982), 145–58; Wallerstein, *The Modern World-System I (1974)*; P. McMichael, "Incorporating Comparison Within a World-Historical Perspective," *American Sociological Review* 55, no. 2 (1990): 385–97.

56   D. Tomich, *Slavery in the Circuit of Sugar* (Baltimore: Johns Hopkins University Press, 1990).

57   Wallerstein, *The Modern World-System I* (1974); G. Arrighi, *The Long Twentieth Century* (London: Verso, 1994).

58   Marx, *Capital,* Vol. I (1977), 638.

humanity's relation *to* nature as if relations between humans were not, already, relations *of* nature.) To organize a historical analysis around such a relational and holistic perspective necessitates transcending an epistemic rift through which nature becomes Nature: a violent abstraction, an object, an ontologically separate "base" upon which the "superstructure" of Society develops.

CAPITALISM/NATURE/CRISIS

At stake is an interpretation of global crisis appropriate to our times, and relevant to our era's movements for liberation. It is an open question as to whether we are facing a *developmental crisis* of capitalism—one open to resolution through new rounds of primitive accumulation and commodification—or an *epochal crisis*, one marked by an irreversible decline in capital's capacity to restructure its way out of great crises. From the twin crises of global urbanization and industrialization signified by "surplus humanity," to the faltering productivist behemoth of industrial agriculture, to the seemingly endless commodity boom in food, metals, and energy, there are good reasons for considering that an epochal crisis may well be on the horizon.

This is a book about crisis, but not about "social" and "ecological" crisis as conventionally understood. As I will make clear, I do not believe "Society" and "Nature" exist, at least not in their dominant usage: humans without nature and nature without humans. Nor do I believe these are mere "social constructions." They are, rather, abstractions at once violent and real. They are *violent*, in the sense that they abstract too much reality in the interests of conceptual clarity.[59] And they are *real*, in the sense that Society and Nature are in fact operative forces,[60] both in our knowledge structures and in capitalism's actually existing relations of power and production. Eschewing this, modernity's most sacred binary, I understand *all* forms of crisis—understood as turning points in the systemic organization of power and production—as bundles of human and extra-human nature. This is a big statement that implies manifold processes, the key point of which turns the conventional wisdom on its head: The crises of capitalism-in-nature are crises of what nature *does for* capitalism, rather more than what capitalism *does to* nature. This point of entry offers not only a fresh perspective—one that includes, centrally, the work of *human* natures—but also provides an opportunity for synthesizing two great streams of radical thought since the 1970s: the theory of accumulation crisis and the study of environmental crisis. For all the extraordinary work in both fields, the accounts of "how

---

59   Sayer, *The Violence of Abstraction* (1987).
60   Toscano, "The Open Secret of Real Abstraction" (2008).

capitalism works" and "how capitalism creates planetary crisis" have not been synthesized, even by our most insightful theorists.[61]

Capitalism in the Web of Life is animated by the desire to translate the philosophy of humanity-in-nature into workable methodological frames, conceptual vocabularies, and narrative strategies for world-historical change. This is the core of the world-ecology perspective, which is just that—a *perspective*, not a theory. And certainly not a theory of everything. World-ecology is a *method* of bounding and bundling the human/extra-human/web of life relation—a manifold and multi-layered relation that encompasses everything from the micro-biome to the biosphere. And it is a *framework* for theorizing manifold forms of the human experience, past and present. No perspective can be the work of an individual; its development must be collective and cooperative. I encourage readers to consider this book not as a series of closed formulations—as is too often the case (for readers and authors like). Rather, I have written this book as a series of proposals and reflections on how to move beyond the Cartesian dualism that has so deeply fragmented our understanding of power, exploitation, work, and liberation. Some of these proposals will surely work better than others. As best I can, I have presented the historically grounded theorizations in this book—clustered around capital accumulation, global value-relations, and agro-ecological change—to demonstrate the kinds of questions that world-ecology can open up. To see "Wall Street as a way of organizing nature," for instance, opens up questions that are prematurely—and unnecessarily—foreclosed by the dualisms of contemporary economic and ecological thought.

The argument can now be reprised. If humans are a part of nature, historical change—including the present as history—must be understood through dialectical movements of humans making environments, and environments making humans. The two acting units—humanity/environments—are not independent but interpenetrated at every level, from the body to the biosphere. Perhaps most of all, it means that relations that seemingly occur purely between humans—say, culture, or political power—are already "natural" relations, and they are always *bundled* with the rest of nature, flowing inside, outside, and through human bodies and histories. And in this flow of flows, we are dealing with much more than microbes and metals and the rest of "material life"; we are dealing as well with ideas as material forces. In this, human history is understood as an "unbroken circle" of being, knowing, and doing.[62]

Many environmental scholars worry that, in abandoning "the" environment as a singular rather than manifold object, we risk giving up the powerful insights of environmental studies. I think the opposite rings truer: the real relational

---

61   J.B. Foster et al., *The Ecological Rift* (2010).
62   H. Maturana and F. Varela, *The Tree of Knowledge* (Berkeley: Shambhala, 1987).

movements of nature as a whole are obscured by the *a priori* fragmentation of Nature/Society. This breaks with the Green convention of tacking factors of an external Nature—what I will call "nature in general"—onto modern social relations. Nature is not a variable. Instead, we can begin by demonstrating that particular historical processes—in this book, world accumulation—are bundles of human and extra-human nature. These bundles are symbolically and materially enacted. And the limits that emerge are limits not of Nature or Society but limits of the *oikeios* in particular historical-geographical circumstances.

CONCLUSION

What if to say *historical* capitalism implies—*necessitates*—historical nature? And what if to say *historical nature*—since the long sixteenth century—implies and necessitates historical capitalism? These are the fundamental questions posed by the double internality. This line of questioning encourages, even compels, us to go beyond the now-commonplace and rarely specified invocation of Nature as one of several crises facing Humanity today. It asks us to examine how the web of life reshapes human organization—*as* a force of nature—and how civilizations forge power, production and reproduction as ways of organizing nature. It asks us to reflect upon our well-worn conceptualizations of capitalism: as economic system, as social system, as commodity system. For if the production of capital has been the strategic pivot of capitalism, to an even greater extent accumulation has unfolded through the appropriation of planetary work/energy. Such appropriation—of cheap resources, yes ("taps"), but also of cheap garbage ("sinks")—does not produce capital as "value"; but it does produce the relations, spaces, and work/energy that make value possible. Capitalism *does* generalize commodity relations, but the actual extent of such generalization depends on an even greater generalization: the appropriation of unpaid work/energy.

This even greater generalization has today reached a boiling point. For the appropriation of Cheap Nature has not only compelled capital to seek out new sources of cheap labor-power, food, energy, and raw materials, but to enclose the atmosphere as a gigantic dumping ground for greenhouse gases. This enclosure—a relation of capital-in-nature—is today generating barriers to capital accumulation that are unprecedented, especially in agriculture. And at the risk of putting too fine a point on matters, this enclosure of the atmosphere is a *class* relation: not only as cause-effect sequence ("the capitalists did it!") but as a necessary condition of world class relations over the past two centuries.

This way of thinking through the relations of capital-in-nature gives us an alternative to the "nature as external limit" model that dominates Red and Green thinking about ecological crisis, and about climate change in particular. The problem with such thinking is that it has closed down, rather than opened up, the big questions about the geographical flexibility and historical evolution of capitalism as world-ecology. The limits are real enough. But what is the best way to identify, to narrate, and to explain the emergence of these limits?

The choice is between a Cartesian paradigm that locates capitalism outside of nature, acting upon it, and a way of seeing capitalism as project and process within the web of life. If the destructive character of capitalism's world-ecological revolutions has widely registered—the "what" and the "why" of capitalism-in-nature—there has been far too little investigation of *how* humans have made modernity through successive, radical reconfigurations of all nature. *How* capitalism has worked *through*, rather than *upon* nature, makes all the difference. We have, I believe, arrived at a powerful educative moment. It is one that allows us to erase old boundaries and open new vistas, one where we can reconstitute each of these processes on the basis of the historically evolving *oikeios*. It allows for an understanding of modernity's historically specific natures as webs of liberation and limitation for the accumulation of capital, itself a way of organizing nature. The point can scarcely be overemphasized if we are to take seriously the idea that all limits to capital emerge historically, out of the relations of humans with the rest of nature. And in equal measure, so do all projects for the liberation of humanity and our neighbors on planet earth.

Part I

FROM DUALISM TO DIALECTICS:
CAPITALISM AS WORLD-ECOLOGY

From Object to *Oikeios:*
Environment-Making in
the Capitalist World-Ecology

Words are like empty balloons, inviting us to fill them up with associations.
As they fill they begin to gain intrinsic force and at last to shape
our perceptions and expectations. So with the word "ecology" . . .

(Worster, 1994)

For nearly half a century, Green Thought has wrestled with a double question. Is nature exogenous to the essential relations of human history, for the most part playing roles as tap (raw materials) and sink (pollution)? Or is nature a web of life encompassing all of human activity, comprising taps and sinks, but also much beyond? Is nature, in other words, a set of objects that humans act upon, or is it a web of life that human relations develop *through*?

The vast Green literatures that have emerged since the 1970s—political ecology, environmental history and environmental sociology, ecological economics, systems ecology, and many more—have developed by answering "yes" (in one form or another) to both questions. On the one hand, most scholars agree that humanity is indeed part of nature. They reject the Cartesian dualism that puts Society (without natures) in one box and Nature (without humans) in another. On the other hand, the conceptual vocabularies and analytical frameworks that govern our empirical investigations remain firmly entrenched in the *interaction* of these two basic, impenetrable units—Nature and Society. This "double yes" poses a real puzzle: How do we translate a materialist, dialectical, and holistic philosophy of humans-*in*-nature into workable (and work*ing*) conceptual vocabularies and analytical frameworks?

The arithmetic of Nature plus Society has been the bread and butter of environmental studies since the 1970s. The arithmetic bears distinctive linguistic inflections across the historical social sciences, and across the Two Cultures. Earth-system scientists talk about "coupled human-natural systems";[1] Marxist ecologists speak of the "nature-society dialectic";[2] cultural studies highlights

---

1   J. Liu, et al., "Coupled Human and Natural Systems," *Ambio* 36, no. 8 (2007): 639–48.

2   B. Clark and R. York, "Carbon Metabolism," *Theory and Society* 34 (2005): 391–428.

hybrids, assemblages, and networks.[3] Establishing this arithmetic as a legitimate domain of scholarly activity has been Green Thought's greatest contribution. The environmental humanities and social sciences brought to light the other, previously forgotten or marginalized, side of the Cartesian binary: the world of environmental impacts. No small accomplishment, this. "The environment" is now firmly established as a legitimate and relevant object of analysis.

About this signal accomplishment, I would make two observations. First, the work of bringing nature as factor into the study of global change is now largely complete. It is increasingly difficult to address core issues in social theory and social change without *some* reference to environmental change. There remains considerable unevenness, across the historical social sciences, in how environmentally oriented research is valorized (or not). But the core project of Green Thought, from the time it gathered steam in the 1970s, has been successful: the legitimacy and relevance of environmental research is no longer in question. This project was always infused with a dialectical sensibility.[4] But its operationalization turned on an affirmation of the first question we posed at the outset—environment as object—rather than nature as the web of life. This prioritization—could it have been otherwise?—resulted in the disjuncture we encounter today: between humanity-in-nature (as philosophical proposition) and humanity *and* nature (as analytical procedure). This disjuncture lies at the core of the impasse in environmental studies today: an impasse characterized by a flood of empirical research and an unwillingness to move beyond environment as object. Nature with a capital "N" has been prized over the web of life. This impasse may be understood in terms of a generalized reluctance to refigure modernity as producer and product of the web of life.

My second observation therefore turns on the exhaustion of the Cartesian binary to deepen our understanding of capitalism, historically and in the present crisis. Today, that binary obscures, more than it illuminates, humanity's place in the web of life. "Nature plus Society" appears especially unsuited to dealing with today's proliferating crises—not least those linked to climate change and financialization—and also with the origins and development of these crisis tendencies over the broad sweep of modern world history.

Is it now necessary to move beyond the environment as object? Can the project of writing environmental histories *of* social processes adequately capture the manifold ways in which these processes are not only producers of environments,

3   B. Latour, *We Have Never Been Modern* (Cambridge, MA: Harvard University Press, 1993); J. Bennett, "The Agency of Assemblages and the North American Blackout," *Public Culture* 17, no. 3 (2005): 445–65.

4   Cf. R. Williams, "Ideas of Nature" (1972); D. Harvey, "Population, Resources, and the Ideology of Science" (1974); R. A. Walker, "Human-Environment Relations: Editor's Introduction," *Antipode* 11, no. 2 (1979): 1–16.

but also products of them? The idea that social organization carries with it environmental consequences has taken us far, but it is unclear just how much farther Green Arithmetic can take us.

But if Green Arithmetic cannot get us to where we need to go today, what can?

My response begins with a simple proposal. Needed, and I think implied by an important layer of Green Thought, is a concept that moves from the *interaction* of independent units—Nature and Society—to the dialectics of humans in the web of life. Such a concept would focus our attention on the concrete dialectics of the messily bundled, interpenetrating, and interdependent relations of human and extra-human natures. Needed, in other words, is a concept that allows a proliferating vocabulary of humanity-in-nature, rather than one premised on humanity *and* nature.

THE *OIKEIOS*: INTERACTION, DIALECTICS, AND THE PROBLEM OF AGENCY

I propose that we begin with the *oikeios*.

Oikeios is a way of naming the creative, historical, and dialectical relation between, and also always within, human and extra-human natures. The *oikeios* is shorthand: for *oikeios topos*, or "favorable place," a term coined by the Greek philosopher-botanist Theophrastus. For Theophrastus, the *oikeios topos* indicated "the *relationship* between a plant species and the environment."[5] Properly speaking, *oikeios* is an adjective. But in the long journey towards a vocabulary that transcends the Two Cultures (the physical and human sciences), I hope the reader might excuse a few liberties with the language.

Neologisms come a dime a dozen in Green Thought. We needn't not look far for concepts aiming to fuse or combine the relations of human and extra-human nature.[6] And yet, after decades of vigorous Green theorizing and analysis, we still lack an approach that puts the *oikeios* at the center. Such a perspective would situate the creative and generative relation of species and environment as the ontological pivot—*and methodological premise*—of historical change. This reorientation opens up the question of nature—as matrix rather than resource or

---

5   J. Donald Hughes, "Theophrastus as Ecologist," *Environmental Review: ER* 9, no. 4 (1985): 296–306; *Pan's Travail* (Baltimore: Johns Hopkins University Press, 1994), 4. Emphasis added.

6   Some of the most imaginative conceptualizations (cyborg, natureculture) have come from Haraway's groundbreaking work, whose particularizing thrust ought not to distract us from their world-ecological implications. D. Haraway, *Simians, Cyborgs, and Women* (New York: Routledge, 1991); *When Species Meet* (Minneapolis: University of Minnesota Press, 2008).

enabling condition—for historical analysis; it allows the reconstruction of humanity's great movements, from warfare to literature to scientific-technological revolutions, as if nature matters to the whole of the historical process, not merely as its context, or its unsavory consequences.

This is the intended contribution of the *oikeios*. Naming the relation through which humans (and other species) create the conditions of life—"definite modes of life" in Marx and Engels' nicely-turned phrase[7]—immediately directs our attention to the relations that activate definite configurations of acting units and acted-upon objects. The *oikeios* is a multi-layered dialectic, comprising flora and fauna, but also our planet's manifold geological and biospheric configurations, cycles, and movements. Through the *oikeios* form and re-form the relations and conditions that create and destroy humanity's mosaic of cooperation and conflict: what is typically called "social" organization. Nature-as-*oikeios* is, then, not offered as an additional *factor*, to be placed alongside culture or society or economy. Nature, instead, becomes the matrix within which human activity unfolds, and the field upon which historical agency operates. From such a vantage point, the problems of food, water, oil (and so much more!) become relational problems first, and object problems second; through the relations of specific civilizations, food, water, and oil become real historical actors.

From the perspective of the *oikeios*, civilizations (another shorthand) do not "interact" with nature as resource (or as garbage can); they develop *through* nature-as-matrix. Climate change is a good example. Civilizations develop by internalizing extant climate realities, favorable and unfavorable. "Climate" is not a historical agent *as such*; it is no more a historical agent, in itself, than empires or classes abstracted from the web of life. *Historical* agency is irreducibly bundled in and through the *oikeios*. To lean on Marx, a species (or biospheric process) that does not have its agency outside itself does not exist.[8] Agency, in others words, is not a property of Nature and (or) Society—not even of humanity's spectacular forms of sociality. Agency is, rather, an emergent property of definite configurations of human activity with the rest of life. And vice versa.

Agency is clearly a key question for left ecology. Here I take agency as the capacity to induce historical change (to produce ruptures), or to reproduce extant historical arrangements (to reproduce equilibrium). It is a crude but useful distinction. To say that nature is a "historical protagonist"[9] sounds quite attractive. But

7   F. Engels, "The Part Played by Labor in the Transition from Ape to Man," in *The Origin of the Family, Private Property, and the State* (New York: International Publishers, 1970).

8   Marx, *Economic and Philosophical Manuscripts of 1844* (Mineola, NY: Dover Publications, 2007).

9   B. Campbell, "Nature as Historical Protagonist," *Economic History Review* 63, no. 2 (2010): 281–314.

what does it really mean? Are we simply adding nature to a long list of historical actors? Or does recognition of nature-as-*oikeios* imply a fundamental rethinking of agency itself? We can read many arguments that seek to elucidate nature's agency.[10] It is not, however, clear how nature's agency—whether conceived in Cartesian or dialectical terms—might clarify the making of the modern world. Does nature, say climate, "have" agency in the same way that classes or empires "make" history?

Yes and no. Part of the problem is the temptation to assign agency to both sides of the Cartesian binary. Climate, weeds, disease, in such assignments, "have" agency in a manner analogous to classes, capital, and empire. There has been a certain arithmetic logic to these assignments: if humans have agency, can we not say the same thing about extra-human natures? That sounds right, but does not, I think, adequately capture how agency unfolds. For relations of class, capital, and empire are *already* bundled with extra-human natures; they are configurations of human and extra-human natures. From this it follows that *agency is a relational property* of specific bundles of human and extra-human nature. Class power (and not only the agency of classes) derives and unfolds through specific configurations of power and (re)production in the web of life.

If nature is indeed a historical protagonist, its agency can be comprehended adequately only by stepping out of the Cartesian binary. The issue is emphatically not one of the agency of Nature *and* the agency of Humans. These are unthinkable without each other. Rather, the issue is how human and extra-human natures get bundled. Yes, diseases make history, but only as epidemiological vectors bound to commerce and empire. This is, too often, left out of arguments of nature's agency: the capacity to make history turns on specific configurations of human and extra-human actors. Human agency is always within, and dialectically bound to, nature as a whole—which is to say, human agency is not purely human at all. It is bundled with the rest of nature.

The world-ecological alternative takes these bundles of human/extra-human activity as its starting point. Civilizations are big, expressive examples of this dialectical bundling. From the large-scale and long-run patterns of human-led environment-making, we can discern historical facts from the practical infinitude of basic facts. Climate change, in this scheme of things, becomes a vector of planetary change woven into the very fabric of civilizational power and production (class, empire, agriculture, etc.). Hardly a recent phenomenon, this socio-ecological fabric stretches back millennia.[11] This is the spirit, if not always

---

10   T. Steinberg, "Down to Earth," *The American Historical Review* 107, no. 3 (2002): 798–820; J. Herron, "Because Antelope Can't Talk," *Historical Reflections* 36, no. 1 (2010): 33–52.

11   W. F. Ruddiman, *Plows, Plagues, and Petroleum* (Princeton: Princeton University Press, 2005).

the letter, of much climate historiography.[12] When climate changes, so too change the structures of power and production. However, this is not because climate *interacts* with civilizational structures, causing problems at some point in these structures' otherwise independent lives. We might do better to reorient our vision, to see climate conditions as present at, and implicated in, the birth of these structures. Civilizations are unthinkable in the absence of climate—itself (yet another) shorthand for a diversity of atmospheric processes that co-produce relations of power and production. As such, climate is but one bundle of determin*ations*—not determin*isms*—that push, pull, and transform the rich totalities of historical change. When climate has changed dramatically, the outcomes have often been dramatic and epochal. Consider, for example, the eclipse of Rome after the passing of the Roman Climatic Optimum around 300 C.E., or the breakdown of feudal civilization with the coming of the Little Ice Age a thousand years later.[13] But consider also those climate shifts favorable to the ascent of Roman power (c. 300 B.C.E.) or the dawning of the Medieval Warm Period (c. 800–900) and the rapid multiplication of new "charter states" across Eurasia, from France to Cambodia.[14]

The point is not to argue against climate change as historical vector; it is, rather, to situate that vector within the *oikeios*, and its successive historical natures.

The ontological point calls for its epistemological corollary. If climate's agency is a bundle of human and extra-human natures, these bundles are unevenly refracted through particular historical-geographical formations. Climate change (and climate is always changing) is a fact. Climate change is not, in itself, a *historical* fact, any more than population and production data. It belongs to the

---

12   Cf. M. Davis, *Late Victorian Holocausts* (London: Verso, 2001); B. Fagan, *The Great Warming* (New York: Bloomsbury Press, 2008); D. Chakrabarty, "The Climate of History," *Critical Inquiry* 35 (2009): 197–222. Scholars addressing the contemporary dynamics of capitalism and climate have gone further, advancing distinctive world-ecology syntheses whose paradigmatic implications remain, at least for now, underappreciated. Here I am thinking, above all, of Larry Lohmann's analyses of carbon markets and financialization and Christian Parenti's interwoven narrative of climate, class, and conflict in the early twenty-first century. L. Lohmann, "Financialization, Commodification and Carbon: The Contradictions of Neoliberal Climate Policy," in *Socialist Register 2012: The Crisis and the Left*, ed. L. Panitch, et al. (London: Merlin, 2012), 85–107; C. Parenti, *Tropic of Chaos* (New York: Nation Books, 2011).

13   C. Crumley, "The Ecology of Conquest," in *Historical Ecology*, ed. C. Crumley (Santa Fe, NM: School of American Research Press, 1994), 183–201; J.W. Moore, *Ecology in the Making (and Unmaking) of Feudal Civilization* (Unpublished book manuscript, Department of Sociology, Binghamton University, 2013).

14   V. Lieberman, *Strange Parallels: Southeast Asia in Global Context, c. 800–1830*, Vol. 2 (Cambridge: Cambridge University Press, 2009).

category of *basic* facts; these are the raw materials of historical explanation.[15] Basic facts become *historical* through our interpretive frames. These frames—whether Cartesian, world-ecological, or something else—offer a way of sorting out basic facts, and assigning them to one or another category. One quite fashionable approach is to evade the thorny issue of historical facts altogether and declare oneself in favor of a flat ontology in which nothing necessarily causes anything else.[16]

But this will hardly be satisfying for those seeking explanations of crisis and change in historical capitalism. This has been the strength of a Red-Green Cartesian approach to global capitalism and global environmental change.[17] Not so long ago, virtually all narratives of human history were organized as if nature—even in a Cartesian sense!—did not matter. Today, this has changed. A broadly conceived environmental history perspective has triumphed. Here the accumulating impacts of biospheric change have met up with the accumulating accomplishments of Green politics and Green Thought to produce a vast but weak hegemony in the world university system. It is no longer possible to ignore the status of "nature" in social theory, and it is increasingly difficult to ignore the problem of nature in the history of capitalism at any scale. This hegemony says, in effect, that any attempt to interpret the broad contours and contradictions of world history without due attention to environmental conditions and changes is inadequate.

This is a major accomplishment. It is also one that has occurred within a limited frame. Green Thought has rarely challenged the hegemony of the Cartesian binary over the core conceptual language of historical change. Transcending the Nature/Society binary has been one thing to do philosophically, theoretically[18] and through regional- and national-scale history.[19] It has been quite a different enterprise for world-historical change.[20] Environmental change has been added to the history of capitalism, but not synthesized.

Weiner is surely correct when he identifies the spirit of the environmental

---

15   E.H. Carr, *What is History?* (New York: Penguin, 1962); R.C. Lewontin, "Facts and the Factitious in Natural Sciences," *Critical Inquiry* 18, no. 1 (1991): 140–53.

16   Latour, *We Have Never Been Modern* (1993); J. Bennett, "The Agency of Assemblages" (2005).

17   Foster, et al., *The Ecological Rift* (2010).

18   Cf. Smith, *Uneven Development* (1984); B. Braun and N. Castree, eds., *Remaking Reality* (New York: Routledge, 1998).

19   Cf. R. White, *The Organic Machine* (New York: Hill & Wang, 1996); J. Kosek, *Understories* (Durham: Duke University Press, 2006); J. Scott, *Seeing Like a State* (New Haven: Yale University Press, 1998).

20   See Moore, "Nature and the Transition from Feudalism to Capitalism," *Review* 26, no. 2 (2003): 97–172.

history project in the twenty-first century: "We are all postructuralists now."[21] By this, he means that environmental historians have come to see nature as irreducibly intertwined with the fundamental relations of historical change.[22] (Whether this relation is best described as *poststructuralist* is another question.) But this now-common political ecology perspective has been reluctant to challenge the Cartesian binary on the terrain of historical capitalism. *Accumulation* is reckoned as a social process with environmental consequences, rather than a way of bundling human and extra-human natures.[23] Global political ecology and environmental history has embraced an environmental perspective that emphasizes the environmental history *of* social relations (Nature-plus-Society), rather than modernity's "social" relations *as* producers and products of the web of life (society-in-nature/nature-in-society). Are we all postructuralists now? Perhaps. But when it comes to historical capitalism, dualism retains its hegemony.

This is perhaps most evident in the populist notion of "converging" crises as a way of articulating the global turbulence of the twenty-first century.[24] Insofar as this breaks with the crisis discourse of the 1970s—in which biophysical contradictions were hived off from the crises of capital and class[25]—the language of converging crises is an important advance. In another sense, however, the radical critique of capitalism since 2008 has proceeded in terms entirely agreeable to the Cartesian sorting out of crisis tendencies. One can now add "climate" or "ecology" to the proliferating list of significant fractures

---

21   D.R. Weiner, "A Death-Defying Attempt to Articulate a Coherent Definition of Environmental History," *Environmental History* 10, no. 3 (2005): 404–20.

22   Cf. R. White, "'Are you an Environmentalist or Do You Work for a Living?'" in *Uncommon Ground*, ed. W. Cronon (New York: W.W. Norton, 1995).

23   At its best, political ecology recognizes global political economy as co-constitutive, and poses the right questions: How are "*specific* environmental conditions" produced, and when, where, and how are these conditions "entangled [or not] with the tendencies of global capitalism . . . : accumulation, growth, and crisis" (Peet, et al., eds. *Global Political Ecology,* (2011), 29)? But for all of political ecology's incantations of the *global* (ibid.), the world-system remains a theoretical rather than historical construction, a generality relegated to the "context" of *specific* conditions—as if capitalism itself is not a specific place with its own specific conditions of production and power! (See especially Moore, "'Amsterdam Is Standing on Norway' Part I," *Journal of Agrarian Change* 10, no. 1 (2010): 35–71). Contextualizing, rather than specifying, world-historical dynamics has left political ecology with a social-reductionist political economy rather than a set of propositions concerning capital accumulation as socio-ecological process.

24   Cf. S. George, "Converging Crises" (2010); P. McMichael, "The Land Grab" (2012).

25   Compare for example D.H. Meadows, et al., *The Limits to Growth* (New York: Signet/Mentor, 1972); with G. Arrighi, "Towards a Theory of Capitalist Crisis," *New Left Review*, no. 111 (1978; 1972 original): 3–24.

in twenty-first century capitalism. "Nature plus Capitalism" is increasingly less productive, because the approach is *additive* rather than *synthetic*. The "red" critique is now closely paired with the "green" critique, but neither Greens nor Reds have moved towards a synthesis that demonstrates a *relational* reconceptualization of "economy-making" in light of "environment-making" and vice versa.[26]

The synthesis that might unify the recognition of global capitalism as a "real" historical place and as a real bundle of human and extra-human natures has been slow to materialize. Cartesian thinking in global studies has been especially resilient. The key concepts of historical change remain embedded in an ontology that few of us, today, agree with: that notion that humans are independent of the rest of nature. The idea persists that conceptual renovation can occur through the promiscuous deployment of adjectives—environmental, ecological, and all manner of cognates—that assume precisely what needs to be explained. Thus we have environmental justice and social justice; ecological imperialism and economic imperialism; the exploitation of nature and the exploitation of labor; economic crisis and ecological crisis. The stylized list could be multiplied endlessly. The addition of ecological adjectives is surely an advance upon older, social reductionist historiographies and analytical frames for which nature—in any sense of the term—really did not matter.

Today, however, the model of Nature plus Society is increasingly self-limiting. We can add environmental factors and consequences indefinitely. But concrete historical wholes—such as capitalism—cannot be constructed by "adding up" the Social and Environmental parts. Nor can capitalism be aggregated through regional case studies that theorectically (rather than historically) construct the modern world-system.

WORLD-ECOLOGICAL IMAGINATIONS: TOWARDS CAPITALISM-IN-NATURE

Although Theophrastus seems to have used the *oikeios topos* in a fairly conventional way, to signify what we would call an ecological niche, a dialectical alternative is suggested by nearly a century of holistic thought.[27] In this

---

26   But see Lohmann's breathtaking analyses of carbon markets, climate change, and world accumulation: L. Lohmann, "When Markets are Poison: Learning about Climate Policy" (2009); "Financialization, Commodification and Carbon: The Contradictions of Neoliberal Climate Policy" (2012).

27   J.C. Smuts, *Holism and Evolution* (New York: Macmillan, 1926); Capra, *The Turning Point* (1982); J.B. Foster, *Marx's Ecology* (2000); Harvey, "Population, Resources, and the Ideology of Science" (1974); Harvey, "The Nature of Environment" (1993); R.

dialectical and holistic alternative, the *oikeios* informs a perspective on historical change in the web of life as simultaneously *enfolding* and *unfolding*.[28] This alternative is the world-ecology synthesis. Like many other Green perspectives, the world-ecology approach offers a philosophy of history premised on humanity-in-nature.[29] World-ecology's distinctiveness lies in its attempt to translate the philosophical premise into world-historical method, emphasizing the bundling of human and extra-human natures through the *oikeios*. Such bundling necessarily carries us far beyond the (so-called) "environmental" *dimensions* of human activity. Our concern is human relations as always already interpenetrated with the rest of nature, and therefore always already both producers and products of change in the web of life.[30] The manifold projects and processes of humanity-in-nature—including imperialisms and anti-imperialism, class struggles from above and below, capital accumulation in its booms and crises—are always products of the *oikeios*, even as they create new relations of power and production within it.

World-ecology is, then, a framework for theorizing those strategic bundles of relations fundamental to capitalist civilization. These strategic relations—above all value/capital as abstract labor-in-nature—are typically viewed as social relations: as relations between humans first, and, only subsequently, as interactions with the rest of nature. Environmental history, from its origins, sought to resolve this social determinism in a new formulation. Four decades ago, Crosby argued that humans are biological entities first, before they are Catholics, capitalists, colonizers, or anything else.[31] Alas, Crosby's groundbreaking argument did not resolve the problem of social determinism so much as invert it. For humanity's biological existence is collective and collaborative, turning on species-specific capacities for symbolic production and collective memory. Biology and sociality are not separate, and to suppose so is to opt for a Hobson's choice of biological determinism or social reductionism. Happily, the *oikeios* gives us a real choice. Here we take "the first premise[s] of all human history" as producer/product relations in the web of life.[32] Thus food-getting and family-making were (and are) affairs of culture/sociality as a ways of

---

Levins and R. Lewontin, *The Dialectical Biologist* (1985); E. Odum, "The Emergence of Ecology as a New Integrative Discipline," *Science* 195 (1977); B. Ollman, *Alienation* (1971).

28   D. Bohm, *The Essential David Bohm*, ed. L. Nichol (New York: Routledge, 2003).

29   Cf. Capra, *The Turning Point* (1982); C. Folke, et al. "Resilience Thinking," *Ecology and Society* 15, no. 4 (2010), http:// www.ecologyandsociety.org/vol15/iss4/art20/.

30   Williams, "Ideas of Nature" (1972).

31   A.W. Crosby, Jr., *The Columbian Exchange* (Westport, CT: Greenwood Press, 1972).

32   Marx and Engels, *The German Ideology* (1970), 42.

negotiating biological and geographical relations; they are ways of environ-ment-making. They are not the "natural base[s]" in a mechanical base/superstructure model of historical change, but rather the constitutive relation "with the rest of nature" through which humans produce (and are products of) "definite mode[s] of life."[33]

The observation applies not only to the relations of everyday life but also to the large-scale patterns of power and production in the modern world-system. The idea that capitalism acts upon nature, rather than develops through the web of life, is prevalent in critical environmental studies today. It is the analytical practice of a broadly-defined global political ecology—even when the philo-sophical premise is explicitly relational.[34] We now have a robust political economy *of* the environment, but few reconstructions of capital accumulation *in* the web of life.[35]

This has allowed for all manner of neo-Malthusian tendencies—as in the "fossil capitalism" argument[36]—to creep into left ecology. They are neo-Malthu-sian because they reproduce Malthus's original error, which was less about population than it was about taking the dynamics of nature out of history. In this scheme, limits are external—rather than co-produced. As global political econ-omy and political ecology developed, scholars tended to accept (implicitly) or reject (explicitly) this conception of limits. But there was little reconceptualiza-tion of capitalism's limits as produced through the *oikeios*.

The view that resources are things unto themselves—and that the limits of capitalism are external constraints rather than internal contradictions—is of course not new to our era. It was not new even in the 1970s. It is a view that locates the taproot of capitalism's limits not only outside of the strategic relations of capitalism, but importantly, outside of historical change. Social limits, in this scheme of things, are historical, flexible, open to revision; Natural limits are, effectively, outside of history. As with agency, we may ask: Is the best procedure for ascertaining civilizational limits one of assigning limiting power to one or the other side of the Cartesian binary? Among the consequences of such Nature/Society models is a pronounced tendency towards an "externalist" view of limits. The obverse of social reductionism in thinking capitalism's limits is biospheric determinism. Such has been the argument of left catastrophists, reintroducing

---

33 Ibid.

34 Foster, et al., *The Ecological Rift* (2010); N. Heynen, et al., eds. *Neoliberal Environments* (New York: Routledge, 2007); Peet, et al., eds., *Global Political Ecology* (2011).

35 But cf. Burkett, *Marx and Nature* (1999).

36 A. Malm, "The Origins of Fossil Capital: From Water to Steam in the British Cotton Industry," *Historical Materialism* 21, no. 1 (2013): 15–68; E. Altvater, "The Social and Natural Environment of Fossil Capitalism," in *Coming to Terms with Nature: Socialist Register 2007*, ed. L. Panitch and C. Leys (London: Merlin Press, 2006).

biospheric determinism under the veil of climate change—whose trajectory is transforming the conditions of planetary life, but whose transformations cannot be explained by treating climate as external force.

The biosphere *is* a kind of limit. But it is a limit of what and not how. To say "limits" is to invoke the external but to implicate the *oikeios*. Historical limits can be explained only through *historical* abstractions, not general ones. And so "nature in general" is of little immediate use. The general abstraction—Nature—cannot take us to a deeper understanding of biospheric limits as products of the double internality: the internalization of biospheric relations within capitalist civilization, and the internalization of value-relations in biospheric reproduction.

Historical nature moves us from the commonplace view of nature as object to nature as matrix, the field within which capitalism unfolds. We are still interested in those objects—what we call resources. Building on Marx's relational ontology, we can see resources as relational and therefore histori-cal.[37] Geology is real enough. But it becomes *geo-history* through definite relations of power and production in which geological dispositions are immanent. Geology cannot "directly determine" the organization of produc-tion,[38] precisely because production relations are co-produced. Articulations of production and reproduction are mediated through the *oikeios*, not least the dialectic of organic life and inorganic environments.[39] Geology, in other words, co-produces power and production as it bundles with historically specific human relations. These specific relations, including geology, undergo successive transformations. One epoch-shaping instance was the re-bundling of human activity in the nineteenth century North Atlantic as the energy regime shifted from charcoal and peat to coal. In this view, geol-ogy is at once subject and object. Civilizations move *through*, not around, the web of life.

We can, through the *oikeios*, implicate the widest range of meta-pro-cesses in the modern world as socio-ecological, from family formation to racial orders to industrialization, imperialism, and proletarianization. From this perspective, capitalism does not develop upon global nature so much as it emerges through the messy and contingent relations of humans with the rest of nature. There is no question that, for most of us, these great processes of world history look like hybrids or fusions. These terms make

---

37   Marx, *Capital*, Vol. I (1977); Ollmann, *Alienation* (1971); Harvey, "Population, Resources, and the Ideology of Science" (1974).

38   S.G. Bunker and P.S. Ciccantell, "Economic Ascent and the Global Environment," in *Ecology and the World-System*, ed. W.L. Goldfrank, et al. (Westport, CT: Greenwood Press, 1999), 25.

39   Birch and Cobb, *The Liberation of Life* (1981).

sense, however, only if we presume an originary separation of Society and Nature. Once we start to look closely at these historical processes—energy regimes and agricultural revolutions, yes, but also nationalisms, developmentalist projects, national literatures, financializations—we begin to see just how deeply rooted in the *oikeios* they really are. Through this movement of *oikeios*-bundling, we may encompass the concerns of the environmental studies—writing environmental histories *of* social processes—while demonstrating that the social processes, too, are products of the web of life. This is the transition from environmental histories *of* modernity, to modernity *as* environmental history. And to accomplish this involves a transition from seeing capitalism as a social system to seeing capitalism as *world-ecology*, joining capital, power and nature in a "rich totality of many determinations."[40]

FROM ENVIRONMENT TO ENVIRONMENT-MAKING

In this way of seeing, the "ecology" in world-ecology is not a noun modified by a geographical adjective, much less a synonym for interactions within extra-human natures. Rather, our ecology derives from the *oikeios*, within and through which species make—and always remake—multiple environments. Nature can neither be saved nor destroyed, only transformed. The *oikeios* represents a radical elaboration of the dialectical logic immanent in Marx's concept of metabolism (*Stoffwechsel*).[41] *Stoffwechsel* signifies "a metabolism of nature . . . in which neither society nor nature can be stabilized with the fixity implied by their ideological separation."[42] In this dialectical elaboration, species and environments are at once making and unmaking each other, always and at every turn. All life makes environments. All environments make life.

This implies a shift from environment to environment-*making*: the ever-changing, interpenetrating, and interchanging dialectic of humans and environments in historical change. We are looking at the *relations* that guide environment-making, and also the processes that compel new rules of environment-making, as in the long transition from feudalism to capitalism.[43] And, at the risk of putting too fine a point on it, "environments" are not only fields and

---

40 Marx, *Grundrisse* (1973), 100.

41 Marx, *Capital,* Vol. I (1977).

42 N. Smith, "Nature as Accumulation Strategy," in *Socialist Register 2007: Coming to Terms with Nature,* ed. L. Panitch and C. Leys (London: Merlin Press, 2006), xiv.

43 Moore, "The Modern World-System as Environmental History?", *Theory and Society* 32, no. 3 (2003): 307–77; "Ecology and the Rise of Capitalism" (2007); "'Amsterdam Is Standing on Norway' Part I" (2010); "'Amsterdam Is Standing on Norway' Part II"(2010).

forests; they are homes, factories, office towers, airports, and all manner of built environments, rural and urban.

Capitalism takes shape through the co-production of nature, the pursuit of power, and the accumulation of capital. These are not, however, three independent blocks of relations that may then be interconnected through feedback links. Rather, these three moments interpenetrate each other in the making of historical capitalism—and in its unraveling today. We are charting the emergence of definite historical relations through the *oikeios* that bring together (bundle) definite human and extra-human activities and movements. When Marx observes that humans "act upon *external* nature, and in this way . . . simultaneously changes [our] own nature,"[44] he is making a point about the centrality of the labor process as "bundled" in a world-ecological sense. "External nature" is not outside the labor process but constitutive of it. The pivotal relation, in turns liberating and limiting, is between human and extra-human natures. Environment-making is an activity of *all* life; and humans, too, inhabit and rework environments "made" by extra-human agencies.

To be sure, humans are unusually effective at environment-making: reconfiguring the web of life to accommodate, and to enable, definite relations of power and production. In world-ecological perspective, civilizations do not act *upon* nature but *develop through* the *oikeios*. Civilizations are bundles of relations between human and extra-human natures. These bundles are formed, stabilized, and periodically disrupted in and through the *oikeios*. Humans relate to nature as a whole from within, not from outside. Undoubtedly, humans are an especially powerful environment-making species. But this hardly exempts human activity from the rest of the nature. We are shaped by the environment-making activities of extra-human life, for whom humans (individually and collectively) are "environments" to be made, and also to be unmade.[45] "To say that man's physical and mental life is linked to nature simply means that nature is linked to itself, for man is a part of nature."[46]

If all relations between humans, all human activity, unfold through the *oikeios* (which itself enfolds), it follows that these relations are always and everywhere a relation with the rest of nature. It is a dialectic that works simultaneously inside-out and outside-in: the earth is an environment for humans, and humans are environments (and environment-makers) for the rest of life on planet earth. The usual approach to these questions is to view the dialectic of human and extra-human natures as one of interaction. But the interactionist model is premised on a grand—and I think unwarranted—reductionism. Humans, in themselves, are

---

44   Marx, *Capital*, Vol. I (1977), 283. Emphasis added.
45   Levins and Lewontin, *The Dialectical Biologist* (1985).
46   Marx, *Economic and Philosophical Manuscripts of 1844* (2007), 107.

complex webs of biophysical determination: we are, among other things, an "environment" for the trillions of microbial symbionts (the micro-biome) that inhabit us, and that make our life-activity possible. We are dealing, in other words, with "worlds within worlds."[47]

The problem is more than reductionism, however. Dialectics is about more than interaction. The difference is one with major implications for how we see historical change. Even among radical critics, the Cartesian binary of Society (humans without nature) and Nature (environments without humans) holds sway.[48] From the perspective of the *oikeios*, the Cartesian view is theoretically arbitrary and empirically misleading. Try drawing a line around the "social" and the "natural" in the cultivation and consumption of food. In a rice paddy or a wheat field, in a cattle feedlot or on our dinner table, where does the natural process end, and the social process begin? The question itself speaks to the tenuous purchase of our Cartesian vocabulary on the everyday realities that we live, and seek to analyze. One can say that we are social and natural beings, but this merely begs the question: When are humans "social" beings, when are we "natural" creatures, and what are the relations that govern these shifting boundaries? When it comes to food (and not just food), every step in the process is bundled. The question becomes not one of "Is it social or natural?" but one of, "How do human and extra-human natures *fit together*?" Any adequate response to the question must flow through some form of dialectical-*oikeios* reasoning.

This reasoning leads us to see capitalism as a specific dialectic of *project* and *process*. On the one hand, the projects of capitalist agencies—capital and empires, to keep it simple—confront the rest of nature as external obstacles, and also as sources of wealth and power. On the other hand, these projects are also co-produced through processes, the unruly movements of bundled natures, through which civilizational projects discover spectacular contradictions: global warming in the twenty-first century, or the mid-fourteenth century confluence of agro-ecological exhaustion, disease, and (yet again) climate change. In this light, civilizations internalize the relations of nature in contingent, yet quasi-linear, fashion—and they do so within the processes and through the projects of (so-called) human history.

Highlighting this dialectic of project and process is a means of guarding against our tendency to accept capital's ontology: the notion that humans (or human organization) act upon nature rather than enter a ceaseless cascade of mutual transformation within it. And, crucially, it is a means of highlighting the *real historical power* of ontological and epistemic dualisms. Nature may be a violent abstraction—a concept in which essential relations are abstracted

---

47   Ley et al., "Worlds within Worlds" (2008).
48   Cf. Foster et al., *The Ecological Rift* (2010).

from the reality in question[49]—but it is also a *real* abstraction, an operative force in the world.[50] To be sure, Nature/Society is not the only dualism, but it is the originary dualism. The separation of the peasant from the land and the symbolic separation of Humans and Nature were a singular process. The emergence of Nature as a violent, but real, abstraction was fundamental to the cascading symbolic-material transformations of primitive accumulation in the rise of capitalism.

The capacity to make history is an expression not only of internally differentiated conditions and relations within human populations, but also of the differentiated conditions and relations of the biosphere. Humanity, too, is an object for the historical movements and fluxes of life and the geophysical movements of our planet. Thus, these capacities to make history may be turned outside-in *and* inside-out. (Our double internality.) Does anyone today seriously doubt that diseases, or climates, or plants make history as much as any empire? At the same time, is it possible to articulate the role of diseases, plants, or climate abstracted from accumulation, empire, or class? This line of questioning allows us to go beyond a view of nature as a place where one leaves a footprint. It encourages a way of seeing nature as an active movement of the whole, one comprising deforestations and toxifications and all the rest but not reducible to these. It is through the *oikeios* that we can see—and reconstruct historically—nature as far more than an aggregate of *consequences* (deforestation, soil erosion, pollution, etc.). The movements and cycles of extra-human natures are producers/products of historical change, *internal to the movements of historical change*. Nature-as-matrix is cause, active condition, and constituting (bundled) agent in the history of civilizations.

It is already quite challenging to make these arguments on the terrain of philosophy and regional history. Constructing narratives of the *longue durée* as if nature matters—as producer no less than product—is more challenging still. This is the challenge that world-ecology meets head on. If nature matters ontologically in our philosophy of history, then we are led to engage analytically the human-biospheric double internality. Humans simultaneously create and destroy environments (as do all species), and our relations are therefore simultaneously—if differentially through time and across space—being created and destroyed with and by the rest of nature. Through this optic, nature's status undergoes a radical shift: a transition from nature as resource to nature as matrix. Nature can be neither destroyed nor saved, only reconfigured in ways that are more or less emancipatory, more or less oppressive. But take note: our terms "emancipatory" and "oppressive" are offered not from the standpoint of

49   Sayer, *The Violence of Abstraction* (1987).
50   Toscano, "The Open Secret of Real Abstraction" (2008).

humans narrowly, but through the *oikeios*, the pulsing and renewing dialectic of humans and the rest of nature. At stake now—perhaps in a more salient way than ever before in the history of our species—is exactly this: emancipation or oppression not from the standpoint of humanity *and* nature but from the perspective of humanity-*in*-nature . . . and nature-in-humanity.

CHAPTER 2

Value in the Web of Life

Every civilization must decide what is valuable. The Marxist tradition makes occasional reference to a "law of value"—but this "law" can scarcely be detected in most radical analyses of capitalism, its historical movements, and its relation to the web of life. Greens, even Marxist Greens, tend to avoid the question of value in some ways, but embrace it in others. Indeed, the spirit of the "law of value" is fundamental to the Green critique, which asks: How do we view nature, in part or as a whole, as valuable? What are the ethics of a sustainable civilization? How are the valuations of nature practiced—through markets, states, and ideas—in the modern world? What I wish to suggest is the possibility for a productive synthesis of Marxist and Green thinking along these lines. I pursue this synthesis by asking: How does a reading of Marx's law of value through the *oikeios* help us understand the development, crises, and restructurings of capitalism, from its origins to the present?

Civilizations are shaped and defined by their priorities: by deciding what things and what relations are valuable. Their rules of reproducing power and wealth turn on these choices of what is—and what is not—valuable. For capitalism, the choice has been clear, and peculiar. "Value" is determined by labor productivity in commodity production: the average labor-time embedded in the average commodity. This kind of value was unprecedented, and its expressions were spectacular. For feudalism, and "tributary" civilizations in general, wealth turned on land productivity. Never before had any civilization negotiated the transition from land productivity to labor productivity as the metric of wealth. The difference is between how many bushels of wheat, or rice, or maize can be grown in the average worker-hour, and how many bushels can be grown on a hectare (or furlong, or *mu*) of land.

Of course, such contrasts are about more than who produces what, and from where and to whom the surplus flows. "Laws" of value speak also to dominant ethico-political judgments about what is valuable. A capitalist looks at a forest and sees dollar signs; an environmentalist sees trees and birds and soils; a world-ecologist sees how humans and other species have co-produced the forest, and how that "bundled" forest simultaneously conditions and constrains capital today. As we shall see in Chapter Ten, the entwining of these ethico-political valuations with capitalism's Cheap Nature strategy has reached a new phase in the early twenty-first century. Their contradictions are generating not only a movement towards a more violent, more toxic, and more oppressive form of capitalism, but also powerful countermovements. These movements are today not only challenging, but offering alternatives to, capitalism's law of value.

VALUE RELATIONS IN THE CAPITALIST WORLD-ECOLOGY: AN OUTLINE

Just what is that law of value? First, let us be clear that we get "law" as a term from Marx, who got it from Hegel. *Law*, in this sense, is a not an iron law of determination, but rather a law in the "Hegelian sense of the 'abstract.'"[1] To speak of a *law* of value, then, is not to encage history in a prison house of structural abstraction, but to advance a working proposition about a durable pattern of power and production that has obtained over the time and space of historical capitalism. To pick up on one of Marx's favored metaphors, the law of value acts as a kind of gravitational field, shaping broad patterns, yet allowing significant contingency.

Second, one of the enduring legacies of Cartesian dualism is a privileging of substances over relations in thinking about value. This is true for Marxists as well as Greens. Value is abstract social labor, say the Marxists, and it is determined by socially necessary labor-time: the average labor-time embodied in the average commodity. "But wait!" says the Green thinker. "The average labor-time is just one part of what makes that commodity possible."[2] The Marxist law of value forgets that Nature—with a capital 'N'—contributes to the value of all the products that humans use. To which the Marxist, quite properly, says that the whole basis of Marx's political economy is the distinction between "wealth" and "value."[3] And there, the discussion seems to have stopped. It replays an older discussion with feminist scholars, who, like the Greens, rightly challenged the blindness of Marxists to the foundational contributions of another kind of invisible work: the daily and intergenerational reproduction of human life. Such work, as we know, is overwhelmingly performed by women.[4]

Can we ford this great divide? Between Green and feminist insights into the

---

1   P.M. Sweezy, *The Theory of Capitalist Development* (New York: Monthly Review Press, 1970), 19.

2   Cf. S.G. Bunker, "Modes of Extraction, Unequal Exchange, and the Progressive Underdevelopment of an Extreme Periphery," *American Journal of Sociology* 89, no. 5 (1984): 1017–64.

3   Cf. Burkett, *Marx and Nature* (1999); Foster, *Marx's Ecology* (2000).

4   L. Vogel, *Marxism and the Oppression of Women* (New Brunswick, NJ: Rutgers University Press, 1983); M. Dalla Costa and S. James. *The Power of Women and the Subversion of the Community* (Bristol, UK: Falling Wall Press, 1972); S. Federici, *Wages against Housework* (Bristol, UK: Falling Wall Press, 1973).

centrality of unpaid work/energy for capital accumulation, and the Marxist view that labor productivity is the decisive metric of wealth and competitive fitness under capitalism?

I think we can. And I think the way forward looks something like this. The substance of value *is* socially necessary labor-time. The drive to advance labor productivity *is* fundamental to competitive fitness. This means that the exploitation of commodified labor-power is central to capital accumulation, and to the survival of individual capitalists. But this cannot be the end of the story. For the relations necessary to accumulate abstract social labor are—*necessarily*—more expansive, in scale, scope, speed, and intensity. Capital must not only ceaselessly accumulate and revolutionize commodity production; it must ceaselessly search for, and find ways to produce, Cheap Natures: a rising stream of low-cost food, labor-power, energy, and raw materials to the factory gates (or office doors, or . . .). These are the Four Cheaps. The law of value in capitalism is a law of Cheap Nature.

What this law says, in effect, is that that every great wave of accumulation turns on Cheap Nature, understood as use-values produced with a below-average value-composition. In systemic terms, Cheap Nature is produced when the interlocking agencies of capital, science, and empire—blunt categories, yes—succeed in releasing new sources of free or low-cost human and extra-human natures for capital. The Four Cheaps are at the core of such Cheap Natures, reproduced cyclically across the history of capitalism. "Cheap Nature" is punctuated here—with an emphatically uppercase "C" and "N"—because we are focusing on capitalism's way of seeing the world. The bourgeois vision supposes that the web of life can be fragmented, that its moments can be valued through calculations of price and value.

Cheap Nature is "cheap" in a historically specific sense, defined by the periodic, and radical, reduction in the socially necessary labor-time of these Big Four inputs: food, labor-power, energy, and raw materials.[5] Cheap Nature, as an accumulation strategy, works by reducing the value composition—but increasing the technical composition—of capital as a whole; by opening new opportunities for the investment; and, in its qualitative dimension, by allowing technologies and new kinds of nature to transform extant structures of capital accumulation and world power. In all this, *commodity frontiers*—frontiers of appropriation—are central. Thus, the tightly connective movements of

---

5   Many colleagues have insisted on a "Fifth" Cheap Element: Cheap Money. This is undeniably true. *However*, Cheap Money—whose maintenance is the strategic priority of leading capitalist interests today—works only through its capacity to restore Cheap Nature. Cheap Money serves to re/produce Cheap Nature; it is not Cheap Nature as such. Nevertheless, the constitutive relations between money/capital/nature-as-*oikeios* merit sustained investigation and conceptual elaboration.

"internal" restructuring and geographical expansion that restore and reconfig-ure the Four Cheaps. The great expansions of the long nineteenth and twentieth centuries, for instance turned on cheap coal and oil, cheap metals, cheap food, alongside the massive destabilization of peasant societies from eastern Europe to East Asia.

But, and here is the key point: the movements creating the necessary relations and conditions of Cheap Nature cannot be reduced to the immediate processes of production, or even commodity production and exchange as a whole. These are crucial and indispensable. But they are not sufficient. For capitalism depends on a repertoire of strategies for *appropriating* the unpaid work/energy of humans and the rest of nature outside the commodity system. These strategies cannot be reduced to so-called economic relations but are enabled by a mix of science, power, and culture. I know these are blunt instruments, but they will suffice. The reality is interpenetrated, messy, and complex. Crucially, science, power, and culture operate within value's gravitational field, *and are co-constitutive of it.*

The implication is explosive: the law of value represents a determination of socially necessary labor-time, which occurs simultaneously through organiza-tional and technical innovation *and* through strategies of appropriating the unpaid work/energy of "women, nature, and colonies."[6] Absent massive streams of unpaid work/energy from the rest of nature—including that delivered by women—the costs of production would rise, and accumulation would slow. Every act of exploitation (of commodified labor-power) therefore depends on an even greater act of appropriation (of unpaid work/energy). Wage-workers are exploited; everyone else, human and extra-human, is appropriated. And lest the reader think I am letting capitalism off the hook, let me rephrase an old Marxist joke: The only thing worse than being exploited is . . . *being appropriated.* The history of capitalism flows through islands of commodity production, develop-ing within oceans of unpaid work/energy. These movements of appropriation produce the necessary conditions for the endless accumulation of capital (value-in-motion).

In other words: Value does not work unless most *work* is not valued.

The law of value under capitalism is, then, comprised of two moments. One is the endless accumulation of capital as abstract social labor. The other, the ceaseless expansion of the relations of exploitation and appropriation, joined as an organic whole. This perspective stresses the historical and logical *non-identity* between the value-form and its necessarily more expansive value-relations. While Marxist political economy has taken value to be an *economic* phenomenon with systemic implications, the inverse formulation may be more plausible: value-relations are a *systemic* phenomenon with a

---

6   M. Mies, *Patriarchy and Accumulation on a World Scale* (London: Zed, 1986), 77.

pivotal economic moment. Far from denying the centrality of socially necessary labor-time to capitalist civilization, such an approach affirms Marx's
greatest contribution within a theoretical frame implicit in the dialectical
method. Thinking of value as a systemic phenomenon with a pivotal economic
moment allows to us to connect the production and accumulation of surplus
value with its necessary conditions of reproduction. It recognizes, moreover,
that these conditions extend beyond the circuit of capital: the accumulation of
abstract social labor is possible through the appropriation of unpaid work
(human and extra-human). The value-form (the commodity) and its substance
(abstract social labor) depend upon value-relations that configure wage-labor
with its necessarily more expansive conditions of reproduction: unpaid work.
Importantly, capital's appropriation of unpaid work transcends the Cartesian
divide, encompassing both human and extra-human work outside, but necessary to, the circuit of capital and the production of value.

VALUE AS METHOD: CAPITAL, CLASS, AND NATURE

The law of value is not only a law of Cheap Nature but a terrain of class struggle.
As I have argued elsewhere, the rise of capitalism and the formation of a peculiar
law of value over the long sixteenth century was a process of class struggle; the
great frontier expansions, encompassing both the "global Baltic" and the global
Atlantic, were in part motivated by the strength of the western European peasantry in beating back feudal restoration. This value regime emerged only as class
struggles blocked feudal restoration in west-central Europe and propelled the
expansion of commodity production and exchange overseas. Where and when
value-relations reached into the European heartland, the class struggle quickly
reached a boiling point. This was the case in the Central European mining and
metallurgy boom and the ensuing German Peasants' War (1525), only the most
dramatic of a series of class struggles involving workers and peasants against
capital and the state.[7]

Value, then, cannot be regarded a discrete empirical process alongside that of
class struggle and class formation—no more than value-relations can be understood as social process independent of the web of life. There is no recipe that can
deliver us from either abstract structuralism or abstract voluntarism; the only
guide that I have found useful is to hold in one's analytical hands the active
tension between the logic of capital and the history of capitalism, between the

---

7 Moore, "Nature and the Transition from Feudalism to Capitalism" (2003); "The
Modern World-System as Environmental History?" (2003); "Ecology and the Rise of
Capitalism" (2007); "'Amsterdam Is Standing on Norway' Part I" and "Part II" (2010).

apparently "social" and the seemingly "environmental." Only then can we think through and with "the muddle of messy living and dying" in human history.[8]

My approach is to take the emergent contradictions of the accumulation process as the point of departure for a larger project: unifying the history of capitals, natures, and class struggles as mutually relational movements in the modern world-system. Just as social reductionism and environmental determinism represent twin perils, so do abstract generalism and abstract particularism.[9] My alternative takes capitalism's value-relations as a point of entry, a means of opening new questions about power, re/production, and nature in the modern world. It is undeniable that the contradictions of capital do not tell the whole story historical change in the modern world. But all is not happenstance; there *are* patterns, and these patterns cohere—and diverge—through definite relations of power and production. These relations are guided, shaped, influenced—and over time increasingly so—by the law of value.

My argument emerges from three observations.

First, the law of value, established through capital's ruthless drive to commodify and to appropriate the web of life, establishes the durable "stakes of the game."[10] These have been struggled over since the sixteenth century. Just as the history of class struggle in the feudal era emerges in and through the contest over the rate of seigneurial levy,[11] so the struggles of capitalism unfold through the contest over the rate of surplus value. I do not mean to suggest that this is the end of the story; but it is hard to begin the story without reference to these stakes.

Second, value as world-historical project presupposes something false: that all of nature can be reduced to an interchangeable part. Such falsification powerfully effects the very real, if partial, transformation of nature into simplified spaces, such as cash-crop monocultures. Perhaps most significantly, the emergence and development of the law of value as historical-material movement is inconceivable without the symbolic and scientific revolutions that "discovered" the homogeneity of time and space in early modern Europe. Progressively consolidated as the metric of wealth in the modern world—after 1450 there would be no systemic reversals of commodification—the value form enabled all

---

8   Donna J. Haraway, "Staying with the Trouble: Anthropocene, Capitalocene, Chthulucene," in *Anthropocene or Capitalocene?*, ed. J.W. Moore (Oakland: PM Press, forthcoming).

9   F. Araghi and P. McMichael, "Contextualizing (Post)modernity" (Paper presented to the Annual Meeting of the American Sociological Association, 2004).

10   P. Bourdieu and L. Wacquant, *An Invitation to Reflexive Sociology* (Chicago: University of Chicago Press, 1992), 177.

11   G. Bois, "Against the Neo-Malthusian Orthodoxy," *Past and Present* 79 (1978); 60–9.

manner of "metrical revolutions" outside the immediate circuit of capital,[12] but clearly homologous to value's simplifying thrust. Foucault's biopolitical "power of regularization"[13] is unimaginable except in a symbolic-material world orbiting around value's fantasies of homogenizable time and space. Indeed, successive revolutions in the "measure of reality"[14] have been the necessary precondition for subsequent movements of widening and deepening the capitalization and appropriation of all life.

Finally, a historically grounded approach to value allows us to resolve an interpretive problem. On the one hand, advocates of a relational ontology of capitalism-in-nature have been reluctant to move towards an interpretation of capitalism as world-historical and world-ecological process.[15] Environmental historians, on the other hand, are (quite reasonably) focused on landscape change, energy consumption, pollution, and so forth, but have been wary to move from "environment" to *oikeios* and back again.[16] A world-historical recuperation of value theory offers a fruitful way forward without abandoning the insights of either camp. With Marx, I will move from the analysis of what makes capital to what capital makes, from the logic of capital to the history of capitalism.

Why Marx's value theory? Is this not an anti-ecological formulation that explicitly denies nature's contribution to capitalist development? I don't think so, for two big reasons. First, value is a historically specific form of wealth—whose "original sources" are land and labor.[17] Marx's conception of value, *already*, entwines human and extra-human work and their constitutive relations. Second, the historical specificity of value-relations encompasses not only wage-work but also the mobilization

---

12   W. Kula, *Measures and Men* (Princeton: Princeton University Press, 1986).

13   M. Foucault, *Society Must Be Defended* (New York: Picador, 2003).

14   A.W. Crosby, *The Measure of Reality* (Cambridge: Cambridge University Press, 1997).

15   Cf. Smith, *Uneven Development* (1984); Braun and Castree, eds., *Remaking Reality* (1998); Peet et al., *Global Political Ecology* (2011).

16   Pivots of discussion in environmental history include W. Cronon, *Changes in the Land* (New York: W.W. Norton, 1983); idem., *Nature's Metropolis* (New York: W.W. Norton, 1991); idem. *Uncommon Ground*, New York: W.W. Norton,1996); Crosby, *The Columbian Exchange* (1972); idem., *Ecological Imperialism* (Cambridge: Cambridge University Press, 1986); W. Dean, *With Broad Ax and Firebrand* (Berkeley: University of California Press, 1995); M. Gadgil and R. Guha, *This Fissured Land* (Berkeley: University of California Press, 1992); R.H. Grove, *Green Imperialism* (Cambridge: Cambridge University Press, 1995); J.R. McNeill, *Something New Under the Sun* (New York: W.W. Norton, 2000); Merchant, *Death of Nature* (1980); idem. *Ecological Revolutions* (Chapel Hill: University of North Carolina Press, 1989); R. White, *Organic Machine* (1995); D. Worster, *Rivers of Empire* (Oxford: Oxford University Press, 1985).

17   Marx, *Capital*, Vol. I (1977), 638.

of uncapitalized natures—soils, women's work, peasant re/production, and so forth—as a fundamental to the rate of exploitation. Nevertheless, value in capitalism remains peculiar and arbitrary—but historically patterned. Assigning value-creation to labor-power within commodity production, the pattern compelled ceaseless geographical expansion and restructuring. This occurred, necessarily, not only to expand the reserve army of labor, but to entrain ever-wider spheres of uncapitalized nature in service to advancing labor productivity.

If "land productivity" enjoyed primacy in pre-capitalist civilizations, "labor productivity" became the metric of wealth in the capitalist era. It is a simple, and simplifying, logic. More and more extra-human nature attaches to every quantum of socially necessary labor-time. Fewer people produce more: more calories, more shoes, more cars, more *stuff*.

This labor productivity metric—a rough and ready shorthand for Marx's law of value—has and has not been central to Green critique since the 1970s. This is most evident in the critique of industrial agriculture's colossal energy- and nutritional-inefficiency.[18] Capital-intensive agriculture has become more, not less, central to rising energy consumption in the Global North since the 1970s, contributing a stunning "80 percent of energy flow increases" in the U.S. between 1997 and 2002.[19] The flip side of such profligate energy consumption was a more than eightfold increase in the labor productivity of advanced capitalist agriculture between 1945 and the mid-1980s.[20] What the more or less conventional Green critique is unable to explain is how this colossal inefficiency is not merely an output of the system, but constitutive of it. For this peculiar valuation of wealth as abstract social labor—labor productivity—favors socio-ecological developments that reward the rapid exhaustion of nature (including human nature), so long as external supplies can be secured.

A PECULIAR WAY OF ORGANIZING NATURE

Modernity's law of value is an exceedingly peculiar way of organizing life. Born amid the rise of capitalism after 1450, the law of value enabled an unprecedented historical transition: from land productivity to labor productivity as the metric of wealth and power. It was an ingenious civilizational strategy, for it enabled the

---

18   M. Perelman, *Farming for Profit in a Hungry World* (Montclair, NJ: Allanheld, Osmun & Co., 1977); D. Pimentel, et al., "Food Production and the Energy Crisis," *Science* 182 (1973): 443–9.

19   P. Canning, et al., "Energy Use in the U.S. Food System" (Economic Research Report Number 94, Washington: United States Department of Agriculture, 2010), 1.

20   P. Bairoch, "Les Trois Révolutions Agricoles du Monde Développé," *Annales: É.S.C.* 44, no. 2 (1989): 317–53.

deployment of capitalist *technics*—crystallizations of tools and ideas, power and nature—to appropriate the wealth of uncommodified nature in service to advancing labor productivity. The great leap forward in the scale, scope, and speed of landscape and biological transformations in the three centuries after 1450 may be understood in this light, as we see in Chapter Seven.

We can glimpse the emergence of this peculiar valuation from the earliest moments of the transition to capitalism. From the sixteenth century, the law of value began to take shape out of the global extensions of commodity production and exchange, stretching from the silver mines of Saxony and Potosí to the sugar plantations of Brazil and Barbados, and the timber frontiers of Scandinavia and the Baltic. This was early capitalism's commodity frontier strategy, and it was central to an epochal shift because it raised labor productivity by treating uncapitalized nature as a substitute for machinery. At every turn, land (forests, silver veins, fertile soils) was organized by empires, planters, seigneurs, yeoman farmers, and others as a force of production in servitude to the commodity form—as a mechanism for advancing the productivity of labor. Treating the whole of uncapitalized nature as a force of production, early capitalism was able to remake planetary natures in epochal fashion.[21]

Long before capitalism came around, civilizations had been remaking natures on a large scale: feudal Europe, the Greek city-states, the Romans, successive Chinese empires, the Sumerians, and many others. In every instance, there were vital clusters of commercial activity and commodity production and of course huge imperial projects: the Great Wall, the Pyramids. What changed after 1450 were the relevant units, and organization, of time and space. Pre-modern civilizations transformed regions over the span of centuries. Capitalism transformed regional landscapes in mere decades. Through the capacities of monetary capital to command, and indeed to produce, space, there emerged a fundamentally globalizing mode of producing wealth, nature, and power, centered on the commodity form. As central to its era as railroads or automobiles were to theirs, sugar production moved rapidly across the Atlantic world after 1450, from Madeira to São Tome, enclosing in successive turns Pernambuco, Bahia, Barbados, and from there, the wider Caribbean. Silver mining flowered in central Europe, moving restlessly from one site to another. It then relocated through the alchemies of empire and finance to Potosí, half a world away, only to give way in turn to the great silver mines of Zacatecas and Guanajuato in the eighteenth century. Commodity frontiers premised on forest products, on fish, on iron and copper, on cereals and flax, moved with the same socio-spatial rhythm (not in lockstep, but as a dance), occupying, producing, and exhausting

---

21   Moore, "Ecology and the Rise of Capitalism"; "'Amsterdam Is Standing on Norway' Part I" and "Part II" (2010).

the ecological formations of the North Atlantic, from the shores of Newfoundland to southern Norway, the banks of the Vistula and the foothills of the Urals.[22] In contrast to the view of early capitalism as technologically or socially inert, every movement of global occupation and transformation signaled a new phase of social organization, technical deployment, and landscape discipline. Never before had any world-ecological regime moved so fast, so far. Something decisive had changed.

To call that "something" Nature/Society would merely restate the problem we seek to answer. But if we can accept, even provisionally, that Marx's value theory identifies a "deep structure" of historical capitalism, we have a clue to how human and extra-human nature work is entwined. This weave of the human and extra-human—a "law" of value—gives priority to labor productivity, and mobilizes uncapitalized natures without regard for their reproduction. Here we have more than a simple restatement of the problem. We have the possibility of understanding capitalism as premised on a fundamental disequilibrium in the (value) relation of capitalization and appropriation in the web of life. If we, moreover, follow Marx and identify the external vent (the frontier) as central—recall how he moves in successive chapters at the end of *Capital* from the "conquest" of the national "home market" to the "commercial wars . . . which [have] the globe as its battlefield," to the "growth of the international character of the capitalist regime" and its mounting systemic contradictions[23]—then we may begin to see the successive resolutions of the disequilibrating tendency as essentially self-limiting. To explore this self-limiting movement, one must move from the logic of capital to the history of capitalism.

This analytic possibility is vitally important because it will help to answer the greatest question of our times: What are the limits to capitalist civilization, and how are these limits constituted by humans and the rest of nature? It would be mystifying to say that the limits of capitalism are ultimately determined by the biosphere itself, although in an abstract sense this is true. This is a view of Nature as an independent system. Yet, this view is insufficient for understanding *how* capitalism reaches limits, *how* capitalism has transcended limits historically, and *how* capitalism has remade successive historical natures in a way that may pose intractable problems for its survival today. How do we pose, and try to answer productively, the "how" of capitalism-in-nature?

Marx's conception of value seems to offer a useful way to answer these questions. It allows us to discern not merely the patterns of power, re/reproduction, and accumulation over the *longue durée*, but the logic animating these patterns' emergence and evolution. I call this method *eductive* because we are locating

---

22   Moore, "'Amsterdam Is Standing on Norway' Part I" and "Part II" (2010).

23   Marx, *Capital*, Vol. I (1977), 913, 915, 929.

value as a gravitational field. The patterns that take shape through this field move at once in quasi-linear and contingent fashion. In all this, money is of course of very important, and not just to capitalist civilization. What money *represents*, however, is not nearly so obvious. Money is so important in historical capitalism because it is central to three interconnected processes: 1) the carving out of a part of human activity, paid work, and giving it special value; 2) the de-valuing of the rest of nature, so as to put these natures to work for free, or low cost; 3) governing the evolving boundary between capitalization and appropriation, between "economy," its constitutive relations, and the web of life. For monetary accumulation ("into which all commodities dissolve themselves") at once imprints and registers the material transformation of commodity production (where money "dissolves itself into all commodities").[24] Recognizing capital accumulation as both objective process and subjective project, Marx's value thinking offers a promising way to comprehend the inner connections between accumulation, biophysical change, and modernity as a whole.

VALUE AND THE CENTRALITY OF SOCIALLY NECESSARY UNPAID WORK

These inner connections could be glimpsed from the origins of modernity. They underpinned the epoch-making transformations of land and labor in early modern capitalism (see Chapter Seven, "Anthropocene or Capitalocene?"). These transformations were not, however, the straightforward result of capital in its economic expression. This strange metric—value—oriented the whole of west-central Europe towards an equally strange conquest of space. The geographical movements of commodification and appropriation were mutually determined by a symbolic-material reworking of space through value. Marx calls this strange reworking the "annihilation of space by time."[25] Across the long sixteenth century we can see a new form of time—abstract time—emerging. While all civilizations in some sense are built to expand across varied topographies, none represented these topographies as external and progressively abstracted in the ways that dominated early capitalism's geographical praxis. The genius of capitalism's Cheap Nature strategy was to represent time as linear, space as flat, and nature as external.[26] It was a civilizational inflection of the

---

24   Marx, *Grundrisse* (1973), 142.

25   Ibid., 424.

26   L. Mumford, *Technics and Civilization* (London: Routledge and Kegan Paul, 1934); C. Merchant, *The Death of Nature* (1980); J. Pickles, *A History of Spaces* (New York: Routledge, 2004).

"God-trick,"[27] with bourgeois knowledge representing its special brand of quantifying; and scientific reason as a mirror of the world—the same world then being reshaped by early modernity's scientific revolutions in alliance with empires and capitals. The God-trick was producer and product of abstract social nature: the co-production of Nature as something to be mapped, rationalized, quantified, and above all, *controlled* in ways that eased the endless accumulation of capital.

With abstract time, in other words, comes abstract space.[28] They were the indispensable corollaries to the weird crystallization of nature as abstract social labor. It was this ascendant law of value—operating as gravitational field rather than mechanism—that underpinned the extraordinary landscape and biological revolutions of early modernity. In these centuries we find the origins of capitalism's Cheap Nature strategy, the very strategy that underpins today's biospheric turbulence. This strategy enables advancing labor productivity in great bursts by means of effecting even greater bursts in the production of the Four Cheaps: labor-power, food, energy, and raw materials. The catch is that capital-labor relations are not well-equipped to map, code, survey, quantify and otherwise identify and facilitate *new* sources of Cheap Nature. This latter has involved all manner of knowledge-practices, closely linked but not reducible to territorial power, in which the expanded reproduction of the capital-*un*paid work relation has been central. This is the terrain of abstract social nature and accumulation by appropriation.

The idea of nature as external has worked so effectively because the condition for capital's "self"-expansion is the location and production of natures external to capital. (A palpably co-productive process.) Because these natures are historical and therefore finite, the exhaustion of one historical nature quickly prompts the "discovery" of new natures that deliver qualitatively new and quantitatively larger sources of unpaid work. Thus did the Kew Gardens of British hegemony yield to the International Agricultural Research Centers of American hegemony, which in turn were superseded by the bioprospecting, rent-seeking, and genomic mapping practices of the neoliberal era.[29]

But the origins of Nature go back to the sixteenth century. Early capitalism's world-praxis, fusing symbolic coding and material inscription, moved forward an audacious fetishization of nature, crystallized in the era's cartographic, scientific, and quantifying revolutions. These were the symbolic moments of

---

27   D. Haraway, "Situated Knowledges," *Feminist Studies* 14, no. 3 (1988): 575–599.

28   Lefebvre, *The Production of Space* (1991).

29   L.H. Brockway, *Science and Colonial Expansion* (New York: Academic Press, 1978); J. R. Kloppenburg, Jr., *First the Seed* (Cambridge: Cambridge University Press, 1988); K. McAfee, "Neoliberalism on the Molecular Scale," *Geoforum* 34, no. 2 (2003): 203–219.

primitive accumulation, creating a new intellectual system whose presumption, personified by Descartes, was the separation of humans from the rest of nature.

The origins of Cheap Nature are, of course, more than intellectual and symbolic. The transgression of medieval intellectual frontiers was paired with the transgression of medieval territoriality. While civilizational expansion is in some sense fundamental to all, there emerged in early modern Europe a specific geographical thrust. While all civilizations had frontiers of a sort, capitalism did something very different. Before the sixteenth century, civilizational frontiers—such as feudal Europe's drive east of the Elbe—were more-or-less an output of the system. With the rise of capitalism, frontier-making was much more fundamental: not merely a safety valve, but a constitutive spatial moment unlocking the epoch-making potential of endless accumulation. The extension of capitalist power to new, uncommodified spaces became the lifeblood of capitalism. I have elsewhere considered the historical geographies of early capitalism's commodity frontiers.[30] For the moment, I wish to highlight two relational axes of these frontiers. First, commodity frontier movements were not merely about the extension of commodity relations, although this was central. They were also, crucially, about the deployment of territorial power and geographical knowledges necessary for the commodity-oriented appropriation of unpaid work/energy. This unpaid work could be delivered by humans—women or slaves, for example—or by extra-human natures, such as forests, soils, or rivers. Second, from the very beginning such frontiers were essential to creating forms of Cheap Nature specific to capitalism.

What are the implications of this line of thought for a post-Cartesian historical method, one that takes the law of value as a co-production of humans bundled with the rest of nature?

For Marx, use- and exchange-value represent "on the surface" the "internal opposition of use-value and value."[31] Marx's discussion in these opening pages of *Capital* is pitched at so high a level of abstraction that the significance of this "internal opposition" has been insufficiently grasped. To say that value and use-value are *internally related* is to say that the value relation encompasses the relation value/use-value in a way that necessarily extends beyond the immediate

---

30   Moore, "Sugar and the Expansion of the Early Modern World-Economy," *Review* 23, no 3. (2000); "Nature and the Transition from Feudalism to Capitalism"; "The Modern World-System as Environmental History?" (2003); "Madeira, Sugar, and the Conquest of Nature in the 'First' Sixteenth Century, Part I"; "'Amsterdam Is Standing on Norway' Part I" and "Part II"; "Madeira, Sugar, and the Conquest of Nature in the 'First' Sixteenth Century, Part II" (2010).

31   Marx, *Capital*, Vol. I (1977), 153, 209.

process of production. Here is a connection that allows us to join definite "modes of production" and definite "modes of life" in concrete historical unities.[32]

This means that capitalism can be comprehended through the shifting configuration of the exploitation of labor-power and the appropriation of Cheap Nature. This dialectic of paid and unpaid work demands a disproportionate expansion of the latter (appropriation) in relation to the former (exploitation). The reality is suggested by those widely cited estimates on the contribution of unpaid work performed by humans[33] and the rest of nature ("ecosystem services").[34] The quantitative reckonings for unpaid human work—overwhelmingly delivered by women—vary between 70 and 80 percent of world GDP; for "ecosystem services," between 70 and 250 percent of GDP. The relations between these two moments are rarely grasped,[35] and their role in long waves of accumulation rarely discussed.[36] Importantly, unpaid work comprises more than ongoing contributions to the daily reproduction of labor-power and the production cycles of agriculture and forestry. It also encompasses the appropriation of *accumulated* unpaid work, in the form of children raised to adulthood largely outside the commodity system (e.g., in peasant formations) and subsequently pushed or pulled into wage-work; and in the form of fossil fuels produced through biogeological processes.

The appropriation of unpaid work signifies something beyond the important—but still too partial—notion of environmental costs and externalities as "missing" from the determination of value.[37] For capitalism is not merely a system of unpaid costs ("externalities"). It is a system of unpaid work ("invisibilities"). Here we may borrow a core insight from feminist Marxism: the contribution of unpaid work is not "just there," but actively produced through complex (yet patterned) relations of power, (re)production, and accumulation. I risk pedantry here in saying that the "free gifts" of nature are not "low-hanging fruit" that can simply be picked without much time or

32   Marx and Engels, *The German Ideology* (1970), 42.

33   UNDP [United Nations Development Programme], *Human Development Report 1995* (Oxford: Oxford University Press, 1995); M. Safri and J. Graham, "The Global Household," *Signs* 36, no. 1 (2010): 16.

34   R. Costanza, et al., "The Value of the World's Ecosystem Services and Natural Capital," (1997); "Changes in the Global Value of Ecosystem Services," *Global Environmental Change* 26 (2014): 152–8.

35   But cf. P. Perkins, "Feminist Ecological Economics and Sustainability," *Journal of Bioeconomics* 9 (2007): 227–44.

36   On unpaid human work, cf. P.A. O'Hara, "Household Labor, the Family, and Macroeconomic Instability in the United States: 1940s-1990s," *Review of Social Economy* 53, no. 1 (1995): 89–120.

37   Cf. R. Patel, *The Value of Nothing* (New York: Picador, 2009).

effort. Cheap Natures are actively produced. All life is actively, creatively, incessantly engaged in environment-making—such that, in the modern world, human ingenuity (such as it is) and human activity (such as it has been) must *activate* the work of particular natures in order to appropriate particular streams of unpaid work. Such activation is co-produced, bundling the life-activities of human and extra-human nature, in the present and accumulated over time.

What are the implications for a historically grounded theory of value? On the one hand, capitalism lives and dies on the expanded reproduction of capital: value-in-motion. The substance of value is abstract social labor, or socially necessary labor-time. On the other hand, this production of value is particular—it does not value everything, only labor-power in the circuit of capital—and therefore rests upon a series of devaluations. Plenty of work—the majority of work in the orbit of capitalism—does not register as valuable. Work by humans, especially women; but also "work" performed by extra-human natures. Quite reasonably, Hribal asks, "Are animals part of the working class?"[38] The question itself illuminates the law of value's absurd, yet consistent, praxis. Although confusion persists on the matter, it is now clear that Marx understood that extra-human natures perform all sorts of useful (but not specifically *valuable*) work for capitalist production, and that such useful work was *immanent* to the capital-relation.[39] Marx's reading of value was, in other words, eminently post-Cartesian.

All of these de- and un-valued forms of work are, however, outside the value form (the commodity). They do not directly produce value. And yet—it is a very big *and yet*—value as abstract labor cannot be produced except through unpaid work/energy. This leads me to an unavoidable conclusion: the value *form* and the value *relation* are non-identical. The "commodification of everything" can only be sustained through incessant revolutionizing—yes, of the forces of production, but also of the *relations of reproduction*. The relations of reproduction cut across the paid/unpaid work and human/extra-human boundaries. In this, the historical condition for socially necessary labor-time is socially necessary unpaid work.

De-valued work becomes an "immanent . . . antithesis" within the generalization of commodity production and exchange.[40] In this contradiction, between the expanded reproduction of capital and the reproduction of life, we have "two universes, two ways of life foreign to each other yet whose

---

38   J. Hribal, "Animals are Part of the Working Class: A Challenge to Labor History," *Labor History* 44, no. 4 (2003): 435–54.

39   Burkett, *Marx and Nature* (1999).

40   Marx, *Capital*, Vol. I (1977), 209.

wholes explain one another."[41] And what is the geographical implication of this enabling and constraining tension between paid and unpaid work? The necessity of frontier-making. Recurrent waves of ·socio-ecological exhaustion—understood as the inability of a given bundle of human/extra-human natures to deliver more work to capital—motivate recurrent waves of geographical expansion. The commodity frontier strategy has been epoch-making not because of the extension of commodity production and exchange as such—a common misunderstanding of commodity frontier theory.[42] Rather, commodity frontiers were so epoch-making because they extended the zone of appropriation *faster* than the zone of commodification. Marx puts his finger on the crucial dialectic when he addresses the contradictions of the working day, the tendency towards manifold "industrial patholog[ies]," and the necessity of incorporating "physically uncorrupted" human natures into the world proletariat (see Chapter Nine).[43]

It will consequently not suffice to identify the influence of abstract social labor as an "economic" phenomenon, although this remains pivotal. The endless frontier strategy of historical capitalism is premised on a vision of the world as interminable: this is the conceit of capital and its theology of limitless substitutability.[44] At best, substitutability occurs within definite limits, primarily those of energy flows and the geographical flexibility they offer. The history of capitalism is one of relentless flexibility rather than endless substitutability. The conditions through which successive world-ecological revolutions have been realized—each yielding a quantum leap in the mass of "physical bodies" and making new streams of unpaid work/energy available for commodity production—may be understood as a succession of one-off affairs. Capitalism has moved from peat and charcoal to coal to oil; from the breadbaskets of the Vistula, southern England, and the American Midwest; to labor frontiers in Europe and Africa, Latin America, and South and East Asia. These are not repeatable events. Substitutability does not unfold through infinite time and space.

Abstract social labor, in this reading, is the *economic expression* of the law of

41   F. Braudel, *Afterthoughts on Material Civilization and Capitalism* (Baltimore: Johns Hopkins University Press, 1977), 6.

42   Moore, "Sugar and the Expansion of the Early Modern World-Economy" (2000): 409–33; "El Auge de la Ecologia-Mundo Capitalista, I," *Laberinto* 38 (2013): 9–26. "El Auge de la Ecologia-Mundo Capitalista, II," *Laberinto* 39 (2013), 6–14.

43   Marx, *Capital*, Vol. I (1977), 380.

44   Much of ecological economics can be read as a sustained critique of this theology. A useful introduction is found in H.E. Daly and J. Farley, *Ecological Economics* (Washington, D.C.: Island Press, 2004); also M. Perelman, "Scarcity and Environmental Disaster" (2007).

value. That law is unworkable historically without strategies of appropriating Cheap Nature. Why? Because the creation of socially necessary labor-time is constituted through a shifting balance of human and extra-human work. Socially necessary labor-time, in other words, is co-produced. If climate change suppresses agricultural productivity, as it has been doing for some time now,[45] the value-composition of production shifts accordingly—and not only in agriculture. Socially necessary labor-time forms and re-forms in and through the web of life.[46] Early capitalism's landscape transformations, in their epoch-making totality, were unthinkable without new ways of mapping space, controlling time, and cataloging external nature—and they are inexplicable solely in terms of world-market or class-structural change. The law of value, far from reducible to abstract social labor, finds its necessary conditions of self-expansion through the creation and subsequent appropriation of Cheap Natures. These movements of appropriation must, if capital is to forestall the rising costs of production, be secured through extra-economic procedures and processes.

By this I mean something more than the recurrent waves of primitive accumulation that we have come to accept as a cyclical phenomenon of capitalism.[47] These also remain crucial. But between our now cherished dialectic of "expanded reproduction" and "accumulation by dispossession"[48] are those knowledges and associated practices committed to the mapping, quantifying, and rationalizing natures in service to capital accumulation. Thus the trinity: abstract social labor, abstract social nature, primitive accumulation. This is the relational core of capitalist world-praxis. And the work of this unholy trinity? Produce Cheap Natures. Extend the zone of appropriation. In sum, deliver labor, food, energy, and raw materials—the Four Cheaps—faster than the accumulating mass of surplus capital derived from the exploitation of labor-power. Why? Because the rate of exploitation of labor-power (within the commodity system) tends to exhaust the life-making capacities that enter into the immediate production of value:

> Capital asks no questions about the length of life of labor-power. What interests it is purely and simply the maximum of labour-power that can be set in motion in a working day. It attains this objective by shortening the life of

---

45   D.B. Lobell, et al., "Climate Trends and Global Crop Production since 1980," *Science* 333, no. 6042 (2011): 616–620.

46   "[T]he process of reproduction has to be considered from the standpoint of the replacement of the individual components of C′ both in value and in material." (Marx, *Capital*, Vol. II [1978], 469).

47   M. de Angelis, *The Beginning of History* (London: Pluto, 2007).

48   D. Harvey, *The New Imperialism* (Oxford: Oxford University Press, 2003).

labour-power, *in the same way* as a greedy farmer snatches more produce from the soil by robbing it of its fertility.[49]

Exhaustion might take the form of an obvious withering of "vital forces."[50] More often, however, exhaustion manifests in the inability of a given production complex to yield a rising stream of unpaid work—performed by human and extra-human natures alike. This latter form of exhaustion typically issues from some combination of class struggle, biophysical change, and the tendentially rising "geographical inertia" of regional built environments.[51] In a world treated as boundless, capital as a whole has evinced a cumulative, but cyclically punctuated, tendency to search out and appropriate new, "physically uncorrupted" zones of Cheap labor, food, energy, and raw materials. Exhaustion signals a rising value composition of capital, and the inflection point of decline for a given production complex to supply more and more unpaid work to regional accumulation.[52] To the degree that "foreign preserves" can be identified and dominated, the relative "degeneration of the industrial population" matters little.[53] Has it been so different for extra-human natures? English agriculture, though not necessarily physically depleted, was certainly exhausted in terms of its capacity to send a rising stream of Cheap Food to metropolitan capital by the early decades of the nineteenth century.[54] Not surprisingly, British capitalism at its mid-century apex would nourish itself on the basis of cheap calories—grain and sugar—supplied from New World frontier zones in North America and the Caribbean.[55]

We can now connect the dots between the rise of capitalism and the emergence of the law of value. Value relations incorporate a double movement to exploitation and appropriation. Within the commodity system, the exploitation of labor-power reigns supreme. But this supremacy is only possible, given its tendency towards self-exhaustion, to the degree that the appropriation of

---

49   Marx, *Capital*, Vol. I (1977), 376. Emphasis added.

50   Ibid., 380.

51   From D. Harvey, *The Limits to Capital* (London: Verso, 1982), 428–9.

52   This explains something of the recurrent waves of financialization that redounded to the benefit of the declining world hegemon—in their respective *belle époques*, the Dutch, British, and American hegemonies each enjoyed a renewal of accumulation by capitalists in their respective geographical loci by deploying financial means to secure the fruits of agro-industrial expansions, based on new appropriations of cheap nature elsewhere in the world (Arrighi, *The Long Twentieth Century* [1994]).

53   J. Cairnes, *The Slave Power* (London: Parker, Son and Bourn, 1862), quoted in Marx, *Capital*, Vol. I, 377.

54   Thomas, *The Industrial Revolution and the Atlantic Economy* (1993).

55   Cronon, *Nature's Metropolis* (1991); Mintz, *Sweetness and Power* (New York: Penguin, 1985).

uncommodified natures counteracts this tendency. This has been difficult to discern because value *relations* are necessarily much broader than the immediate production of commodities. The generalization of commodity production has proceeded through an expansionary web of value relations whose scope and scale extends well beyond production. The problem of capitalist development is one of the uneven globalization of wage-work *dialectically joined to* the "generalization of its conditions of reproduction."[56] The centrality of wage-work in certain Marxist perspectives is not wrong but partial, given the unsustainability of the circuit of capital as closed system. The difficulty in pursuing this alternative analysis has been rooted in the dualisms immanent to modern thought; for to construct capitalism in the fashion that I have suggested is to transcend the man/woman, nature/society boundaries upon which the whole edifice of modernist thought depends.[57] Not only do we need to unify the distinctive but mutually formative dialectics of human work under capitalism through the nexus paid/unpaid work—"productive" and "reproductive" work. We also need to recognize that capitalism's dynamism has owed everything to appropriating and co-producing ever more creative configurations of human and extra-human work across the *longue durée*.

If we take the nexus of paid/unpaid work as our premise, capitalism and value relations cannot be reduced to a relation between the owners of capital and the possessors of labor-power. *The historical condition of socially necessary labor-time is socially necessary unpaid work.* This observation opens a vista on capitalism as a contradictory unity of production and reproduction that crosses the Cartesian boundary. The meaningful distinction is between the zone of paid work (the exploitation of commodified labor-power) and the zone of unpaid work (the reproduction of life). This contradictory unity works by creating a relatively narrow sphere of commodity production within which labor-power can be said to yield either rising or falling productivity, represented (imperfectly) through input-output calculations. This narrow sphere, premised on the exploitation of labor-power within commodity production, operates in relation to a much more expansive sphere of appropriation, through which the diversity of nature's "free gifts"—including the reproduction of life from the family to the biosphere—may be taken up into commodity production, but not fully capitalized. Why not? Because the capitalization of reproduction is subject to the exhaustive tendencies we have just discussed, which imply a rising value composition of capital and signal a situation in which capital must bear a greater share of its own costs.

---

56   P. McMichael, "Slavery in Capitalism," *Theory and Society*, 20, no. 3 (1991): 343.

57   V. Plumwood, *Feminism and the Mastery of Nature* (New York: Routledge, 1993), 41–68; M. Waring, *If Women Counted* (San Francisco: Harper and Row, 1988).

This new law of value, turning on socially necessary labor-time within commodity production, required an expansive (*and expanding*) domain of appropriating cheap natures. Early capitalism excelled at this: developing technologies and knowledges unusually well-suited to identifying, coding, and rationalizing Cheap Natures. Here the new way of seeing the world—inaugurated by the emergence of Renaissance perspective—decisively conditioned a new organizing *technics* for the capitalist world-ecology, manifesting in the cartographic-shipbuilding revolution of early modernity, from the Portolan maps and caravels to Mercator globes and galleons, and much beyond.

Appropriating cheap natures was and is a far more creative act than the *dependencia* language of plunder allows.[58] "Appropriation" represents a productive activity every bit as much as "exploitation." The outright seizure of basic wealth—clearly not an invention of the sixteenth century— could not provide a durable basis for the endless accumulation of capital. But the new praxis of Cheap Nature did. Here appropriative practices combined with the world market and technological innovations oriented towards global expansion. These practices comprised quite conscious colonial strategies to reorganize indigenous populations into strategic hamlets that functioned as labor reserves: the *reducciones* in the Andes and the *aldeias* in Brazil during the sixteenth century.[59] The practices enabled a rising rate of surplus value by treating the land, *simultaneously*, as a force of production and a "free gift." It did not matter that horrific levels of mortality accompanied this rising labor productivity so long as the costs of appropriation—through indigenous and African slave trades—were sufficiently low.[60]

This speaks to a problem not only of economic historiography but also of Marxist political economy. We are, in the conventional reading of Marx, offered two categories for the production of surplus value: absolute (more hours worked) and relative (more commodities produced in the same number of hours). Marx focused on the basic tendencies at play in the rise of large-scale industry, and this focus has been reproduced ever since. But Marx also points towards a theory of the rate of exploitation that is grounded in the dialectic of human and extra-human natures. In this, soil fertility may "act like an increase of fixed capital."[61] We can take this reference to soil fertility as a shorthand for the life-making

58   Cf. B. Clark and J.B. Foster. "Ecological Imperialism and the Global Metabolic Rift," *International Journal of Comparative Sociology* 50, nos. 3–4 (2009): 311–34.

59   D.W. Gade and M. Escobar. "Village Settlement and the Colonial Legacy in Southern Peru," *Geographical Review* 72, no. 4 (1982): 430–49; S.B. Schwartz, "Indian Labor and New World Plantations," *American Historical Review* 83, no. 1 (1978): 43–79.

60   S.B. Schwartz, *Sugar Plantations in the Formation of Brazilian Society* (Cambridge: Cambridge University Press, 1985); Moore, "Ecology and the Rise of Capitalism" (2007).

61   Marx, *Capital*, Vol. I (1977), 238, 636–8; *Grundrisse*, 748.

capacities of human and extra-human natures. Even where extraordinary soil fertility was in some sense "given," it was equally co-produced: as in the fertility of seventeenth-century Bahia or the nineteenth-century American Midwest and Great Plains. Absent the cartographic-shipbuilding revolution of the long sixteenth century, or the railroad revolution and the rationalization of American territory in the long nineteenth century, the bounty of these frontiers was no more than *potential*. These "hard" and "soft" technologies of production advanced labor productivity by harnessing the capacities of these natures to work for free. But it took work to get these natures to work for free. *This* was the innovation of early capitalist technical advance. Sugar and wheat frontiers remade the world only through extraordinary movements of capital, knowledge, and humans, each movement a mighty expenditure of energy aimed at transforming nature's *work* into the bourgeoisie's *value*. Yes, coal and oil are dramatic examples of this process of appropriating unpaid work. But this observation—namely, that fossil fuels have been central to rising labor productivity—is turned into a fetish when the same processes are not applied to early capitalism.

The consequence is a massive blind spot in radical thought: the great labor productivity revolution of early capitalism is almost universally ignored.[62] I suspect this has happened because our metrics and narrative frames have been largely unable to bring unpaid work into value-relations. The challenge is to internalize, in our narrative frames and analytical strategies, the ways that configurations of paid and unpaid work stabilize, and are cyclically restructured, through successive productivity regimes. Returning to our early modern frame, we might ask how to internalize, analytically, the fertility windfalls of *massapé* soils in seventeenth century Brazil? Or the contributions of the families of the *mitayos* (forced wage-workers) traveling to the Potosí mines? Or those of Norwegian and Baltic forests to the shipbuilding centers of the Dutch Republic? Or peasant cultivation to the off-season iron-making work of Swedish peasants, whose labor costs were correspondingly much lower than their English competitors? And perhaps most spectacularly—I am again transgressing the Cartesian boundary—the work of African families whose sons and daughters were impressed into slavery?

This early modern labor productivity revolution turned not only on Smithian specialization, technological change, and organizational innovation, but also on the new *technics* of value through which cheap natures were mapped, organized, and appropriated. The "fertility" of Cheap Natures was the pedestal for productivity advance within the commodity zone. Perhaps inadvertently, Clark offers an illuminating contrast about labor productivity informed by a caloric metric.

---

62   This revolution is largely unacknowledged, although sometimes hinted at (cf. D. Landes, *The Wealth and Poverty of Nations* [New York: W.W. Norton, 1998]).

In a passage that would resonate with any energy-centered critic of industrial agriculture, Clark notes that the average "worker-hour" in English agriculture around 1800 yielded about 2,600 calories, premised on wheat, milk, and wheat staples.[63] In contrast, the average "worker-hour" in swidden agriculture in early nineteenth century Brazil, cultivating manioc, maize, and sweet potatoes, yielded anywhere between 7,000 and 17,600 calories.[64]

What does this tell us? Most of all, it tells us that early capitalism triumphed because of its ability to appropriate the astounding realities, and realize the extraordinary potentialities, of uncommodified natures worldwide. If sixteenth-century Europe was exceptional in any technological sense, it was in this domain. Food works well as an example, because the metrics are easy, but one could multiply the appropriations of worker-hour windfalls to all sectors of early capitalism. How would work-hour productivity in timber vary between, say, coppiced English forests and the relatively unmanaged Norwegian forests of the late sixteenth century? Or between long-exploited Central European silver mines and Potosí's Cerro Rico around 1550? These differences were not "produced" in any straightforward, linear sense. But neither were these bountiful frontiers simply there for the taking. *They were co-produced.*

There was necessarily a mix of serendipity and strategy at play in early capitalism's productivity revolution: serendipity, insofar as New World crops such as maize, potatoes, and manioc were high-yielding; and strategy, insofar as the new commodity frontiers (sugar and silver especially) actively constructed production systems around such high-yielding crops. But even where Old World crops were introduced—the Spaniards in colonial Peru loved wheat—the initial yields were extraordinarily high (an order of magnitude greater than the Europe average) and remained so for the first long wave of colonial domination (c.1545–1640).[65] The point can scarcely be overstated: the introduction of "Cheap" food, as civilizational strategy, "acts like an increase in fixed capital." The declining price (value composition) of food equals advancing labor productivity equals the rising rate of exploitation.

The catch? The cheapening of food—along with raw materials and energy—cannot be accomplished by economic and territorial means alone. Cheap Food, and Cheap Nature as capitalist project, could be realized only through the symbolic regimes of abstract social nature. These encompassed the

---

63   G. Clark, *Farewell to Alms* (Princeton: Princeton University Press, 2007), 67–8.

64   Ibid.

65   J.C. Super, *Food, Conquest, and Colonization in Sixteenth-Century Spanish America* (Albuquerque: University of New Mexico Press, 1988); J.W. Moore, "'This Lofty Mountain of Silver Could Conquer the Whole World,'" *Journal of Philosophical Economics* 4, no. 1 (2010): 58–103.

"primitive accumulation of botanical knowledge" organized by Iberian botanical gardens,[66] the emergence of a new "map consciousness,"[67] the "death of nature" inaugurated by early modern materialism,[68] and much more. We will have both motive and opportunity to return to the question of abstract social nature later in this book.

The law of value-in-formation during early capitalism—*and since*—unfolded through two simultaneous movements, corresponding to the dialectic of value/use-value. The latter is "produced" through the zone of appropriation—the condition for *value*—encompassing the unpaid work/energy of human and extra-human natures. Historical capitalism has been able to resolve its recurrent crises because territorialist and capitalist agencies have extended the zone of appropriation faster than the zone of exploitation. This has allowed capitalism to successively overcome seemingly insuperable "natural limits" through the coercively enforced and scientifically enabled restoration of the Four Cheaps: labor-power, food, energy, and raw materials. The Four Cheaps are produced by effecting "accumulation by appropriation" faster than "accumulation by capitalization." This is possible on a planet where capitalization is limited and most life reproduces without the help of capital: the reality of early but not twenty-first-century capitalism. Hence, the centrality of the frontier and imperialism in capital accumulation. Significant enlargements in the zone of appropriation resolve capitalism's crises by simultaneously reducing the value composition of production, expanding physical output, and opening new spheres of capital investment. All of that can proceed so long as capitalization is checked, and appropriation liberated. This is, indeed, the history of capital, empire, and science in the modern world: every new era of capitalism brings with it a new industrialization, a new imperialism, a new science.

CONCLUSION

Taking value as an eductive method acknowledges the increasing centrality of value relations in the modern world-system over the past five centuries. Value emerges in and through Braudel's "market economy,"[69] weaving together the ethereal valences of finance capital and the prosaic routines of everyday life in new world-historical crystallizations of power and profit, pivoting on the

---

66   J. Cañizares-Esguerra, "Iberian Science in the Renaissance," *Perspectives on Science* 12, no. 1 (2004): 86–124.

67   Pickles, *A History of Spaces* (2004).

68   Merchant, *The Death of Nature* (1980).

69   F. Braudel, *The Wheels of Commerce*, trans. Siân Reynolds (New York: Harper & Row, 1982).

commodity. In this light, the apparently external relations of capitalism to nature are revealed as inner relations (capitalism-in-nature), constitutive of new, and profoundly restless, socio-ecological configurations.

Having opened the possibility for a view of value-in-nature, another challenge presents itself: to see value as a way to investigate the singular metabolism of modernity. To this challenge we may now turn.

CHAPTER 3

Towards a Singular Metabolism: From Dualism to Dialectics in the Capitalist World-Ecology

Dialectics does not consider fixed artifacts, formations and objects, the entire complex of both the material world of things and that of ideas . . . to be something original and autonomous. It does not accept them in their ready-made form, but subjects them to investigation in which the reified forms of the objective and the ideal worlds dissolve, [and] lose their fixed and natural character. (Kosík, 1976)

Metabolism is a seductive metaphor. As critical environmental studies across the humanities and social sciences boomed over the past decade, metabolism and its cognates—above all, the "metabolic rift"—has enjoyed a special place in Green and Red-Green thought. Mainstream and radical metabolism arguments have highlighted the importance of a historical perspective on the linkage of global capitalism (or industrial society) and global environmental change.[1] We can say two things about this special place. On the one hand, Marx's conception of social metabolism has been re-interpreted as the "metabolism of nature and society."[2] On the other hand, there has been virtually no critical interrogation of social metabolism as the metabolic exchange between two entities: "nature" and "society." Social metabolism has been cleansed of its double internality.

Why should this be a problem?

Metabolism-centered studies face an unresolved contradiction: between a philosophical-discursive embrace of a relational ontology (humanity-*in*-nature) and a practical-analytical acceptance of the Nature/Society dualism (humanity *and* nature). Indeed, the rise of metabolism as a "conceptual star" in the late 1990s owed much to its promise of fording the Nature/Society divide.[3] At the

---

1   Respectively, the "global metabolism" school of thought of Fischer-Kowalski and her colleagues; and the "metabolic rift" perspective of Foster, Richard York, Brett Clark, and their students. See M. Fischer-Kowalski, et al., "A Sociometabolic Reading of the Anthropocene," *The Anthropocene Review* 1, no. 1 (2014): 8–33; Foster et al., *The Ecological Rift* (2010).

2   Foster, *Marx's Ecology* (2000).

3   M. Fischer-Kowalski, "Society's Metabolism," in *The International Handbook of Environmental Sociology*, ed. M.R. Redclift and G. Woodgate (Cheltenham, UK: Edward Elgar, 1997) 119–37.

time—and still today—metabolism promised a way of bringing nature, as *oikeios*, into the core of how we see and think about historical change.

But it has not delivered on that promise. Rather than ford the Cartesian divide, metabolism approaches have reinforced it. Marx's "interdependent process of social metabolism" became the "metabolism of nature *and* society."[4] Metabolism as "rift" became a metaphor of separation, premised on material flows *between* Nature and Society. Thus did metabolic *rift* triumph over metabolic *shift* as a means of unifying humanity-in-nature within unified metabolisms of power, wealth, and nature. Meanwhile, our Red-Green "conceptual star" resisted the tendency of dialectical praxis to dissolve its analytical objects (Nature/Society), and to create new categories suitable to comprehending the messiness and interpenetration of humans with the rest of nature.

One of Cartesian dualism's essential features is the tendency to circumscribe truth claims by drawing hard and fast lines between what is human and what is "natural." We might call this an *epistemic rift*.[5] At the core of this epistemic rift is a series of violent abstractions implicated in the creation and reproduction of two separate epistemic domains: "Nature" and "Society." The abstractions are "violent" because they remove essential relations from each node in the interests of narrative or theoretical coherence.[6] Not for nothing was this symbolic divorce of Nature and Society consolidated in early capitalism. The epistemic rift was an expression—and, through new forms of symbolic praxis, an agent—of the world-shaking material divorce of the direct producers from the means of production.

If metabolism is not an exchange between quasi-independent objects—Nature/Society—but instead a process of life-making within the biosphere and its human-initiated processes, new possibilities emerge. The epistemic rift might be transcended. A singular metabolism of humanity-in-nature might allow us to chart a course beyond dualism.

This is, in a very general sense, an uncontroversial statement. Of course! Does not everyone wish to transcend dualism? The question often meets with widespread affirmation, especially but not only among critical scholars. But the

---

4   Quotations from, respectively, K. Marx, *Capital*, Vol. III., trans. D. Fernbach (New York: Pelican, 1981), 949; J.B. Foster, *Marx's Ecology* (2000), chapter five.

5   The term is indebted to Vetter, and Schneider and McMichael. Their independent formulations are, however, distinct from epistemic rift as epistemological dualism. J. Vetter, "Expertise, 'Epistemic Rift,' and Environmental Knowledge in Mining and Agriculture in the U.S. Great Plains and Rocky Mountains" (Paper presented to the Annual Meeting of the American Society for Environmental History, March 29, 2012); M. Schneider and P. McMichael, "Deepening, and Repairing, the Metabolic Rift," *Journal of Peasant Studies* 37, no. 3 (2010): 461–84.

6   Sayer, *The Violence of Abstraction* (1987).

affirmation requires no real action in the absence of a method—what I am calling the double internality—that enables and encourages new analytics as if nature matters. Even today, the spirit of this double internality remains largely outside the methodological frames, theoretical propositions, and narrative strategies of the humanities and social sciences. They remain captive to the logic of human exceptionalism: the curious notion that humanity "alone is not a spatial and temporal web of interspecies dependencies."[7] In this logic, relations between humans are regarded as ontologically prior to the relations of nature, a metatheoretical procedure that allows one to speak of modernity as a set of social relations that act upon, rather than develop through, the web of life.

Emphasizing disruption and separation, rather than reconfiguration and unity, the metabolic rift has come to signify "a disruption in the exchange between social systems and natural systems."[8] Social systems, in this framework, are separate from natural systems. Social systems *disrupt* natural systems. As capitalism develops, the disruption of nature escalates, leading to "planetary crisis." Catastrophe ensues.

It all makes a certain amount of sense is it *good* sense? Is nature really best considered as external to—and an external limit of—capitalism? Or is capitalism, *and its limits*, co-produced through shifting configurations of human and extra-human nature?

If one begins with the *oikeios* and the double internality, we may reconceptualize metabolism as a flow of power, capital, and material nature characterized by an "unbroken coincidence of our being, our doing, and our knowing."[9] To recast our narrative on the basis of this "unbroken coincidence" implies a movement from "the" environment as object to environment-making—as we saw in Chapter One. For humanity in the era of historical capitalism, environment-making has reached a stage of development capable of facilitating a new geological era. This is usually called the Anthropocene ("Age of Man"), but is more accurately called the Capitalocene ("Age of Capital"). It is certain that the twenty-first century is a moment of extraordinary global change.

The task of interpreting these extraordinary global changes is daunting, and complicated by more than the facts on the ground. For the epistemic rift between the "economic" and the "environmental" limits our capacity to understand the present conjuncture; it constrains our understanding of how capitalism has created and resolved crises over the *longue durée*. A concept of metabolism that transcends this epistemic rift may, however, liberate us from these constraints.

---

7   Haraway, *When Species Meet* (2008), 11.

8   R. York, "Metabolic Rift," in *Encyclopedia of the Earth*, ed. C.J. Cleveland, (2010), http://www.eoearth.org/view/article/154577/, accessed March 8, 2014.

9   Maturana and Varela, *The Tree of Knowledge* (1987), 250.

Metabolism may then become more than a way of seeing flows "between." It can become a way of seeing flows *through*. In what follows, we consider a reconstruction of metabolism as a means to unify modernity's differentiated flows of capital, power, and life.

FROM GREEN ARITHMETIC TO DIALECTICAL REASON

The turbulence of the twenty-first century confounds the old models of historical change. Even when such models recognize environmental change, they are premised on the idea that capitalism develops *upon* Nature—not *through* the web of life. But financialization, global warming, the rise of China, the end of Cheap Food—and much beyond these—cannot be understood in the old terms. They are neither social nor environmental processes, as conventionally understood. They *are* bundles of human and extra-human nature whose fundamental connections turn on the configuration of power and re/production in the web of life. In this frame, it is not the humanity's separation *from* Nature that matters. It is humanity's place *within* the web of life. Humanity is differentiated and plural; its diversity cohered through capitalism's re-shaping of the *oikeios*. This approach offers something that the well-worn trope of humanity's separation from Nature cannot: the possibility of discerning the conditions of capitalist renewal (if any) and crisis in the twenty-first century. For I think many of us understand intuitively—even if our analytical frames still lag behind—that capitalism is more than an "economic" system, and even more than a social system. Capitalism is a way of organizing nature.

Such a perspective immediately draws our attention towards two great organizing moments. This is the double internality of historical change. On the one hand, capitalism internalizes—however partially—the relations of the biosphere. In the process, the agencies of capital and empire (but not only these) seek to turn the work/energy of the biosphere into capital (abstract social labor). On the other hand, the biosphere internalizes the relations of capital. These are asymmetrical relations, of course; their valences and vectors change over time. In this, the philosophical point shapes the historical observation: capitalism, like all civilizations, is constituted through a double internalization. Hence capitalism-in-nature/nature-in-capitalism. To say human activity of any sort "organizes" nature is to say that human activity is ontologically coincident with, and constituted through, specifically bundled relations with the rest of nature. "Society" is not only a producer of changes in the web of life but also a *product* of it; this is the heart of a co-evolutionary method in which human history is always bundled with the rest of nature.

The production of nature is therefore always the *co-production* of nature—a co-production not of two ontologically independent units (Humanity plus Nature) but of an evolving mosaic of interdependent flows, forces, conditions, and relations. (Humans are surely distinctive in this mosaic, a point to which we will return.) This means that the accumulation of capital and the pursuit of power in the modern world-system do not *have* an ecological dimension. They are, rather, ways of human organization moving, representing, channeling, and reworking a singular metabolism: the web of life. And in the very act of moving, representing, channeling, and reworking, human organization *acquires new properties*, undergoes cumulative and sometimes fundamental change, and brings new contradictions to the fore.

In this, *all* human activity is environment-making. This extends far beyond what I would call earth-moving: urbanization, agricultural expansion, mining, and so forth. Environment-making includes those symbolic, cultural, and scientific processes central to modernity's reworking of the *oikeios*. The "thinking" and the "doing" of environment-making are two moments of a singular process. Ideas of nature are fundamental to earth-moving. Environment-making is, consequently, not limited to earth-moving. It encompasses those epoch-making revolutions in cartography, mathematics, agronomy, economic botany, quantification, and rationalizing endeavors of all kinds—the relations of *abstract social nature*. In this perspective, "capitalism" names those long-run and large-scale patterns of environment-making that encompass *and are necessary to sustain* a project of endless commodification. Earth-moving always works *through* the extra-economic procedures of mapping and quantifying reality, *through* new "measures of reality" (see Chapter Eight).[10]

By contrast, metabolism arguments have avoided the active role of cultural process and scientific knowledge in the history of capitalism. They have consequently facilitated a kind of materialism that dramatically understates the role of ideas in historical change. This favors explanations of crisis premised on an exogenous breakdown model, in which overpopulation, resource scarcity, earth-system breakdown, and increasingly global warming, will cause either planetary disaster or the end of civilization as we know it.

The result is a curious state of affairs in thinking capitalism's historical limits, and considering Marx's "ecological" thought in the study of historical change. For much of Left Ecology, "Marxist ecology = society + nature": an arithmetic rather than dialectical procedure. There are social limits, and there are natural limits. But the boundaries between the two units—Nature/Society—are nowhere specified; and the ways in which Social limits make

---

10   A.W. Crosby, Jr., *The Measure of Reality* (Cambridge: Cambridge University Press, 1997).

Natural limits, and vice versa, are unexplored. The *history* of each limit is asserted rather than historically constructed.[11] By and large, the metabolism argument has painted a picture of capitalism sending Nature into the abyss . . . with little sense of *how* history is co-produced by humans in the web of life. (And does not our politics turn on this "how"?) The consequence is a static and ahistorical theory of natural limits, in which Humans (not-Nature) ultimately push Nature (not-Humans) too far, whereupon nature exacts its "revenge."[12] Too often, however, the revenge of Nature appears as impending cataclysm, and too rarely, as a "normal" cyclical phenomenon of capitalism. This narrow view of limits undermines the consideration of how capitalism has overcome its socio-ecological limits historically, and what might be different today.

The one-size-fits-all model of ecological crisis is a problem if we acknowledge nature as a constitutive field and force in modern world history. This history is replete with instances of capitalism overcoming "natural" limits. Any account of capitalist development unable to come to grips with capitalism's cyclical crises—*developmental crises*—will be unable to frame a theory of capitalism's *cumulative* limits today. Ignoring the "normal" operation of capitalism's world-ecological reorganizations, a dual systems approach to metabolism gives us only one flavor of crisis—the apocalypse.[13] In the absence of a rigorous historical approach to the bundling of human and extra-human natures in the accumulation process, arguments for an *epochal* crisis today will tend to fall back on arithmetic rather than dialectical reason.

This fetishization of natural limits is problematic analytically, because it blinds us to the ways that capitalism unfolds historically through the web of life. Positing two metabolisms, one Social and one Natural, the Marxist metabolism school forgets to answer the really revolutionary question: How are distinctive metabolisms of capital, power, and production *unified*, however unevenly, across the long arc of capitalist history?

Such a question hardly rules out the specification of distinctive metabolisms. But it *does* rule out the *a priori* designation of metabolism as an exchange between the mythic categories Nature/Society. In Foster's pioneering work, metabolism moved from an open question—how can categories of class and capital be reworked in light of biophysical flows?—towards a hardening of distinctions: "the metabolism of nature and society." Through Foster's reading,[14] Marx's ecological insights have been taken up by a significant layer

---

11   For example, Foster, et al., *The Ecological Rift* (2010).

12   Engels, "The Part Played by Labor in the Transition from Ape to Man" (1970).

13   Larry Lohmann, "Fetishisms of Apocalypse," *Occupied Times*, 30 October (2014).

14   Foster, *Marx's Ecology* (2000).

of critical scholarship in highly dualist fashion. There is no denying the contribution of Foster's elaboration of the metabolic rift: in its time, the rift concept opened new questions for critical environmental studies. At the same time, Foster's ambivalent dualism blunted the possibilities for a dialectical synthesis.

Such a synthesis confronted other obstacles as well. The formulation of social metabolism as the metabolism of Nature *and* Society has won such great popularity among social scientists because it leaves untouched the sacred category of Society. In channeling research into the metabolism of Nature *and* Society, the radical metabolism perspective has reduced nature to flows and stocks within and between pre-formed units. This has, in turn, driven a wedge between Marx's historical materialism and Marx's theory of value.

And why should this matter? Because capitalism's metabolism of capital, power, and nature is governed by a logic of value accumulation, which reduces the world to zones of exploitation (surplus-value) and appropriation (of unpaid work). A reading of metabolism that takes seriously the centrality of value as a logic of re/producing the flow of life helps us to see how capitalism has created and transcended limits. Taking an expanded conception of value-relations, we can better interpret the ways in which the worlds of humanity-in-nature became valued and de-valued over the past five centuries, converting the globe into a vast storehouse of unpaid work/energy. This Cheap Nature strategy has been the basis for advancing labor productivity within the commodity system. Marx's conception of value-relations, in other words, provides a way of seeing the exploitation of labor-power and the appropriation of unpaid work as a singular metabolism of many determinations. The exclusion of value-relations from the historical materialism of nature has the virtue of never specifying how capital works through nature— something sure to enhance the metabolic rift's appeal (for now), but at the cost of a necessary clarity.

FROM DUALISM TO DIALECTICS: METABOLIC RIFT TO METABOLIC SHIFT

Adding "the environment" to a laundry list is precisely that: additive, and not synthetic. This "soft" dualism tends to justify social-reductionist analyses of neoliberalism's crisis tendencies. Nature, in the dominant critical approach, does not call for any fundamental rethinking of the patterns of recurrence, evolution, and crisis in historical capitalism. For world-historical scholars too, environmental factors are now widely recognized, but again in additive fashion: "the" environment can now be added to a long list of consequential factors in modern world history. The web of life has been transformed into a variable. It is this Green Arithmetic—"Nature plus Society"—that insulates critical political economy and world-historical studies from a view of modernity as producer and product of the web of life. And it is this arithmetic that leads Foster to conclude in 2002—shaping a decade of metabolic rift analysis—that there is no "feedback mechanism that . . . turns environmental destruction into increasing costs for capital itself."[15]

But what if nature matters as more than consequence, as more than variable? How then do we go about reshaping our methodological premises, conceptual vocabulary, and analytical frames to show capitalism-in-nature at work? Any effective response must pursue a translation of the philosophical claim (humanity-in-nature) into workable analytics for the history of capitalism—including, of course, the history of the present.

For the world-ecology synthesis, the historical task is not one of explaining the separation of humanity and nature. The priority is to specify the historical forms of humanity-in-nature, and therefore nature-in-humanity. Humanity's species-being is located at once inside and outside. Marx's "system of nature" is immediately internalized through our life-activity, which, through embodied thought, simultaneously externalizes our experiences and mental constructs in a never-ending, yet asymmetrical and contingent, circle of life.[16]

A world-ecological method unfolds from the premise of a fundamental unity between human activity and the rest of nature. The historical specificity of human organization derives from its co-produced relation within the web of life. There is no ontological divide between the web of life and civilizations, only distinctive variations and configurations. Civilizations are specific forms of power and re/production, which is to say they are producers and products of specific historical natures. Even when environments are in some abstract sense pre-formed (the distribution of the continents, for example), historical change works through the encounters of humans with those environments. That relation is fundamentally co-productive. A mountain range or an ocean is an environmental, not historical, fact. *Historical* change begins when we move from environmental facts to environment-making, through which humans make environments and vice versa. Here we recognize that humanity's environment-making proceeds through the nexus of production and reproduction, a process in which humanity "can only proceed as nature does herself," by "chang[ing] the form of the materials."[17] Such a mode of analysis

15   J.B. Foster, *The Ecological Revolution* (New York: Monthly Review Press, 2009), 206.

16   Marx, *Economic and Philosophical Manuscripts* (2007), 157.

17   Marx, *Capital*, Vol. I (1977) 107.

gives analytical—not just moral—teeth to radicals' now-ritualized denuncia-tions of capitalism's destruction, degradation, and disruption of nature. It allows us to shift to the "reordering of matter" through the *oikeios* in its succes-sive historical-geographical forms.[18] The notion that humans relate to nature from within, in our "physical and mental life . . . simply means that nature is linked to itself."[19] From this perspective, the problem is not metabolic *rift*, but metabolic *shift*.

TOWARDS A SINGULAR METABOLISM: GEOGRAPHY, NATURE, AND THE LIMITS TO CAPITAL

The pursuit of such a holistic and relational perspective implies a transition from dualism to dialectics. The virtue of the metabolic rift as a heuristic intervention was to highlight the irreducibly geographical character of human activity, always interdependent within the web of life. Metabolisms are always geographical. Capitalist relations move through, not upon, space—which is to say, through and not upon nature as a whole.

Indeed, a closr reading of Foster's original formulation of metabolic rift opens the possibility for thinking through a singular metabolism of power, nature, and capital. Foster originally formulated the rift in three registers. First, there is a "rift between human production and its natural conditions." Second, there is a "material estrangement [alienation] of human beings in capitalist society from the natural conditions of their existence." And third, this rift finds geographical expression in a new town-country antagonism.[20] Foster took the *rift* in metabolic rift to signify the rechanneling of food and resources produced in agrarian zones into urban-industrial spaces. Although metabolic *rift* today is almost universally understood as a metaphor of separa-tion, the original argument suggested something different: rift as reconfiguration and shift.

In this, Foster broke new ground and assembled the elements of a new synthe-sis. This new synthesis promised not only a revitalized and reworked historical materialism in line with Marx's system of thought. It would also actively pursue the renewal of value-relational thinking—the law of value as co-produced by humans and the rest of nature—offered by Burkett's pioneering *Marx and Nature*, a companion to *Marx's Ecology*.[21] The potential was tantalizing. The

---

18   P. Verri, quoted in ibid.
19   Marx, *Economic and Philosophical Manuscripts*, 133.
20   Foster, "Marx's Theory of Metabolic Rift," (1999), 370, 383–4.
21   Cf. Foster, *Marx's Ecology* (2000), 282n; Burkett, *Marx and Nature* (1999).

incorporation of an ecologically informed theory of value into historical materialism—the synthesis made possible by reading *Marx's Ecology* and *Marx and Nature* as a singular argument—would be a "groundbreaking" contribution. Its core insight? A theory of the "alienation of nature and the alienation of human production *as two sides of a single contradiction*."[22] This would allow us to see the history of capitalism as a world history in which nature matters not merely as consequence, but as constitutive and active in the accumulation of abstract social labor.

Foster's enduring contribution,[23] then, was to suggest how we might read Marx to join capital, class, and metabolism as an organic whole. From this perspective, all social relations are spatial relations and relations within the web of life. Metabolism becomes a way to discern *shifts* (provisional and specific unifications), not *rifts* (cumulative separation). In these terms, the apparent solidity of town and country, bourgeois and proletarian, and above all Society and Nature, begins to melt. Metabolism, liberated from dualisms, acts as a solvent. For if metabolism as a whole is a flow of flows in which life and matter enter into specific historical-geographical arrangements, we are called to construct a much more supple and historically sensitive family of concepts, unified by a dialectical method that transcends all manner of dualisms—not least, but not only, Nature/Society.

What does this mean for the question of limits? Foster's insight was to posit capitalism as an open-flow metabolism, one that requires more and more Cheap Nature just to stay in place: not just nature as input (e.g., cheap fertilizer) but also nature as waste frontier (e.g., greenhouse gas emissions). Many of the most powerful implications of metabolic rift thinking, however, remain fettered by the very dualisms that Foster initially challenged. Not least is an unduly narrow view of accumulation as an "economic" process (it is surely much more than this) and an undue emphasis on the rarely specified "destruction" of nature.[24]

Historical natures *are* subject to broadly entropic processes—the degradation of nature—but these are also reversible within certain limits. Much of this reversibility turns on capitalism's frontiers of appropriation. Thus the centrality of the "Great Frontier." Walter Prescott Webb coined the term to describe the great shift in the labor-land ratio that inaugurated the rise of capitalism in the sixteenth century.[25] The Great Frontier was, Webb reminded us, the source

22   Foster, "Marx's Ecological Value Analysis," *Monthly Review* 52, no. 4 (2000), emphasis added.

23   Foster, *Marx's Ecology*.

24   Foster, et al., *The Ecological Rift* (2010); Foster, *The Ecological Revolution* (2009).

25   W.P. Webb, *The Great Frontier* (Austin: University of Texas Press, 1964).

of unprecedented "windfall profits." These windfalls began—but did not end—with the plunder of gold and silver. The opening of the Great Frontier marked the rise of a civilization that had begun to pivot on the cash nexus. But the new frontiers offered much, much more than a one-time windfall: they offered up the possibility of an entire historical epoch based on windfall profits. Webb thought the modern world was the product of a great "boom" of economic prosperity that lasted for four centuries. On closer inspection, thanks to the vertical frontiers of coal and then oil, this Great Boom appears to have lasted until the dawn of the twenty-first century (with signs of exhaustion apparent by the 1970s). Although the specifics of Webb's analysis have often been super-seded in the half-century since he wrote it, the basic argument remains as sound as ever: modernity's epoch-making reorganizations of labor and land were premised on ruthless conquest and the *ongoing appropriation* of wealth on the frontier.

The frontier of what? Of commodification and global value relations. For central to the great arc of modern world history has been the voracious consumption of, and relentless quest for, Cheap Natures—"cheap" in relation to the accumulation of capital and its curious privileging of wage-work as the only thing worth valuing. A civilizational conceit of this sort could only emerge on the basis of devaluing both human work outside the commodity system—much of it so-called women's work—and the "work" of extra-human natures.

What this line of thought suggests is that the investigation of capitalism and the "end of cheap nature" has been hobbled by its Cartesian sorting out of the problem. Too often, "nature" remains the stuff of metals and oil and corn, to the exclusion of human natures, and to the exclusion of the constitutive relations between them. So I would recommend that our analyses of capitalism's metabolism and its limits begin by unifying the processes of "surplus humanity" and the end of cheap energy, food, and raw materials. We can dispense with the notion that something like climate change can be analyzed in its quasi-independent social and natural dimensions. And we can embrace the understanding that, with climate change, financialization, or warfare, we are dealing with bundles of human and extra-human natures. These are varied and bundled "determinations of one essence."[26] Such an embrace would take "limits talk" as a methodological proposition rather than an empirical claim, setting aside the millenarian language of catastrophe and privileging a more hopeful and historical view of limits and crises. Crises are full of danger, to be sure. But they are also, as the Chinese would remind us, full of opportunity.

The limits suggested by a monist and relational view of metabolism bring into

---

26   Marx, "Critique of Hegel's Philosophy of Right," (1843), www.marxists.org/archive/marx/works/1843/critique-hpr/cho5.htm.

focus the historical agency of extra-human natures as internal to capitalism's crises. Capitalism as world-ecology defies the convenient and Cartesian notion that capital, power, and production can be placed into their bloodless and disembodied boxes, next to another, bigger but still quite tidy box: Nature. And if we still recognize that the capitalist project creates something called Nature in discrete forms (resources, genes, etc.), a world-ecological view of metabolism reveals this view of compartmentalized natures as a "God-trick": please *do* pay attention to the Man behind the Curtain.

The promise of a singular metabolism perspective is this. It recognizes that the realities signified by capital, power, and nature cannot be encaged within dualist categories. It dissolves those categories and opens the possibility for new, more relevant and practical, concepts. Capital and power (and more than this, of course) unfold within the web of life, a totality that is shaped by manifold civilizational projects. These projects are not infinitely contingent. Foster and his colleagues are right about the "what" of capitalism's coherence. Nevertheless, their dualism—an ontological and epistemic rift—keeps them from seeing how value-relations, which are themselves co-produced, make that coherence. These value-relations create quasi-law-like rules of reproduction that necessarily admit contingency: capitalism's greatest strength has been its flexibility in mobilizing and recombining parts of nature in the interests of endless accumulation. And because value has been premised on valuing some nature (e.g., wage-labor) and not-valuing most nature ("women, nature, colonies"), it necessitated a powerfully alienating conception of Nature as external.

At the core of the capitalist project, from its sixteenth century origins, was the scientific and symbolic creation of nature in its modern form, as something that could be mapped, abstracted, quantified, and otherwise subjected to linear control. This was external nature; it is what we have come to call Nature, even if many of us no longer believe in a Nature that is independent of the Anthropos. (And is not the Anthropos as violent an abstraction as Nature?) It is easy to talk about the "limits to growth" as if they were imposed by this (external) Nature. But the reality is thornier, more complex—and also more hopeful. The limits of capitalist civilization include biophysical realities, but are not reducible to them. And if the limits of capitalism today are limits of a particular way of organizing nature, we are confronted with the possibility of changing humanity's relation to nature—which is to say also humanity's relation to itself. We are frequently warned of the alleged dangers of civilizational "collapse." But is the "collapse" of capitalism—a civilization that plunges more than a third of its population into malnutrition—really something to be feared? Historical experience suggests not. The Fall of Rome after the fifth century, and the collapse of feudal power in Western Europe in the fourteenth century, ushered in golden ages in living standards for the vast majority.[27] We should be wary of making too much of such parallels. But neither should we ignore them.

I have long thought that the most pessimistic view is one that hopes for the survival of modernity in something like its present form. But this is impossible, because capitalism's metabolism is inherently an open-flow system that continually exhausts its sources of nourishment. There are limits to how much new work capitalism can squeeze out of new working classes, forests, aquifers, oilfields, coal seams, and everything else. Nature is finite. Capital is premised on the infinite. And both are *historical* in a very specific sense: what worked at one historical juncture will not necessarily work at the next. Thus the centrality of the Great Frontier in the history of capitalism, and the centrality of the end of the last frontiers—Cheap oil in the Middle East, Cheap labor-power in China, Cheap food everywhere—in the present conjuncture. It was this Great Frontier that inaugurated a civilizational metabolism in which most nature, including most humans, was sacrificed in service to the productivity of wage-labor. These frontiers of appropriation were the major way of making others, outside the circuit of capital but within reach of capitalist power, foot the bill for endless accumulation. The great secret and the great accomplishment of capitalist civilization has been to *not* pay its bills. Frontiers made that possible. Their closure is the end of Cheap Nature—and with it, the end of capitalism's free ride.

27   C. Wickham, *Framing the Middle Ages* (Oxford: Oxford University Press, 2005); Wallerstein, *The Modern World-System I* (1974).

Part II

HISTORICAL CAPITALISM, HISTORICAL NATURE

CHAPTER 4

The Tendency of the Ecological Surplus to Fall

Everyone knows why capitalism runs itself into crisis, right? Too many commodities chasing too few customers. Economists call this the problem of "effective demand." For Marxists, the emphasis lies squarely within the zone of production and investment: overproduction and overaccumulation. For both, the problem of crisis unfolds within the zone of commodification. My argument in this chapter says something different: the problem of crisis unfolds through the unifying relations between the zone of commodification and the zone of reproduction. The tendency of surplus capital to rise, and of the world-ecological surplus to fall, are entwined.

The entwined character of capital accumulation in the web of life has been recognized for a long time.[1] But the process of crisis-formation in the *oikeios* has so far eluded us. This will be our focus for the next three chapters.

We may begin with the basics. Capitalism is a system of endless accumulation. Because accumulated capital flows disproportionately into the hands of ... well, *capitalists*, a big problem presents itself. Marx called this the "general law of capitalist accumulation": the accumulation of capital in hands of the few, the accumulation of poverty in the hands of the many.[2] At some point, the goods and services produced in the "real economy" cannot be purchased in a rising volume by those in "real life." In one sense, this is an *overproduction* problem: too many factories produce too many cars, or refrigerators, or computers that cannot be purchased in sufficient volumes to maintain the rate of profit. In another sense, it is an *overaccumulation* problem: the rate of profit in existing investment lines begins to fall, and new, more profitable investment opportunities have not emerged.

So far, so good. What has happened—in both radical and mainstream economic thinking—is a curious conflation of overaccumulation and overproduction. Why this should be so is no mystery. The formation of Marxist and neoclassical thought across the long twentieth century occurred during the long fossil fuel boom. That boom made possible a series of innovations and transformations

---

1   O'Connor, *Natural Causes* (1998); R. Luxemburg, *The Accumulation of Capital* (New York: Routledge, 2003 [1913 orig.]).

2   Marx, *Capital*, Vol. I (1977).

that propelled rising labor productivity, new agricultural and resource frontiers, and the radical extension of value relations worldwide, setting hundreds of millions of peasants "free" to work for wages. It seemed to abolish the specter of crisis haunting early capitalism: underproduction. Thus, overproduction was the necessary and immediate problem that needed to be explained. And it became very easy to conflate overproduction with overaccumulation.

It was especially easy to conflate the two if one assumed that capitalism begins around 1800. This is what I call the "Two Century Model." It has obscured the revolutionary shift in environment-making that occurred after 1450, as we will see. Early capitalism was indeed real capitalism in every major respect: labor productivity increased, commodification widened and deepened with no systemic reversals, proletarianization accelerated sharply, capital moved into production, from farming to heavy industry, and a new scale, scope and speed of environment-making altered regional ecologies across the planet.

Early capitalism's dominant crisis tendency was not overproduction, but *under*production—the insufficient flow of labor, food, energy, and materials relative to the demands of value production. Early capitalism's greatest problem centered on the delivery of cheap inputs to the factory gates, not on selling the commodities that issued from manufacturing centers. To be clear, we are dealing with configurational weight: underproduction and overproduction always operate simultaneously. The Dutch Republic was the seventeenth century's "model capitalist nation"[3] because it organized and led a world-ecological regime that delivered Cheap grain (from Poland), Cheap energy (from domestic peat), and Cheap timber (from Norway and the Baltic) to the northern Netherlands. When this regime faltered, definitively by the 1760s, the British married technical ingenuity with geological good fortune to move from increasingly expensive wood fuel to increasingly cheap coal.[4] This marriage solved—but did not abolish—the problem of underproduction, setting the stage for two centuries of remarkable expansion.

MARX'S GENERAL LAW OF UNDERPRODUCTION

Marx did not like to write about scarcity. Malthus ruined the question for him. But it's not true that Marx avoided the problem. Arguably, Marx's general model

---

3   Marx, *Capital*, Vol. I, 916.

4   Properly speaking, the price per BTU of coal energy in early modern England remained steady in the face of sharply rising output. R.C. Allen, "The British Industrial Revolution in Global Perspective" (Unpublished paper, Department of Economics, Oxford University, 2006).

of accumulation crisis is grounded in capital's co-production of value. The organic composition of capital, writes Perelman with some exaggeration, was "a code for scarcity . . . In the back of Marx's mind, [capitalism's co-production of] scarcity was [partly] responsible for the falling rate of profit."[5]

Scarcity probably isn't the best word for what we have seen in the history of capitalism. I'm with Marx on this one—there is a better conceptual language we can use. Marx's choice was "underproduction." And among Marx's many "general laws," the least appreciated is the general law of *under*production.[6] The general law of underproduction identifies the circuit of capital *as* a socio-ecological relation, albeit one whose substance (value) is necessarily blind to "natural distinctness."[7] In this model, "the rate of profit is inversely proportional to the value of the raw materials":[8] The cheaper the raw materials and energy, the higher the rate of profit. Why? Because "constant" capital is comprised of two moments. One is fixed capital, comprising machinery, but also other extra-human forces of production, including animals, that outlast the production cycle.[9] The other is *circulating* constant capital, not to be confused with the *circulation* (and circuit) of capital. Circulating capital is the forgotten moment in Marx's model—a casualty of dualist habits of thought. It consists of energy and raw materials used up during a production cycle. The dynamism of capitalist production, observes Marx, leads the "portion of constant capital that consists of fixed capital . . . [to] run significantly ahead of the portion consisting of organic raw materials, so that the demand for these raw materials grows more rapidly than their supply."[10] Marx goes still further. Not only does fixed capital in industrial production tend to "run ahead" of raw materials sectors, the *condition* for large-scale industrial production is Cheap Nature: "it was only the large fall in the price of cotton which enabled the cotton industry to develop in the way that it did."[11] In sum: the "overproduction" of machinery (fixed capital) finds its

5   M. Perelman, "Marx and Resource Scarcity," in *The Greening of Marxism*, ed., T. Benton (New York: Guilford Press, 2006), 73.

6   Marx, *Capital*, ed. F. Engels, Vol. III (New York: International Publishers, 1967), 111.

7   Marx, *Grundrisse* (1973), 141.

8   Marx, *Capital*, Vol. III (1967), 111.

9   Hribal and Haraway are correct to argue for non-human animals as central to the production of surplus value—but err in assigning animals to the working class. This is not, in any event, how capital views animals, which are either circulating or fixed capital. Indeed, the very condition for variable capital (*human* labor-power) is capital's designation of non-human animals as non-workers. Hribal, "Animals are Part of the Working Class" (2003); Haraway, *When Species Meet* (2008), 55.

10   Marx, *Capital*, Vol. III (1967), 118–19.

11   K. Marx, *Theories of Surplus Value*, Vol. III (Moscow: Progress Publishers, 1971), 368.

dialectical antagonism in the "underproduction" of raw materials (circulating capital).[12] This law, like the tendency of the rate of profit to fall, is a dialectic of tendencies and counter-tendencies, in which the latter are *endogenous*. This endogeneity of nature—through the double internality—sets Marx's perspective as a clear contrast to the Malthusian program.

The issue is therefore not overproduction *or* underproduction. It is how the two *fit together* in successive eras of accumulation. Underproduction is of course much more than the overproduction of machinery and the underproduction of inputs. The model is too simple. We cannot, however, get to the complexities without it. The overproduction of machinery and the underproduction of raw materials is where long cycles of accumulation end up: overcapacity and rising raw materials prices.[13] If there is nothing particularly revolutionary in the observation, it points us in two promising directions. The first is how the "normal" accumulation of capital drives the rising costs of production through the progressive exhaustion of the natures within both the circuit of capital (exploitation) and in the orbit of capitalist power (appropriation). The second is how underproduction fetters—or threatens to fetter—accumulation, and how it has been resolved through great waves of geographical restructuring. Thus, eras that mark the demise of one long wave of accumulation and the rise of another tend to be accompanied by "new" imperialisms and "new" scientific revolutions. In these periods, as capitalist and territorialist agencies seek to find, secure, and appropriate Cheap Natures that can resolve the problems of the old order.

How do we go about unifying overproduction and underproduction in our model of accumulation? This is a vexing question, because it asks us to move into the thicket of the *oikeios*. We will begin to answer at a fairly high level of abstraction. I ask the reader to withhold judgment until we put some skin and muscle on the skeletal model we now explore.

The World-Ecological Surplus and Phases of Capitalist Development

Capital engages the world as something to be reduced to an interchangeable part. These reductions are at once symbolic and material. They comprise both "economic" and "non-economic" simplifications.[14] Crucially, the tendential generalization of value relations works through a dialectic of capitalizing production and appropriating reproduction. Value is encoded simultaneously

12   Marx, *Capital*, Vol. III (1967), 119.

13   E. Mandel, *Late Capitalism* (London: New Left Books, 1975); W.W. Rostow, *The World Economy* (Austin: University of Texas Press, 1978).

14   H. Braverman, *Labor and Monopoly Capital* (New York: Monthly Review Press, 1974); D. Worster, "Transformations of the Earth," *Journal of American History* 76, no. 4 (1990): 1087–106; Scott, *Seeing Like a State* (1998).

through the *exploitation* of labor-power in commodity production, and through the *appropriation* of nature's life-making capacities. *Accumulation by appropriation* involves those extra-economic processes—perhaps directly coercive, but also cultural and calculative—through which capital gains access to minimally or non-commodified natures for free, or as close to free as it can get. If appropriation is partly about primitive accumulation, it is equally about the cultural hegemonies and scientific-technical repertoires that allow for unpaid work/energy to be mobilized, on a sustained but not sustainable basis, for capital accumulation. Such accumulation proceeds vigorously when unpaid work/energy is appropriated in service to commodity production, and opens new opportunities for capital investment. This occurs through geographical expansion, and is most effective when empires and states do the hard work of imposing order—cultural, scientific, juridical, and the rest—on new spaces. Such geographical expansion, in other words, must involve capitalist power and rationality in rather heavier doses than capitalization itself. Appropriation works through projects to control, rationalize, and channel potentially unruly human and extra-human sources of unpaid work/energy, *without immediately capitalizing these sources.*

Modernity is a therefore mighty control project. It effects all manner of quantifying and categorizing procedures oriented towards identifying, securing, and regulating historical natures in service to accumulation. Counter-intuitively, these procedures are not primarily aimed at directly commodifying natures. They are aimed at appropriating unpaid work/energy. Commodification can and does occur. But it must be kept in check, and if accumlation is to revive, must serve the "greater good" of appropriation. When capitalists can set in motion *small* amounts of capital and appropriate *large* volumes of unpaid work/energy, the costs of production fall and the rate of profit rises.[15] In these situations, there is a high *world-ecological surplus* (or simply, "ecological surplus"). This ecological surplus is the ratio of the system-wide mass of capital to the system-wide appropriation of unpaid work/energy.[16] In this, the "mass of capital" involves not only fixed capital, but also relations of human and extra-human reproduction that are increasingly capitalized: labor-power, tree plantations, factory farms.

The ecological surplus is suggested, albeit too narrowly, by the EROI

---

15   I am using a simplified model of capital and nature, understood in world-ecological terms as the contradiction between the expanded accumulation of capital and the simple reproduction of life. One would naturally wish, given the opportunity, to extend and elaborate this simple model into a series of world-historical specifications and revisions based on richer totalities of many determinations, bringing into the capital-nature model issues of state power, class struggles, cultural transformations, and much more.

16   This is an imperfect formulation, precisely because the condition for quantification within the commodity system (units of labor-time) is a world of unpaid work that cannot be quantified.

ratio—energy returned on energy invested—pioneered by ecological econo-mists.[17] Its decline is suggested by the declining energy efficiency of industrial agriculture, a longtime staple of Green critique. This orients us to the centrality of unpaid work/energy in the rise and demise of successive accumulation cycles. EROI gets us closer to an understanding of the world-ecological surplus, however, only when we move from EROI to EROCI: energy returned on *capital* invested. EROCI's decline is suggested by mounting evidence of rising produc-tion costs and slowing labor productivity growth over the past two decades—in agriculture, extraction, and industry. That decline suggests a powerful question: Has capitalism entered a new era of secular decline in the ecological surplus, and therefore in it capacity to achieve a significant advance in system-wide labor productivity?

Historically, "great depressions" have been resolved through world-ecological revolutions that create opportunities for windfall profits. These new opportu-nities depend upon the restoration of the Four Cheaps, the core of the world-ecological surplus. It is a "surplus" relative to the average costs of production in capitalism, which take many forms but are ultimately rooted in the productivity of labor. Such productivity is, however, decisively linked to the production of new historical natures and their chief historical forms: successive waves of enclosure, imperial expansion, scientific practice, and dispossessionary movements. These combine with technical change to appro-priate unpaid work/energy faster than the tendentially rising capitalization of global nature.

When the ecological surplus is very high, as it was after World War II, produc-tivity revolutions occur and long expansions commence. Naturally, this is not merely a story of appropriation, but also of capitalization and socio-technical innovation. The ecological surplus emerges as new accumulation regimes combine plunder and productivity, joining the enclosure of new geographical frontiers (including subterranean resources) and new scientific-technological revolutions in labor productivity. Great advances in labor productivity, express-ing the rising material throughput of an average hour of work, have been possible through great expansions of the ecological surplus. The assembly line of classic Fordism, for instance, was unthinkable without Cheap steel, rubber, and oil. It is impossible to overstate the irreducibly socio-ecological character of this surplus, which comprises not only food, energy, and raw materials, but also human nature as labor-power and domestic labor. The origins of the long twentieth century were found not only in the mass production systems of the "second industrial revolution," but also in multiple appropriations of human and extra-human natures: of the soil and water resources of the American Midwest;

---

17   C.J. Cleveland, et al., "Energy and the US Economy," *Science* 225 (1984): 890–97.

of Eastern European and South Asian peasantries; of the forests, fields, and resource veins of the colonial and semi-colonial worlds.

The ecological surplus declines over the course of every long wave of accumulation. It falls for four big reasons. First, there is wear and tear on the *oikeios*—on the specific historical natures in play. This is an entropy problem: matter/energy move from more useful to less useful forms within the prevailing configuration of the *oikeios*. The "law of entropy"—whereby "all economic process[es] . . . transform valuable matter and energy into waste"[18]—operates within specific patterns of power and production. It is not determined by the biosphere in the abstract. From the standpoint of historical nature, entropy is reversible and cyclical—but subject to rising entropy within specific civilizational logics. Capitalism's logic of appropriating work/energy therefore allows recurrent fixes to rising entropy by locating uncapitalized natures on the frontier.

Second, even if there was *no* wear and tear, the ecological surplus would tend to decline. The mass of accumulated capital tends to rise faster than the appropriation of unpaid work/energy—a necessary implication of Marx's general law of underproduction. (Capital's bets on the future grow faster than the practical activity of locating new Cheap Natures.) Even in the exceptional circumstances of the "second" industrial revolution and the post-World War II golden age—when the appropriation of unpaid work/energy was at an all-time high—the cheapening of food, raw materials, and energy required extraordinary effort and was sometimes reversed. The cyclical movement towards rising costs, like the entropy problem, can be reversed, but the space for such reversals narrows over capitalism's *longue durée*. In this light, Marx's general law of underproduction may be formulated as tendency for the rate of accumulation to decline as the mass of capitalized nature rises. It finds historical expression in recurrent waves of financialization, the chief expression of the overaccumulated capital that piles up as opportunities for appropriation decline.

Third, the ecological surplus declines through the contradiction between the reproduction time of capital and the reproduction times of the rest of nature. Capital's dystopian drive towards temporal instantaneity manifests by finding "short cuts" to compress the reproduction times of manifold natures. Not all human-initiated compressions are violent; but nearly all of capitalism's are. Capitalist agriculture, with its monocultures and labor productivity fetish, is a prime example. The capitalization of nature proceeds because this confers a competitive advantage over the short run. Capitalizing nature yields short-run gains for particular capitalists, but middle-run costs. These costs are externalized wherever possible, but ultimately new sources of work/energy must be

---

18   N. Georgescu-Roegen, "Energy and Economic Myths," *Southern Economic Journal* 41, no. 3: 347–81.

found, and appropriated. Thus every long accumulation cycle unfolds through new commodity frontiers.

Finally, the share of unpaid work/energy tends to fall relative to the mass of capital not only because of entropy, capitalization, and temporal disproportionality, but also because the accumulation of capital becomes more wasteful over time. This dimension is cyclical, but the least cyclically problematic. (Until now.) It is arguably the most cumulatively significant. One form is the colossal energy-inefficiency of industrial agriculture. Another, epoch-making dimension of waste production concerns the ways that massive energy- and chemical-use is toxifying the biosphere, and activating *negative-value*: the emergence of historical natures that are increasingly hostile to capital accumulation, and which can be temporarily fixed (if at all) only through increasingly costly and toxic strategies. The rise of negative-value—expressed starkly in contemporary climate change—suggests a significant and rapid erosion of the ecological surplus in the early twenty-first century (see Chapter Ten).

This means that capital, over time, must pay a greater share of its costs of doing business. In formal terms, every great wave of accumulation begins with a high ecological surplus, which is created through combinations of capital, science, and power.[19] We may associate these moments with abstract social labor, abstract social nature, and primitive accumulation. This "triple helix" of accumulation works by developing new ways of advancing labor productivity, alongside the securing of new and greatly expanded sources of unpaid work in service to accumulation.[20] This is the dialectical counter-point to the traditional rendering of Marx's so-called primitive accumulation as a process of class formation (bourgeois and proletarian). Class formation is one result of primitive accumulation. This result depends upon, and is co-produced through, the appropriation of unpaid work by "women, nature, and colonies." But the processes of identifying, mapping, and rationalizing those new sources of unpaid work/energy cannot be explained by economic forces alone; they depend upon state and science to make them work. Thus, primitive accumulation and the geographical expansion of capitalism is about more than the transfer of wealth from the non-capitalist to the capitalist world. And it is about more than the relation of bourgeois and proletarian. *Primitive accumulation is equally about the restructuring of the relations of reproduction—human and extra-human alike—so as to allow the renewed and expanded flow of Cheap labor, food, energy, and raw materials into the commodity system.*

---

19   These three categories—"science" most of all—are tremendously blunt instruments.
20   Special thanks to my friend Richard Walker for "triple helix."

THE DIALECTIC OF CAPITALIZATION AND APPROPRIATION

Let us now consider capitalization and appropriation not merely as accumulation strategies, but as relations of reproduction. From there, we may consider the relations between the two. First, the capitalization of relations of reproduction has occurred most conspicuously through the proletarianization of human labor. "Proletarianization" is another way of saying that the reproduction of labor-power flows through capital, largely in the form of paid work.[21] Of course, even proletarian households in the Global North continue to rely upon significant expenditures of unpaid work (laundry, cooking, raising children, etc.). Humans transform the rest of nature only through work, and the commodification of work—directly and indirectly—is therefore pivotal to the capitalization of extra-human natures.

But it is not just the reproduction of labor-power that has become capitalized; it is also the reproduction of extra-human natures. Flows of nutrients, flows of humans, and flows of capital make a historical totality, in which each flow implies the other. Modern agriculture, from its genesis in the sugar plantations of the long sixteenth century, reveals cash-crop agro-ecologies as a process of appropriating nutrients, energy, and water through global capital flows, credit especially.[22] The extraordinary shift that occurred in the twentieth century—through successive hybridization, chemical, and biotechnological "revolutions"—has been the rising capitalization of nature. But it has been non-linear, and consequently obscured until recently, because of the radical cheapening of energy. Nitrogen-fixation was of course central, but so were mechanization, pesticides, and electrification. As we will see in Chapter Ten, the liberation of capitalist agriculture from its dependence on local energy sources significantly *reduced* capitalization for a quarter-century after World War II—and modestly after 1970s. But recently, this process has boomeranged, significantly *advancing* capitalism over the past decade. At some point, every agricultural revolution faces a "blowback": from human-centered revolts to extra-human resistance (e.g., "superweeds"). The dynamic is captured, albeit partially, in discussions of capitalist agriculture's "technological treadmill," as farmers are locked into a regime of rising costs

---

21   I say "largely in the form of paid work," because the relation of bourgeois and proletarian assumes many concrete forms, including that of master and slave in the early modern sugar plantation (Mintz, "Was the Plantation Slave a Proletarian?" [1978]). In relation to the late twentieth-century capitalist farmer, Lewontin suggests (with some exaggeration) that the farmer has become a proletarian (R.C. Lewontin, "The Maturing of Capitalist Agriculture." *Monthly Review* 50, no. 3 [1998]: 72–84).

22   Moore, "Ecology and the Rise of Capitalism" (2007).

through dependence on commodified seeds, machines, and poisons.[23] But the "treadmill" expands beyond the forces of production. It is a treadmill of capital, tools, and nature—the *technics* of agro-industrial capitalism. The farm family must strive to produce more and yet more to satisfy the debt obligations of an agro-ecological model that is increasingly "reproduced within the circuits of capital accumulation."[24] The capitalization of agriculture today—in contrast to a century ago—is now exceeding cash-crop agriculture's appropriation of unpaid work/energy. The ecological surplus is contracting.

Capitalization transcends the Cartesian binary. So too does the appropriation of unpaid work/energy. This dialectic allows us to see beyond the reductionist language of Humanity and Nature. For in capitalism, the crucial divide is *not* between Humanity and Nature—it is between capitalization and the web of life. Capitalism's arrogance is to assign value to life-activity within the commodity system (and an alienating value at that) while de-valuing, and simultaneously drawing its lifeblood from, uncommodified life-activity within reach of capitalist power.

These movements of capitalization and appropriation mutually determine socially necessary labor-time. The first movement occurs within the "organic whole" of commodity production, comprising distribution, exchange, and distribution, alongside immediate production.[25] The other is the "organic whole" of appropriating unpaid work in service to advancing labor productivity. In other words, the rate of exploitation under the law of value is determined not only by the class struggle within commodity production (between capitalist and the direct producers), and not only by the organization and value composition of commodity production. *It is also determined by the contribution of unpaid work*, performed by human and extra-human natures alike.

Regimes of abstract social labor therefore turn on the active reconfiguration of production and reproduction. In this view, value relations unfold through the dialectic of paid and unpaid work, directly implicated in new accumulation regimes. This means that capitalism's *technics*—understood as specific crystallizations of tools, nature, and power[26]—do more than pick the low-hanging fruit. Capitalist *technics* seek to mobilize and to appropriate the (unpaid) "forces of nature" so as to make the (paid) "forces of labor" productive in their modern form: the production of surplus value. This is the significance of the *production*

23   Kloppenburg, *First the Seed* (1988).

24   W. Boyd, et al., "Industrial Dynamics and the Problem of Nature," *Society and Natural Resources* 14 (2001): 560.

25   Marx, *Grundrisse* (1973), 100.

26   L. Mumford, *Technics and Civilization* (1934).

of nature; nature is not a pre-formed object for capital. Rather, historical natures are those webs of relations that capital reshapes—through the double internality of the *oikeios*—so as to advance the contributions of biospheric "work" for capital accumulation.

The appropriation of unpaid work—manifested in the cyclical rise and decline of the Four Cheaps—is consequently central to conceptualizing and investigating capitalism's limits. This is because the *real historical limits* of capitalism derive from capital as a relation of capitalization and appropriation. The "limits to growth"[27] are not external, but derive from relations internal to capitalism. Why internal? Clearly, we are not speaking of "internal" as a fixed boundary, but rather of capitalism as an *internalizing* civilization. We are speaking of *internal* as methodological premise, not descriptive statement. Ecological economists often speak of how capitalism "externalizes" costs. The conversion of the atmosphere to a dumping ground for greenhouse gases is a prime example. Such externalization of costs is also the internalization of spaces necessary for capital accumulation. The atmosphere, for instance, must be put to work as capital's unpaid garbage man. These spaces may or may not be *directly* within the circuit of capital. Such spaces may be oilfields (internal to capital) or they may be frontier zones, where waste is dumped, or unpaid work appropriated. While waste frontiers are now partially recognized, the internalizing character of capitalist civilization goes still further, precisely because the accumulation of capital depends upon the active incorporation of "physically uncorrupted" sources of work/energy.[28]

When opportunities for appropriation decline relative to the mass of accumulated capital, a familiar train of events ensues. The costs of production rise. Workers, soils, forests, and other dimensions of unpaid work become physically exhausted or collectively uncooperative. The share of paid work rises, and the profitability of the old regional production complexes declines. Finally, the possibility of renewed capital accumulation, in a particular sector or for capital as a whole, depends upon finding new frontiers of appropriation. New production complexes emerge. Not coincidentally, every new era of capitalism begins with a "new imperialism" and a new industrialization.[29]

Why do new imperialisms, new industrializations, new agricultural revolutions, and new scientific revolutions go hand in hand? Because the (capitalized) forces of production rely on the (appropriated) conditions of re/production: the

27 D.H. Meadows, et al., *The Limits to Growth* (1972).

28 Marx, *Capital*, Vol. I, 380.

29 Harvey, *The New Imperialism* (2003); P.J. Cain and A.G. Hopkins, "Gentlemanly Capitalism and British Expansion Overseas II," *Economic History Review* 40, no. 1 (1987): 1–26.

Four Cheaps. Our focus on the Big Four inputs in value-relational terms allows us to see paid and unpaid work/energy in their historical configurations. As these configurations tilt towards appropriation, world accumulation revives and a "golden age" begins. When these configurations shift towards capitalization, opportunities for investment at (or above) the average rate of profit decline, and various symptoms of capitalist stagnation appear—rising inequality, financialization, etc.

This inverts the usual thinking about capitalist development. Capitalism expands *not* to expand the domain of commodification as such; it expands to shift the balance of world accumulation towards appropriation. Thus, capitalism's geographical expansions only sometimes—and only partially—privilege commodification. Most often, the priority is the projection of capitalist power into uncapitalized domains of reproduction: of uncommodified human and extra-human natures. These latter have been continually invaded, penetrated, and subsumed by capital, but always partially—and always partially for a good reason. Great advances in labor productivity—the British-led Industrial Revolution and American-led Fordism in the long nineteenth and twentieth centuries—have been strongly conditioned on gigantic appropriations of *unpaid* work, performed by human natures (domestic labor) and extra-human natures (geological accumulations) alike. Such industrializations depend on a configuration of rising labor productivity (rate of exploitation) in commodity production, alongside a *disproportionately greater* appropriation of unpaid work. The implication is crucial and merits emphasis: *the relation between exploitation and appropriation is asymmetrical.* Rising labor productivity in commodity production implies an even greater augmentation of the volume of energy and raw materials (circulating capital) for every unit of labor-time. Accumulated unpaid work/energy is especially important. The British- and American-led industrial revolutions, for example, unfolded through epoch-making appropriations of the accumulated work/energy of fossil fuel formation (coal, then oil) and the accumulated work/energy of humans raised to adulthood outside the commodity system (dispossessed peasants).

This highlights the historical unity of the reproduction of human and extra-human natures. From this perspective, *work* encompasses much more than direct participation in commodity production. Rather, work encompasses the totality of waged and unwaged activity performed by humans and the rest of nature within reach of capitalist power. The *unpaid* "work of nature"—over the short-run of agriculture, the intergenerational time of childrearing, the geological time of fossil fuel creation—is the pedestal upon which the *paid* "work of capital" unfolds. Both moments are inscribed in the law of value. While the value form (the commodity) emerges in the immediate process of production, the value relation—*including the systemic determination of socially necessary labor-time[30]—encompasses not only production relations, but also the broader relations of appropriation necessary to the expanded production of surplus value. The rate of exploitation is fundamentally conditioned by the scale, speed, and scope of appropriation of nature's work/energy, provided "free of charge," or as close to free as possible.*[31]

As the Four Cheaps materialize, new opportunities for capital accumulation appear: for instance, the railroad revolution of the nineteenth century or the automobile revolution of the twentieth century. Over time, the Four Cheaps cease being Cheap. The squeezing out of unpaid work/energy in the upswing of an accumulation cycle exhausts the resilience of uncommodified relations of reproduction. Meanwhile, workers and peasants find new ways to contest capital and the world market. Labor costs rise, along with food, energy, and raw materials prices. (Historically, in uneven fashion.) As Cheap inputs stop being cheap and start being dear, the opportunities for accumulation in the zone of material production stagnate, and begin to contract. Financial expansions tend to commence as appropriation falters, and the value composition of labor-power, food, energy, and raw materials rises rather than falls. Thus, financial expansions inaugurate new eras of primitive accumulation, as capitalists and states pursue the restoration of Cheap Nature.

The grand alternation of great phases of industrial and financial expansion therefore implicates the co-production of Cheap Natures in a fundamental way. Arrighi calls these two moments "material" and "financial" expansions.[32] Together they constitute an accumulation cycle. In the first moment, capital invests in labor-power, machinery, and raw materials: M-C-M'.[33] In the second, capital divests from M-C-M' and pursues accumulation through financial channels: M-M'. As we consider more fully in Chapter Six, these moments are overlapping, and the emergence of new centers of industrialization (M-C-M') has occurred during moments of financialization (M-M'). The timing, geography, and organizational form of these successive material and financial expansions implicates the value composition of the Big Four inputs.

The food/labor nexus is especially important, because Cheap Food and Cheap

---

30   "If, say in consequence of the exhaustion of flax-growing soil, the labour-time necessary for the production of the linen be doubled, the value of the linen will also be doubled" (Marx, *Capital*, Vol. I [1967], 67).

31   Ibid., 751.

32   Arrighi, *The Long Twentieth Century* (1994).

33   In "M-C-M' . . . [m]oney capital (M) means liquidity, flexibility, freedom of choice. Commodity capital (C) means capital invested in a particular input-output combination in view of a profit. Hence, it means concreteness, rigidity, and a narrowing down or closing of options. M' means *expanded* liquidity, flexibility, and freedom of choice" (*The Long Twentieth Century* [1994], 5).

Labor are determined by transformations of commodity production (through the capital-intensive moment of agricultural revolutions) and by the degree to which capital can secure new opportunities for appropriating unpaid work *outside* the commodity system. This was the genius of the American-led "family farm" revolution of the later nineteenth century (c. 1840–1900). This revolution combined unpaid family labor with the unpaid work of extra-human natures, especially those frontier soils of western North America, accumulated over millennia and largely untouched by agriculture. Cheap Energy is crucial because, especially since the steam power revolution, labor productivity advances with abundant energy, and stagnates with rising energy prices, as occurred in the 1970s.[34] (Recessions in the North Atlantic core have been closely linked to oil prices since the 1970s.[35]) Finally, Cheap Energy and Labor depend upon abundant (Cheap) raw materials to be worked into manufactured commodities.

Haunting capital's productive dynamism is the specter of underproduction. There is, consequently, a strong impulse to dissolve the boundaries between the Big Four inputs: to turn food into energy and raw materials, energy into food, and of course energy into labor-power. Here is capital's project to create Nature in its own image, endlessly quantifiable and interchangeable. One moment of this project is directly bio-material. Maize is a paradigm case, leading the way for all manner of "flex crops." It provides the raw materials for, seemingly, just about everything: ethanol, food (or "food-like products"), and raw materials in construction and industrial production.[36] Another moment is the generalization of energy-intensive nitrogen fertilizers in world agriculture, compelling a growing share of humanity to "eat" fossil fuels.[37] And let us not forget that capitalism is premised on the dissolution of human specificity—craft knowledge and the like—that is embodied in the incessant drive to replace "living" with "dead" labor.

The movement towards the increasing fungibility of extra-human nature is also calculative. The financialization of commodities since the turn of the millennium is another key moment in this dissolution of the boundaries between the Big Four inputs. Perhaps most spectacularly is the recent history of global primary commodity markets. Before the twenty-first century, these were largely independent "from outside financial markets and from each other"—for example, the price of oil was not necessarily correlated with the price of copper. After

34   D.W. Jorgenson, "The Role of Energy in Productivity," *American Economic Review* 74, no. 2 (1984): 26–30; C.J. Cleveland, et al., "Energy and the US Economy" (1984).

35   J.D. Hamilton, "Causes and Consequences of the Oil Shock of 2007–08," *Brookings Papers on Economic Activity*, 1 (2009): 215–61.

36   M. Pollan, *The Omnivore's Dilemma* (New York: Penguin, 2006); *In Defense of Food* (New York: Penguin, 2008).

37   R. Manning, "The Oil We Eat," *Harper's* 308 (February, 2004): 37–45.

2000, however, finance actors, index investors especially, "precipitated a funda-mental process of financialization among commodities markets, through which commodity prices became more correlated with prices of financial assets and with each other . . . As a result of [this] financialization . . . *the price of an indi-vidual commodity is no longer simply determined by its supply and demand.*"[38] This combination of bio-material and financial restructuring suggests a twenty-first-century scenario in which the tendency towards underproduction reasserts itself, through an unusual and unstable combination of physical depletion, climate change, new anti-systemic movements, and financialization.

Underproduction signifies a *conjoncture*—the downslope of a bell-shaped curve—in which one or more of the Big Four inputs becomes increasingly costly, and begins to fetter the accumulation process. In this, underproduction is an immanent contradiction of overproduction. This means that underpro-duction is not about "scarcities" that reside in an external nature—a neo-Malthusian view. Rather, underproduction takes shape through the rela-tions that obtain, cyclically and cumulatively, in historical capitalism and historical nature (our double internality). Underproduction is co-produced by human and extra-human natures, and historically specific. "Scarcity" for one civilization may not be for another. Capitalism's scarcities are imposed through price—the food price inflation that began in 2003 is not a function of inade-quate world food supplies, but of distribution, power, and capital. This allows us to see the *really relational* sources of hunger and other forms of deprivation and oppression. But the analysis cannot stop there. We need a way to see how changes in the biosphere translate into deepening contradictions in capital-ism—and vice versa.

Peak appropriation

Depletion is real enough. Its most salient contemporary expression is probably energy. Here, the geographical retreat of easy-to-extract big oilfields is clearly a contest over the terms of the double internality. Will capitalism's internalization of nature produce new geographies that allow for Cheap Energy's return? Or will nature's internalization of capital produce new geographies that make such a return impossible? We have been distracted from this double internality by the terms of the "peak everything" debate. These terms pose a question about

---

38   K. Tang and W. Xiong "Index investment and Financialization of Commodities" (Working paper, Department of Economics, Princeton University, March 2011). Emphasis added. Accessed March 17, 2011, www.princeton.edu/~wxiong/papers/commodity.pdf.

substances, not relations: Have we reached a "peak" in global output for oil, coal, phosphorous, even soil, from which a "post-peak" world of scarcity ensues?[39]

What happens if we approach the problem of depletion from a relational perspective? Here we find more useful a different kind of peak: peak *appropriation*. Peak appropriation may be visualized as the maximal inflection point of a bell-shaped curve in which the share of unpaid work/energy peaks relative to the capitalization of nature: that "peak" represents the world-ecological surplus at its highest point. Of course the visualization is merely a thought-exercise. Cyclical changes and sectoral shifts alter the picture in significant ways. Since the early nineteenth century, moreover, the relative ease with which Cheap Energy could be mapped, extracted, and put to work has smoothed the transition from one phase of capitalism to another.

Peak appropriation is one way of building on EROI (energy returned on energy invested) analyses.[40] It allows for the enfolding of resource and energy measures in a historical and relational frame. The movement towards peak appropriation, as we've noted, sees a rising ecological surplus. Post-peak appropriation is characterized by a falling ecological surplus. But EROI cannot get us to a model of accumulation that unifies energy/capital. For this we need EROCI.

Appropriation and the cyclical movements of the ecological surplus direct our attention not only to EROI but to *Energy Returned on Capital Invested* (EROCI): calories or joules per dollar. EROCI puts the relative contributions of paid and unpaid work/energy at the center. The *peak* in question is not, then, a peak in output—of energy, or some other primary commodity. It is, rather, the peak "gap" between the capital set in motion to produce a given commodity and the work/energy embodied in that commodity: dollars per bushel, or ton, or barrel, or horse, or hour of labor-power. Even here, the language is imprecise, precisely because we are dealing with an incommensurable mix of specific work/ energies. Quantification can illuminate but not adequately capture these specifics. Energy and material flows can be measured; but within capitalism, they cannot be *counted*—for the secret of capital's dynamism is that it counts only what it values (labor productivity). Peak appropriation is, moreover, not simply about particular commodities, but about the ways that certain primary commodities—coal and oil are paradigm examples—"diffuse" Cheap Natures across the whole accumulation process. Cheap Food after the 1930s, for instance, became "petro-farming," its prodigious appropriations of soil, water, and life increasingly mediated through Cheap Energy.

For long waves of capital accumulation, peak appropriation occurs when the contribution of appropriated natures "peaks" relative to capitalized natures. Thus

39   Cf. R. Heinberg, *Peak Everything* (Gabriola Island, BC: New Society, 2007).
40   Cleveland, et al., "Energy and the US Economy" (1984).

Marx's insight on soil fertility as "fixed capital."[41] Of course Marx understood fertility as not so natural (fixed) as Ricardo believed; fertility could be increased through the application of fertilizers as circulating capital.[42] But where fertility was given, prior to the advance of capitalist agriculture, the windfalls of peak appropriation could be epoch-making. The American grain frontiers of the nineteenth century appropriated nutrients accumulated over millennia. When combined with the capital-intensive family farm, they revolutionized not only American capitalism but also flooded Europe with Cheap Food, "freeing" Cheap Labor for American industrialization. As with early capitalism's sugar plantations, we see the precocious combination of cutting-edge industrial production and frontier appropriation. The potential consequences of rising capital-intensity—rising production costs—could be offset through new appropriations and enclosures. These allowed capital to advance labor productivity while reducing (or checking) the tendentially rising value composition of production. The technical composition of production—the mass of machinery and raw materials relative to labor-power—could rise without undermining the rate of profit.

Capitalism, we have seen, is a frontier process: endless accumulation and endless geographical appropriation are joined at the hip. Relative to premodern civilizations, such geographical expansion works for capitalism in a radically novel way because of capital's alienated unification of labor and land productivity. From this perspective, the problem with energy production today is not EROI but EROCI: a declining ecological surplus. Production costs continue to rise—sharply. Curiously, rising costs did not stop oil prices from falling by 50 percent in the nine months after July 2014. How did this happen, absent a significant industrial depression and rising costs of production? In two words: Cheap Money.

The neoliberal era is in some sense defined by Cheap Money—with real interest rates plummeting in the three decades after 1981.[43] The history of energy production and prices since 2006 conveys a special sense of how this played out around the Money/Energy nexus. As interest rates declined and energy prices surged, it became possible to bring high-cost production—largely from shale—into play. American oil production rose dramatically. Shale output grew sixfold between 2005 and 2014.[44] This was largely realized through massive borrowing by mid-size US energy firms, whose debt grew from $1 trillion in 2006 to $2.5 trillion in 2014. As prices began to slide in July 2014, the downward movement was amplified by indebted

41   K. Marx, *Grundrisse*, (1973), 748.

42   K. Marx, *The Poverty of Philosophy* (New York: International, 1963), 162–63.

43   A. Shaikh, "The First Great Depression of the 21st Century," in *The Crisis this Time: Socialist Register 2011*, eds. L. Panitch, G. Albo and V. Chibber. London: Merlin Press (2011), 44–63.

44   A. Sieminski, "Outlook for U.S. Shale Oil and Gas," U.S. Energy Information Administration, 2014, www.eia.gov/pressroom/presentations/sieminski_01042014.pdf.

producers seeking to weather the storm by pumping more oil.[45] By early 2015, the major private oil companies too had embarked on a borrowing spree, taking on $63 billion in new debt during the first two months of the year.[46] All of which points towards a very short era of Cheap Energy this time around. It is exceedingly unlikely that oil will dip much below $90–100/barrel *averaged* over the next decade— approximately three times higher than the average for the two decades after 1983.[47] And it *is* possible that there will be a massive collapse of industrial production that would allow for a more durable collapse in energy prices. But this would not restore Cheap Energy in the old way, by reducing the costs of production.

All of which tells us that are dealing with a new era: the end of Cheap Nature. The old logic of "pour money in, cheap oil comes out," is not working as it once did. Non-OPEC investment in oil exploration and production more than quadrupled between 1999 and 2012, rising from $40 billion to $180 billion annually.[48] New investment in oil and gas exploration and production reached $900 billion in 2014.[49] This investment has not returned Cheap Oil—and does not promise to. Quite the contrary! New oil and other energy are, in historical terms, very expensive to extract and to make useful. In this oil sector, capital expenditure (Capex) per new barrel—reflecting a declining EROCI—increased 10.9 percent annually between 1999 and 2013. Is that a lot? Between 1985 and 1999, capex per new barrel grew at just 0.9 percent annually.[50] New projects in unconventional oils—shale and tar sands—do not promise to reverse the trend. Meanwhile, OPEC's oil output, whose production costs remain low, did not increase between 2005 and 2013. Across the world energy sector, production costs are rising.[51] The world energy sector is moving through a transition from a net subsidizer of the costs of production to a net contributor, as production costs rise—a momentous transition indeed.

Are rising production costs about scarcity? Depletion translates into scarcity only through the capitalist market, and that market is determined by all manner of mediations: social unrest, international conflict, state policies,

---

45   D. Domanski, et al., "Oil and Debt," *BIS Quarterly Review* (March, 2015): 55–65.

46   C. Adams, "Oil majors pile on record debt to plug cash shortfalls," *Financial Times* (March 22, 2015).

47   BP, *Statistical Review of World Energy 2014* (London: BP, 2014), 15, bp.com/statisticalreview.

48   R. Weijermars, et al., "Competing and Partnering for Resources and Profits," *Energy Strategy Reviews* (online first, 2014).

49   Ibid., and Domanski et al., "Oil and Debt."

50   S. Kopits, "Oil and Economic Growth: A Supply-Constrained View" (Presentation to the Center on Global Energy Policy, Columbia University, February 11, 2014), 43.

51   Ibid; Goldman Sachs, "Higher Long-Term Prices Required by a Troubled Industry," *Equity Research, Goldman Sachs* (April 12, 2013); R. Weijermars, et al., "Competing and Partnering for Resources and Profits" (2014).

petro-developmentalism, financialization, etc. Indeed, energy "markets" are among those that least conform to the ideal-type of the economists.[52] In recognizing depletion of a narrow kind as implicated in underproduction, I would underscore that capital recognizes scarcity only through price, and that price (exchange-value) expresses middle- and long-run tendencies in the production of value. If the value composition of energy production rises because of depletion—more labor-power required per unit of energy—this will induce non-linear shifts in the value composition of capital as a whole. As we have learned, nearly everything in our world depends on Cheap Energy: everything we associate with "economic development" turns on fossil fuels. And yet, depletion is *not* everything. Price signals also reflect contradictions within capital—such as the financialization of commodities—as well as the contradictions of class, empire, and national developmentalist projects.

Thus, the geography of depletion is important, but scarcely determining. Since 2000, the high price of oil has surely been conditioned by geological realities that have propelled rising exploration and production costs. But these do not stand alone. American-led imperialist adventures and occupations, the galloping industrialization of the Global South, the petro-developmentalism of oil-producing states—these too are fundamental to the ongoing demise of Cheap Nature. In sum, the price of the Big Four inputs is conditioned by the geology, geography, and biophysicality of extra-human natures, and is simultaneously co-determined by human-initiated relations class, empire, and development. These moments are always bundled. The implication is simple and paradigm-making: the "limits to growth" in the capitalist era are neither "natural" nor "social." They are, rather, the limits of capitalism as *oikeios*. They are the limits of capitalization, the focus of our next chapter.

52   T. Mitchell, *Carbon Democracy* (London: Verso, 2011).

CHAPTER 5

The Capitalization of Nature, or, the Limits of Historical Nature

Capitalism is, and is not at the same time, anthropocentric. On the one hand, capital is about the value of labor-power, and labor-power can only be delivered by humans. On the other hand, most humans are not exploited for their labor-power—even today. For the most part, capitalism appropriates human activity just as it does the rest of nature. Human natures are at only oddly elevated and systematically alienated—and violated—in capitalist civilization. Recognizing this combined and uneven model of development tells us something very important about limits: that the limits of capital and the limits of nature are much more tightly connected than our usual narratives of impending catastrophe and collapse would have it. There is a more interesting story to tell, and also a more hopeful one.

The cyclical restoration of the Four Cheaps, and the renewal of the Four Cheaps, is a combined and uneven process. As we have seen, accumulation by appropriation works through the extra-economic mobilization of work/energy streams. These mobilizations tend to exhaust the "natural conditions" of re/production, as when newly cleared forest is planted with sugar or soy, followed by relative soil exhaustion. The progressive exhaustion of these earlier conditions leads to capitalization; a rising share of production comes to depend on the circuit of capital. Accumulation by capitalization works by simplifying, rationalizing, and reorganizing production—within the commodity zone. Capitalization therefore has two priorities. One is to squeeze more work/energy out of older, appropriated zones, as in postwar American agriculture. Another is to render more efficient the industrial processing of Cheap Natures appropriated elsewhere, as in successive industrial revolutions. Capitalization is never really a fix to accumulation crisis, since such crises can only be resolved through new appropriations of Cheap Nature; and yet, new forms of Cheap Nature imply and necessitate new industrial systems. Accumulation by capitalization therefore works in complex ways that simultaneously increase and reduce costs.

The tendency of the ecological surplus to fall is no iron law. Capitalization counteracts the rising costs of production by making the most of particular Cheap Natures, and diffusing their particular surpluses to the system as a whole. The greatest illustration of this process is the history of fossil fuels. Decisive since the eighteenth century, Cheap Energy has radically counteracted socio-ecological exhaustion in the re/production of labor, food, and raw materi-als—at first largely through new transport networks, and later, through the rise of petro-farming, our focus in Chapter Ten. In this chapter, we concentrate on the capitalization of extra-human natures, and how this informs a theory of systemic crisis co-produced through the *oikeios*.

CAPITALIZATION AND THE PRAXIS OF EXTERNAL NATURE

The history of capitalism is the history of revolutionizing nature. Capitalist civili-zation therefore does not *have* an ecological regime; it *is* an ecological regime. Capitalism is a way of shaping, channeling, and negotiating the terms of the *oikeios*. This is, of course, not something specific to capitalism. All civilizations do this in one way or another. Capitalism's distinctiveness lies in how it organizes quasi-stable relations between humans and the rest of nature in service to endless accumulation. The most durable form of this relation is the *praxis* of external Nature. Through this *praxis* capitalist and territorialist agencies seek to create new Natures as objects of power and production, and as new and expanded sources of unpaid work/energy.

Endless accumulation poses a number of problems for this *praxis*. For the present discussion, we can reduce these to just two. The first is between the finite character of the biosphere and the infinite character of capital's demands. The second is between capital's need to expand and to accelerate the uptake of work/energy relative to the reproductive requirements of varied elements of the web of life. Readers may note that both moments are quantitative. Capital knows only one qualitative relation: capital-labor, premised as we have seen on capital/nature. Everything else is reducible, not only through calculative rationalities, but also through practical reconstruction: monocultures, assembly lines, "flex" crops, and so on. Capital values only what it can count.

Nevertheless, capital's quantism must be remade in successive eras. This occurs because historical natures that initially liberate a wave of accumulation become exhausted. The Four Cheaps become dearer. Exhausting the possibilities for reproducing Cheap Nature means one of two things, often in combination. One is that historical nature gets "wiped out" in some way. Forests may get cleared to such a degree that fuel-intensive commodity production is no longer profitable. This was exceptional, but occurred on Madeira in the "first" sixteenth century.[1] Another is that nature gets "maxed out" and continues to deliver work/

---

1   Moore, "Madeira, Sugar, and the Conquest of Nature in the 'First' Sixteenth Century, Part I," *Review* 32, no. 4 (2009): 345–90; "Madeira, Sugar, and the Conquest of Nature in the 'First' Sixteenth Century, Part II," *Review* 33, no. 1 (2010): 1–24.

energy, but at a volume and cost that no longer sustains accumulation. World energy production looks like this today: output remains high, and will rise in the coming decade, but the costs of production continue to soar.[2] The same process of exhaustion works its logic through national working classes, too, as we see in Chapter Nine.

Much of the emphasis in Green Thought has focused on the first moment, where parts of Nature are *wiped out*. Capitalism wages war on the earth and all that. I wish to suggest, however, that the more interesting—and practically relevant—problem is how nature gets *maxed out*. The problem is vexing because it goes against grain of how we think about capitalism: as a system that acts upon an external Nature.

The problem of how capital puts nature to work and how, over time, nature gets maxed out helps us go beyond the usual thinking about accumulation crises. Putting these historical questions of work/energy/value at the center allows us to see that the problem of surplus capital in new light. For the problem is not simply one of too much capital chasing too few investment opportunities. This is true, but we can go further. The problem of surplus capital is one of capital putting nature to work, and then failing because uncapitalized nature balks at working overtime. That "failure" materializes in overaccumulation crises: too much capital with too few (profitable) places to go. A rising ecological surplus, in contrast, makes all sorts of capital investment attractive, because lots of free nature can work lots of cheap overtime.

Capitalism revolutionizes the *oikeios*, but all is not flux. The historical capitalism/historical nature dialectic stabilizes—it must stabilize—for capital accumulation to revive. Thus successive eras of capitalist development are "governed"—if this is the right term for it—by world-ecological regimes that establish definite relations and rules of reproduction. These are regimes in an institutional sense, pivoting on successive world hegemonies,[3] but also regimes in a hegemonic sense: establishing norms through which labor-power is organized, food is grown and exchanged, resources extracted, and knowledge developed. These rules and relations are not static but subject to cyclical revolutions within a cumulative trend towards commodification. The capitalization of nature is cumulative, but the cumulative trend depends on a series of revolutions: world-ecological revolutions. These are turning points in the prevailing organizational structures, scientific practices, and cultural norms of reproducing capital, power, and nature. They are necessitated by *developmental crises*, expressed in the economic decline of the old centers of power and production, a

2   Goldman Sachs, "Higher Long-Term Prices Required by a Troubled Industry" (2013); S. Kopits, "Oil and Economic Growth" (2014).

3   Arrighi, *The Long Twentieth Century* (1994).

faltering rate of world accumulation, and the temporary upward ratchet in the costs of production.

This upward ratchet is the expression of the tendentially rising capitalization of nature. Capitalized nature depends on the circuit of capital—crudely, either M-C-M′ or M-M′—for its daily and intergenerational reproduction. (We are of course dealing with dialectical primacy here: capitalization and appropriation operate simultaneously.) For capitalized natures, including labor-power, the circuit of capital directly shapes the rules of reproduction. A good example is the capital-intensive family farm that first developed in the U.S. after 1865, and which was progressively globalized as the Green Revolution model after World War II. An Iowa corn farm producing for ethanol refineries is highly capitalized nature. As for highly capitalized human natures, these can be found in the proletarianized households of metropolitan accumulation—households that depend on wages for most income (see Chapters Nine and Ten).

The capitalization of nature is the obverse of the tendency of the ecological surplus to fall. There are two big movements during the rising capitalization of nature. One is that the accumulation of capital depends on the rising technical composition of capital: a rising physical mass of production. Here we find a corollary to Marx's general law of underproduction. As the technical composition of capital rises, so does its value composition, *except* under conditions of the rapid appropriation of Cheap Nature. The crucial word here is *except*. It is crucial, because the apparent ease with which capital has appropriated global natures over the past two centuries has made it easy to forget the centrality of appropriation in capital accumulation. It is not easy to rapidly appropriate the massive streams of work/energy that can turn the Big Four inputs into the Four Cheaps. Our caveat—*except under conditions of rapid appropriation*—points towards the historical reality that a relative cheapening of energy and raw materials reduces not only the value composition of circulating, but also, of fixed capital. Cheap metals, for example, reduce not only raw material costs but also the costs of machinery.

The second factor behind the rising capitalization of nature is the corrosive effect of capitalization and appropriation. At first liberating new flows of unpaid work/energy, capitalization progressively limits those flows. This corrosion occurs through capital's interlinked temporal and spatial reorganizations of primary production. Capitalist agriculture is a key example. Not only are agro-ecosystems subjected to rising nutrient withdrawals, monocultures reorganize space in a manner favorable to pests and weeds. This spatio-temporal corrosion undermines a given region's capacity to deliver a rising stream of unpaid work/energy. Thus the tendency of surplus capital to rise, and of ecological surplus to fall, constitute an irreconcilable contradiction between the project of capital and the work of the natures that make that project possible. Irreconcilable, that is, within the geographically given boundaries of capitalization and appropriation. The frontier always beckons.

Capital's world-historical challenge has been to strike the right balance between regularizing supply (which must always rise) and making those supplies Cheap enough to permit expanded accumulation. It is complicated by the punctuated development of historical capitalism and historical nature, through which new resources are located, extracted, and brought into the accumulation process. Rising capital intensity tends to regularize supply but does so by accelerating the place-specific exhaustion of profitability—usually over the middle-run of fifty to sixty years.

Capitalism has been remarkably adept at finding ways to overcome such exhaustion. Through capital intensification and socio-technical innovation, capitalist agencies have found ways to make more out of less. But more out of less is not something for nothing. The counter-tendency within the general law of underproduction has therefore been a frontier movement. From the sixteenth century, the appropriation of biophysically rich frontiers, combined with uncapitalized labor-power and sufficiently mobile capital, has periodically resolved the underlying contradiction. The question to consider, as we move into the second half of this book, is this: Are today's frontiers of appropriation of sufficiently great mass—in terms of work/energy—that they can restore the Four Cheaps, provide investment outlets for now massively overaccumulated capital, and revive accumulation? And if they are of sufficiently great mass, how long can such a revival be sustained?

Capitalizing what nature?: from nature "in general" to historical nature

We begin with a banal observation. Nature is not just there. We know nature only through our life-activity. Through this life-activity occurs a triple transformation: of ourselves, of external nature, of our relation with other humans and the rest of nature. This holds, too, for human organization. The very largest of these are civilizations, understood as patterns of power and re/production that obtain over long-time and large-space. Civilizations co-produce *historical natures* specific to these patterns, and to their developmental phases. Crucially, these patterns are not merely about earth-moving, but also about ways of seeing and knowing nature. We call these latter "symbolic" but they are tightly bundled with the material. Ways of earth-moving and ways of knowing form an unbroken—if uneven—circle. To say that humans know only historical natures is not to deny nature in general but to situate our thinking of nature—and the historical practices that unfold from specific ways of knowing nature—within the double internality. From this perspective, nature "in general" exists as

> a noumenon, a category of the last instance, without any qualification or characterization. For [capitalism, however], nature is an object of labor, a resource, a manifold, an attic, or a cellar, or a boxroom to be ransacked . . . It is a potential to be actualized by different epochs with different goals, different priorities, different cosmologies, different worldviews and agendas. The metaphysical basis of reality, of experience, of investigation, changes. Ontologies change, epistemologies change, methodologies change. At a more mundane academic level, there are paradigms, research programmes, disciplines, grand theories—all of which are formed and constituted by the contradictions and moving resolution of class forces of different epochs. This is a dynamic, dialectical historical process, born in conflict and struggle.[4]

There are two layers of historical nature specific to capitalism. The first is a historical nature specific to capitalism as a whole. The second is the succession of historical natures co-produced through the law of value. As we have seen, this law of value is a law of Cheap Nature. It is a dynamic relation compelling the cyclically punctuated realignments of abstract social labor and abstract social nature. The rise of globalizing value relations was concurrent with the incessant revolutionizing of time, space, and nature that has been central to capitalism from its origins.[5] That these revolutions were fundamentally socio-ecological is easily overlooked. And yet, the universalization of money capital as a storehouse of value is unthinkable except as a part of a world-ecological revolution that enabled European states and capitals to perceive, represent, and act upon a Nature that was cheap and external.

"Nature in general" is as dangerous as it is unavoidable. On the one hand, there is clearly a web of life whose *durée* is reckoned in the billions of years. Capitalism is barely the blink of an eye in such a scheme. On the other hand, time is always multi-layered, and those layers are not all created equal for the particular problems humanity faces today. The interpenetration of these layers of historical time is fundamental, and shapes how we see capitalism's crises— past and present. A view of capitalism that proceeds from nature-in-general absent the interpenetration of historical time is therefore extraordinarily limiting. Nature-in-general tends to flatten not only our understanding of the web of

---

4   Young, "Is Nature a Labor Process?" (1985).

5   Harvey, *The Condition of Postmodernity* (1989); Moore, "Ecology and the Rise of Capitalism" (2007).

life—as something whose energies are inexorably drawn down—but also our conception of capitalism. Nature and capitalism become structurally invariant in such a rendering. This does a disservice to both. The survival of capitalism has turned on its unusual flexibility.[6] Where Braudel stressed capital's capacity to move from one sector to another—say, from industry to finance—we might highlight an even more fundamental form of flexibility: the capacity to move from one historical nature to another.

Capitalism has survived the rising capitalization of nature because it revolutionizes the *oikeios*. Every phase of capitalism not only makes a quantum leap in its material throughput, but makes that quantum leap through the co-production of a historically-specific nature. The quantitative expansion of capital accumulation occurs through the qualitative reconstruction of historical nature. Just as the imperialism and great firms of the seventeenth century are not equivalent to the imperialism and great firms of the twenty-first century, so, too, the historical natures of these eras. There is a quantitative moment that merits careful scrutiny: the exponential growth curves of twentieth century resource use are a powerful illustration.[7] We now have an important literature on energy history for early capitalism, too.[8] But the qualitative moment that allowed these growth curves cannot be abstracted.

Not only has capital sustained itself on the basis of Cheap inputs (the quantitative moment); it has also revolutionized the socio-ecological relations of production (the qualitative moment). In this fashion, leading capitalists and imperial states have mobilized a succession of "great leaps forward" in the ecological surplus: the rising share of appropriated unpaid work/energy relative to the mass of accumulated capital. The cumulative trend of geometrically rising throughput is embedded in a cyclical moment: the production of new configurations of paid and unpaid work within the *oikeios*. Hence the significance of *historical nature*. Industrial capitalism gave us Darwin and the Kew Gardens; neoliberal capitalism, Gould and biotechnology firms. In Chapter Eight, we will turn to the symbolic and scientific moments of co-producing historical nature. In the rest of this chapter, we explore the historical patterns and tendencies that drive the capitalization, and subsequent exhaustion, of extra-human natures in successive ecological regimes. This is a story of how the historical nature that is

---

6   Braudel, *The Wheels of Commerce* (1982).

7   Cf. McNeill, *Something New Under the Sun* (2000); Costanza, et al., "The Value of the World's Ecosystem Services" (1997).

8   Allen, "The British Industrial Revolution in Global Perspective" (2006); P. Malanima, "Energy Crisis and Growth 1650–1850: The European Deviation in a Comparative Perspective," *Journal of Global History* 1, no.1 (2006): 101–21; "The Path Towards the Modern Economy: The Role of Energy," *Rivista di Politica Economica* 2 (2011): 77–105.

created at the outset of an accumulation cycle—(re)launching the Four Cheaps with a high rate and mass of appropriation of unpaid work/energy—experiences contradictions that must be resolved through new world-ecological revolutions. And it is a story of how capitalism's revolutionizing of nature is premised on historical limits of its own making.

The Oikeios, Relational Exhaustion, and the Long Wave

The normal course of capital accumulation tends to exhaust the establishing relations of re/production that inaugurate a great wave of accumulation. These establishing relations encompass all manner of scientific, botanical and agronomic, cartographic, and technological innovations that we consider in subsequent chapters. For now, I will elaborate a simplified model. The emergence of new major centers of production—with their distinctive patterns of industrial organization and rising labor productivity—is premised on the emergence of more expansive nets of appropriating the unpaid work/energy of human and extra-human natures. These configurations of capitalization (within the circuit of capital) and appropriation (outside that circuit but within reach of capitalist power) allow for long waves of accumulation to unfold. They enable the rate of accumulation to rise at the same time as the costs of production fall.[9] Thus, Cheap Nature, in the specific form of the Four Cheaps (food, labor-power, energy, and raw materials), is the necessary condition for every great wave of accumulation. Over time, the value composition of these Big Four inputs begins to rise, the rate of accumulation slows, and capital must find new ways to reconfigure the *oikeios* and restore the Four Cheaps. The rise and fall of the ecological surplus therefore shapes the cyclical and cumulative development of capitalism.

To this point, we have evaded a crucial question: How do we periodize, even provisionally, those "long centuries" of development?

The phases of capitalism literature is impossibly vast and extraordinarily diverse. But its diversity has unfolded within a common, social reductionist, frame: phases of capitalism are defined by some combination of (geo)political power, technological development, class relations, the world market, capitalist organization, and so forth. Within a Cartesian frame, it is possible to render plausible conceptualizations of capitalism's stadial development. In a world-ecological frame, however, neither the dualist conceptualization of the parts

---

9   Alternatively, primary commodity prices might remain stable as output rises sharply, as with English coal in the sixteenth and seventeenth centuries (R.C. Allen, "The British Industrial Revolution in Global Perspective" [2006]) , or copper in the later nineteenth century (C. Schmitz, "The Rise of Big Business in the World Copper Industry, 1870–1930," *Economic History Review* 39, no. 3 [1986]: 392–410).

(technology, class, etc.) nor the conceptualization of wholes (eras of capitalism), makes sense. All are implicitly world-ecological in the terms that I have laid out. Their explicit reconstruction awaits. This book is a contribution to such reconstruction.

The question of periodization cannot be evaded. I take Arrighi's scheme of successive "long centuries" of capital accumulation as a guiding thread.[10] But I have woven Arrighi's threads with a number of my own. The result is a comradely but distinct synthesis. Arrighi's model of capitalism unfolded from the premise of "input-output" combinations,[11] rather than value as a co-productive relation of capital/nature. The core of his approach was therefore substantialist, a view that confused the capitalist project with its process, and one that reduced extra-human nature to substances. This led to a historical error with significant theoretical and methodological consequences. For Arrighi did not see that early capitalism was not *real* capitalism. He is hardly alone in this mistake. As we shall see, early capitalism was, *in every major respect*, "real" capitalism, premised above all on the law of value as a law of Cheap Nature: a law that prioritized rising labor productivity in commodity production and exchange. These productivity advances were realized through the unprecedented appropriation of unpaid work/energy. Failing to see the appropriation of Cheap Nature as central to world accumulation has led to a major mis-recognition of capitalism's laws of motion: namely, that these laws of motion work exclusively within the circuit of capital, and that socio-ecological relations outside the circuit of capital are contextual, and not constitutive. This mis-recognition has prevented Marxists and Greens alike from seeing how nature-as-*oikeios* matters. Social reductionism has prevented too many scholars from seeing that frontiers and strategies of appropriating unpaid work/energy have "acted like an increase in fixed capital" in the history of capitalism.[12] Indeed, the great mechanizations of the past five centuries are dwarfed by the contribution of Cheap Nature to world accumulation. Appropriated nature is a force of production.

With Arrighi, I see successive long centuries of capitalist development as central to the story of capitalism: capitalism does not "automatically" restructure.[13] My periodization—readers will detect a family resemblance to Arrighi's model—looks something like this: 1) a Germanic-Iberian cycle (c. 1451–1648), in which the expansionary phase turns to relative decline after the 1557 financial

10   Arrighi, *The Long Twentieth Century* (1994).
11   Ibid., 5.
12   Marx, *Grundrisse*, 748.
13   B. Silver and E. Slater, "The Social Origins of World Hegemonies," in *Chaos and Governance in the Modern World-System*, ed. G. Arrighi, et al. (Minneapolis: University of Minnesota Press, 1999).

crisis; 2) a Dutch-led cycle (c. 1560s–1740s), in which decline sets in after 1680; 3) a British-led cycle, c. 1680s–1910s), with relative decline after 1873; 4) an American-led cycle (c. 1870s–1980s), with relative decline after 1971; and 5) a neoliberal cycle (it could just as easily be called neo-mercantilist) that commenced in the 1970s. Naming and periodizing is a tricky business, and I make no pretense that these are the best possible; they are simply the most reasonable I could find. This book does not reconstruct the narrative because I do not think we know—yet!—how to reconstruct that narrative in a way that recognizes the double internality of capitalism-in-nature/nature-in-capitalism. Such reconstructions are crucial if we are to understand the limits of capitalism today. They will be most effective as they emerge through a sustained conversation among scholars committed to a synthesis in which nature matters. As such, this periodization is a provisional model to allow for reconstructive critique. It is invitation as much as definition.

Marx's theory of underproduction, sketched in Chapter Four, was of course provisional. Capitalism's productive dynamism is undeniably important here. As capitalist production demands a geometrically rising throughput, supply crunches are inevitable—even as the severity and duration of such crunches is uneven. But the story of underproduction cannot be told through investment flows and industrial production alone. Simply putting more capital in play does not *necessarily* call forth Cheap Nature, as capitalists in the world energy and metals sectors are discovering today.[14] The tendency towards underproduction is also a story of how capitalism unfolds through the *oikeios*, and how capitalization exhausts the work/energy streams that open new opportunities for expanded accumulation. Simply put, the problem of exhaustion is a problem of how capitalism puts nature to work.

Why do the costs of production rise over long waves of accumulation? There are certainly many factors involved, not least those swirling about Marx's general law of underproduction. In the rush to accumulate capital, and to outcompete other firms, capitalists are not only compelled to invest in more machinery, but to advance labor productivity at every step. Rising labor productivity is rising material throughput per unit of labor-time. (More widgets per hour.) Manufacturing is therefore intimately connected with extractive systems in energy, forestry, agriculture, and mining.[15] These modes of extraction, however, do not quickly respond to changing industrial and urban demand. There are

---

14   S. Kopits, "Oil and Economic Growth" (2014); P. Stevens, et al., *Conflict and Coexistence in the Extractive Industries* (London: Chatham House, 2013); D. Humphreys, "The Great Metals Boom," *Resources Policy* 35, no. 1 (2010): 1–13.

15   This is a preliminary distinction. Agriculture internalizes elements of both categories, and there is a distinction to be made between primarily organic extraction (farming, forestry) and inorganic extraction (coal mining, oil drilling).

distinct temporalities in play, which have to do with the different ways that primary and industrial production are bundled, geographically and materially, through the *oikeios*. The most famous of these distinctions—and arguably the most important—is the difference between the production time of agriculture, regulated by the seasons, and its labor-time, such that the continuous flow of manufacture is counterposed to the cyclical flow of cultivation.[16] If industrial work at the point of production involves the immediate interaction of "living" with "dead" labor—workers, machinery, and inputs—agro-extractive work involves these and more: living labor with unpaid (but living) work/energy. Working up the raw materials is easier than getting them out of the ground in the first place; it is easier to cook a hamburger than it is to butcher a cow. There is, then, a necessarily sticky supply response involved in the delivery of raw materials (circulating capital) to the factory gates. As capitalism developed, that sticky response became more fluid. *But only for a time.* The accumulating contradictions of capitalism-in-nature began to reimpose such "stickiness" by the end of the twentieth century, when climate change, superweeds, and other signs of a revolt of extra-human nature began to register as formidable barriers to the old models of accumulation (see Chapter Ten).

Regional Exhaustion and Historical Nature: From Commodity Frontier to Commodity Bust

Here we can begin to talk about exhaustion in a more tangible sense, because the general law of underproduction is not merely about supply response. We can begin with mining, because this is the most obvious case and in many ways serves as a popular metaphor for ecological crises. In fact, even extractive systems are not reducible to a physical depletion model.

Digging into the earth and extracting metals from it is not easy. Success tends to make it harder to extract more with the same—never mind less!—effort.[17] This is where historical capitalism has excelled. It turned the long decline in metal production characteristic of pre-capitalist civilizations into the opposite: a centuries-long boom in metal output. Indeed, the origins of capitalism are partly to be found in Central Europe's mining boom after 1450. New industrial organization and technological innovations allowed for a fivefold (or greater) increase in the output of such key metals as silver, copper, lead, and iron. By the 1530s, the pace of expansion slackened, and by the 1550s

16   Marx, *Capital*, Vol. II (1967); S. Mann, *Agrarian Capitalism in Theory and Practice* (Chapel Hill: University of North Carolina Press, 1990).

17   Bunker, "Modes of Extraction, Unequal Exchange, and the Progressive Underdevelopment of an Extreme Periphery" (1984).

Central Europe's mining complex no longer stood atop the world's metals economy. Production moved elsewhere: copper to Sweden, iron to England, silver to Peru. This movement was not a straightforward process of geology limiting capital. The pace of expansion slowed—even before contraction set in—not because ore quality declined *as such*. It declined because Central Europe's extractive complex was increasingly exhausted in its capacity to advance (or even sustain) labor productivity. This *capacity to advance labor productivity*—the rate of exploitation—is a co-production of human and extra-human natures. In sixteenth-century Central Europe, ore quality was part of this. So were geographical challenges, such as the construction of ever-deeper pits and attendant problems of flooding. But so were problems of rising wages and labor unrest, and of rising fuelwood and timber costs arising from confluence of metallurgical demand, urbanization, and deforestation. These bundled together to exhaust the region's capacity for advancing labor productivity in mining and metallurgy.[18]

As we know, such episodes of regional exhaustion have appeared—and been "fixed"—a great many times since the sixteenth century. In the pivotal case of silver, the exhaustion of Central European mining was resolved by turning to Potosí. Production boomed after Spain's enclosure of the Cerro Rico ("Rich Mountain") after 1545: ores were rich, fuel plentiful, and labor cheap. Within two decades, however, production collapsed. Ore quality declined, which made smelting fuel-intensive and increasingly costly, and indigenous smelters no longer found it worthwhile to produce silver for the Empire. The regional production complex was exhausted. The configuration of historical capitalism/historical nature no longer worked. Silver output collapsed.

This ushered in one of early capitalism's most spectacular episodes of socio-ecological transformation. The arrival of a new Viceroy, Francisco de Toledo, in 1571 was followed by a far-ranging transformation. A new method of extracting silver, mercury amalgamation, was instituted. A radical process of agrarian restructuring—centering on the *reducciones* (village resettlement) and the *mita* (a labor draft)—was launched to ensure a steady supply of cheap labor-power for the mines. Vast hydraulic infrastructures were built to power the mills that ground ore preparatory to amalgamation. And labor organization moved from arms-length sharecropping to more direct forms of labor control. Output was quickly restored, resolving Spain's fiscal crisis, but more importantly feeding the rise of Dutch capitalism. By the 1630s, exhaustion would again set in—driven no less by a crisis of (human) reproduction than by declining ore quality and faltering demand. And though silver output later revived in Potosí, the

---

18   F. Braudel, *The Structures of Everyday Life* (New York: Harper & Row, 1981); Moore, "Ecology and the Rise of Capitalism" (2007).

center of the world silver economy would migrate once again, to New Spain in the eighteenth century.[19]

What we see in this historical vignette is a recurring problem: the exhaustion of the relations of appropriation that make possible regional booms. These booms are tightly articulated with the global centers of accumulation, power, and production. Crucially, *exhaustion* does not reside in—to stick with our example—ore quality or mine depth or deforestation, but rather in the *oikeios* as it obtains in particular times and places. The question becomes one of how ore quality or mine depth or deforestation impacts labor productivity in commodity production. Thus, in seventeenth century Peru, there was a continual hemorrhaging of the sources of Cheap Labor, as population contracted and the *mita's* forced wage-workers fled both mines and villages, which reinforced difficulties in extracting and processing ore at the point of production.

Exhaustion is therefore about how we have "mixed our labor with the earth," as Williams might say.[20] It is not "capitalism" or "nature" that gets exhausted, but, as in colonial Peru, regionally specific relations of capitalization and appropriation. Both boom and exhaustion characterize phases in the regional development of definite relations of human and extra-human natures organized to advance the rate of exploitation, either by making labor more productive, by suppressing labor's income, by appropriating unpaid work— or, most often, all three at once. That project—to produce more use-value with less labor-power—unfolds within the *oikeios*, whose specific configurations shape the range of possibility and constraint. The initial restructuring of the *oikeios* that enables a regional boom to occur generates contradictions that bring that boom to an end: not because of human organization *or* natural limits, but because of how capitalist organization produces, and is produced by, the web of life.

Exhaustion: Substantial or Relational?

I have sketched the regional moment of exhaustion because it gives us a way to cut into the world-historical problem without making it all unfathomably abstract.[21] In such an enterprise, of course, some measure of abstraction is

---

19   Cf. Moore, "'Amsterdam Is Standing on Norway'" Parts I and II; "'This Lofty Mountain of Silver Could Conquer the Whole World'" (2010).

20   Williams, "Ideas of Nature" (1972).

21   To be clear, we are not dealing with "macro" and "micro"—yet another dualism that obscures more than clarifies— but rather with the co-production of world history through relations that are, simultaneously, local, regional, and systemic. Global-local dualism renders modernity's specific weaving of everyday life and world accumulation incomprehensible (cf. Tomich, *Slavery in the Circuit of Sugar* (1990); Moore, "'Amsterdam Is Standing on Norway'", Parts I and II).

unavoidable, because the conflation of "depletion" with the "limits to growth" is so deeply ingrained in our thinking. This conflation encourages an unproductive either/or discussion about how the web of life is a source of limits. The alternative recognizes that there *are* limits, and that these limits do not reside in Nature, any more than they reside in Society. They emerge in the ways that a particular civilization organizes—and *seeks to organize*—the *oikeios*. Capitalism's value project does indeed produce and provoke definite obstacles to its own survival, just as it also produces definite strategies for overcoming those obstacles through an ingenious combination of technology and frontier-making: the dialectic of productivity and plunder. These strategies have one big thing in common: they rely on the existence of uncapitalized natures that can be appropriated cheaply.

Exhaustion consequently involves, but cannot be reduced to, stocks and flows. Exhaustion is not a historical property of particular natures-as-substances—as when a forest is cleared and can no longer deliver timber. That reality speaks to exhaustion, but of course it is entirely possible for specific mineral veins or specific forests to be wiped out in a biophysical sense without provoking a capitalist crisis. Why? Because the hallmark of capitalism is its constant enlargement—and revolutionizing—of the geographies of *potential* accumulation and appropriation. The flows and stocks of particular substances are part of the dynamic. But exhaustion is not a substantial property. It is a *relational* property of the specifically capitalist *oikeios*.

From the standpoint of world accumulation, exhaustion emerges through the relation between two moments. On the one hand, the endless accumulation of capital entrains competition in the market and within production to produce more and more commodities with less and less labor-time. The endless accumulation of capital is the ceaseless expansion of material throughput. *But this can only occur if food, labor-power, energy, and raw materials prices can be contained.* That is, the Four Cheaps must remain cheap, or relatively so. This is challenging, because supply volumes must be relentlessly increased and supply prices must be constantly reduced. On the other hand, the accumulation of capital weighs heavily on the capacity of particular natures to deliver a rising—or even constant—stream of work/energy into the circuit of capital. This can happen directly, through exploitation (of labor-power) and capitalization (of the rest of nature). Or it can happen indirectly, through the appropriation of the work/energy of "women, nature, and colonies,"[22] outside the circuit of capital but within reach of capitalist power. *Exhaustion* occurs when particular natures—crystallized in specific re/production complexes—can no longer deliver more and more work/energy. At this point, the share of unpaid work/energy in a given

---

22   Mies, *Patriarchy and Accumulation* (1986), 77.

production complex falters, and the share of capitalized work/energy rises. The rising capitalization of re/production registers in rising prices for the Big Four inputs—almost always unevenly—unless new sources of unpaid work/energy can be located.

Developmental crises—as turning points in the historical configuration of capital, power, and nature—are "developmental" because they can be resolved through a double movement. First, a slowdown in the rate of accumulation can be "fixed" by opening new investment arenas, and expanding the scale and scope of commodification. This depends upon the opening of new, more expansive, arenas of appropriation, and expanding not just the scale of appropriation but its scope: not just more, but more and *new* forms of nature. This is capitalism's cardinal rule of systemic reproduction: commodify Nature, but appropriate even faster.

WORLD-ECOLOGICAL CRISES: EPOCHAL AND DEVELOPMENTAL

The radical critique of what modernity has done *to* nature has been a powerful one. It has been less successful in showing how the co-production of nature *works for* capitalism in its successive phases of development. This is a problem, because the strategies for remaking global nature—and for establishing new and expanded conditions for appropriating Cheap Nature—must be clarified if we are to understand the crisis today. Is it developmental, and subject to resolution through renewed capitalization and appropriation? Or is it epochal, and likely to lead to a fundamentally new historical configuration of wealth, power, and nature?

Here we can think about two great forms of world-ecological crisis. These are not "ecological" crises in a Cartesian sense, but crises that signify more or less fundamental turning points—between or within modes of re/producing wealth, nature, and power. The first is an *epochal* crisis. Such crises are so serious that one mode of producing wealth, nature, and power gives way to another. The crisis of feudalism in the "long" fourteenth century (c. 1290–1450) was one such epochal crisis. The second is a *developmental* crisis. These crises qualitatively transform the relations of power, wealth, and nature within a given mode of production. The "feudal revolution" around 1000 A.D. is a good example.[23] In the history of capitalism, developmental crises punctuate the transition from one phase of capitalism to the next. This is the history of

---

23   J. Poly and E. Bournazel, *The Feudal Transformation, 900–1200* (New York: Holmes & Meier, 1997); Moore, *Ecology in the Making (and Unmaking) of Feudal Civilization* (2013).

world-ecological revolutions—captured in historiographies on agricultural, industrial, commercial, scientific, and other "revolutions"—since the sixteenth century. Through *developmental crises*, new ways of commodifying and configuring the *oikeios* take shape. We may consider these two crises in their respective turns.

First, capitalism emerged out of the epochal crisis of feudalism.[24] This was the crisis of the long fourteenth century, which marked the end of European feudalism. No biophysical crisis in a narrow sense of soil and climate, the late medieval era marked a complex transition in the dominant bundles of seigneurial, territorial, and merchant power. The seigneurs, states, and merchants faced increasingly intractable problems reproducing themselves. Why intractable? Because feudal relations, from the agricultural revolution of the long eighth century, were bundled with the climate conditions of the Medieval Warm Period—as we saw in Chapter One. And because the *longue durée* tendencies of feudal agriculture implied a long-term stagnation of agricultural productivity, counteracted by increasingly less effective movements of geographical and demographic expansion.

The problem faced by feudal Europe was not one of abstract population overwhelming an abstract carrying capacity—*just as the problem today is not one of an abstract capitalism overwhelming an abstract nature*. Rather, the key contradiction turned on the failure of agricultural productivity to grow at a pace necessary to sustain the medieval demographic regime—understood as a class-structured process of production and reproduction.[25] This regime tended towards a widening sphere of "amino-starvation" and inadequate nutrition, even as the seigneurs' demands (and reproduction costs) grew over time.[26] It was feudal Europe's bad luck that the opportunities for frontier expansion—especially those easy frontier zones within the northwestern core—began to contract just as the Little Ice Age made its presence known. Thus, the crisis of feudalism was co-produced through class, climate, and a demography in which the prevailing class structure offered few opportunities for a turn towards greater "resilience." As Bois makes clear, the crisis was one of class, not carrying capacity. As opportunities contracted for reclaiming land in Normandy around 1250,

---

24   Moore, "Environmental Crises and the Metabolic Rift" (2000); "Nature and the Transition from Feudalism to Capitalism" (2003); "Ecology and the Rise of Capitalism" (2007).

25   W. Seccombe, *A Millennium of Family Change* (London: Verso, 1992).

26   L. White, Jr., *Medieval Technology and Social Change* (Oxford: Oxford University Press, 1962), 75; G. Duby, *Rural Economy and Country Life in the Medieval West* (Philadelphia: University of Pennsylvania Press, 1968), 233–5; R. Hilton, *The English Peasantry in the Late Middle Ages* (Oxford: Oxford University Press, 1975), 177.

the long, slow advance in agricultural production ran out of steam and then stopped ... [T]he Norman rural economy [had] reached a ceiling of growth ... The conquest of agricultural growth had arrived at its final stage: forest and pasture had receded to an astonishing extent ... *The ceiling was certainly not absolute* ... [In a peasant mode of production] an intensification of production was conceivable. If the traditional [feudal] system of cultivation had been abandoned to grow garden produce for example, the Norman land would have been able to produce more and feed a population two or three times larger.[27]

The crucial relation was between a class structure and its logic of surplus extraction on the one hand, and on the other, the regime of agrarian re/production—wherein both logic and regime were constituted through the web of life. The path to crisis unfolds through the unwillingness of ruling strata to make those "more or less painful internal adjustments" that would allow for a "long plateau of stabilization" or gradual decline.[28] That these contradictions and vulnerabilities led ultimately, under the pressure of the Black Death, to an epochal shift is understood, at least in its broad outlines. Bois' reasoning—there are certainly striking parallels to the early twenty-first century—points to the ways that class structures, even civilizations, enforce specific patterns of environment-making that are necessary to the reproduction of extant relations of power and production, and which progressively undermine those relations.

The essential point is elementary, yet rarely taken to heart: the "limits to growth" are historically specific. They are limits of historical nature. Just as feudalism's crisis marked the breakdown of a lord-peasant relation that had developed over six centuries, so we might look more closely at the erosion of the capital-labor relation in the early twenty-first century. This erosion signifies the capital-labor *relation's* withering capacity to transcend obstacles to accumulation posed by the rising need for appropriating natures and declining opportunities for doing so. This signals the end of the Great Frontier first opened in the sixteenth century.[29] The conventional view is to think of ecological crisis in terms of diminishing flows of substances—not enough food, not enough oil—but it may well be more productive to think of crisis as a process through which fundamentally new ways of ordering the relations between humans and the rest of nature take shape.

---

27   G. Bois, *The Crisis of Feudalism: Economy and Society in Eastern Normandy c. 1300–1550* (Cambridge: Cambridge University Press, 1984), 264.

28   Ibid.

29   Webb, *The Great Frontier* (1964).

Developmental Crises: The Origins of the Long Nineteenth Century

Capitalism's first great developmental crisis began in the mid-eighteenth century. The 1760s marked the end of the "first" agricultural revolution that established the conditions for English industrialization—largely by flooding the cities with Cheap food and labor-power.[30] Just 39 percent of the English workforce was employed in agriculture by 1700.[31] But this agricultural revolution was faltering by 1750. Over the next half-century, English agriculture failed to sustain the surging productivity of the previous century, either in terms of labor productivity or yields.[32] As early as the 1740s, English "agriculture . . . did not increase supplies of food and raw materials to match the rapidly growing demands of the urban industrial economy."[33] Agricultural productivity growth stagnated after 1760, and food prices began to increase. Even with sharply rising imports from Ireland,[34] English food prices increased twice as fast as the industrial price index at the end of the eighteenth century.[35] Relative to textiles and coal, food prices increased by 66 percent and 48 percent, respectively, between 1770 and 1795.[36]

Nor was this a narrowly English phenomenon. Productivity slowed, inequality widened, and food prices increased throughout the Atlantic world. Output per worker was either falling or stagnant across much of western Europe in the

---

30   R. Brenner, "The Agrarian Roots of European Capitalism," in *The Brenner Debate*, ed. T.H. Aston and C.H.E. Philpin (Cambridge: Cambridge University Press, 1985), 213–327; R.C. Allen, "Tracking the Agricultural Revolution in England" (1999).

31   S. Broadberry, et al., "When did Britain Industrialise?" *Explorations in Economic History* 50, no. 1 (2013): 23.

32   Agricultural labor productivity fell from .57 percent annually in 1700–59 to .41 percent between 1759 and 1801 (calculated from Broadberry, et al., "When did Britain Industrialise?", 23). For wheat, yield growth per acre averaged .38 percent annually over the period 1500–1700—.32 percent for the first half of the eighteenth century—but only .17 percent in 1759–1801. For rye—the poor man's cereal—yields actually fell, .13 percent annually in 1759–1801, after rising .47 percent annually for the two centuries after 1550 (S. Broadberry, et al., "British Economic Growth, 1270–1870" [Unpublished paper, Department of Economic History, London School of Economics, 2011], 37). Allen thinks output per worker in English agriculture declined in the second half of the eighteenth century (R.C. Allen, "Economic Structure and Agricultural Productivity in Europe, 1300–1800" (2000), 37).

33   P.K. O'Brien, "Agriculture and the Industrial Revolution," *Economic History Review* 30, no. 1 (1977): 175.

34   B. Thomas, "Feeding England during the Industrial Revolution," *Agricultural History* 56, no. 1 (1982): 328–42.

35   P.K. O'Brien, "Agriculture and the Home Market for English Industry, 1660–1820," *English History Review* 100 (1985): 776.

36   G. Clark, et al., "A British Food Puzzle, 1770–1850," *Economic History Review* 48, no. 2 (1995): 233.

half-century after 1750.[37] In France, food prices, mainly bread, shot up 65 percent—three times faster than wages—in the two decades before 1789.[38] In central Mexico, too, yields declined and prices rose—maize, by nearly 50 percent—in the later eighteenth century.[39] Abel dates the onset of the downturn from the 1730s, inaugurating eighty years of rising food prices, accelerating sharply around 1770. Across Europe, between 1730 and 1810, the price of the "chief bread grains" (wheat and rye) skyrocketed:

> By about 250 percent in England, 205 percent in northern Italy, 210 percent in Germany, 163 percent in France, 283 percent in Denmark . . . 265 percent in the Netherlands, 259 percent in Austria, and 215 percent in Sweden. In Denmark, the Netherlands, and Austria *this was the highest point reached [up to this time] in the long-term ascent of prices.*[40]

England took the lead in its "capacity to augment output while releasing labour for employment in industry and services":[41] in other words, in its capacity to prioritize labor over land productivity. This was, of course, the English moment— and a dramatic one at that—of a worldwide surge of primitive accumulation across the Atlantic world-ecology, prompting peasant rebellions from Russia to the Americas.[42] The turning point in the English countryside was reached by 1760. The scale and tempo of Parliamentary Enclosure jumped sharply:[43] a sixfold increase in the number and acreage of enclosure acts in the three decades after 1760 relative to the three decades prior.[44] In the century following 1750,

---

37   Allen, "Economic Structure and Agricultural Productivity" (2000), 20.

38   O. Hufton, "Social Conflict and the Grain Supply in Eighteenth-Century France," *Journal of Interdisciplinary History* 14, no. 2 (1983): 304.

39   S. Lipsett-Rivera, "Puebla's Eighteenth-Century Agrarian Decline," *Hispanic American Historical Review* 70, no. 3 (1990): 463–81; L. Arroyo Abad, et al., "Real wages and Demographic Change in Spanish America, 1530–1820," *Explorations in Economic History* 49, no. 2 (2012): 149–66.

40   W. Abel, *Agricultural Fluctuations in Europe* (New York: St. Martin's Press, 1980 [1966 orig.]), 197–8. Emphasis added.

41   O'Brien, "Agriculture and the Home Market," 775.

42   I. Wallerstein, *The Modern World-System III* (San Diego: Academic Press, 1989), 193–256; T.P. Slaughter, *The Whiskey Rebellion* (Oxford: Oxford University Press, 1986); C.A. Bayly, *The Birth of the Modern World 1780–1914* (Oxford: Blackwell, 2004), 86–120.

43   Ross, "The Malthus Factor" (2000), 3.

44   B.H. Slicher van Bath, *The Agrarian History of Western Europe, 500–1850 A.D.* (New York: St. Martin's Press, 1963), 319; P. Mantoux, *The Industrial Revolution in the Eighteenth Century* (New York: Harper & Row, 1961), 141–2; R.V. Jackson, "Growth and Deceleration in English Agriculture, 1660–1790," *Economic History Review* 38 (1985): 333–51.

fully one-quarter of "England's cultivated acreage was transformed from open field, common land or waste land into private property."[45] Agriculture's occupational share declined .23 percent annually between 1522 and 1700, but accelerated to .35 percent a year between 1759–1801.[46] The food price spikes— or long swings, in the period 1740–1815—were therefore not only biophysical and "economic," but, *also and at the same time*, crucial moments in the world class struggle. Long inflationary swings have been, in the long history of capitalism, moments through which the bourgeoisie deploys the power of the market—backed by the power of the state, as during the Parliamentary Enclosures after 1760[47] —to redistribute value from the producers to the accumulators of surplus value. Income inequality—a rough proxy and an effective, if temporary, "fix" for capital accumulation—rose sharply. The English bourgeoisie—the top 5 percent—"gained enormously at the expense of the middle and upper-middle classes" over the next century. Meanwhile, the poverty rate grew by more than 50 percent after 1759, encompassing a fifth of the population by 1801.[48]

This was not the first time such a redistribution of value had occurred. The "price revolution" after 1470 also redistributed value from workers to capitalists, issuing in part from the forcible suppression of peasant and proletarian diets.[49] Indeed, English per capita food consumption declined across the sixteenth and seventeenth centuries (and not only English).[50] Then as now, "forced underconsumption" offered a crucial subsidy to world accumulation.[51]

In the *conjoncture* of accelerating dispossession and proletarianization combined with stagnating productivity, there were two possibilities. One was that rising food prices would drive up the wage-bill for capital, enacting a kind of wage-squeeze on accumulation. The other was the road of forced

---

45   We should take care not to collapse two processes here: the "specific device of the Enclosure Act" and the "general phenomenon of agricultural concentration" (E.J. Hobsbawm, *Industry and Empire* (New York: Penguin, 1968), 101.

46   Calculated from Broadberry (S. Broadberry, et al., "When did Britain Industrialise?", 23).

47   M. Turner, *Enclosures in Britain, 1750–1830* (London: Palgrave Macmillan, 1984).

48   P.H. Lindert and J.G. Williamson. "Reinterpreting Britain's Social Tables, 1688–1913," *Explorations in Economic History* 20, no. 1 (1983): 104.

49   F. Braudel and F. Spooner, "Prices in Europe from 1450 to 1750," in *The Cambridge Economic History of Europe*, Vol. IV, ed. E.E Rich and C.H. Wilson (London: Cambridge University Press, 1967), 378–486; Wallerstein, *The Modern World-System I* (1974).

50   Allen, "Tracking the Agricultural Revolution in England," 216–217.

51   F. Arrighi, "Accumulation by Displacement," *Review* 32, no. 1 (2009): 113–46.

underconsumption, whereby working-class food budgets were instead squeezed. This probably resulted in a net caloric and nutritional decline for proletarian diets—certainly in England but probably well beyond.[52] The proposition finds support in widespread declining physical stature in the half-century after 1760.[53] What bears emphasizing is that the redistribution of value through food price movements is a middle-run strategy. Consumption can only be driven down so far. At some point, the world-ecological surplus must be expanded and not simply maintained—the mass of unpaid work/energy must rise relative to the mass of accumulated capital. New frontiers must be opened, their "free gifts" identified and mapped, secured and appropriated.

And what about energy and raw materials? Like food/labor-power, energy and raw materials were tightly bound to each other. The principal, indispensable, raw materials in early capitalism were iron and timber. Both came from the forests, directly or indirectly. (Iron was early capitalism's greatest consumer of wood fuel after domestic heating.) But here the immediate barriers to *systemic* accumulation were much less intractable than is commonly supposed.[54] Given the geographical concentration of coal supplies in England, and the robust movement of the iron-making commodity frontier—which, in the eighteenth century, incorporated Swedish and Russian iron exporting zones—the underproduction tendency was readily checked after 1760. (Though not for English iron producers, who saw their production costs rise significantly in the mid-eighteenth century.)[55] What stands out in this era is the ability of capitalists, states, and commodity markets to sustain Cheap iron and energy—by extending the zone of appropriation. Cheap Food, in contrast, posed thornier problems.

And what about energy? Capitalism's energy systems have done two big things. On the one hand, they have reduced the value composition of production, by reducing the costs of raw materials (circulating capital). Coal and peat were cheaper alternatives to charcoal, and proved indispensable in key sectors

---

52   O'Brien, "Agriculture and the Home Market"; Allen, "Tracking the Agricultural Revolution."

53   J. Komlos, "Shrinking in a Growing Economy?" *Journal of Economic History* 58, no. 3 (1998): 779–802; F. Cinnirella, "Optimists or Pessimists? A Reconsideration of Nutritional Status in Britain, 1740–1865," *European Review of Economic History* 12, no. 3 (2008): 325–54.

54   See the neo-Malthusian assumptions on energy limits offered by E.A. Wrigley, *Energy and the English Industrial Revolution* (Cambridge: Cambridge University Press, 2010); and K. Pomeranz, *The Great Divergence* (2000).

55   C.K. Hyde, "Technological Change in the British Wrought Iron Industry, 1750–1815," *Economic History Review* 27, no. 2 (1974): 190–206.

such as salt refining, construction (e.g., brick-making), baking and brewing, and textiles.[56] But, and here is the crucial point, they were also more productive in terms of labor-power (variable capital). That Cheap Energy allowed for the simultaneous decline of input costs and the advance of labor productivity is no small thing, since rising labor productivity is the rising material throughput per hour of socially necessary labor-time.

Modernity's energy revolutions do not date—as sometimes supposed—from the eighteenth century, but rather from the long sixteenth century. England's astounding increase in coal production began in the 1530s.[57] By 1660, coal covered more than a third of the country's energy output; by 1700, half.[58] The Dutch, too, found new ways to extract peat, a kind of proto-coal, beginning in the 1530s. Both movements unfolded as wood-based energy prices in England and the Low Countries moved sharply upwards after 1530.[59] The Dutch model of fossil capitalism, which had flourished with Cheap Energy—and Cheap food and timber—began to stumble around 1660, just when domestic peat output declined and English coal output soared. The very success of the Dutch model, meanwhile, had given the Republic's capitalists the highest wage-bill in Europe by this point—it would move still higher by 1680—without any easy way out. Mechanization could and did occur, but the relative rise of energy prices placed limits on productivity-advancing innovations that would expel labor from production and drive down the wage-bill, which remained high until the 1740s.[60] The English, too, faced rising real wages, starting at a lower point than the Dutch but increasing much faster in the century after 1625.[61] As in the Republic, English wages were "remarkably high."[62] But in England, energy was remarkably cheap: "This wage and price history was a fundamental reason for the technological breakthroughs of the

---

56   J.W. de Zeeuw, "Peat and the Dutch Golden Age," *A.A.G. Bijdragen* 21 (1978): 3–31; E.A. Wrigley, *Poverty, Progress and Population* (Cambridge: Cambridge University Press, 2004).

57   J.U. Nef, *The Rise of the British Coal Industry* (London: Routledge, 1966 [1932 orig.]).

58   R.C. Allen, "Energy Transitions in History: The Shift to Coal" in *Energy Transitions in History*, ed. R.W. Unger (Munich: Rachel Carson Center/Federal Ministry of Education and Research), 11; P. Malanima, "The Path Towards the Modern Economy" (2011).

59   R.C. Allen, "The British Industrial Revolution in Global Perspective" (2006); P. Malanima, "Energy Crisis and Growth 1650–1850" (2006); J. de Vries and A. van der Woude, *The First Modern Economy* (Cambridge: Cambridge University Press, 1997), 37–9.

60   J. de Vries and A. van der Woude, *The First Modern Economy*, 674–6ff; J.W. Moore, "'Amsterdam Is Standing on Norway' Part II."

61   R.M. Smith, "Fertility, Economy, and Household Formation in England over Three Centuries," *Population and Development Review* 7, no. 4 (1981): 601.

62   Allen, "The British Industrial Revolution in Global Perspective" (2006).

eighteenth century [enabled by Cheap energy] whose object was to substitute capital and energy for labour."[63]

The achievement of the late eighteenth century was the marriage of mass-produced coal and iron through coke, a coal derivative known since the seventeenth century but made practical only after Darby's breakthrough in 1707–1709. Just 7 percent of English iron came from coke-fired blast furnaces in 1750; by 1784, when coke was used in all phases of production, the figure reached 90 percent.[64] This was a breakthrough because it allowed for a radical cheapening of *fixed* capital at the same time as new machinery was massively deployed. Not for nothing does von Tunzelmann characterize this period as one of capital-saving as much as labor-saving.[65] Iron, and increasingly steel, tools and machinery could be deployed on a gargantuan scale. The trinity of fixed, circulating, and variable capital could therefore enjoy a virtuous circle of accumulation. Its pedestal was a vicious circle of appropriation.

Of course, Cheap Energy was not everything. It depended on cheapening labor-power, which was accomplished after mid-century (and would not be reversed until the 1820s) through Parliamentary Enclosures. Here again, the decisive turning point occurred a century before, as the relative slowdown of the seventeenth century world-economy owed much to "a marked labor shortage from 1625–1750," registered in rising wages across the northern European core.[66] But in contrast to the epochal crisis of the long fourteenth century, the "B phase" of the long seventeenth century saw the rapid expansion—not contraction—of the proletariat.[67] The process had begun earlier—in the Netherlands by the fifteenth century and in England by the sixteenth, reaching critical mass by 1750. The European proletariat swelled by one-third in absolute numbers in the second half of the eighteenth century, as expulsion from agricultural production and a new demographic regime took shape.[68] England, by this point, was in the

---

63   Ibid., 2.

64   R. Fremdling, "Industrialization And Scientific And Technological Progress," in *History Of Humanity*, Vol. VI, ed. P. Mathias and N. Todorov (New York: Routledge, 2005), 80–94.

65   G.N. von Tunzelmann, "Technological Progress During the Industrial Revolution," in *The Economic History of Britain since 1700*, Vol. 1, ed. R. Floud and D. McCloskey, 143–63 (Cambridge: Cambridge University Press, 1981).

66   W. Abel, *Crises Agraires en Europe (XIIIe-XXe Siecle)*, 2d ed. (Paris: Flammarion, 1973), 225; Quoted in Wallerstein, *The Modern World-System II* (1980), 16; R.C. Allen, "The British Industrial Revolution in Global Perspective."

67   Seccombe, *A Millennium of Family Change* (1992), 193ff; C. Tilly, "Demographic Origins of the European Proletariat" (CRSO Working Paper No. 207, Center for Research on Social Organization, University of Michigan, 1979).

68   Ibid.

vanguard. Crucially, Parliamentary Enclosures after 1760 were profoundly gendered, disproportionately proletarianizing women, and yielding a kind of "gendered surplus" to capital in the form of lower remuneration relative to men.[69] Thus did Britain combine demographic, industrial, and energy revolutions, pointing the way towards a new world-ecological regime. The threat of underproduction had receded.

But it did not disappear.

UNDERPRODUCTION IN THE ERA OF PEAK APPROPRIATION

What "work" did all this coal perform for an emergent industrial capitalist order? The now-conventional answer is that "coal and colonies" rescued an emergent capitalism from a Malthusian trap.[70] And there is some merit to the argument, even if the Malthusian language misleads: another dualism that blinds us to the dynamics of early capitalism. The real contribution of coal, iron, and steam power is found in the ways that it dealt with four interconnected phenomena. The first resolved the problem of overaccumulated capital. By 1860, the railroads soaked up four times as much capital as textile production.[71] The second resolved the production of iron, necessary to the widest range of productive and infrastructural developments, from machinery to bridges. Output skyrocketed after the perfection of coke-smelting in 1784: high-quality (and fuel-intensive) wrought iron production increased 500 percent between 1788 and 1815; Britain's iron exports increased from 57,000 tons a year in 1814 to over a million in 1852.[72] The third resolved the problem of labor productivity. How much of this increase came from steam power directly? This is hard to say. But even Clark,[73] a pessimist on the matter, sees a tenfold increase in cotton spinning and weaving productivity between 1810 and 1860. Steam accounted for a growing share of this rising productivity, especially as steam displaced water mills after 1830.[74] Even here, the trend favored steam for transport more

69   M. Berg, *The Age of Manufactures, 1700–1820*, 2nd ed. (New York: Routledge, 1994), 117–44. Thanks to Andy Pragacz for the concept of a "gendered surplus."

70   K. Pomeranz, *The Great Divergence* (2000).

71   N. Crafts, "Productivity Growth in the Industrial Revolution," *Journal of Economic History* 64, no. 2 (2004): 530.

72   E. Moe, *Governance, growth and global leadership: the role of the state in technological progress, 1750–2000* (Burlington, VT: Ashgate, 2007), 84.

73   G. Clark, "The Secret History of the Industrial Revolution" (Unpublished paper, Department of Economics, University of California-Davis, 2001).

74   N. Crafts, "Steam as a General Purpose Technology," *Economic Journal* 114 (2004): 338–51.

than for factories in the mid-century golden age: railroads already used 30 percent of total steam power in 1840; by 1870, this had increased to 60 percent.[75] Finally, the potential contradictions of rising capitalization and rising commodity production were offset by the construction of a global rail and steamship network that—apace with ongoing primitive accumulation in North America and elsewhere—greatly expanded the scale, scope, and *speed* of appropriating work/energy.

There is no question that steam power augmented the capacities of capitalist agencies to transform space. A modest amount of capital mobilized a relatively vast energy surplus, some—but not all—of which turned on coal. (In the U.S., coal dethroned charcoal as the principal energy source only after 1880!)[76] This enabled capital to appropriate new frontiers faster than its productive dynamism could exhaust extant reserves of resources and labor-power. In other words, accumulation by capitalization, as in the Manchester textile mills, was accompanied by a truly earth-shaking revolution in accumulation by appropriation.

The revolution in appropriation reached a definitive turning point after 1830. For the commodity frontier strategy that enabled the rise of capitalism was, by the middle of the nineteenth century, propelled to new heights by the coal/steam power nexus. This nexus came into its own—for capitalism as a whole—with the first major wave of railroad and steamship expansion beginning in 1830. By 1860, 107,000 kilometers of railroad track had been laid and 803,000 tons of steamships were afloat.[77] From the standpoint of appropriation, the flashpoint of this movement was clearly North America. Already by 1840, the U.S. had twice as much track as Britain, a gap that continued to widen, as American railroads grew nearly eightfold between 1845 and 1860.[78] This facilitated an explosion of internal trade—merchant shipping on rivers in the trans-Appalachian west increased nearly tenfold between 1830 and 1860—facilitating the export of cheap cotton to the English mills. By 1860, some 70 percent of American cotton was exported, with 70 percent going to England.[79] Raw cotton prices for English importers dropped by a whopping 80 percent between 1814 and 1843.[80] Cheap Nature, indeed.

---

75   Rostow, *The World Economy* (153).

76   C. Ponting, *A Green History of the World* (New York: St. Martin's Press, 1991), 284.

77   E.J. Hobsbawm, *The Age of Capital 1848–1875* (New York: Meridian, 1975), 310.

78   D.R. Headrick, *The Tentacles of Progress* (Oxford: Oxford University Press, 1988), 55; P.J. Hugill, *World Trade Since 1431* (Baltimore: Johns Hopkins University Press, 1995), 173.

79   P.J. Hugill, *World Trade Since 1431*, 169–70.

80   A.G. Kenwood et al., *Growth of the International Economy, 1820–2015* (New York: Routledge, 2013), 148.

Even here, we should take care to situate the coal-iron-steam power trinity within definite bounds. Coal did not resolve the agro-ecological crisis of the later eighteenth century: that was the work of imperialism and ongoing primitive accumulation. As English agriculture stagnated after 1760, grain was imported in growing volumes, at first from Ireland and, after the 1846 repeal of the Corn Laws, increasingly from North America. Britain's mid-nineteenth-century zenith as the "workshop of the world" was closely linked to the agricultural revolution of the American Midwest. North American grain replaced the relative exhaustion of England's "agricultural district" in Ireland (c. 1780–1840). In time, American grain would be complemented by new supplies in Russia, India, and elsewhere. Between 1846 and the downturn of the 1870s, Britain's grain imports increased 254 percent. Grain poured in from the U.S. even faster: fortyfold, from 25,000 tons to over a million tons a year, providing more than half of Britain's imports by 1873.[81] It is true that grain prices fell only modestly in this golden age of British capitalism[82]—a major accomplishment in light of England's rapid population growth (from 16 to 23 million) and rapid industrialization (one-third of world manufacturing). Prices tumbled after 1873—a bushel of imported wheat in 1896 cost less than half what it did in 1873—even as England came to consume 80 percent of its daily bread from external sources.[83] Supply outpaced demand, which reduced food costs, while the appropriation of manifold frontiers outpaced supply, making agricultural expansion profitable *enough*. This was not the work of coal alone: steamships did not displace sails for most commodities—save cotton—until the 1850s, and even then slowly, until the 1870s.[84] If the 1830s marked a turning point in textiles, even as late as the 1860s "preindustrial" innovations and practices—should we not say "pre-steam"?—held sway in transport. The special character of fossil fuels cannot explain it all.

Whatever coal's immediate role in nineteenth century developments, it was

---

81   Calculated from M. Atkin, *The International Grain Trade* (Cambridge: Woodhead, 1992), 17–18.

82   D.G. Barnes, *A History of English Corn Laws* (Abingdon, UK: Routledge, 1930), 290.

83   M.G. Mulhall, *The Dictionary of Statistics* (London: Routledge, 1892), 444; B. Thomas, "Feeding England during the Industrial Revolution" (1982): 336; K.H. O'Rourke, "The European Grain Invasion, 1870–1913," *Journal of Economic History* 57, no. 4 (1997): 775–801; W. Page, ed., *Commerce and Industry: Tables of Statistics for the British Empire from 1815* (London: Constable, 1919), 219.

84   Headrick, *The Tentacles of Progress* (1988), 18–48; P. Sharp, "Pushing Wheat" (Discussion Paper 08–08, Department of Economics, University of Copenhagen, 2008); D.S. Jacks and K. Pendakur, "Global Trade and the Maritime Transport Revolution," *Review of Economics and Statistics* 92, no. 4 (2010): 745–55; C. Knick Harley, "Ocean Freight Rates and Productivity, 1740–1913," *Journal of Economic History* 48, no. 4 (1988): 851–76.

clearly central to a shift in the locus of capitalist crisis from underproduction to overproduction. A combination of underproduction—crop failures, and the potato blight in Ireland—and overproduction was at work in Europe's economic and political turbulence of 1845–1850.[85] But the bias continued to move towards overproduction. Indeed, the whole period from 1817 to 1896 is marked by a "protracted and sharp deflation" driven by the productivity advances generalized after 1820.[86] The balance had tipped towards overproduction as the principal axis of accumulation crisis.

This tipping point was an extraordinary accomplishment. For the first time in human history, planetary life came to be governed by single logic of wealth, power, and nature: the law of value. I have said that coal was not everything— but the scale, speed, and scope of planetary transformation surely owed much to the transformation of coal into capital. Capitalism as a planetary system became possible through the production of a globe-encircling railroad and steamship network. This established the conditions for two tightly connected developments: 1) the *global* hegemony of value relations, previously contained within the Atlantic world; and 2) the unprecedented appropriation, in absolute terms, of planetary work/energy. Planetary work as a whole—nearly all unpaid—was now *potentially* available for conscription into the armies of capital. The dominance of overproduction was realized through an unprecedented disproportionality between paid and unpaid work. This was the world-historical "peak" of the world-ecological surplus: peak appropriation. The gap would slowly close over the next century (c. 1870–1970), then show signs of more rapid decline. The era's productivity advances—the "second" and "Fordist" industrial revolutions—owed their revolutionary character to the even greater appropriation of planetary work. This dialectic of productivity and plunder—of accumulation by capitalization and accumulation by appropriation—is at the heart of how capitalism has survived and sustained itself over the past five centuries. It is how early capitalism survived underproduction crises, and how industrial capitalism seemed to have banished them.

This transition to overproduction as the dominant crisis tendency in the mid-nineteenth century weighs heavily on our thinking about crisis. Certainly, metropolitan capital has been hugely successful in securing Cheap Nature since the nineteenth century. This has an awful lot to do with the production and transportation efficiencies enabled by Cheap fossil fuels. Nevertheless, for all their undeniable contributions to the appropriation of nature's free gifts, fossil fuels eased, but did

---

85   E. Vanhaute, et al., "The European Subsistence Crisis of 1845–1850," in *When the Potato Failed*, ed. E. Vanhaute, et al. (Turnhout, Belgium: Brepols, 2007).

86   D. Landes, *Prometheus Unbound* (Cambridge: Cambridge University Press, 1969), 233–34.

not resolve, the basic contradiction. Here we may return to Marx's theory of under-production, which basically says two things. First, capital seeks to drive down the value composition of raw materials (circulating capital) relative to machinery and buildings (fixed capital), even as it geometrically expands material throughput. Second, capital's inner dynamism undermines the conditions of reproduction that allow it to deliver cheap inputs. This is why new frontiers of appropriation have been central to launching, and sustaining, long waves of accumulation.

I have argued that underproduction and overproduction are dialectically bound, and that our investigations ought to focus on their shifting configurations. The "great depression" of the late nineteenth century is arguably the paradigmatic example. Prices for Britain's raw materials began to rise sharply during the 1860s and 1870s, at the very moment of its peak industrial suprema-cy.[87] The inflationary moment was, as we know, quickly turned inside out. World market prices generally declined quite sharply after 1873. At the same time, an inflationary undercurrent was in play. The era was punctuated by successive (if partial) moments of underproduction in such key raw materials as cotton, indigo, rubber, palm oil, copper, nickel, lead, tin, jute, and sisal.[88] These infla-tionary undercurrents were set in motion by the rise of new industrial powers, Germany and the U.S. They were amplified further still by the qualitative shifts inscribed in the "second" industrial revolution's production of nature, premised on oil and petrochemicals, and the auto, steel, and electrical industries.

The underproductionist tendency was consequently checked, but not abol-ished, by the second industrial revolution. Insofar as we restrict our attention to the new industrializers, the inner contradiction between value accumulation and the underproduction of inputs was intensified. The contradiction was resolved through the dialectic of plunder and productivity characteristic of capi-talism's successive global ecological fixes: 1) the radical enlargement of the geographical arena, with the rapid acceleration of colonial and white settler expansion; and 2) the "massive penetration of capital into the production of raw materials," especially in these newly incorporated zones.[89] Metals such as copper were especially important to late nineteenth-century industrialization, and the pace of technological innovation was fast and furious. Of the "new" industrial-izers, Germany's advantage was the application of science and capital to new production processes, while America's edge was the rapid appropriation of

---

87   Hobsbawm, *The Age of Capital 1848–1875* (1975), 310; Rostow, *The World Economy* (1978); Mandel, *Late Capitalism* (1975).

88   Headrick, *The Tentacles of Progress* (1988); Brockway, *Science and Colonial Expansion* (1978); N. Bukharin, *Imperialism and World Economy* (New York: International Publishers, 1929 [1917 orig.]); H. Magdoff, *Age of Imperialism* (New York: Monthly Review Press, 1969), 33–40.

89   Mandel, *Late Capitalism* (1975), 61.

Cheap Nature on a continental scale, and, through migration, its importation of Cheap labor-power from the rest of the world. The fate of the first half of the twentieth century would turn on this difference.

What bears emphasizing is that the moment of "productivity" (capitalization) was enabled by one of "plunder" (appropriation). The massive flow of investment was possible because the rapid geographical expansion signified the rapid expansion of opportunities for accumulation by appropriation. The surplus profits enjoyed by metropolitan capital in this era were consequently remarkably high, resting on the appropriation of unpaid work/energy above the system-wide average. And yet, for all the dynamism of production and restless commodity frontiers, the tendency towards underproduction would not go away. Copper production surged tenfold between 1870 and 1914 without any price decline—a stark contrast to the eightfold increase in American cotton output and sharply falling prices in the three decades after 1814.[90] This, despite massive capital investment and a dynamic commodity frontier that reached from sub-Saharan Africa to Chile and the American West.[91] At the dawn of the long twentieth century, Malaysian rubber and tin, Chilean nitrates, Australian copper and gold, and Canadian nickel all entered the world-historical stage as key moments in an ecological revolution that was "far quicker, far more prodigious in its results, far more revolutionary in its effects on people's lives and outlooks" than anything previously known.[92]

This century after 1870 was characterized by an unusual state of affairs. This was the century of *peak appropriation*—the maximal mobilization of unpaid work/energy per quanta of value (abstract social labor). Technological progress, capitalist power, and modern science produced a perfect storm of appropriation. The relatively contained character of capitalist power in the North Atlantic core now gave to way tentacles of power, capitalization, and appropriation that brought the whole of uncapitalized nature within reach. Thus, peak appropriation represents the "peak" of the world-ecological surplus, the ratio of the mass of unpaid work/energy to the mass of accumulated capital. Here we are talking

---

90   J.L. Watkins, *King Cotton: A Historical and Statistical Review, 1790 to 1908* (New York: J.L. Watkins & Sons, 1908), 299; Kenwood et al., *Growth of the International Economy* (2013), 148.

91   G. Bridge, "What Drives the Extractive Frontier?" Paper presented to the 1st World Congress of Environmental History, Copenhagen, August 3–8, 2009); J. Leitner, "Red Metal in the Age of Capital," *Review* 24, no. 3 (2001): 373–437; T. Frederiksen, "Unearthing Rule"(Paper presented to the 1st World Congress of Environmental History, Copenhagen, August 3–8, 2009); Schmitz, "The Rise of Big Business in the World Copper Industry" (1986).

92   G. Barraclough, *An Introduction to Contemporary History* (New York: Penguin, 1967), 44.

about peak appropriation in systemic and cumulative terms—a "peak" moment for capitalism as a whole—but such peaks can also be identified for each long cycle of accumulation, and for particular regional production complexes.

Peak *appropriation* views the problem as relational—between and within human and extra-human natures at the same time. There is no need for geological reductionism. Peak appropriation enfolds the geological and biophysical moments highlighted by "peak everything" arguments into one that understands the limits of civilizations—capitalism not least!—as historically inscribed in their strategic organizing principles. Those principles—for instance, capitalism's insistence on labor productivity as the metric of wealth—are not exogenous to nature but rather represent specific projects and processes that internalize, in contingent yet durable ways, the relations of all nature.

CONCLUSION

How does capital accumulation work in an era of *post*-peak appropriation? This question unfolds within the cumulative and cyclical expressions of capitalist crisis over the *longue durée*. In the next chapter, we look at how capitalism has dealt with its recurrent developmental crises, and how those have been overcome through successive world-ecological revolutions.

CHAPTER 6

World-Ecological Crises: From Revolutions to Regimes

Does capitalism today face an epochal or developmental crisis? Is the ongoing restructuring of neoliberal capitalism likely to yield a new "golden age" of capitalism? Or is a terminal exhaustion of capitalist strategies of commodification and appropriation more likely? For some measure of guidance, we may look to the ways that capitalism has restructured over successive long centuries of accumulation and crisis. These are eras of world-ecological revolution.

Ecological revolutions resolve developmental crises by reducing the capitalization of nature, and finding new quantitative—*and qualitative*—means of appropriating the biosphere's work/energy. These revolutions rework the specifically capitalist *oikeios*. In so doing, they revolutionize both human ("society," "economy," "culture," and so forth) and extra-human natures. By driving down the capitalized share of world nature and increasing the share that can be freely appropriated, revolutions of the capitalist *oikeios* "work" by expanding the ecological surplus. This surplus finds its chief expression in the Four Cheaps—cheap, in a world-historical sense, to the degree that they expand and increase the appropriation of unpaid work relative to its capitalization.

We will unpack this argument in two major phases. First, we consider the dynamics of accumulation and crisis by linking the tendentially rising value composition of capital with the rising capitalization of world nature. Next, we consider the restructuring of world accumulation and world commodity production through successive world-ecological revolutions.

VALUE, NATURE, AND WORLD ACCUMULATION

We can begin with Marx on the tendency of the rate of profit to fall. As capitalists invest in constant capital (machinery and inputs), its share of production rises, and with it, labor productivity. Consequently, labor's share (variable capital) falls. In this, rising capital intensity—the rising organic composition of capital—places downward pressure on the general rate of profit. The operative assumption here is that aggregate profit, on balance, flows from aggregate surplus value, which is generated and distributed unevenly.[1] Why then does the rate of profit fall?

> The argument is simple. It is because the numerator in the profit equation, surplus value, is outrun by the denominator, capital stock (both measured in annual terms) . . . That is, too much capital stock builds up in factories and equipment around the world, pitting companies against each other in an ever-fiercer competitive brawl for markets. This holds prices down, leads commodity output to outrun demand at prevailing prices, and/or lowers capacity utilization rates—thereby lowering profit margins, leaving goods unsold and running equipment at less efficient levels.[2]

How does profitability revive? Marxists usually respond by emphasizing the role of crises in propelling creative destruction. In these accounts there are three big themes. One is the devaluation of fixed capital, as when factories close. Another is the introduction of productivity-maximizing technical or organizational innovations that increase the rate of exploitation. A third is the implementation of coercive-intensive policies that redistribute wealth from the direct producers to the accumulators of capital.[3] There is, of course, enormous debate over the relation between accumulation crisis and the falling rate of profit, conceptually and empirically.[4]

To these three moments, I would add a fourth. This turns on circulating capital (inputs), but with important implications for variable capital (labor-power). Marx's "most important law"[5] can be more fully grasped—and its explanatory power radically extended—by taking as a whole two tightly linked sets of contradictions: 1) those between "first" and "second" nature (the supply of inputs relative to machinery); and 2) those within second nature (constant relative to variable capital). In what follows, I treat Marx's "progressive tendency" towards

---

1   Marx, *Capital*, Vol. I (1977); *Capital*, Vol. III (1981).

2   R.A. Walker, "The Global Agitator, or Capitalism's Recurrent Self-Criticism" (Working Paper, Department of Geography, University of California, Berkeley, 1998), http://geography.berkeley.edu/ProjectsResources/Publications/Global_Economic_Crisis.html.

3   D. Harvey, *The Limits to Capital* (London: Verso, 1982); D. Harvey, *The New Imperialsm* (2003); E. Mandel, *Late Capitalism* (1975); McNally, *Global Slump* (2011); R.A. Walker, "Capitalim's Recurrent Self-Criticism," *Historical Materialism*, 5 (2000): 179–210.

4   Useful surveys can be found in E. Mandel, "Introduction," in Karl Marx, *Capital*, Vol. III (New York: Penguin, 1981) 9–90; and B. Fine and A. Saad-Filho, *Marx's Capital*, 4th ed. (London: Pluto, 2004).

5   Marx, *Grundrisse* (1973), 748.

a "gradual fall in the general rate of profit"[6] as a guiding thread for comprehending the historical dynamics underpinning the tendentially rising capitalization of nature. I am therefore less concerned with the precise operationalization of this general law at a sectoral or national level, and rather more with how it helps us think through the big picture: How does this tendency illuminate a decisive point of fracture in the *longue durée* movements of capitalism as world-ecology? My working answer is this: the *value* composition of production—Marx's concept of value for the "organic whole" of capital accumulation—is conditioned by the appropriation of Cheap Natures.

I am tempted to say that the crucial weakness in falling-rate-of-profit arguments has not been the theory itself, but an overemphasis on one moment of constant capital—on *fixed* rather than *circulating* capital. Could it be that since the 1830s, capitalism has forged agro-extractive complexes capable of outrunning the tendency towards the underproduction of inputs? If a sufficient mass of Cheap energy and raw materials can be mobilized, the rising value composition of capital can be attenuated—especially if "capital saving" innovations run strongly alongside labor saving movements.[7] When this occurs, the tendency towards a falling rate of profit is not only checked, but (for a time) reversed. A rising rate of appropriation tends to reduce the value composition of production and counteracts the tendency. *However*, if capitalization rises faster than the appropriation of unpaid work—a situation that characterizes capitalist agriculture today, for instance (see Chapter Ten)—the accumulation process will slow. A declining rate of appropriation shapes the declining rate of profit.

The costs of production tend to rise over the course of long waves of accumulation. They rise because the normal course of accumulation tends towards the capitalization of everyday life, so that more and more the elements of daily reproduction depend on commodities. (Thus, successive "consumer revolutions.") They rise because the exploitation of labor-power tends to favor new solidarities that challenge capital, even if these have, as yet, been a far cry from socialist revolution. And they rise because the capitalization of the relations of reproduction—for human and extra-human nature—tends to exhaust their capacities to yield a rising stream of work/energy into the circuit of capital. This last moment is our focus here. When these natures are capitalized, the short-run effect is to generate an enhanced stream of unpaid work/energy, as new techniques and technologies are brought to bear. Over the middle-run, however, capitalization induces rising costs. Socio-ecological reproduction is

6   Marx, *Capital*, Vol. III (1981), 318–19.

7   Between 1980 and 2005, the "relative price of capital goods has declined by between 25 and 40 percent" in the U.S. and Japan Bank of International Settlements, *767th Annual Report* (Basil: 2006), www.bis.org/publ/ardpf/ar2006e.htm.

progressively internalized within the circuit of capital. Even when work/energy flows increase, the rate of increase slows relative to rising re/production costs. Late capitalist agriculture is one expression of this tendency; the (heavily feminized) proliferation of "second" and "third" shifts is another (as we see in Part Four).

The focus on the capitalization of natures give us a fruitful angle of vision from which to consider accumulation crisis. The rising value composition of production operates only partly in industry. Significantly, the pace of capitalization increases faster in primary production—farming, forestry, mining, and the rest—relative to secondary and tertiary sectors, which are *already* highly capitalized. Thus, the key check to the rising capitalized composition of world-nature is the rising rate of appropriation on the frontiers. (*Commodity frontiers.*) These frontiers of appropriation are bundles of uncapitalized work/energy that can be mobilized, with minimal capital outlays, in service to rising labor productivity in the commodity sphere. Such frontiers can be found on the outer geographical boundaries of the system, as in the early modern sugar/slave complex, or they can be found within the heartlands of commodification, as in the proletarianization of women across the long twentieth century.

The tendency towards the rising capitalization of nature is therefore the obverse of the tendency of the ecological surplus to fall. The systemic point is counterintuitive, because the greatest commodity frontiers have often appeared highly capital-intensive. Consider the Caribbean sugar mill and plantation system in the seventeenth century; the giant hydraulic ore-crushers of colonial Potosí; or the mechanized family farm of late nineteenth-century Iowa. Contrast this with hyper-capitalized resource extraction today—cyanide gold mining, strip mining, shale oil production.

This is where the language of industrialization misleads. The distinctively *modern* form of industrialization begins not in cities but in the countrysides. Agrarian, not urban, spaces offer the most fruitful terrain for accumulation by appropriation. This is why the forerunners of large-scale industry were found in zones where mechanization allowed for the rapid appropriation of unpaid work/energy. In this, the sugar plantation and the mining and metallurgical complexes of early modern capitalism were key;[8] so too were sectors, such as Dutch shipbuilding after 1570, where Cheap timber was readily secured. Such episodes of capitalization enabled a *rising* world-ecological surplus: the mass of capital increased slower than the appropriation of unpaid work/energy. Was this not also the case for the Industrial Revolution in its formative decades? This is the secret of capital accumulation: to capitalize the *oikeios,* so as to enable more expansive appropriations of nature. But that only works if there are big frontiers

---

8   Moore, "Ecology and the Rise of Capitalism" (2007).

somewhere "out there." Thus, calls for capital to pay the "true costs" of resource-use—an impossibility, since no metric can capture the differentiated activity of the web of life—are to be welcomed, because such calls directly contradict capital's fundamental logic. To call for capital to pay its own way is to call for the abolition of capitalism.

Capitalism's enduring priority has been to negotiate the value composition of production so that capitalization taps into new, more expansive streams of unpaid work/energy. This is why the Marxist critique of value remains so powerful today: it illuminates the inner rationality and complete absurdity of a system that consumes unpaid natures as a condition of its existence. In terms of constant capital—recalling its fixed and circulating moments—capital's priority has been to reduce the value share of raw materials relative to machinery while increasing physical throughput. This drives down the value composition of production even as its technical composition rises.[9] Hence the centrality of frontiers of appropriation—commodity frontiers—throughout the history of capitalism. Not only has capital sustained itself on the basis of Cheap inputs, but by revolutionizing the socio-ecological relations of production on a system-wide level, it has restored and recreated an expanded ecological surplus.

Fossil fuels have been central to this ecological surplus for the past three centuries. But these energy sources did not make capitalism so much as capitalism remade itself through their incorporation.[10] To paraphrase Marx, coal is coal. It becomes fossil fuel "*only in certain relations*."[11] These "certain relations" pivot on appropriation. Accumulation by appropriation signifies a range of processes through which capital puts the *oikeios* to work: to maximize labor productivity without, however, capitalizing the relations of reproduction for those webs of life. At its core, appropriation is less about the mechanism of extraction—neoliberal privatizations, colonial taxation, enclosures old and

---

9   "A certain quantity of labour-power, represented by a certain number of workers, is required to produce a certain volume of products in a day, for example, and this involves putting a certain definite mass of means of production in motion and consuming them productively—machines, raw materials, etc. A definite number of workers corresponds to a definite quantity of means of production, and thus a definite amount of living labour to a definite amount of labour already objectified in means of production. This proportion . . . constitutes the technical composition of capital, and is the actual basis of its organic composition" (Marx, *Capital*, Vol. III [1981]).

10   "'[R]esources' can be defined only in relationship to the mode of production which seeks to make use of them and which simultaneously 'produces'; them through both the physical and mental activity of the users. There is, therefore, no such thing as a resource in abstract or a resource which exists as a 'thing in itself'" (Harvey, "Population, Resources, and the Ideology of Science" (1974): 265.

11   Marx, *Wage-Labor and Capital* (New York: International Publishers, 1971).

new—and more about how capitalism reduces its basic costs of production: food, energy and raw materials, and labor-power.

Appropriation and capitalization, then, are not directly implicated in the physical shares of machinery relative to labor-power in production (Marx's *technical* composition of capital). "Industrial" agriculture, for instance, has been, variously, highly capitalized and highly appropriative in different eras, even when agricultural enterprises were highly mechanized, as in the case of American agriculture since the mid-nineteenth century or early modern sugar plantations. The capital-intensive farming of the American Midwest developed through the epoch-making appropriations of Cheap water, Cheap soil, and Cheap energy. For a long time American industrial agriculture was highly "industrial," but nevertheless appropriated unpaid work/energy even faster than its capitalization. These appropriations are now coming to an end,[12] as the cost of securing these vital inputs moves closer to the systemic average.

Costs rise because appropriation imposes a peculiar temporal logic on nature. This temporal discipline undermines daily and intergenerational reproductive conditions by enforcing the systemic disciplines of "socially necessary turnover time."[13] The temporal discipline is, moreover, tightly linked to the spatial remaking of nature into a storehouse of interchangeable parts. These spatio-temporal compulsions drive capital to accelerate the extraction of work/energy, but at the cost of destabilizing the webs of relations necessary to sustain rising physical output. This temporal revolution was present from the origins of capitalism, revealing itself in rapid and large-scale landscape changes, such as deforestation, that moved in decades, not centuries—as was the case for feudalism. As Marx recognizes in his treatment of the working day,[14] these frontiers of appropriation have been as necessary for labor-power as they have been for energy, food, and raw materials.

Appropriation assumes two principal material forms. The first pivots on processes of biophysical reproduction (labor-power, forestry, agriculture); the second, on geological extractions (energy and minerals). In ecological revolutions, both appropriations raise labor productivity above the prevailing system-wide average without a corresponding increase in constant capital (machinery and inputs). They also reduce the costs of reproducing labor-power in highly capitalized zones of the system. Cheap energy, for instance, made possible the highly suburbanized and automobilized working classes of North America,[15] while

---

12   T. Weis, *The Global Food Economy* (London: Zed, 2007); T. Weis, "The Accelerating Biophysical Contradictions of Industrial Capitalist Agriculture," *Journal of Agrarian Change*, 10, no. 3 (2010): 315–41.

13   D. Harvey, *Spaces of Capital* (New York: Routledge, 2001), 327.

14   Marx, Capital, Vol. I (1977), 377–8.

15   M.T. Huber, *Lifeblood* (Minneapolis: University of Minnesota Press, 2013).

Cheap food in the neoliberal era made possible the wage repression of the Global North and the massive expansion of the world proletariat after 1980.

We may consider these in their respective turns. The first comprises the appropriation of socio-ecological relations whose reproduction is relatively autonomous of the circuit of capital. This process is captured in capitalism's long history of depeasantization. Labor-power "produced" by peasant formations within the reach of capitalist power, but not yet reproduced through the cash nexus, is labor-power with a low value composition. Like a coal deposit, it is *accumulated* work/energy. If capitals and empires can secure new frontiers with bountiful supplies of such accumulated work/energy—in this case, potential labor-power, which also depend on extra-human webs of reproduction—the effect on the accumulation process is tantamount to a global wage cut or a rising rate of exploitation. In the rise of capitalism, when peasantries across much of Europe effectively resisted feudal restoration, the African slave trade, eastern Europe's "second serfdom," and colonial labor regimes such as Peru's *mita* played a role similar to this dispossession of peasantries.[16] The same story can be told, with different backdrops and casts of characters, for all manner of primary commodity frontiers—the great forests of North America and Atlantic Brazil, whaling grounds and fisheries, cash-crop agricultures such as, historically, sugar and cotton, and even soybeans today.

The second great moment of appropriation pivots on "non-renewable" resources, and above all energy. From the standpoint of world accumulation, the phase of appropriation spans that era when the value of strategic resources is significantly reduced. These are phases of "peak appropriation" when Cheap Natures reduce the system-wide costs of production. These strategic resources are *mass commodities*, "markers for entire historical epochs."[17] Among inorganic natures, silver and iron, coal, and then oil have served this function in successive long centuries of accumulation.

Energy sources are especially important because both heat and mechanical energy allow labor productivity to rise. Just as the value of food is closely linked to the reproduction costs of labor-power, the value of energy (and its specific forms) is closely linked to the productivity of that labor-power. Rising energy prices and stagnant labor productivity growth are closely linked.[18] So too is rising energy throughput and rising labor productivity.[19] Although geological conditions are obviously crucial, this form of appropriation is not essentially

16   Moore, "Ecology and the Rise of Capitalism"; "'Amsterdam Is Standing on Norway' Part I"; "'Amsterdam Is Standing on Norway' Part II" (2010).

17   Retort, *Afflicted Powers* (London: Verso, 2005).

18   D.W. Jorgenson, "The Role of Energy in Productivity," *American Economic Review* 74, no. 2 (1984): 26–30.

19   Cleveland, et al., "Energy and the US Economy," *Science* 225 (1984): 890–7.

(but only relationally) a geological affair. Coal, as we have seen, was epoch-making because it facilitated capitalization *and* appropriation in the long nineteenth century. Through the *technics* of industrial capitalism, coal was central to the rapid advance of labor productivity, and, thanks to steam power on land and sea, to the opening of vast new frontiers for appropriation. Significantly, these appropriations included depeasantized labor flows from China, India, and eastern Europe moving towards North America, the Caribbean, and white settler zones worldwide.[20]

For oil, arguably the most important mass commodity of the postwar era, peak appropriation is now past. Production costs have been rising over the past decade—fast.[21] Since 2000, operating costs in the world oil sector "more than doubled," exploration costs quadrupled, and the marginal cost of producing a barrel of oil increased tenfold between 1991 and 2007.[22] These marginal costs— that is, the cost of producing on the worst fields (often in the U.S., as luck would have it)—are strongly linked to world price beyond the very short run.[23]

This dynamic of rising costs is the kernel of truth in the popular notion of "the end of cheap oil."[24] Depletion certainly plays a role in the rising costs of production, influencing oil prices. But financialization is also an increasingly important socio-ecological vector. The rising attractiveness of financial activity over investment in the real economy (M-M′) induced protracted "underinvestment" in the extractive apparatus proper.[25] That underinvestment was reversed around 2003, but returned just one-tenth of the production increment—new oil per dollar invested—as it did in the 1980s and 1990s.[26]

Financialization not only exerts upward pressure on oil prices and encourages

20   D. Northrup, *Indentured Labor in the Age of Imperialism* (Cambridge: Cambridge University Press, 1995); E.R. Wolf, *Europe and the People without History* (Berkeley: University of California Press, 1982).

21   Goldman Sachs, "Higher Long-Term Prices Required by a Troubled Industry" (April 12, 2013); S. Kopits, "Oil and Economic Growth: A Supply-Constrained View" (Presentation to the Center on Global Energy Policy, Columbia University, February 11, 2014).

22   World Bank, *Global Economic Prospects 2009* (Washington, D.C: World Bank, 2009), 60; J. Simpkins, "The 'Cheap Oil Era' is Ending Soon . . ." *Money Morning* (January 10, 2006), http://www.moneymorning.com/2009/01/10/cheap-oil-era/; IMF [International Monetary Fund], *World Economic Outlook* (Washington, D.C.: International Monetary Fund, 2008), 95.

23   C. Bina, "Limits of OPEC Pricing," *OPEC Review* 14, no. 1 (1990): 55–73.

24   C.J. Campbell, and J.H. Laherrère, "The end of cheap oil," *Scientific American* 278, no. 3 (1998): 60–5.

25   IEA [International Energy Agency], *Energy Technology Perspectives* (Paris: International Energy Agency, 2008).

26   Kopits, "Oil and Economic Growth" (2014).

market volatility. To the extent that financial activities are more profitable than investing in exploration and extraction, it renders the latter insufficiently profitable, an effect homologous to (and reinforcing) the rising costs of production stemming from depletion. Financialization's logic has, moreover, given rise to all manner of cost cutting—efforts to reduce the organic composition of capital—whose consequences have become horrifically evident in such events as the 2010 explosion of the Deepwater Horizon offshore oil rig in the Gulf of Mexico. For oil, gas, and coal, the transition from appropriation to capitalization has brought with it a monstrous turn towards toxification on a gigantic scale—from unprecedented oil spills, to the "hydraulic fracturing" of natural gas exploitation, to coal's mountaintop removals, energy production in late capitalism increasingly manifests as a qualitative erosion of the conditions of human, never mind extra-human, well-being.

WORLD-ECOLOGICAL REVOLUTIONS

World-ecological revolutions deliver a rising ecological surplus. The "surplus" represents the gap between appropriated and capitalized natures. This surplus becomes "revolutionary" to the degree that accumulation by appropriation issues a significant middle-run (forty to sixty years) reduction in the value composition of food, labor, and inputs. Just as capital benefits from employing workers located in semi-proletarian households, where necessary income and means of subsistence derive from outside the wage relation,[27] so does capital prefer to mobilize extra-human natures capable of reproducing themselves outside the cash nexus. (But within reach of capitalist power.)

A large ecological surplus is found whenever a relatively modest amount of capital sets in motion a very large mass of work/energy. When the volume of appropriated natures (unpaid work/energy) is sufficiently large, it reduces the share of the *oikeios*—within reach of capitalist power—that depends on the circuit of capital for its daily and intergenerational reproduction. This is why frontiers of minimal or non-existent commodification—commodity frontiers—have been so important in the history of capitalism, from early modern sugar plantations to the soy frontiers of late capitalist Brazil.

This work/energy is often discussed in terms of use-value. But this elides a necessary transformation: from work/energy to use-value. Use-value is not, as many radical critics have assumed, "just there": it is not a pre-given utility to be used (and used up) by capital.[28] Capitalism's law of value has been remarkably

---

27   I. Wallerstein, *Historical Capitalism* (London: Verso, 1983).

28   Cf. S.G. Bunker and P.S. Ciccantell, *Globalization and the Race for Resources* (Baltimore: Johns Hopkins University Press, 2005).

flexible because it has been able to take its one structurally invariant law—advancing labor productivity in the zone of commodification—and co-produce, in rapid succession, a cascade of new historical natures. This means that new use-values come into being through world-ecological revolutions that create and sustain new configurations of capital, power, and nature. Use-values, in other words, are themselves historically specific through the evolution of value-relations. Thus, the low-capital-to-high-unpaid-work ratio (the ecological surplus) is only a necessary point of departure. It reflects the logic of capital and the project of Cheap Nature, not the history of capitalism proper. That history can begin to emerge by investigating how capitalist agencies—science, capital, and empire—have gone about mapping the world through successive ecological revolutions that qualitatively transform the natures within capital's gravitational field. Quantity affects quality. Quality affects quantity.

These qualitative transformations—world-ecological revolutions—are the moments when new historical natures take shape. These historical natures are not "produced" in linear fashion but co-produced by the biosphere and capitalism; historical natures are products of capitalism, but also producers of new capitalist arrangements. An ecological revolution occurs when the innovations of capital, science, and empire forge a new unity of abstract social labor, abstract social nature, and primitive accumulation. These unities are world-ecological regimes. Technical and organizational innovations allow for rising labor productivity. Ways of mapping, quantifying, and discovering new historical natures—and new use-values—allow for the rising appropriation of unpaid work/energy. And the coercive-intensive processes of territorial conquest and dispossession open new, largely uncommodified, natures to the penetration of global value-relations. This trinity—agro-industrial revolutions, scientific revolutions, and "new" imperialisms—forms the core of capitalism's *world-praxis*. These three moments are always uneven, but tend to converge during periods of systemic crisis. Their successful convergence restores the Four Cheaps.

This changes our usual thinking about technology, not least the relations of fossil fueled-machinery to the modern world. *Technics*, not technology, leads the way.[29] The distinction is fundamental, since the isolation of technology—or a technology/energy nexus—as the driver of ecological crisis is so deeply ingrained in environmentalist thought. Just as capitalism has its own "special laws of population,"[30] so too does it have its own "special laws of technology." Of course new machines matter: they "reveal the active relation of man with Nature."[31] But *how*

---

29   Here and throughout, Mumford's influence shines, see Mumford, *Technics and Civilization*.

30   Marx, *Capital*, Vol. I (1977), 784.

31   Ibid., 493n.

does technology matter? Not just for the production of value, but by revealing the "process of production by which he sustains his life, and thereby also lay[ing] bare the mode of formation of his social relations, *and of the mental conceptions that flow from them*."[32] Here Marx anticipates the present argument: that we are dealing with production and reproduction, abstract social labor and abstract social nature.

This is indeed the history of capitalism's epochal innovations—from ship-building and cartography to the steam and internal combustion engines. These allowed the revolutionary increase in material throughput: throughput that *includes* humans (e.g., slavery and its "veiled" forms). They allowed, as we know so well, for a succession of revolutionary shifts in what are usually considered social relations: of class, politics, culture, and so forth. But were not these social relations much more than Social? The remaking of human sociality—class, politics, and culture—were rooted in a succession of revolutionary shifts in the "nature" of the material throughput itself. These shifts, in turn, were unthinkable without revolutions in ways of seeing, knowing, and quantifying planetary natures. Thus, *technics*, combining capital, power, and knowledge, allows us to more clearly discern the revolutionary impact of particular machines, and to understand the fundamental basis of these epochal inventions in the co-production of Cheap Nature.

Each long century of accumulation does not "tap" an eternal and external Nature. Each such long wave creates—and is created by—a historical nature that offers a new, specific set of constraints and opportunities. The accumulation strategies that work at the beginning of a cycle—creating particular historical natures through science, technology, and new forms of territoriality and governance—progressively exhaust the relations of re/production that supply the Four Cheaps. At some point, this exhaustion registers in rising commodity prices.

Capitalism's great problem is therefore *historical* nature, not "nature in general." The crux of the problem lies in specific limits of condition and constraint posed by a historical nature that capitalism itself co-produces. The problem for capital is that the specific strategies that create the Four Cheaps, in any given era, are "one-off" affairs. You cannot discover something twice.

By driving down the capitalized share of historical nature, and increasing the share that can be freely appropriated, world-ecological revolutions have worked in three major ways. First, they have expanded the ecological surplus specific to the ongoing transformation of production: more coal for more steam engines. Second, they produced new kinds of nature: not just more coal for existing engines, but oil and gasoline for new, internal combustion, engines, and thence an extraordinary array of petro-chemical use-values. Third, and relatedly, they

---

32   Ibid. Emphasis added.

produced new historical natures on a progressively more globalized scale: as in the "massive taxonomical exercise[s]" of early capitalism that culminated with Linnaeus's classifications, or the planetary surveillance of remote sensing in recent decades.[33] Every great era of primitive accumulation is accompanied by new agronomic, botanical, and cartographic knowledges (*inter alia*) appropriate to the new geographies of appropriation and capitalization.[34] These taxonomical and other scientific projects have been crucial to successive reimaginings of global nature as a warehouse of free gifts. Identifying and quantifying new sources of extra-human wealth, these successive scientific, cartographic, and metrical revolutions enabled that crucial achievement of world-ecological revolutions: an increase in the share of appropriated work/energy relative to capitalized nature, and therefore a decrease in the capitalized composition of world-nature. By reducing system-wide capitalization through global appropriations, these revolutions have allowed a rising volume of nature's bounty to attach to a given unit of capital. This checked—directly and indirectly—the tendency towards the rising organic composition of capital. This happened directly, through the cheapening of raw materials (circulating capital), and indirectly, through the effects of Cheap inputs on fixed capital (e.g., cheaper steel meant cheaper fixed capital). In so doing, these revolutions created the conditions for new "long waves" of accumulation.

This dialectic of appropriation and capitalization turns our usual thinking about capitalism's long waves inside out. The great problem of capitalism, in effect, has not been too little capitalization, but *too much*. Its greatest strength has not been its move towards capitalization "all the way down" to the genome,[35] but rather appropriation . . . *all the way down, across, and through*. The socio-technical innovations associated with capitalism's long history of industrial and agricultural revolutions were successful because they dramatically expanded the opportunities for the appropriation of unpaid work/energy, *especially the accumulated work/energy* of fossil fuels (over millions of years), soil fertility (over millennia), and humans "fresh off the farms" of peasant societies (generationally). It is true that one finds concentrations of highly capitalized production in each of these revolutions, from Amsterdam to Manchester to

---

33   J.F. Richards, *The Unending Frontier* (Berkeley: University of California Press, 2003), 19; T.W. Luke, "Developing Planetarian Accountancy," in *Nature, Knowledge and Negation (Current Perspectives in Social Theory)*, Vol. 26, ed. H. Dahms (New York: Emerald Group Publishing, 2009), 129–59.

34   Far from a base/superstructure relation, these moments of capitalization, primitive accumulation, and abstract social nature must be taken as a cascading series of contingent, but also quasi-determined and "teleconnected" processes.

35   N. Smith, "Nature as Accumulation Strategy," in *Socialist Register 2007: Coming to Terms with Nature*, ed. L. Panitch and C. Leys (London: Merlin Press, 2006), 16–36.

Detroit. These technological revolutions, however, became epoch-making only when joined to those imperial and scientific projects that revolutionized world-ecological space. If technological dynamism alone was enough, Germany likely would have won out over Britain *and* the U.S. in the late nineteenth century. Instead, the American vertically integrated firm with its continental geography, and British commercial and financial supremacy, combined to make Germany—arguably the era's leading scientific power—the odd man out.

Capitalism's world-ecological revolutions combine capitalization and appropriation in pursuit of Cheap Nature, reducing the capitalization of the *oikeios* within reach of capitalist power. One of the most spectacular examples of this logic, as we have seen, is the global railroad and steamship revolution of the "second" nineteenth century (c. 1846–1914), during the apogee and *belle époque* of British world hegemony. Its crowning achievement was a revolutionary advance in appropriation, as capital's steel tentacles penetrated far-flung peasant formations from South Asia to Eastern Europe, setting free vast rivers of Cheap labor-power.[36] Within North America, railroads made the antebellum revolution in property relations a continental reality.[37] The capital-intensive family farm, integrated into international markets, was of a piece with railroadization—the latter making possible the former's audacious appropriation of soil and water, formed over millennia.[38] The epoch-making character of railroadization consequently turned on the radical extension of appropriation, creating new conditions for Cheap Nature—and especially Cheap Food. Cheap Food, in turn, disorganized European peasantries and sent millions to North America and beyond. Once arrived, they worked in factories that were competitive on the basis of Cheap (highly appropriated) energy and Cheap resources mobilized through railroadization. Here was the *appropriation* of space by time, central to American hegemonic ascent.

Rising capital intensity in the technical division of labor enters into dialectical tension with a distinctive, if broadly homologous, process within the social division of labor. This is where the rising organic composition of capital meets up with the capitalization of world-nature. Of course, nature can never be fully capitalized; it cannot even come close. Capitalization raises the middle-run costs of extracting work/energy by exhausting the relations that deliver that work/energy, typically resulting in relative stagnation rather than absolute decline.

---

36   Northrup, *Indentured Labor in the Age of Imperialism* (1995); Wolf, *Europe and the People without History* (1982).

37   C. Post, *The American Road to Capitalism* (Leiden: Brill, 2011); J.W. Moore, "Remaking Work, Remaking Space," *Antipode* 34, no. 2 (2002): 176–204.

38   H. Friedmann, "World Market, State, and Family Farm", *Comparative Studies in Society and History* 20, no. 4 (1978): 545–86; Friedmann, "What on Earth is the Modern World-System?" (2000).

And yet, capital is compelled to capitalize an ever-growing share of world-nature, whose greatest gifts can be enjoyed so long as they remain uncapitalized. The "coercive laws of competition" drive capital to remake the rest of nature according to the logic of socially necessary turnover time—a far cry from the reproduction time of forests and fields, not to mention mines, oilfields, and aquifers.[39] In order to keep socially necessary turnover time from rising, capitalism has cyclically extended the sphere of appropriated nature in recurrent, great bursts of global expansion. There is, then, a tension between that quantum of socio-ecological relations dependent on the circulation of capital and that which is dominated by capitalist power, but whose reproduction is not yet capital-dependent.

Productivity-maximizing technologies revive system-wide accumulation when they set in motion a vast appropriation of uncapitalized nature. For every Amsterdam there is a Vistula Basin. For every Manchester, a Mississippi Delta. This is why early capitalism was propelled by the "proto-industrial" appropriation of peasant work/energy—through which the fruits of simple manufacture could be appropriated without undermining the fertility rate.[40] This is also why twentieth-century Fordism was unthinkable without the North American and Middle Eastern oil frontiers (Cheap Energy).

The relative contraction of opportunities for appropriation therefore tells us something important about neoliberal capitalism. The class offensives of metropolitan ruling strata after the downturn of the 1970s, the acceleration of dispossession and its shock doctrines, and the financial expansion were of a piece. All aimed at redistributing wealth in the face of the progressive dilapidation of metropolitan "real economies," manifested in the non-appearance of the "third" scientific–technological revolution and its promise of a quantum leap in labor productivity.[41] The savage nature of this neoliberal counter-revolution surely owes something to the relative contraction of opportunities for appropriation.

The long history of colonialism, enclosure, and "accumulation by dispossession"—aimed at producing abstract social nature without the costs and risks associated with M-C-M′ (capitalization)—may be understood in this light. The ecological surplus is therefore a relational movement: between capital and labor, between town and country, between metropoles and frontiers, between capitalization and appropriation. If the value of any given commodity is determined by its abstract social labor, and if this average quantum of social labor embedded in

---

39   Marx, *Capital*, Vol. I (1977), 44; Harvey, *Spaces of Capital*.

40   W. Seccombe, *A Millennium of Family Change* (London: Verso, 1992).

41   G. Balakrishnan, "Speculations on the Stationary State," *New Left Review* II, no. 59 (2009): 5–26.

commodities determines price movements over the long run, then high labor productivity is the first priority of any capitalist enterprise. High labor productivity allows the capitalist, via the market, to capture the surplus value of competing production units with lower productivity. The great catch to this, as we have seen, is that rising labor productivity is often mediated through rising capital intensity (the value composition of capital). This sets in motion the tendency towards a falling rate of profit.[42] If, however, a means can be found to increase labor productivity without a corresponding increase in constant capital, a new set of possibilities emerges.

These possibilities take shape through the vast frontiers of appropriation that have characterized capitalism's greatest waves of accumulation. By reducing the capitalization of world-nature through global appropriations, world-ecological revolutions have checked the tendency towards the rising value composition of capital. Directly, such revolutions cheapened raw materials (circulating capital) and, indirectly, reduced the value composition of fixed capital itself. Cheap coal, for instance, made possible Cheap iron and, especially after the 1860s, Cheap steel. As American steel output skyrocketed—rising fortyfold between 1865 and 1895—the price of fixed capital collapsed. The price of steel rails fell by more than 80 percent.[43] Small surprise, then, that American labor productivity surged to an all-time high between 1890 and 1970,[44] precisely when "peak appropriation" maximally checked the rising value composition of capital.

Capital therefore depends on the Four Cheaps, and there is only one way to get this Cheap Nature fix: the frontier. The response to this imperative has been endless geographical expansion and endless innovation. They are not independent of each other. The great innovations that have enabled capital accumulation have been "great" to the degree that they have enabled the rapid appropriation of heretofore-uncapitalized unpaid work/energy. The history of "capital-intensive," epoch-making innovations—the early modern shipbuilding-cartographic revolution, the nineteenth century steam engine, and the internal combustion engine of the twentieth century—have been characterized by important technical advances that ratcheted upwards the capital-intensity of production in specific places, especially in the heartlands of the Dutch, British, and American hegemonies.

These innovations in commodity production have owed their epoch-making character to new global appropriations of work/energy. The Industrial Revolution is a prime example. Manchester's textile mills were dialectically bound to the American South's cotton frontier. This frontier was, in turn, bound to Whitney's

---

42   Marx, *Capital*, Vol. III (1981).
43   Rostow, *The World Economy* (1978), 179.
44   Gordon, "Is U.S. Economic Growth Over?" (2012).

cotton gin, enabling the rapid geographical expansion of short-staple cotton. And this expansion was made possible by the globalizing credit chains pioneered by Scottish factories and the City of London's financial institutions.[45] Here we can bring into focus the combined and uneven development of highly capitalized pockets of production and the globalizing appropriation of nature as a dialectical unity. "Technological" revolutions became epoch-making through their generative relations with hegemonic projects, revolutionizing world-ecological space, and creating a rising ecological surplus. In these three great hegemonic eras—the Dutch, the British, and the American—timber, coal, and oil were freely appropriated, with relatively minimal capital outlay. Each epoch-making innovation has joined productivity and plunder in a world-historical act that drove down, for a time, the share of historical nature directly dependent on the circuit of capital.

This explains some measure of why and how the great technical fixes of capitalism have entwined with movements of global expansion. Every technical fix is a geographical fix is a world-ecological fix. This is easily forgotten today, in the rush to find a technical solutions to the unfolding destabilization of the biosphere and crisis of capitalism. Technology under capitalism is a specific manifestation of capitalist *technics*—which presume a highly selective and wasteful transformation of work/energy into value. The history of capitalist technology within this *technics*—the dialectic of capitalization and appropriation—can be reduced to a two-phase process: (1) skimming the most easily-won surpluses, such as Amazonian rubber tapping prior to Malaysia's plantation revolution in the early twentieth century;[46] and (2) reorganizing a widening sphere of world nature on an increasingly capitalist basis, such as the progressive rationalization of forest-product industries worldwide since the end of the nineteenth century.[47]

It would, however, be a mistake to see this simply as a logical-historical succession. The capitalization of nature that characterizes this second phase issues short-run windfalls, to be sure. It is an eminently modern variant of the "yield honeymoon" that early modern planters enjoyed when their slaves planted Eurasian cane on New World soils.[48] The concert of favorable biophysical conditions with cutting-edge agronomy issues yield bursts that invariably turn bust over the course of 50–75 years (more quickly in late capitalism). The very

45   P. McMichael, "Slavery in Capitalism," *Theory and Society*, 20, no. 3 (1991): 321–49.

46   L.H. Brockway, "Science and Colonial Expansion," *American Ethnologist* 6, no. 3 (1979): 449–65; R.P. Tucker, *Insatiable Appetite* (Berkeley: University of California Press, 2000).

47   R.A. Rajala, *Clearcutting the Pacific Rain Forest* (Vancouver: University of British Columbia Press, 1998).

48   P. Dark and H. Gent. "Pests and Diseases of Prehistoric Crops," *Oxford Journal of Archaeology* 20, no. 1 (2001): 59–78; Moore, "Ecology and the Rise of Capitalism" (2007).

innovations that create yield booms invariably undermine supply conditions over the middle run. From the standpoint of the *oikeios*, these contradictions are unified, while their expressions diverge, comprising "social" transformations (in, say, the global agro-food regime) no less than "biophysical" feedbacks (as in weed control). As these contradictions unfold in ways that limit accumulation, the search for new frontiers reappears with savage power. If frontiers are unavailable, ferocious acts of redistribution are visited upon those populations least able to offer effective resistance—from poor to rich (as in neoliberalism), or from peasantries to heavy industrialization (as in Soviet collectivization).

The central problem posed by the capitalization of nature can be overcome to the extent that the inner contradiction finds an outer vent. The rising organic composition of capital tends towards socio-ecological disequilibrium, whose systemic expression is the rising capitalized composition of world-nature. As we have seen, this is the tendency of the ecological surplus to fall. It can be counteracted through geographical expansion, understood both quantitatively (more space) and qualitatively (new historical natures). But take note of the relational process. It is not simply that a large mass of use-values is now easily skimmed once geographical expansion reaches critical mass. More to the point, once critical mass is reached, the quantum of socialized nature dependent on the cash nexus declines. This was the case in the long sixteenth century, and at the beginning of the long twentieth century, in the classic instance of the "new imperialism." Today, that old model of geographical expansion is no longer working.

Nature within reach of capitalist power may be socialized without (yet) being capitalized. The extension of capitalist power into new frontiers works to propel world accumulation so long as two conditions hold: (1) the newly incorporated formations reproduce themselves relatively independently of capital, but deliver sizeable contributions to the ecological surplus; and (2) the mass of use-values taken up is sufficiently large, relative to value accumulation, so as to reduce the capitalized share of work/energy in commodity product. As geographical expansion slows, relative to rising capitalization, the quantum of socialized nature dependent on the cash nexus increases. Over time, the advance of commodification reaches a tipping point, and socialized natures give way to capitalized natures. This is the moment of capitalist transformation, at which neither governing structures nor production systems, nor the (newly transformed) forests, fields, households, and other ecologies can reproduce themselves except through the cash nexus.

The more that social ecologies—fields, forests, fisheries, and so forth—become capitalized ecologies, the more their reproduction is entrained within the reproduction of capital. Rising capitalization tends to produce short- and medium-run windfalls, but undermines systemic conditions of accumulation in the middle- to long-run. If "natural fertility" may act like fixed capital, and therefore check the tendency towards a falling rate of profit, soil exhaustion and resource depletion can set the stage for a dramatic reversal of profitability—an underappreciated moment of long waves of accumulation.

If expansion across space (appropriation) represents one fix to the falling rate of profit, innovation through time (capitalization) represents the second. Neither can be amplified endlessly. Global space is not only relational, but asymptotic and finite from the standpoint of endless accumulation. On the one hand, competition drives capitalism to expand geographically, to zones where commodification is low, and the opportunities for appropriation high. To the degree that capital can "jump scale," always in some concert with states and empires, it can drive down the cost of inputs and labor-power, and in so doing, increase the rate of profit. On the other hand, this accelerates the uptake of external natures into a geometrically expansive production process, which intensifies the drive towards geographical expansion as input and labor costs rise in established zones of production. In this way, capitalism's ever-accelerating transformation of biophysical and geological natures (the conquest of time) is joined to its voracious appetite for new frontiers of appropriation (the conquest of space).

WORLD-ECOLOGICAL REGIMES

To reprise: capitalism does not *have* an ecological regime; it *is* an ecological regime.

By ecological regime, I highlight those relatively durable patterns of governance (formal and informal), technological innovations, class structures, and organizational forms that have sustained and propelled successive phases of world accumulation since the long sixteenth century. At a minimum, these regimes comprise those markets, productive and institutional mechanisms necessary to ensure adequate flows of Cheap energy, food, raw material, and labor-power to the organizing centers of world accumulation. But the story does not end here. We should also attend to the re/production complexes that consume these surpluses and set in motion new (and contradictory) demands upon the rest of nature. That is to say, the town-country antagonism—overlapping with, but distinct from the core/periphery divide—is the pivotal geographical relation. In this, ecological *regimes* signify the historically stabilized process and conditions of extended accumulation; ecological *revolutions* mark the turbulent demise and renewal of these provisionally stabilized processes and conditions.

How might we begin to move from the logic of capital to the history of capitalism? If the construct of "ecological regime" is to prove useful, it must be more than a large descriptive category. In what sense can this perspective explain something of the rise and future demise of the modern world-system? For guidance, we might turn to Giovanni Arrighi's "systemic cycles of accumulation" perspective,[49] and to Harvey's theory of the spatial fix.[50]

For Arrighi, ascendant world powers—the Dutch, British, and Americans—have risen to global preeminence (hegemony) through varied "organizational revolutions" in the structures of capitalist and territorial power. Arrighi's model of capital accumulation across successive "long centuries" of expansion and contraction runs like this. Accumulation crises take shape out of the contradictions of capital and world power, whose specific forms vary from one long century to the next. The way out of such crises is offered by organizational and technical innovations that are incubated by emergent world powers—for instance, the American mass production model relative to British industry in the later nineteenth century. These innovations allow for the revival of capital accumulation through phases of "material expansion." These are expansionary in terms of rising physical output of commodities, capital accumulation, and geographical expansion. Characterized by rising returns to capital in the "real" economy, these phases of material expansion mark the beginning of a systemic cycle of accumulation. Over time, the material expansion sets in motion new competitors from outside the hegemonic center. These competitors erode the hegemon's surplus profits, equalizing profit rates across the core, and exhausting profit-making opportunities within the productive circuit (M-C-M′). Within the hegemonic center, diminishing returns to capital lead to a rising volume of surplus capital that cannot be (re)invested profitably in material expansion. As profitability falters, capitalists reallocate capital from production to finance (M-M′). This reallocation brings about "financial expansions"—the most recent began in the 1970s—which are "symptomatic of a situation in which the investment of money in the expansion of trade and production [M-C-M′] no longer serves the purpose of increasing the cash flow to the capitalist stratum as effectively as pure financial deals can. In such a situation, capital invested in trade and production tends to revert to its money form and accumulate more directly": M-M′.[51] Such expansions are sustained by the escalating geopolitical competition that accompanies the end of material expansion. These financial expansions set the stage for a new round of innovations, brought about by new alliances of territorial and capitalist agencies in geographically more expansive hegemonic centers.

Relevant to the present exploration is Arrighi's view of systemic crisis as constituted through the exhaustion of the very "organizational structures" that

49   Arrighi, *The Long Twentieth Century* (1994).
50   Harvey, *The Limits to Capital* (1982).
51   Arrighi, *The Long Twentieth Century* (1994), 8–9.

once liberated "material" accumulation.[52] Out of this exhaustion form the creative responses—*organizational revolutions*—of classes, states, and business organizations to the great crises of their times. For Arrighi, these revolutions cannot be reduced to industrialization; industrial transformations become world-historical facts through innovations in capitalist and territorial organization. Although this is nearly always understood in social reductionist terms, Arrighi saw it differently. Each long wave of accumulation was made possible by organizational revolutions that gave the new hegemonic power "unprecedented command over the world's human and natural resources."[53] This new, unprecedented command, could only be realized through territorialist and capital organization expansively conceived, comprising "science regimes" co-produced in and through capital, state, and nature.[54] To "command" nature, and therefore to accumulate capital rapidly, involves difficult and protracted processes of making nature legible to accumulation: the production of abstract social nature, which we consider in Chapter Eight.

These organizational revolutions possess a dual character. On the one hand, they produce a competitive edge, for the emerging hegemonic power, in the exercise of politico-military and economic power. On the other hand, they create a hegemonic development model emulated by rivals. In so doing, these revolutions make possible renewed and expanded accumulation over successive long centuries, only to generate renewed and expanded contradictions. As a hegemon reaps the rewards of its organizational revolution, its success leads rivals to emulate, then to innovate, with increasingly greater success. The very successes of the initial revolution become an iron cage from which the hegemon cannot escape. Flexibility in youth turns to sclerosis in old age.

The organizational moment in Arrighi's scheme—fusing territorial and capitalist organization with technical innovation—is complemented by a spatio-temporal moment. Influenced by Harvey,[55] Arrighi makes time and space central to the making and unmaking of systemic cycles of accumulation. Here is the crucial opening to a world-ecological reading. Arrighi's approach suggests a *longue durée* contradiction—between the endless accumulation of capital (possible within the logic of capital) and the endless appropriation of space (impossible within the *oikeios*). The *longue durée* therefore frames Arrighi's emphasis on middle-run crises to demonstrate systemic restructuring in its cumulative and cyclical dimensions. Innovations and organizational revolutions unfold within the constraints

---

52   Ibid., 226.

53   Ibid., 223.

54   R. Lave, "Neoliberalism and the production of environmental knowledge," *Environment and Society* 3, (2012): 19–38.

55   Harvey, *The Limits to Capital* (1982).

and possibilities of capitalism's cumulative development, which is spatial and temporal—and which unfolds through the *oikeios*.

This means that the qualitative moment—restructuring and innovation—does not erase the quantitative moment. Organizational revolutions achieve their qualitative shifts in response to—and on the basis of—the accumulating (quantitative) contradictions of the previous era. Cyclical restructuring occurs within cumulative limits. First, the limits to capital's self-expansion manifest geographically, and these geographical limits are produced by the accumulation regime itself. Metropolitan rivals "catch up" by emulating, and seeking to transcend, the hegemon's developmental model. Second, declining investment opportunities within the extant divisions of labor signal overaccumulation. Both moments set in play mounting pressures for restructuring through market-deepening and market-widening. To overcome the crises implicated in the system's always-rising "dynamic density," the organizational revolutions effected by successive hegemonic complexes pioneered a quantum leap forward in the geographical scale of its organizing center. While capital may regard space as an inexhaustible and infinitely substitutable zone of appropriation and commodification, Arrighi reveals each such world-systemic expansion as the production of special stimuli, whose underlying conditions are progressively exhausted over the *longue durée*.

The connection between geographical expansion (appropriation) and those special stimuli—such as the steam and internal combustion engines—is fundamental. It allows us to see that the accumulation of capital is the appropriation of space: which is the appropriation of historical natures. And so the crises generated in successive accumulation cycles have called forth organizing centers of progressively greater geographical breadth—from the Genoese city-state of the sixteenth century to the American continental-state of the long twentieth century. The upshot? *Innovation cannot proceed indefinitely because geographical expansion cannot proceed infinitely.*

How could nature (as *oikeios*) matter to Arrighi's scheme, seemingly oblivious to nature? His model points towards the possibility of integrating daily life with the world-scale relations of power and capital. Arrighi bracketed, but did not foreclose, this connection with material life. To reopen the question of accumulation and everyday life, we might point to a cyclically deepening relation between financialization and material life. The "Age of the Genoese" (1557–1648), for example, was directly linked to the commodity-centered remaking of Andean life, and closely bound to the ecological revolution of the seventeenth century, which stretched from Brazil to Poland to Southeast Asia.[56] The financialization of neoliberal capitalism has, likewise, been realized through a world-ecological revolution unrivaled in scale and scope. The "conversion of the global South into a 'world

---

56   Moore, "'Amsterdam Is Standing on Norway' Part I" and "Part II" (2010).

farm,"[57] the industrialization of the South,[58] and the radical externalization of biophysical costs, giving rise to everything from cancer epidemics to Global Warming—all figure prominently in the unusually expansive character of finance-led appropriations of the *oikeios* during the neoliberal era.

This observation on the relation between financialization and material life is only a beginning. We might consider a further, ecohistorical, twist. Here we can point to Arrighi's fruitful notion that systemic cycles of accumulation pivot on the vitality of "particular organizational structure[s], the vitality of which [is] progressively undermined by the expansion itself."[59] Once we bring the *oikeios* into such a frame, it becomes clear that something more than competition and anti-systemic movements undermines profitability in successive accumulation cycles. Indeed, competition, interstate rivalry, and anti-systemic struggles *are* socio-ecological contests, though not necessary in the obvious form of "resource wars" or environmental justice struggles. It is not the *absolute* exhaustion of an abstract and ahistorical nature that "causes" such crises of profitability. Rather, it is the exhaustion of specific complexes of socio-ecological relations that induce transitions from one systemic cycle to the next. Put simply, there is a simultaneous exhaustion of the organizational structures and of the historical nature specific to the old accumulation regime.

This allows us to step outside of "natural limits" thinking. All "social" and "natural" limits are irreducibly socio-ecological. These limits assume multiple forms, from state regulation and anti-systemic movements to deforestation and climate change. The point—and this is what Marx underscores in arguing that the limit of capital is capital itself—is that all limits are historically constituted through the *oikeios*. The problem is not the "separation" of humans from extra-human nature but how the two fit together. These configurations emerge through specific human projects to remake *all* of nature, which is what Arrighi's organizational revolutions really are.

Recall that, for Arrighi, accumulation crises occur when the organizational structures formed at the onset of a systemic cycle exhaust their capacity to generate rising returns to capital. Here we may reformulate: crises occur when the old organizational structures can no longer sustain a rising flow of unpaid work/energy relative to mass of accumulated capital. The question is one of the exhaustion of the relations organized at the beginning of the cycle. While Arrighi's account is resolutely sociological, there is every reason to re-situate his

57   P. McMichael, "A Food Regime Analysis of the World Food Crisis," *Agriculture and Human Values* 26 (2009): 281–95.

58   G. Arrighi, et al., "Industrial Convergence, Globalization, and the Persistence of the North-South Divide," *Studies in Comparative International Development* 38, no. 1 (2003): 3–31.

59   Arrighi, *The Long Twentieth Century* (1994), 226.

favored axes of change—geopolitical rivalry, inter-capitalist competition, and class conflict—as partial totalities within the historical natures of historical capitalism. This is a far cry from "adding on" environmental factors. World hegemonies do not merely organize resource and food regimes; world hegemonies *are* socio-ecological projects. Dutch hegemony emerged through a world-ecological revolution that stretched from Canada to the spice islands of Southeast Asia; British hegemony, through the coal/steam power and plantation revolutions; American hegemony, through oil frontiers and the industrialization of agriculture it enabled. In each era, old limits were transcended. A socio-ecological limit for each phase of capitalism is not necessarily a limit for the next.

Harvey's theory of spatial fix[60] adds two further connections of the greatest significance. First is the contention that modernity's great financial expansions, so central to Arrighi's perspective, are dialectically connected with "accumulation by dispossession."[61] Highlighting the neoliberal era, Harvey's conception of the "umbilical cord" linking finance, territorial power, and dispossession, points us in the right direction. What:

> dispossession does, is to release a set of assets (including labour power) at very low (and in some instances zero) cost . . . Privatization (of social housing, telecommunications, transportation, water, etc. in Britain, for example) . . . opened up vast fields for overaccumulated capital to seize upon . . . Another way [to resolve the overaccumulation problem is] . . . to release cheap raw materials (such as oil) into the system. *Input costs would be reduced and profits thereby enhanced* . . . What would have happened to overaccumulated capital these last thirty years if these new terrains of accumulation had not opened up?[62]

Second, in Harvey's broader theory of spatial fix, the initial flexibility of capital, and acceleration of turnover time, achieved through a "built environment" (urban spaces) favorable to capital in one era, becomes a fetter upon accumulation in the next. But does not the logic of this argument extend well beyond *built* environments? The historical natures created to liberate accumulation also serve to "imprison the future paths of capitalist development."[63]

Arrighi and Harvey point towards a theory of capitalist development that illuminates the socio-ecological conditions of capitalist boom and bust over the

---

60   Harvey, *The Limits to Capital* (1982).

61   Harvey, *The New Imperialism* (Oxford: Oxford University Press, 2003).

62   Ibid., 149–150, order of quotation changed, emphasis added.

63   D. Harvey, "Geography," in *The Dictionary of Marxist Thought*, ed. T. Bottomore (Cambridge, MA: Basil Blackwell, 1991), 219.

longue durée. To Arrighi, we may add that the organizational revolutions and technical innovation unfold through the *oikeios*. To Harvey, we may say the same thing about the spatial fix, and that "dispossession" works to the degree it facilitates the appropriation of unpaid work/energy and restores the Four Cheaps. In this reckoning, the abstract "limits to growth" give way to the historical conditions and limits of accumulation, directly given in capitalism itself. Successive phases of capitalism have unfolded through ecological revolutions in the dynamics of accumulation (the civilizational project), and the socio-ecological relations within its gravitational field (the historical process). These have been organizational revolutions in the webs of governance enacted by capitalist and territorialist agencies, and revolutions in the built environments of capitalization and appropriation. Their signal accomplishment has been the radical enlargement of the ecological surplus through the radical expansion of opportunities for appropriation relative to capitalization.

To echo Harvey, these world-ecological revolutions at first liberate accumulation. Was not this the world-historical accomplishment of British hegemony in the "first" nineteenth century (c. 1763–1848)? Over time, however, these new ways of organizing historical nature—through political regulation, built environments, industrial organization, agricultural innovation, not to mention class struggles—generate contradictions through the corrosive effects of plunder and productivity, and escalating challenges from ascendant states, capitalists, and dangerous classes. The widening and deepening movements of capitalization undermine the capacities of human and biophysical natures to reproduce themselves independently (or relatively so) from the circuit of capital. Sooner or later, the rules of reproduction change in the direction of capital-dependency. Peasant cultivators become capitalist farmers. Old-growth forests give way to tree plantations. Intergenerational reproduction becomes mediated by the cash nexus. The ecological surplus falls as the capitalization of world nature rises. This undercuts the basis of expanded accumulation, culminating in a developmental crisis.

The ecological regimes emerging out of these developmental crises confronted, and indeed produced, historically specific natures as webs of liberation and limitation. The point can scarcely be overemphasized if we are to take seriously the idea that all "limits to capital" emerge historically, out of the relations of humans with the rest of nature. This historical specification is not idiographic, but rather acknowledges the multi-layered spatio-temporal character of the *oikeios*. The natures that neoliberalism has produced operate within the epochal nature of historical capitalism, and perhaps even a sort of civilizational nature of humankind since the Neolithic revolution. Such a multi-layered comprehension of historical nature (as *oikeios*) opens up the possibilities for distinguishing the cumulative, the cyclical, and the genuinely novel in the present conjuncture.

Here I would repeat: limits for one historical system—or phase of capitalism—may not be a limit for another. Thus may we begin to think of successive phases of capitalism as creating, and created by, an increasingly capitalized world-ecology. The historical limits of the early capitalist ecological regime—for example, agricultural exhaustion and relative energy scarcity throughout central and western Europe—had been reached by the middle of the eighteenth century. These were ecohistorical limits to capital accumulation as it was then organized. Clearly, they were not absolute limits.

CONCLUSION

If the limits of humanity-in-nature are *historical questions*, we may lean on Arrighi's Three Questions: What is cumulative? What is cyclical? What is new? How does the present conjuncture differ from previous socio-ecological crises? From these we may begin to discern the contours of capitalist crisis in the century ahead. These questions suggest that renewed rounds of capitalization—comprising the extension of commodification, technological innovation, and financialization—may not resolve the developmental crisis of neoliberalism. From where will come the next great expansion of the ecological surplus? This is difficult to see. Relative to capital as a whole, the opportunities for appropriation have never been fewer, while the demand for such appropriations has never been greater. Here is a precious clue to understanding the ongoing transformation of capitalism as it confronts the *longue durée* exhaustion of the Great Frontier.

Part III

HISTORICAL NATURE AND THE ORIGINS OF CAPITAL

Anthropocene or Capitalocene?: On the Nature and Origins of Our Ecological Crisis

There is no denying the urgency that many scholars—and many citizens—feel in relation to climate change. There is little question about the pressing realities of climate change, the sixth great extinction of biodiversity, ocean acidification, and a long list of very, very serious problems. But does the urgency to communicate the realities of biospheric change override the need for an adequate historical interpretation of the problem? Conceptualizations of a problem and efforts to resolve that problem are always tightly connected. So, too, are the ways we think about the origins of a problem and how we think through possible solutions.

Over the past decade, one conceptualization has captivated scholarly and popular audiences alike: the Anthropocene. As with all fashionable concepts, the Anthropocene has been subject to a wide spectrum of interpretations.[1] But one is dominant. This one tells us that the origins of the modern world are to be found in England, right around the dawn of the nineteenth century.[2] The

---

1　The argument over the periodization of the Anthropocene rages on. Some archaeologists now argue for converting most or all of the Holocene into the Anthropocene, either from the mega-fauna extinctions at the dawn of the Holocene, or the origins of agriculture, c. 11,000 B.P. (summarized in M. Balter, "Archaeologists Say the 'Anthropocene' Is Here—But It Began Long Ago," *Science*, 340 (April 19, 2013): 261–2; see Ruddiman, *Plows, Plagues, and Petroleum*: (2005); "The Anthropocene," *Annual Reviews in Earth and Planetary Science* 41, nos. 4.1–4.24 ([online first], 2013); J. Gowdy, and L. Krall. "The Ultrasocial Origin of the Anthropocene," *Ecological Economics* 95 (2013): 137–47. Still others argue for an Anthropocene c. 2,000 years B.P. (cf. G. Certini and R. Scalenghe. "Anthropogenic Durées are the Golden spikes for the Anthropocene," *The Holocene* 21, no. 8 [2011]: 1269–74).

While still others argue, albeit weakly, for a post-1945/1960 periodization (J. Zalasiewicz, et al., "Are We Now Living in the Anthropocene?" *GSA Today* 18, no. 2 [2008]: 4–8). Empiricist concepts like the Anthropocene are often a conceptual and historical mess, precisely because they propose to engage reality as bundles of quantitative aggregates prior to discerning the actually existing historical relations within which such numbers can be given historical meaning. Adding up facts does not a *historical* interpretation make (cf. Carr, *What is History?* [1962]).

2　W. Steffen, et al., "The Anthropocene: Are Humans Now Overwhelming the

motive force behind this epochal shift? In two words: coal and steam. The driving force behind coal and steam? Not class. Not capital. Not imperialism. Not even culture . . . you guessed it: the *Anthropos*: Humanity as an undifferentiated whole.

The Anthropocene makes for an easy story. Easy, because it does not challenge the naturalized inequalities, alienation, and violence inscribed in modernity's strategic relations of power and production. It is an easy story to tell because it does not ask us to think about these relations *at all*. The mosaic of human activity in the web of life is reduced to an abstract Humanity: a homogeneous acting unit. Inequality, commodification, imperialism, patriarchy, racial formations, and much more, have been largely removed from consideration. At best, these relations are acknowledged, but as after-the-fact supplements to the framing of the problem. This framing unfolds from an eminently commonsensical, yet I think also profoundly misleading, narrative: one in which the "human enterprise" is set against the "great forces of nature."[3] The taxonomy of "Anthromes"[4]—ecosystems dominated by humans, and consequently not "wild"—*precedes* historical interpretation, substituting highly linear notions of time and space for historical-geographical change. At the same time, Anthropocene scholars cannot escape the conclusion that humans, too, are a "geophysical force"—the singular is important here—that operates *within* nature.[5] This is the "One System/Two Systems" problem common to Green Thought in its mainstream and critical expressions. Philosophically, humanity is recognized as a species within the web of life. But in terms of our methodological frames, analytical strategies, and narrative structures, human activity is treated as separate and independent: humanity becomes Humanity. There are "human constructions" and "natural" constructions[6]—even as humans are recognized as a geophysical force. This dissonance creates rather more fog than light, for the recognition of humanity-in-nature becomes a kind of philosophical cover for reductionist narratives of Humanity *and* Nature.

Great Forces of Nature?" (2007); "The Anthropocene: Conceptual and Historical Perspectives" (2011); "The Anthropocene: From Global Change to Planetary Stewardship" (2011); D. Chakrabarty, "The Climate of History" (2009).

3   Steffen, et al., "The Anthropocene: From Global Change to Planetary Stewardship" (2011); "The Anthropocene: Are Humans Now Overwhelming the Great Forces of Nature?" (2007).

4   E.C. Ellis, et al., "Anthropogenic Transformation of the Biomes, 1700 to 2000," *Global Ecology and Biogeography* 19, no. 5 (2010): 589–606.

5   Steffen, et al., "The Anthropocene: From Global Change to Planetary Stewardship" (2011), 741.

6   J. Zalasiewicz, et al., "The Anthropocene: A New Epoch of Geological Time?" *Philosophical Transactions of the Royal Society A* 369 (2011): 837.

There are two major dimensions of the Anthropocene argument today. One is a strict emphasis on atmospheric and geological change and its proximate drivers. The other is an argument about history, and therefore about the crisis today. There is frequent slippage between the two. In the latter, the dominant Anthropocene argument goes beyond the domain of earth-system science, reaching into the very heart of historical analysis: the dialectically bound questions of historical agency and periodization.

The Anthropocene argument takes biogeological questions and facts—turning on the presence of variously significant stratigraphic signals[7]—as an adequate basis for historical periodization. Two subtle but powerful methodological decisions underpin this approach. In the first instance, empirical focus is narrowed to the consequences of human activity. In this, the Anthropocene argument embodies the *consequentialist bias* of Green Thought. The case for Humanity's domination of the earth is constructed almost entirely on the basis of a significant catalogue of biospheric consequences. The drivers of such consequences are typically reduced to very broad "black box" categories: industrialization, urbanization, population, and so forth.[8]

The second methodological choice turns on the construction of humanity as "collective" actor.[9] Here the historical-geographical patterns of differentiation and coherence are erased in the interests of narrative simplicity. This erasure, and the elevation of the *Anthropos* as a collective actor, has encouraged several important misrecognitions: 1) a neo-Malthusian view of population,[10] ignoring the modern world-system's patterns of family formation and population movement; 2) a view of historical change in which technology-resource complexes drive historical change; 3) a concept of scarcity abstracted from the historical relations of capital, class, and empire; and 4) a meta-theory of humanity as collective agent, without acknowledging the forces of capital and empire that have cohered modern world history.

The two principal framing devices—consequences determine periodization, the *Anthropos* as the driver of these consequences—stem from a philosophical position that we may call Cartesian dualism. As with Descartes, the separation of humans from the rest of nature—"Are humans overwhelming the great forces

---

7   Zalasiewicz, et al., "Are We Now Living in the Anthropocene?" (2008); "Stratigraphy of the Anthropocene" (2011).

8   Steffen, et al., "The Anthropocene: Conceptual and Historical Perspectives" (2011); "The Anthropocene: From Global Change to Planetary Stewardship" (2011).

9   Zalasiewicz, et al., "Stratigraphy of the Anthropocene" (2011).

10   Cf. M. Fischer-Kowalski, et al., "A Sociometabolic Reading of the Anthropocene," *The Anthropocene Review* (2014); E.C. Ellis, et al., "Used Planet," *Proceedings of the National Academy of Sciences* 110, no. 20 (2013): 7978–85.

of nature?"[11]—appears as self-evident reality. In its simplest form, this philosophy locates Human activity in one box; Nature, in another. To be sure, these two acting units interact and influence each other. But the differences between and within each acting unit are not mutually constitutive, such that changes in one imply changes in the other. This dualism leads Anthropocene advocates to construct the historical period since 1800 on an arithmetic basis: "human activity plus significant biospheric change equals the Anthropocene." In this, too, the Anthropocene perspective incorporates the common sense of Green Arithmetic: "Society plus Nature equals environmental studies."

It all makes sense, again up to a point. But the parts do not add up to the whole. Human activity not only produces biospheric change, but relations *between* humans are themselves produced through nature. This nature is not nature-as-resource but rather nature-as matrix. It is a nature that operates not only outside and inside our bodies (from global climate to the micro-biome) but also *through* our bodies, including our embodied minds. Humans produce *intra*-species differentiations, which are fundamental to our history: inequalities of class especially, inflected by all manner of gendered and racialized cosmologies. Those differentiations have made human history—modern world history in particular—full of contingency and rapid change. They have not only produced non-linear shifts. They have also been *produced by* non-linear relations of power and wealth, already bundled with, and within, the web of life.

And it is here—in thinking through the origins of the problem of rapid and fundamental biospheric change—that we find the central *historical, and therefore political*, problem with the Anthropocene argument. If we shift our method from one that unduly prioritizes environmental consequences to one that prioritizes the producer/product relation, a very different view of the Anthropocene problem comes into focus. From this standpoint, the origins of a new pattern of environment-making began in the Atlantic world during the long sixteenth century. Why is this not "merely" a historical problem, but also a political one? In sum, to locate the origins of the modern world with the steam engine and the coal pit is to prioritize shutting down the steam engines and the coal pits (and their twenty-first-century incarnations.) To locate the origins of the modern world with the rise of capitalist civilization after 1450, with its audacious strategies of global conquest, endless commodification, and relentless rationalization, is to prioritize the relations of power, capital, and nature that rendered fossil capitalism so deadly in the first place. Shut down a coal plant, and you can slow global warming for a day; shut down the relations that made the coal plant, and you can stop it for good.

---

11   Steffen, et al., "The Anthropocene: Are Humans Now Overwhelming the Great Forces of Nature?" (2007).

The erasure of capitalism's early modern origins, and its extraordinary reshaping of global natures long before the steam engine, is therefore of some significance to our politics—far beyond the politics of climate change, and even beyond "environmental" politics. How we conceptualize the origins of a crisis has everything to do with how we choose to respond to that crisis. The question of how and when to draw lines around historical eras is therefore no small matter. Ask any historian and she will tell you: how one periodizes history fundamentally shapes the interpretation of events, and one's choice of significant relations. Start the clock in 1784, with James Watt's rotary steam engine,[12] and we have a very different view of history—and a very different view of modernity—than we do if we begin with the English or Dutch agricultural revolutions, with Columbus and the conquest of the Americas, or with the first signs of an epochal transition in landscape transformation after 1450. Are we really living in the *Anthropocene*, with its return to a curiously Eurocentric vista of humanity, and its reliance on well-worn notions of resource- and technological-determinism? Or are we living in the *Capitalocene*, the historical era shaped by relations privileging the endless accumulation of capital?[13]

How one answers these historical questions shapes one's analysis of—and response to—the crises of the present.

CAPITALISM AS A WAY OF ORGANIZING NATURE

To ask about humanity's modern relation with the rest of nature is to shift our focus from the consequences of these relations to the relations that enfold and unfold these consequences. Consequences *are* crucial. Those issuing from climate change are especially salient, perhaps especially in its suppressive impact on labor and land productivity in world agriculture. But to periodize historical change on the basis of consequences—or a highly stylized interpretation of the Industrial Revolution—is to cloud our vision from the outset. Of course we must begin with major shifts in the dominant relations of power and production, of classes and commodities. To leave it at that, however, says nothing new. What the more sophisticated versions of the "coal and capitalism" argument appreciate is that the long nineteenth-century transition in the relations of power and production was one that went beyond relations between humans; it also implied

---

12   P.J. Crutzen, "Geology of Mankind: The Anthropocene," *Nature* 415 (2002): 23.

13   No doubt about it: *capitalocene* is an ugly word in an ugly system. The Age of Capitalism does not merit an aesthetically pleasing moniker. (My thanks to Diana Gildea for the reminder.)

a transition in humanity's relation with the rest of nature—and therefore humanity's relation with itself.[14]

I would go further. History is not a world-historical ping-pong match in which one player, Society, volleys historical forces with another, Nature. Historical change is better reckoned as a cascade of environment-making processes and relations, through which particular bundles of human and extra-human nature flow, upon which these bundles act and re-form as they act. The bundle of transformations that gathered steam in the closing decades of the eighteenth century was *co-produced* by human and extra-human natures (in which the latter are also directly constitutive of so-called "society"). This was true at the level of consequences, and also in terms of capitalism's strategic relations. The patterns of co-production are contingent but also stabilized and cohered. This coherence reveals itself in specific patterns of environment-making that reach well beyond conventional reckonings of landscape change. Such coherence is realized and reproduced through definite rules of reproduction—of power, of capital, of production. For capitalist civilization, these rules embody a *value relation*, quite literally determining what counts as valuable and what does not. As we have seen, different civilizations have different value relations, prioritizing different forms of wealth, power, and production. In historical capitalism, abstract social labor may be accumulated only through a far-flung repertoire of imperialist enclosure and appropriation of nature's "free gifts." Capital is value-in-motion is value-in-nature. Hence the natural fertility of the soil may "act as an increase in fixed capital:"[15] an observation pregnant with socio-ecological implications for the analysis of capital accumulation.

Here we return again to our transformation problem: the dynamics through which capital, science, and state transform work/energy into value. Only some energy becomes work, and only some work becomes value. These broadly entropic transitions highlight the self-consuming character of the capital relation, which tends to burn through its necessary biophysical conditions (included workers) and in so doing jack up the organic composition of capital.[16] Thus, capitalism's Cheap Nature strategy, and the recurrent cyclical movements in favor of ever-cheaper nature until 2003,[17] may be understood in relation to the

---

14   C.f. M.T. Huber, "Energizing Historical Materialism," *Geoforum* 40 (2008): 105–15; A. Malm, "The Origins of Fossil Capital: From Water to Steam in the British Cotton Industry," *Historical Materialism* 21, no. 1 (2013): 15–68.

15   Marx, *Grundrisse* (1973), 748.

16   Marx, *Capital*, Vol. I (1977), 377–380; R. Luxemburg, *The Accumulation of Capital* (2003), 328–47.

17   J. Grantham, "Days of Abundant Resources and Falling Prices Are Over Forever," *GMO Quarterly Newsletter* (April 2011).

cyclical threat of the Four Cheaps turning dear.[18] Costly nature turns cheap through appropriating unpaid work on the commodity frontiers inside and outside the heartlands of commodification.[19] These frontier movements counteracted the capitalization of global nature and its obverse: the tendency of the ecological surplus to fall. Frontiers made it possible for capital to voraciously consume both the geological accumulations and biological configurations of unpaid work without a ruinous increase in the costs of production. The constant danger, given capitalism's industrial dynamism and commitment to expansion, is that the value of inputs will rise, and the rate of profit will fall.

A world-ecological reconstruction calls into question any periodization—such as the Industrial Revolution—premised on a dualistic "social driver plus environmental consequence" model. This remains the hegemonic model within global environmental studies, even as regional studies have long since transcended such dualisms.[20] From this standpoint, the Anthropocene argument is not only philosophically and theoretically problematic—viewing humans as separate from nature and erasing capitalism from the equation—it also offers an unduly narrow conceptualization of historical time. This plays out at two levels. One is an awkward conflation of geological notions of time with the periodization of historical change. The other is the Anthropocene's recuperation of an older historiographical vista, which saw the "real" changes of "real" modernity beginning in the later eighteenth century.

In this respect, the Anthropocene argument feeds into Green Thought's long-standing love affair with the Two Century model of modernity: *industrial* society, *industrial* civilization, *industrial* capitalism. The notion that "It all began with the Industrial Revolution" has been with us for a very long time.[21] The problem with the Two Century model is not just that it left out something crucial, but that it blinded Green Thought to the remarkable remaking of land and labor beginning in the long sixteenth century. Industrialization still appears, in the meta-narratives of Green Thought, as a *deus ex machina* dropped onto the world-historical stage by coal and steam power.

---

18 Mandel, *Late Capitalism* (1975); Rostow, *The World Economy* (1978).

19 A. Hochschild, *The Second Shift* (New York: Viking, 1989); Moore, "Sugar and the Expansion of the Early Modern World-Economy" (2000).

20 White, *Organic Machine*; J. Kosek, *Understories* (Durham: Duke University Press, 2006).

21 The "industrialization thesis" on the origins of ecological crisis is especially popular: Moore, "Nature and the Transition"; see, e.g., Daly and Farley, *Ecological Economics*; Heinberg, *The Party's Over*; D. Jensen, *Endgame, Volume 1: The Problem of Civilization* (New York: Seven Stories Press, 2006); Malm, "The Origins of Fossil Capital"; Steffen, et al., "The Anthropocene" (2007); E.A. Wrigley, *Continuity, Chance and Change* (Cambridge: Cambridge University Press, 1990).

There are two questions here. First, is Industrialization the Big Bang of modernity, or is it instead a cyclical phenomenon of capitalism from the sixteenth century? Second, is Industrialization the most useful concept for explaining large-scale and long-run patterns of capital, power, and nature over the past five centuries? If the first question was tackled during the 1970s and '80s,[22] the second question is rarely posed.

At its best, industrialization is a shorthand for the tensions between technology and power, between the "forces" and "relations" of production. These are hardly novel historical problems. But these tensions have, almost universally, been framed in dualistic terms. This is the problem of Cartesian dualism, one that bears bitter fruit in the hegemonic narrative of industrialization as acting upon, rather than developing through, Nature. At a time when Cartesian dualism, as philosophical construct, finds itself widely questioned across the spectrum of Green Thought,[23] such dualism retains its hegemony over the methods, theory, and narrative frames of world-historical change.

Whereas the Anthropocene argument begins with biospheric consequences and moves towards social history, an unconventional ordering of crises would begin with the dialectic between (and among) humans and the rest of nature, and from there move towards geological and biophysical change. These consequences, in turn, constitute new conditions for successive eras of capitalist restructuring across the *longue durée*. Relations of power and production, themselves co-produced within nature, enfold and unfold consequences. From this perspective, nature stands as the relation of the whole. Humans live as one specifically endowed (*but not special*) environment-making species within the web of life.

To grasp how humans go about making environments—and how power, capital, and nature form an organic whole—we might turn to Mumford's notion of *technics*.[24] Mumford grasped that a new technics emerged in the early modern era—crystallizing tools and knowledge, nature and power, in a new *world-praxis* that reduced both "man" and "nature" to abstractions. For Mumford, power and production in capitalism embodied and reproduced a vast cultural-symbolic repertoire that was cause, condition, and consequence of modernity's *specific form* of technical advance. This was not, Mumford made plain, a story to be celebrated. It was, rather, one to be recognized, and criticized, for its peculiarity:

---

22   I. Wallerstein, "The Industrial Revolution: *Cui Bono?*" *Thesis XI* 13, 67–76.

23   Cf. D. Harvey, *Justice, Nature, and the Geography of Difference* (Oxford: Basil Blackwell, 1996); Latour, *We Have Never Been Modern* (1993); Plumwood, *Feminism and the Mastery of Nature* (1993); Braun and Castree, eds., *Remaking Reality* (1998); N. Castree and B. Braun, eds. *Social Nature* (Oxford: Blackwell Publishers, 2001).

24   L. Mumford, *Technics and Civilization* (London: Routledge and Kegan Paul, 1934).

"The Chinese, the Arabs, the Greeks, long before the Northern European, had taken most of the first steps toward the machine . . . These peoples plainly had an abundance of technical skill . . . *They had machines; but they did not develop 'the machine.'*"[25] Here, Mumford might have stopped, as have so many Green thinkers. But he did not. At the heart of Mumford's argument was the idea that machines, *technics*, and the alienated violence of capitalist civilization move through the web of life. It was the

> *discovery of nature as a whole* [that] was the most important part of that era of discovery which began for the Western World with the Crusades and the travels of Marco Polo and the southward ventures of the Portuguese. . . . [A]s soon as the procedure of exploration was definitely outlined in the philosophy and mechanics of the seventeenth century, man himself was excluded from the picture. Technics perhaps temporarily profited by this exclusion; but in the long run the result was to prove unfortunate. In attempting to seize power, man tended to reduce himself to an abstraction.[26]

Absent a relational conception of *technics*, much of Green Thought conflates the Industrial Revolution with modernity.[27] The question of origins is elided—not resolved—through recourse to a meta-narrative premised on the periodizing implications of rising CO_2 emissions and other eco-consequential phenomena. The question of the origins of world-ecological crisis is axiomatically reduced to a surficial representation of the drivers and consequences of nineteenth-century industrialization.

The fetish of industrialization quickly leads to others. A stylized love affair with machinery leads quickly to a stylized love affair with resources. Even for those on the left who favor a class-relational approach, a certain fossil-fuel fetishism appears, as when Malm proposes coal as the spark that ignites the engine of capital.[28] "Capital," in these accounts, forms independently of the web of life, and intervenes in "nature" as an exogenous force (or vice versa), variously intruding in, and interrupting, a pre-given "traditional balance between

---

25   Ibid., 4. Emphasis added.

26   Ibid., 31. Emphasis added.

27   Steffen, et al., "The Anthropocene: Conceptual and Historical Perspectives" (2011); "The Anthropocene: From Global Change to Planetary Stewardship" (2011); A. Malm, "The Origins of Fossil Capital" (2013).

28   Malm, "The Origins of Fossil Capital" (2013). Also E. Altvater, "The Social and Natural Environment of Fossil Capitalism," in *Coming to Terms with Nature: Socialist Register 2007*, eds. L. Panitch and C. Leys (London: Merlin Press, 2006); M.T. Huber, "Energizing Historical Materialism," *Geoforum* 40 (2009): 105–15.

humanity and nature."[29] This view of capitalism as an exogenous, rather than endogenous, actor in relation to the web of life has had the paradoxical effect of reducing nature to Nature: a substance that can be variously protected or destroyed by Humans.[30]

It is always tempting to "think in terms of realities that can be 'touched with the finger.'"[31] In this way of thinking—Bourdieu calls it "substantialist"[32]—substances form prior *to*, and independently *of*, events and fields of relations, rather than developing *through* environments cohered by definite patterns of events.[33] Substantialism, in this sense, is at the heart a "human exceptionalist" social theory,[34] which isolates humanity from its extra-human conditions of reproduction. The result is a way of thinking about humanity as ontologically independent—a kind of Human substance apart from the "substance" of Earth/Life. Even when the professed goal is holism, substantialism fetters the move towards synthesis.[35] Why? Largely because human exceptionalist social theory—and this is still most social theory[36] —presumes humanity's specificity in the absence of a historical specification of the whole: the natures within which human activity unfolds, and to which human activity actively contributes.[37] In the process, the very procedure that might establish humanity's "dialectical historicity" is denied.[38]

It turns out that (as with pregnancy), one cannot be a little bit Cartesian. For nature is either abstract and external, or it is historical *and* immanent to everything that humans do, including those large-scale and long-run patterns of power and production that we call civilizations. On the terrain staked out by the Anthropocene argument, we might consider how the definite relations of early

29   J.B. Foster, *The Vulnerable Planet* (New York: Monthly Review Press, 1994), 40.

30   Cf. J. Martinez-Alier, *The Environmentalism of the Poor* (Cheltenham, UK: Edward Elgar, 2002).

31   Bourdieu and Wacquant. *An Invitation to Reflexive Sociology* (1992), 228.

32   Ibid.

33   Birch and Cobb, *The Liberation of Life* (1981), 79–96.

34   Haraway, *When Species Meet* (Minneapolis: University of Minnesota Press, 2008).

35   J.B. Foster, "The Epochal Crisis," *Monthly Review* 65, no. 5 (2013): 1–12.

36   G. Ritzer, ed. *Encyclopedia of Social Theory*, 2 vols. (Thousand Oaks, CA: Sage, 2005).

37   It would be silly to deny the signal accomplishment of a broadly Green social theory, which is now significant. Indeed, the present argument is possible precisely because Green social theory has, in its critique of nature-blind theorizations, made possible an argument for transcending the dualism of the "social theory and the environment" tradition (e.g., J. Barry, *Environment and Social Theory*, second ed. [New York: Routledge, 2007]; D. Sonnenfeld, and A.P.J. Mol, eds., *Social Theory and the Environment in the New World (dis)Order*. Special issue of *Global Environmental Change*, 21, no. 3 [2011]: 771–1152).

38   Mészáros, *Marx's Theory of Alienation* (1970).

capitalism—co-produced in the web of life—transformed coal from a rock in the ground to a fossil fuel. We might then ask, how do geological facts become historical processes?

Material flows *do* matter. But their historical significance is best understood through a relational rather than substantialist view of materiality. Flows of resources, the circuits of capital, and the struggles of classes and states form a dialectical whole. Geology is a *basic* fact; it becomes a *historical* fact through the historically co-produced character of resource production, which unfolds through the *oikeios*.[39] Geology, in other words, co-produces power and production as it bundles with human patterns of power and production—hence the re-bundling of capitalist relations across the later eighteenth-century North Atlantic, as the energy regime shifted from charcoal and peat to coal. Specific geological formations, under definite historical circumstances, can become at once objects of human activity and *subjects* of historical change. This allows us to see civilizations moving *through*, not around, the rest of nature.

The relational view gets us away from the resource-determinism that often shapes a Green view of history. It directs our attention to how, say, coal becomes coal through new relations of power and production—and vice versa. One of the most vital Green narratives, as we have seen, tells us the story of "fossil capitalism," beginning sometime around 1800. But the revolution in English coal production began in the sixteenth, not the eighteenth, century. This was—as we shall see presently—intimately connected to a revolution in environment-making that marked the rise of capitalism.

If the Anthropocene begins not in 1800 but in the long sixteenth century, we begin to ask much different questions about the drivers of world-ecological crisis in the twenty-first century. The onset of the English coal revolution around 1530 directs our attention to the relations of primitive accumulation and agrarian class structure, to the formation of the modern world market, to new forms of commodity-centered landscape change, to new machineries of state power. This line of argument only appears to return to "social relations" because the legacy of Cartesian thought continues to tell us that state formation, class structure, commodification, and world markets are all about relations between humans . . . *which they are not*. These too—states, classes, commodity production and exchange—are bundles of human and extra-human nature. They are processes and projects that reconfigure the relations of humanity-in-nature, within large and small geographies alike.

From this standpoint, to stick with coal, we can say that geology co-produces energy regimes as historically specific bundles of relations; geology is at once subject and object. The view that geo-material specificities determine social

39   Carr, *What is History?* (1962).

organization does not, however, highlight geology's role in historical change; it obscures it. This is so for two, tightly linked reasons. First, to say that geology determines historical change is to confuse geological facts for historical facts. Second, to conflate geological facts with historical facts is to engage in environmental determinism of a specific kind: the "arithmetic" of Nature plus Society. And so we may return to our refrain: Nature plus Society does not add up. Perhaps most significantly, environmental determinisms, however partial or sophisticated they may be, leave intact the Cartesian order of things, in which Society and Nature interact rather than interpenetrate. The alternative sees geology co-producing historical change through the *oikeios*. This allows us to see energy regimes—even whole civilizations—moving *through*, not around, the rest of nature. The definite relations of early capitalism—co-produced in the web of life—transformed coal into unpaid work/energy, and unpaid work/energy into capital. Material flows and their particularities matter—quite a bit. But their historical significance is best understood through a relational, rather than substantialist, view of materiality, one in which the flows of resources, circuits of capital, and the struggles of classes and states form a dialectical whole.

Bunker's insight that material particularities shaped industrialization as much as industrialization shaped the rest of nature is an important corrective to the prevailing wisdom.[40] For much of the Green left—one finds little fundamental difference with the Anthropocene argument—industrialization is a matter of Society acting upon the earth, drawing upon fossilized carbon and spewing forth all manner of nasty effluents. This substantialist view of industrialization, and its conflation with capitalism, has encouraged a powerful metabolic fetish, one reproduced even by radical scholars in the critique of "fossil capitalism."[41] In this scheme of things, "material flows" are given ontological priority over the relations that create, enfold, and develop through these flows. The relationality of material flows and class relations (*inter alia*) is denied as a matter of research practicality. Cartesian practicality pushes the movements of classes and capitals from the analysis altogether![42] For radical and mainstream scholars alike, there is a tendency to invoke an exogenous nature that creates an "ahistorical and apolitical bottom line."

The metabolic fetish, and its manifold resource- and energy-determinisms, is easy to justify quantitatively. More energy used, more minerals extracted and metals produced, more urban-industrial workers and fewer agrarian producers,

40   Bunker and Ciccantell, *Globalization and the Race for Resources* (2005).

41   Altvater, "The Social and Natural Environment of Fossil Capitalism" (2006).

42   H. Haberl, et al., "Quantifying and Mapping the Human Appropriation of Net Primary Production in Earth's Terrestrial Ecosystems," *Proceedings of the National Academy of Sciences* 104, no. 31 (2007): 12942–7; "A Socio-Metabolic Transition Towards Sustainability?" *Sustainable Development* 19, no. 1 (2011): 1–14.

and so on. For this reason, perhaps, most environmentally oriented historians of the Industrial Revolution have preferred to analyze energy (rather than, say, parliamentary enclosures) owing to its allure of easy mathematization.[43] But numbers are tricky things. They easily entrain an empiricist logic that blinds its handlers to alternatives capable of enfolding quantitative data within world-relational processes.[44] Gould elegantly reminds us that "numbers suggest, constrain, and refute; they do not, by themselves, specify the content of scientific theories."[45] More poignant still, the confusion of numbers for explanation tends to ensnare "interpreters . . . [in the logic of] their own rhetoric. They [tend to] believe in their own objectivity, and fail to discern the prejudice that leads them to one interpretation among many [others] consistent with their numbers."[46] Thus do we have an Anthropocene line of thought that has given rise to many possible periodizations, with the exception of one: the turning point of the long sixteenth century.[47]

THE ORIGINS OF CAPITALISM: FROM ECOLOGY TO WORLD-ECOLOGY

Capitalism in 1800 was no Athena, bursting forth, fully grown and armed, from the head of a carboniferous Zeus. Civilizations do not form through Big Bang events. They emerge through cascading transformations and bifurcations of human activity in the web of life. This cascade finds its origin in the chaos that followed the epochal crisis of feudal civilization after the Black Death (1347–1353), followed by the emergence of a "vast but weak" capitalism in the long sixteenth century.[48] If we are to put our finger on a new era of human relations with the rest of nature, it is in these centuries. These were the centuries of an extraordinary revolution in human-initiated environment-making, centered

---

43   E.A. Wrigley, *Energy and the English Industrial Revolution* (Cambridge: Cambridge University Press, 2010); R.P. Sieferle, *The Subterranean Forest* (Cambridge: The White Horse Press, 2001); P. Malanima, "Energy Crisis and Growth 1650–1850" (2006).

44   A paradigm instance of such enfolding is on offer in B.J. Silver, *Forces of Labor* (Cambridge: Cambridge University Press, 2003).

45   S.J. Gould, *The Mismeasure of Man* (New York: W.W. Norton, 1981), 106.

46   Ibid.

47   But see S.L. Lewis and M.A. Maslin, "Defining the Anthropocene," *Nature* 511 (2015): 171–80.

48   Moore, "Ecology and the Rise of Capitalism" (2007); Wallerstein, *The Modern World-System I* (1974); M. Małowist, *Western Europe, Eastern Europe and World Development, 13th–18th Centuries* (Leiden: Brill, 2009); Braudel, "European Expansion and Capitalism, 1450–1650," in *Chapters in Western Civilization,* ed. Contemporary Civilization Staff, Columbia College (New York: Columbia University Press, 1961), 245–88.

geographically in the expansive commodity-centered relations of the early modern Atlantic. The rise of capitalism after 1450 marked a turning point in the history of humanity's relation with the rest of nature, greater than any watershed since the rise of agriculture and the first cities—*and in relational terms, greater than the rise of the steam engine.* That significance consequences and quantitative expansions *eventually* follow in the wake of new, epoch-making relations will not surprise any historian. But even the *immediate* consequences were dramatic.

The rise of capitalism after 1450 was made possible by an epochal shift in the scale, speed, and scope of landscape transformation in the Atlantic world and beyond. The long seventeenth century's forest clearances of the Vistula Basin and Brazil's Atlantic Rainforest occurred on a scale, and at a speed, between five and ten times greater than anything seen in medieval Europe.[49] Feudal Europe had taken centuries to deforest large expanses of western and central Europe. After 1450, comparable deforestation occurred in decades, not centuries. To take but one example, in medieval Picardy (northeastern France), it took 200 years to clear 12,000 hectares of forest, beginning in the twelfth century.[50] Four centuries later, in northeastern Brazil at the height of the sugar boom in the 1650s, 12,000 hectares of forest would be cleared in a single year.[51] These are precious clues to an epochal transition in the relations of power, wealth, and nature that occurred over the course of the long medieval crisis, and the expansion that commenced after 1450.

A modest catalogue of early capitalism's transformations of land and labor, from the 1450s to the eve of the Industrial Revolution, would include the following commodity-centered and -influenced changes:

1) the agricultural revolution of the Low Countries (c. 1400–1600)—motivated by the crisis of sinking peat bogs resulting from medieval reclamation—allowed three-quarters of Holland's labor force to work outside of agriculture;[52]

---

49   Moore, "Ecology and the Rise of Capitalism" (2007); "'Amsterdam Is Standing on Norway' Part II" (2010); H.C. Darby, "The Clearing of Woodland in Europe," in *Man's Role in Changing the Face of the Earth*, ed. W.L. Thomas, Jr. (Chicago: University of Illinois Press, 1956), 183–216; M. Williams, *Deforesting the Earth* (Chicago: University of Chicago Press, 2003).

50   R. Fossier, *La Terre et les Hommes en Picardie jusqu'à la Fin du XIIIe Siècle*, 2 vols (Paris: B. Nauwelaerts, 1968), 315.

51   Moore, "Ecology and Rise of Capitalism" (2007), ch. 6.

52   B. van Bavel, "The Medieval Origins of Capitalism in the Netherlands," *BMGN-Low Countries Historical Review* 125, nos. 2–3 (2010): 45–79; R. Brenner, "The Low Countries in the Transition to Capitalism," *Journal of Agrarian Change* 1, no. 2 (2001): 169–241.

2) the mining and metallurgical revolution of Central Europe, which thoroughly transformed the political ecology of forests across the region;[53]

3) the first signs of the modern sugar-slave nexus in Madeira, whose rapid rise and decline (1452–1520s) turned on rapid deforestation;[54]

4) Madeira's crisis was followed quickly by the sugar frontier's movement to São Tomé (1540s–1590s) and the first modern, large-scale plantation system, which deforested one-third of the island by 1600 and encouraged large-scale slave revolts;[55]

5) northeastern Brazil displaced São Tomé at the commanding heights of the world sugar economy after 1570, from which issued the first great wave of clearing Brazil's Atlantic rainforest, unfolding at an unprecedented pace;[56]

6) the African "slaving frontier," meanwhile, shifted from the Gulf of Guinea to Angola and the Congo in the later sixteenth century, marking the first of several major expansions in the slave trade;[57]

7) Potosí emerged as the world's leading silver producer after 1545, and then again with its epochal restructuring after 1571, on the heels of the exhaustion of Saxon and Bohemian silver mining, itself conditioned by deforestation, declining ore quality, and labor unrest;[58]

8) the decline of central European mining and metallurgy also affected iron and copper production by 1550, which favored English iron (to 1620), and especially, the rise of Swedish iron and copper;[59]

---

53   J.U. Nef, *The Conquest of the Material World* (New York: Meridian, 1964); J. Vlachovic, "Slovak Copper Boom in World Markets of the Sixteenth and in the First Quarter of the Seventeenth Centuries," *Studia Historica Slovaca* 1 (1963): 63–95; Moore, "Ecology and the Rise of Capitalism" (2007).

54   Moore, "Madeira, Sugar, and the Conquest of Nature, Part I" (2009); "Madeira, Sugar, and the Conquest of Nature, Part II" (2010).

55   J. Vansina, "Quilombos on São Tomé, or In Search of Original Sources," *History in Africa* 23 (1996): 453–9; B.L. Solow, "Capitalism and Slavery in the Exceedingly Long Run," in *British Capitalism and Caribbean Slavery*, ed. B.L. Solow & S.L. Engerman (Cambridge: Cambridge University Press, 1987), 51–77.

56   S.B. Schwartz, *Sugar Plantations in the Formation of Brazilian Society* (Cambridge: Cambridge University Press, 1985); W. Dean, *With Broad Ax and Firebrand* (Berkeley: University of California Press, 1995).

57   J.C. Miller, *Way of Death: Merchant: Capitalism and the Angolan Slave Trade 1730–1830* (Madison: University of Wisconsin Press, 1988).

58   P. Bakewell, *Miners of the Red Mountain*. Albuquerque: University of New Mexico Press, 1984; Moore, "Madeira, Sugar, and the Conquest of Nature, Part II" (2010).

59   U. Sundberg, "An Energy Analysis of the Production at the Great Copper Mountain of Falun During the Mid-Seventeenth Century," *International Journal of Forest Engineering* 1, no. 3 (1991): 4–16; K-H. Hildebrand, *Swedish Iron in the*

9) American silver depended on European shipbuilding timber, and so Potosí's efflorescence was accompanied by the shift of the forest-products frontier from Poland-Lithuania towards southern Norway in the 1570s, followed by renewed movements into the hinterlands of Danzig (again) by the 1620s, and from there towards Königsberg, Riga and Viborg in successive turns;[60] meanwhile

10) the rise of the Vistula breadbasket in the 1550s, exporting Cheap grain to the maritime Low Countries, was followed by the agro-ecological exhaustion of Polish market-oriented agriculture in the 1630s;[61]

11) any shortfalls from the Polish agro-ecological downturn were quickly made good by the English agricultural revolution, which made England the breadbasket of Europe by 1700, albeit on an agro-ecological basis that faltered after the 1760s, as productivity stagnated;[62]

12) English forests were rapidly appropriated during seventeenth-century expansion, such that pig iron output in 1620 would not be exceeded until 1740 even with rising demand, met by imports— especially from Sweden;

13) and even Sweden's sylvan abundance was quickly diminished, as iron devoured the forests with such speed that the centers of iron production moved quickly towards new forest regions;[63]

14) the stagnation of English iron output after 1620 stimulated iron's movement into Ireland, where fuel costs were much lower. In just a century, the Emerald Isle's forest declined from 12.5 percent to just 2 percent, such that little iron would be produced by the mid-eighteenth century;[64]

Seventeenth and Eighteenth Centuries, trans. P. Britten Austin (Stockholm: Jernkontorets Bergshistoriska Skriftserie, 1992); P. King, "The Production and Consumption of Bar Iron in Early Modern England and Wales," *Economic History Review* 58, no. 1 (2005): 1–33.

60   Moore, "'Amsterdam Is Standing on Norway' Part II" (2010).

61   W. Szcygielski, "Die Okonomische Aktivitat des Polnischen Adels im 16–18. Jahrhundert," *Studia Historiae Oeconomicae* 2 (1967): 83–101; Moore, "'Amsterdam Is Standing on Norway' Part II" (2010).

62   M. Overton, *Agricultural Revolution in England* (Cambridge: Cambridge University Press, 1996); R.V. Jackson, "Growth and Deceleration in English Agriculture, 1660–1790," *Economic History Review* 38 (1985): 333–51.

63   P. King, "The Production and Consumption of Bar Iron in Early Modern England and Wales," *Economic History Review* 58, no. 1 (2005): 1–33; B. Thomas, *The Industrial Revolution and the Atlantic Economy* (New York: Routledge, 1993); R. Fouquet, *Heat, Power and Light: Revolutions in Energy Services* (Northampton, MA: Edward Elgar, 2008), 59–60; P. Mathias, *The First Industrial Nation: The Economic History of Britain, 1700–1914* (London: Methuen & Co., 1969); K-H. Hildebrand, *Swedish Iron in the Seventeenth and Eighteenth Centuries* (Stockholm: Jernkontorets bergshistoriska skriftserie, 1992).

64   R. Kane, *The Industrial Resources of Ireland*, 2d ed. (Dublin: Hodges and Smith,

15) the Dutch energy regime, centered on extracting Cheap domestic peat, reached its high point in the seventeenth century, but easily-tapped zones were quickly depleted, and output fell sharply after 1750;[65]

16) in Southeast Asia, the Dutch imposed a new colonial regime between the 1650s and 1670s, securing a monopoly over the clove trade during the 1650s through the large-scale removal of "unauthorized" clove trees, the large-scale relocation of indigenous populations from the interior into new colonial administrative units suitable for labor drafts, and the establishment of new shipyards outside the Batavian core;[66]

17) from the early seventeenth century, wetlands across the Atlantic world were reclaimed, often by Dutch engineers, from England to Pernambuco and Suriname, Rome to Göteborg;[67]

18) the great burst of Iberian and Italian expansion during the "first" sixteenth century (c. 1450–1557) produced a relative, but widespread, exhaustion of Mediterranean forests—beginning earlier for the Italians and Portuguese, somewhat later for Spain—and especially their capacity to supply quality shipbuilding timber, by the early seventeenth century;[68] resulting in

19) the relocation of Spanish shipbuilding to Cuba, where one-third of the fleet was built by 1700, and the relatively modest yet significant expansion of

---

1845), 3; E. McCracken, *The Irish Woods Since Tudor Times* (Newton Abbot, Ireland: David & Charles, 1971), 15, 51 et passim; E. Neeson, "Woodland in History and Culture," in *Nature in Ireland: A Scientific and Cultural History*, eds. J.W. Foster and H.C.G. Chesney, 143–56 (Montreal: McGill-Queen's University Press, 1997).

65   J.W. de Zeeuw, "Peat and the Dutch Golden Age" (1978).

66   C. Boxer, *The Dutch Seaborne Empire, 1600–1800* (London: Hutchinson, 1965), 111–12; C. Zerner, "Through a Green Lens: The Construction of Customary Environmental Law and Community in Indonesia's Maluku Islands," *Law and Society Review* 28, no. 5 (1994): 1079–122; P. Boomgaard, "Forest Management and Exploitation in Colonial Java, 1677–1897," *Forest and Conservation History* 36, no. 1 (1992): 4–14; N.L. Peluso, *Rich Forests, Poor People* (Berkeley: University of California Press, 1992), 36–43.

67   C.H. Wilson, *The Dutch Republic and the Civilisation of the Seventeenth Century* (New York: McGraw Hill, 1968), 78–81; T.D. Rogers, *The Deepest Wounds* (PhD dissertation, Department of History, Duke University, 2005), 51; J.F. Richards, *The Unending Frontier* (2003), 193–241; P. Boomgaard, "Forest Management and Exploitation in Colonial Java" (1992).

68   Braudel, *The Mediterranean and the Mediterranean World in the Age of Philip II*, Vol. I (1972); C. Cipolla, *Before the Industrial Revolution: European Society 1000–1700* (New York: W.W. Norton, 1976); Moore, "'Amsterdam Is Standing on Norway' Part I" (2010); J.T. Wing, "Keeping Spain Afloat," *Environmental History* 17 (2012): 116–45; F.C. Lane, "Venetian Shipping During the Commercial Revolution," *American Historical Review* 38, no. 2 (1933): 219–39.

Portuguese shipbuilding in Salvador da Bahia and Goa;[69] this was followed in the eighteenth century by

20) the emergence of major shipbuilding centers and significant frontiers for timber and naval stores in North America during the eighteenth century;[70]

21) the relentless geographical expansion of forest product and shipbuilding frontiers were bound up with the increasingly vast fleets of herring, cod, and whaling vessels that searched for and devoured the North Atlantic's sources of maritime protein;[71]

22) the search for fish was complemented by the search for furs. While the fur trade contributed but slightly to world accumulation, its steady advance (and serialized extermination of fur-bearing animals) across North America (Siberia too), stretching by the eighteenth century into the expansive Great Lakes region, encouraged significant infrastructures of colonial power;[72]

23) the expansion of the world sugar market and the relative decline of Brazilian sugar after 1650 favored successive sugar revolutions in the West Indies, leaving a trail of African graves and denuded landscapes in its wake;[73]

24) human ecologies too were transformed in many ways, not least through the sharply uneven "cerealization" of peasant diets—and the "meatification" of aristocratic and bourgeois diets—within Europe after 1550;[74]

25) the resurgence of Mexican silver production in the eighteenth century and the attendant deforestation of already-thin Mexican forests;[75]

26) the revolution in English coal production from 1530;[76] and, perhaps most significantly,

---

69   J.H. Parry, *The Spanish Seaborne Empire* (Berkeley: University of California Press, 1966); F.W.O. Morton, "The Royal Timber in Late Colonial Bahia," *Hispanic American Historical Review* 58, no. 1 (1978): 41–61; C. Boxer, *The Dutch Seaborne Empire* (1965), 56–7.

70   J. Perlin, *A Forest Journey* (Cambridge, MA: Harvard University Press, 1989); Williams, *Deforesting the Earth* (2003).

71   J.F. Richards, *The Unending Frontier* (2003), 547–616; B. Poulsen, "Talking Fish," in *Beyond the Catch*, eds. L. Sicking and D. Abreu-Ferreira (Leiden: Brill, 2008), 387–412.

72   E.R. Wolf, *Europe and the People without History* (Berkeley: University of California Press, 1982), 158–94; Richards, *The Unending Frontier* (2003).

73   Watts, *The West Indies* (1987).

74   Braudel, *The Structures of Everyday Life* (1981), 190–9; J. Komlos, "Height and Social Status in Eighteenth-Century Germany," *Journal of Interdisciplinary History* 20, no. 4 (1990): 607–621; J. Komlos, "Shrinking in a Growing Economy?" (1998).

75   P.J. Bakewell, *Silver Mining and Society in Colonial Mexico* (Cambridge: Cambridge University Press, 1971); D. Studnicki-Gizbert and D. Schecter. "The Environmental Dynamics of a Colonial Fuel-Rush," *Environmental History* 15, no. 1 (2010): 94–119.

76   M. Weissenbacher, *Sources of Power* (New York: Praeger, 2009); J.U. Nef, *The Rise of the British Coal Industry* (London: Routledge, 1966 [1932 orig.]), 19–20, 36, 208.

27) the epoch-making "Columbian exchange," as Old World diseases, animals, and crops flowed into the New World, and New World crops, such as potatoes and maize, flowed into the Old World.[77]

Perhaps, one might object, these landscape transformations were nevertheless the output of an essentially preindustrial civilization? This is the commonsense point of departure for the Anthropocene argument. Let us take industrialization as consisting of two decisive moments of capitalist *technics*. One is industrialization as a shorthand for the rising mass of machinery and inputs relative to labor-time—Marx's rising technical composition of capital. It might be more fruitful to call these processes *mechanization*. The other is industrialization as a shorthand for standardization and rationalization, prefiguring, in embryonic form, the assembly line and Taylorism of the twentieth century.[78] If this rough-and-ready definition holds, we are hardly short of examples in the three centuries before Watt's rotary steam engine: the printing press, perhaps the most prefigurative advance in labor productivity with a two-hundredfold increase after 1450, such that twenty *million* books were printed by 1500;[79] the sugar mill in the colonies, successively boosting labor productivity, and the sugar refinery in the

---

77 Crosby, *The Columbian Exchange* (1972); idem., *Ecological Imperialism* (Cambridge: Cambridge University Press, 1986).

78 This shorthand applies not only to machineries but also the rationalization of human and extra-human relations necessary to work these machines—Taylor's time-and-motion studies in the early twentieth century (1914; also Braverman, *Labor and Monopoly Capital* (1974)) are one indication of the symbolic coding, mapping, and "rational" reorganizations of human/extra-human relations attendant upon capitalism's successive industrial revolutions, but hardly new to the twentieth century. Consider, for example, meatpacking's "dis-assembly lines" in the antebellum United States (Cronon, *Nature's Metropolis* [1991]) or the rationalization of labor processes and landscapes necessary for the early modern sugar plantation (S.W. Mintz, *Sweetness and Power* [New York: Penguin, 1985]; Moore, "Ecology and the Rise of Capitalism" [2007]. Moving beyond the immediate process of production, one can see a long line of such rationalizations in play across the time and space of early capitalism—suggested in various if partial ways by Weber's formal rationality (1947), Foucault's biopolitics, and Sombart's thesis on the "art of calculation" double-entry bookkeeping, a far from exhaustive list! See, respectively, M. Weber, *The Theory of Social and Economic Organization* (New York: Free Press, 1947); M. Foucault, *Society Must be Defended*; W. Sombart, *The Quintessence of Capitalism*, M. Epstein, trans. and ed. (New York: E.P. Dutton & Co., 1915).

79 L. Febvre and H. Martin, *The Coming of the Book* (London: Verso, 1976), 186; A. Maddison, *Growth and Interaction in the World Economy* (Washington, D.C.: AEI Press, 2005), 18.

metropoles);[80] very large blast furnaces in iron-making;[81] new ships, such as the Dutch *fluyt*, leading to a fourfold increase in labor productivity in shipping;[82] a new shipbuilding regime, led by the Dutch, which tripled labor productivity by combining Smithian specialization (simplified tasks), the standardization of parts, organizational innovation (integrated supply systems), and technical change (sawmills to displace costly skilled labor);[83] the rapid expansion of iron implements in agriculture;[84] the mercury-amalgamation process in New World silver production;[85] the elaboration and diffusion of screw-presses;[86] the *saiger-prozess* in the Central European copper-silver metals complex, and after 1540, the rod-engine for effective drainage, which reached Sweden by 1590;[87] the quick diffusion of the "Saxony Wheel" in textile manufacturing, trebling labor productivity, accompanied by the diffusion of fulling and napping mills, advancing productivity still further;[88] the number of water mills, already widely deployed

---

80   J. Daniels and C. Daniels. "The Origin of the Sugarcane Roller Mill," *Technology and Culture* 29, no. 3 (1988): 493–535; A. van der Woude, "Sources of Energy in the Dutch Golden Age: The Case of Holland," *NEHA-Jaarboek voor economische, bedrijfs, en techniekgeschiedenis* 66 (2003): 64–84.

81   Braudel, *The Structures of Everyday Life* (1981), 378–9.

82   R.W. Unger, "Technology and Industrial Organization: Dutch Shipbuilding to 1800," *Business History* 17, no. 1 (1975): 56–72; J. Lucassen, and R.W. Unger, "Shipping, productivity and economic growth," in *Shipping and Economic Growth 1350–1850*, ed. R.W. Unger (Leiden: Brill, 2011), 3–44.

83   The new sawmill technology spread rapidly and "could be found in Brittany by 1621, Sweden in 1635, Manhattan in 1623, and soon after Cochin, Batavia, and Mauritius," P. Warde, "Energy and Natural Resource Dependency in Europe, 1600–1900" (BWPI Working Paper 77, University of Manchester, 2009), 7.

84   R. Wilson, "Transport as a Factor in the History of European Economic Development," *Journal of European Economic History* 2, no. 2 (1973): 320–37; de Vries, "The Labour Market," in *The Dutch Economy in the Golden Age*, eds. K. Davids and L. Noordegraaf (Amsterdam: Nederlandsch Economisch-Historisch Archief 1993): 55–78; L. Noordegraaf, "Dutch industry in the Golden Age," in *The Dutch Economy in the Golden Age*, eds. K. Davids and L. Noordegraaf (Amsterdam: Nederlandsch Economisch-Historisch Archief), 131–57.

85   P. Bairoch, "Agriculture and the Industrial Revolution, 1700–1914," (1973), 452–506.

86   P. Bakewell, "Mining," in *Colonial Spanish America*, edited by L. Bethell (Cambridge: Cambridge University Press, 1987), 203–49.

87   H. Kellenbenz, "Technology in the Age of the Scientific Revolution 1500–1700," in *The Fontana Economic History of Europe, II*, ed. C.M. Cipolla (London: Fontana/Collins, 1974), 177–272.

88   I. Blanchard, *International Lead Production and Trade in the 'Age of the Saigerprozess'* (Wiesbaden: Franz Steiner Verlag, 1995); G. Hollister-Short, "The First Half-Century of the Rod-Engine (c.1540–1600)," *Bulletin of the Peak District Mines Historical Society* 12, no. 3 (1994): 83–90.

in the medieval era, doubled in the three centuries after 1450, tripling of aggregate horsepower;[89] the extraordinary multiplication of spring-driven clocks.[90] Nor does this exhaust the list.

What do these transformations suggest? A general observation would point towards a qualitative shift in the relations between land and labor, production and power. If some of these examples look more like a quantitative amplification of medieval developments, as a totality they embodied a qualitative shift. And if many of these transformations fit nicely into Marx's distinction between manufacturing and machinofacture, some look a lot like modern industry: especially the sugar plantation, shipbuilding, and large-scale metallurgy. Any adequate explanation of this qualitative shift must recognize that there was a transition from control of land as a direct relation of surplus appropriation to control of land as a condition for advancing labor productivity within commodity production. This transition was of course tremendously uneven and messy. Hence, where peasant cultivation persisted across early modern Europe, there was no fundamental rupture with the medieval rhythm of landscape transformation[91]—*except where, as in seventeenth century Poland, peasants were directly pushed towards sylvan zones by cash-crop cultivation.*[92] Swidden is swidden; under capitalist conditions of appropriation, it becomes a commodity frontier. Wherever primary commodity production penetrated, however, the tempo of landscape transformation accelerated. Why should this be? Although the pace of technical change did indeed quicken—and the diffusion of techniques even more so—in the "first" sixteenth century (1450–1557), this was not enough to compel such an epochal shift in landscape transformation. That shift pivoted the inversion of the labor-land relation (land used as a force of production) and the ascendance of labor productivity as a metric of wealth, premised on appropriating Cheap Natures. Here we may glimpse the tenuous and tentative formation of capitalism as a regime of abstract social labor, and the emergent disciplines of socially necessary labor-time.

Towards provisional synthesis: the origins of the Capitalocene

I have said that these transformations are clues to an epochal transition. But clues to what kind of transition, and to what sort of capitalism? Let me offer

---

89   J-C. Debeir, et al., *In the Servitude of Power* (London: Zed, 1991 [1986 orig.]), 90–1, 76.

90   D. Landes, *Revolution in Time* (Cambridge, MA: Harvard University Press, 1983).

91   Cf. N. Plack, "Agrarian Reform and Ecological Change During the Ancien Régime," *French History* 19, no. 2 (2005): 189–210.

92   J. Blum, "Rise of Serfdom in Eastern Europe," *American Historical Review* 62, no. 4 (1957): 807–36; Moore, "'Amsterdam Is Standing on Norway' Part II" (2010).

two working propositions: one explanatory, the other interpretive. First, these transformations represented an early modern revolution in labor productivity within commodity production and exchange. These were products and producers of a revolution in environment-making with a specific priority: accumulation by appropriation. The labor productivity revolution was rendered possible by a revolution in the *technics* of global appropriation— *including* appropriation within Europe. This was manifested not only in the immediate practices and structures of European imperialism; more funda- mentally, the "new" imperialism of early modernity was impossible without a new way of seeing and ordering reality. One could conquer the globe only if one could see it.[93] Here the early forms of external nature, abstract space, and abstract time enabled capitalists and empires to construct global webs of exploitation and appropriation, calculation and credit, property and profit, on an unprecedented scale.[94] The early modern labor productivity revolution turned, in short, on the Great Frontier—a Great Frontier that was not just there, but had to be imagined, conceptualized, and seen.[95] The fact that early capitalism relied on global expansion as the principal means of advancing labor productivity and facilitating world accumulation reveals the remarkable precocity of early capitalism, not its premodern character. This precocity allowed early capitalism to defy the premodern pattern of boom and bust:[96] there would be no system-wide reversal of commodification after 1450, not even during the "crisis" of the seventeenth century. Why? In sum, because early capitalism's *technics*—its crystallization of tools and power, knowledge and production—were *specifically organized* to treat the appropriation of global space as the basis for the accumulation of wealth in its specifically modern form: capital.

This takes us to a second proposition, which turns on our interpretive frame. The three revolutions we have identified—of landscape transformation, of labor

---

93   T. Ingold, "Globes and Spheres," in *Environmentalism*, ed. K. Milton (New York: Routledge, 1993): 31–42; M.L. Pratt, *Imperial Eyes: Travel Writing and Transculturation* (New York: Routledge, 1992).

94   Merchant, *The Death of Nature* (1980); Lefebvre, *The Production of Space* (1991); M. Postone, *Time, Labor, and Social Domination* (Cambridge: Cambridge University Press, 1993); Crosby, *The Measure of Reality* (1997); Pickles, *A History of Spaces* (2004); W. Sombart, *The Quintessence of Capitalism*, trans. and ed. M. Epstein (New York: E.P. Dutton & Co., 1915); P. Chaunu, *European Expansion in the Later Middle Ages* (Amsterdam: North Holland Publishing Company, 1979).

95   Webb, *The Great Frontier* (1964).

96   Brenner, "The Agrarian Roots of European Capitalism" (1985); J.A. Goldstone, "Efflorescences and Economic Growth in World History," *Journal of World History* 13, no. 2 (2002): 323–89.

productivity, of the *technics* of global appropriation—suggest a revision of think-ing about the law of value in ways both orthodox and revolutionary. Crudely put, I think Marxists have *under*stated the significance of value relations in the modern world-system. First, a vast but weak law of value crystallized during the long sixteenth century. In the standard view, value-relations have been defined as a phenomenon reducible to the "economic" form of abstract social labor. But such an interpretation significantly understates the epoch-making influence of value relations. The law of value—understood as a gravitational field exerting durable influence over the long-run and large-scale patterns of the capitalist world-ecology—is not an *economic* phenomenon alone, but a *systemic* process with a pivotal economic moment (abstract social labor). Second, the moment of value accumulation (as abstract labor) is historically materialized through the development of scientific and symbolic regimes necessary to identify, quantify, survey, and otherwise enable not only the advance of commodity production but also the ever-more expansive appropriation of cheap natures.

Cheap Nature, in the modern sense, encompasses the diversity of human and extra-human activity necessary to capitalist development but not directly repro-duced ("paid") through the money economy. Here the Four Cheaps are central. They are the major way that capital prevents the mass of capital from rising too fast in relation to the mass of appropriated nature. When the delivery of the Big Four inputs approaches the average value composition of world commodity production, the *world-ecological surplus* falls and the pace of accumulation slackens. The centrality of Cheap Nature in the era of capital can, then, be adequately interpreted only through a post-Cartesian frame that sees value as a way of organizing nature. Because value relations encompass a contradictory unity of exploitation and appropriation, heedless of a Cartesian divide, only an analysis that proceeds from the essential unity of humanity-in-nature can move us forward. The goal is to focus on the relations of the *oikeios* that form and re-form capitalism's successive contradictory unities of the exploitation of labor-power (paid work) and the appropriation of a global zone of reproduction (unpaid work) from the family to the biosphere.

This line of thinking and investigation leads me to an argument I did not expect to make. I cannot help but see a new law of value in formation in these centuries, expressed by two epoch-making movements. One was the prolifera-tion of knowledges and symbolic regimes that constructed nature as external, space as flat and geometrical, and time as linear (the field of abstract social nature). The other was a new configuration of exploitation (within commodifi-cation) and appropriation (outside commodification but in servitude to it). In this latter (the production and accumulation of value), we have the paradox of valve as self-forming and yet unable to form without its constitutive outside. With abstract social nature, we have clues to how this paradox has been resolved historically. On the one hand, capitalism is a civilization that turns on the zone of commodification and the exploitation of labor-power within it. On the other hand, strategies of commodification and exploitation can work only to the extent that uncommodified natures are somehow put to work, for free or very low cost. In sum, capitalism must commodify life/work but depends upon the "free ride" of uncommodified life/work to do so. Hence, the centrality of the frontier. Historically, this paradox has been resolved partly through brute force, gunboat diplomacy, shock doctrines, and all the rest. But force is expensive. However necessary, brute force has been insufficient on its own to unlock and to mobilize the wealth of nature for the *long-run* accumulation of capital. Beginning with the Iberians, and clear through to the long twentieth century, one of the first things great empires and states do is establish new ways of mapping, categorizing, and surveying the world.[97] These are strategic expressions of the production of abstract social nature, to which we turn in the next chapter. They have been crucial because they allow for the frontier-led appropriations of Cheap Nature that make possible an otherwise self-consuming strategy: commodification. Coercively enforced, to be sure, the world-praxis of appropriating Cheap Natures (humans included) so that a much smaller group of (human) natures could be exploited has provided the decisive condition for advancing labor productivity within the commodity system (the field of abstract social labor). I do not think these two movements of abstract social labor and abstract social nature exhaust the possibilities; but I cannot escape the conclusion that they provide an indispensable basis for unpacking the history of capitalism as a way of organizing nature.

---

97   J. Cañizares-Esguerra, "Iberian Science in the Renaissance" (2004): 86–124; T.J. Barnes and M. Farish, "Science, Militarism, and American Geography from World War to Cold War," *Annals of the Association of American Geographers* 96, no. 4 (2006): 807–26.

CHAPTER 8

Abstract Social Nature and the Limits to Capital

How do we move from the humanity *and* nature towards historical narratives, analytical strategies, and methodological frames of humanity-in-nature? In Chapter Two, we explored a theory of value-relations as a way of organizing nature. Now, we turn to the possibilities of putting this theory to work as a method that enables the historical reconstruction of capitalism as world-ecology. In this reconstruction, I privilege four propositions. First, the accumulation of capital is the transformation of Earth (and its creatures). Second, the *substance* of value is abstract social labor but the *relations* of value encompass and unify the relations of paid and unpaid work/energy. Third, because the production of value is premised on the appropriation of unpaid work outside the circuit of capital but within reach of capitalist power, the law of value is a law of Cheap Nature. If Cheap Nature turns costly, accumulation grinds to a halt. Fourth, the frontiers of Cheap Nature are not "just there" but are actively constituted through symbolic praxis and material transformation, at once unifying and alienating "mental" and "manual" work (base/superstructure).

This reading of value-relations—as a co-production of human and extra-human work—unfolds from Marx's conception of abstract social labor as the substance of value. But I want to go further than this. As we saw in Chapter Two, Marxists have taken value to be an *economic* phenomenon with systemic implications. This, I think, inverts the reality. Value-relations are a *systemic* phenomenon with a pivotal economic moment. There is, crucially, a historical and logical *non-identity* (but constitutive relation) between the value-form (the commodity) and its necessary value-relations. The simplification, rationalization, and homogenization of socio-ecological life that occurs through manifold commodity regimes and production systems—from assembly lines to agro-monocultures—works through a simultaneous process of exploitation (of paid work) and appropriation (of unpaid work/energy). This double (but not dual) process must occur simultaneously, because life-activity within the circuit of capital is subject to relentless exhaustion, as Marx highlights in his discussion of the working day. The condition of some work being valued is that most work is not.

Uncapitalized work/energy is always earned. Nature's gifts are never free. This is the terrain of accumulation by appropriation. It is enabled by regimes of *abstract social nature*, the relational counterpoint to abstract social labor. If the substance of abstract social nature is the production of "real abstractions"—of time (linear), space (flat), and Nature (external)—its historical expressions are found in the family of processes through which capitalists and state-machineries make human and extra-human natures legible to capital accumulation. The historical conditions of Cheap Nature are found not only in the capital-labor relation but also in the production of knowledge-practices necessary to identify and to appropriate unpaid work. Such a framework—unifying the domains of human and extra-human activity, paid and unpaid work—is essential to grasping the crisis today, which is a crisis of capitalization and appropriation as a unity: the exhaustion of Cheap Nature. Such dialectical unification will be key to developing effective analytics and emancipatory politics as modernity unravels in the century ahead.

HISTORICAL NATURES: VALUE, WORLD-PRAXIS, AND ABSTRACT SOCIAL NATURE

Abstract social nature names the family of processes through which states and capitalists map, identify, quantify, measure, and code human and extra-human natures in service to capital accumulation. This family of processes is immanent to capitalism's law of value; it is directly constitutive of those relations that nourish and sustain the long-run self-expansion of capital, whose substance is abstract social labor. This dialectic of abstract nature and abstract labor is at the heart of those *historical natures* that are cause, consequence, and unfolding condition of successive long centuries of accumulation. This approach allows us to kill two birds with one stone. First, it allows us to transcend a Nature/Society dualism and illuminate the historically concrete interpenetration of "paid" and "unpaid" work in the accumulation of capital. Second, it allows us to transcend a base/superstructure dualism in the history of capitalist environment-making. To this latter idea we can now turn.

There is an unsavory undercurrent to the often-exciting literature on global environmental change: a kind of vulgar materialism. This is materialism that strikes me as dismissive of science and culture (*inter alia*) in the making of the modern world. I do not mean to suggest that global environmental scholars are unaware of the importance of science in a broad sense—radical and mainstream arguments alike enthusiastically embrace natural science. But the resulting interpretations of historical change—say of the "Great Acceleration," or the theory of monopoly capitalism[1]—have little room for the flow of ideas

---

1   Steffen, et al., "The Anthropocene: Are Humans Now Overwhelming the Great Forces of Nature?" (2007); Foster, et al., *The Ecological Rift* (2010).

in the history of the modern world.[2] Here we see how the base/superstructure approach of global environmental analysts meets up with Nature/Society dualism. The implication? That human thought is not *really* embodied within the web of life—human thought is somehow exempt. This is the enduring justification for human-exceptionalist social science, and a key stumbling block to understanding humanity-in-nature.

Productive forces *are* tools and technological systems; they are also more than this. For the metabolism of humanity-in-nature is structured by a species-specific and highly plastic mode of sociality: the "application and development of a certain body of social knowledge" towards definite ways of producing and reproducing life.[3] In short, *ideas matter* in the history of capitalism.

But how, exactly, do they matter? We may begin with modernity's recurrent scientific, botanical, cartographic, agronomic, and chemical revolutions. These are immanent to the accumulation of capital. In the modern world, science—like technology—is a "productive force."[4] Yes, the ruling ideas of society are the ideas of the ruling classes. But this hardly clarifies matters. Ruling classes owe their rule to the production of surpluses, but this is never a simple economic process independent of social knowledge. The production of knowledge itself is constitutive of capitalist world-praxis and its trinity—abstract social labor, abstract social nature, primitive accumulation. Without this, the "triple helix" of commodification (labor, land, and the commodities produced) could not develop over large-space and long-time.

Let us consider nature as matrix rather than resource. Does this mean we no longer need to talk about *resources*? Hardly! It means that we recognize the

---

2   But see G. Pálsson, et al., "Reconceptualizing the 'Anthropos' in the Anthropocene," *Environmental Science and Policy* 28 (2013): 3–13.

3   "What then is a 'productive force'? It is all and any of means of production and reproduction of real life. It may be seen as particular kind of agricultural or industrial production, but any such kind is already a certain mode of social co-operation and the application and development of a certain body of social knowledge. The production of this specific social co-operation or of this specific social knowledge is itself carried through by productive forces" (R. Williams, *Marxism and Literature* [Oxford: Oxford University Press, 1977], 71, 91). Neither are productive forces the basic relations upon which power unfolds; to say "power and production in the web of life" is to implicate the interpenetration of these moments in the totality of the biosphere: "There are not first of all relations of production and then, in addition, alongside or on top of these relations, mechanisms of power that modify or disturb them, or make them more consistent, coherent, or stable . . . Mechanisms of power are an intrinsic part of all these relations and, in a circular way, are both their effect and cause (M. Foucault, *Security, Territory, Population* [New York: Picador, 2007], 17). Where Foucault writes production, could we not say *capital*? Where he says mechanisms of power, could we not say *relations of nature*?

4   Marx, *Capital*, Vol. I (1967), 341.

bourgeois representation of nature—of resources as things-in-themselves—as both a fetish and a particular historical project. To move beyond the fetish, we may view resources as bundles of relations rather than geo-biological properties *as such*—without of course denying these properties. The journey from geology to geohistory necessitates a historical method that grasps the material-symbolic formation of power in human organization, itself already constituted relationally in the web of life. Thus a world-ecological view of, say, coal's "agency" since 1800, allows us to distinguish coal's geology from its geohistory—to discern geological from historical facts. Geohistorically speaking, whoever says capital implicates coal in the era of large-scale industry. Those who say that fossil fuels make industrial capitalism are not wrong so much as errant in the insertion of a non-relational object (coal) in the relational process of capital accumulation. By itself, coal is only a *potential* actant; bundled with the relations of class, empire, and appropriation in the nineteenth century, however, coal becomes something quite different. It becomes a way of naming a mass commodity whose presence was felt in every strategic relation of nineteenth-century capitalism. Nineteenth-century capital sweated coal from every pore. Resources, then, are actively co-produced; they are markers and creators of the historical natures that help to define the scope of opportunity and constraint in successive eras of capitalist development. If this sensibility has long been registered theoretically,[5] the historiography of resource extraction has seldom taken the relational point seriously.[6]

Just what would it mean to take the relational point seriously? I would begin with a simple observation: What "counts" as a resource shifts as the terms of the *oikeios* change—as new historical natures emerge. As we have seen, coal is coal. Only under specific conditions does it become fossil fuel, and come to shape entire historical epochs. Historical nature must not be taken as an output of capitalism or any other kind of human organization. Capitalism does not produce an external "historical" nature according to its needs (a functionalist position). Nor does capitalism simply respond to external changes in nature (another functionalist position). Rather, successive phases of capitalist development are at once cause and consequence of fundamental reorganizations of world-ecology. Both "capital" and "nature" *acquire new historical properties* through these reorganizations: this allows us to give the differentiated unity—historical capitalism/historical nature—real *historical* content.

These reorganizations unfold through the interpenetrating patterns of

---

5   Harvey, "Population, Resources, and the Ideology of Science" (1974).

6   Cf, Bunker and Ciccantell, *Globalization and the Race for Resources* (2005); Wrigley, *Energy and the English Industrial Revolution* (2010).

planetary change—forged over Braudel's "very *longue durée*" of geological time[7]—and capitalism's configurations of power and production forged across long centuries of accumulation. Historical natures are, in other words, a dance of the dialectic between part (modes of humanity) and whole (the web of life), through which particular limits and opportunities come to the fore.[8] The question of historical natures is a question of how the layers of historical time shape each other.[9] This history is often told in dualistic terms. But the close relation between climate and the rise and demise of great civilizations—say, Rome over the Roman Climatic Optimum, or feudal Europe during the Medieval Warm Period—suggests a different view of historical natures. In this alternative view, cascading movements of the web of life enter into particular historical-geographical configurations of power and production. If human sociality articulates these relations (in its double meaning: to connect and to give expression to), the biosphere is its integument. Historical natures are those specific part-whole combinations in which specific "geological, hydrographical, climatic, and [biogeographical]" conditions enter into the most intimate, and also the most expansive, domains of human history.[10]

These historical natures are the *fields* upon which the conditions and constraints of capital accumulation unfold in any given era. Such constraints and conditions are best grasped as specifiable bundles of relations—say, agriculture or religion or markets. These enable and express specific configurations of species-environment relations. Relations of capital, labor, and power move *through*, not around, nature; they are "specifically harnessed natural force[s]."[11] Capital does not interact with nature as external object but, rather, is a specifically harnessed natural force. Capital, itself co-produced, in turn co-produces specific historical natures, albeit under conditions that are full of resistances and frictions to capital's desire for a world of fungible, passive, and malleable life. The upshot? World-economies do not interact with world-ecologies; world-economies *are* world-ecologies.

In the modern world, successive historical natures have been produced

---

7   F. Braudel, "History and the Social Sciences: The *Longue Durée*," *Review* 32, no. 3 (2009/1958 orig.): 195.

8   The view of nature as constraint and opportunity for capital accumulation has been articulated by Henderson and Boyd, et al.—but in regional-historical or systemic-theoretical terms, respectively, rather than across the historical-geography of capitalism as a whole (G.L. Henderson, *California and the Fictions of Capital* [Oxford: Oxford University Press, 1998]; Boyd, et al., "Industrial Dynamics and the Problem of Nature," [2001]).

9   Braudel, *The Mediterranean and the Mediterranean World in the Age of Philip II*, Vol. I (1972), 73.

10   Marx and Engels, *The German Ideology* (1970).

11   Marx, *Grundrisse* (1973), 612.

through a dialectic of commodification and appropriation. On the one hand, this has occurred through the monetized transformation of land and labor; on the other, through the harnessing of unpaid life-activity in service to commodification. This latter moment—appropriation—has long been recognized by the theory of imperialism.[12] But it has been only weakly grounded in the theory of accumulation, which has tended to regard the circuit of capital as a closed system. This accounts in part for the nature-blindness of Marxist economic critiques of the post-2008 era.[13]

What makes appropriation possible, and such a powerful moment in the history of capitalism? Part of the answer can be found in a long history of analysis on culture, ideology, and hegemony in the modern world, representing what Shapiro calls the "cultural fix." This cultural fix

> broadly includes Gramscian hegemony and all forms of cultural and social customs, institutions and identity-formation. The cultural fix covers the moments of class compact, as well as mechanisms by which the working class is . . . pitted against [itself]—the moments when capitalism exports its own competition onto the working class. The spatial fix and the cultural fix also frequently overlap, such as when housing struggles include slum clearance and gentrification in ways that alter working-class identities within the urban ecology . . . The role of the cultural fix [comprises, moreover, those] social and cultural matters involving the reproduction of class identities and relations *over time-lengths greater than a single turnover cycle [of capital] are intrinsic, not superficial, to the [accumulation] of capital.*[14]

If cultural fixes cement successive hegemonic agreements between capital and the direct producers,[15] they also extend beyond the sphere of *direct* production. Necessarily, cultural fixes transcend the wage-relation's double boundary with unpaid work. Such fixes naturalize not only capital's appropriation of unpaid work by humans—above all the reproduction of labor-power—but also new epoch-making practices of appropriating unpaid work by extra-human natures. Today's meat-industrial complex, for instance, would be unthinkable to those living in an earlier era of capitalism when the human relation to non-human

---

12   R. Luxemburg, *The Accumulation of Capital* (2003 [1913 orig.]); Wallerstein, *The Modern World-System I* (1974).

13   Cf. J.B. Foster and R.W. McChesney, *The Endless Crisis* (New York: Monthly Review Press, 2012); S. Gindin and L. Panitch, *The Making of Global Capitalism* (2012).

14   S. Shapiro, "The World-System of Capital's Manifolds: Transformation Rips and the Cultural Fix," unpublished paper, Department of English and Comparative Literary Studies, University of Warwick (2013).

15   B. Silver and E. Slater, "The Social Origins of World Hegemonies" (1999).

animals was—symbolically and materially—more direct and intimate.[16] Cultural fixes serve to normalize otherwise unacceptable appropriations of global natures, human and extra-human. Thus are revolutions in gender and nature closely bound, materially instituted and symbolically practiced: "ideas" of nature/ gender are not simply outputs of the system but implicated in the intergenerational reproduction of life and labor-power that capital cannot pay for and must appropriate (lest reproduction costs rise and accumulation falter). This tendency found epochal expression in early modernity's complementary movements of scientific revolution and "proto-industrial" demographic restructuring.[17] Cultural fixes, in this light, appear as the necessary symbolic condition for the "long wave" appropriations of the Four Cheaps.

If cultural fixes naturalize capitalism's punctuated transitions in the relations of power, capital, and nature, the production of abstract social natures make those transitions possible.

Abstract social nature signifies those relations of appropriation—through scientific practice and their institutional forms—that are directly implicated in making the world legible for capital accumulation. Socially necessary labor-time forms through the dialectic of capital-labor relations and the appropriation of unpaid work, made possible through abstract social nature. The language is clunky. The Cartesian vocabulary of social change dies hard. To be clear, we are working with a double internality: of labor-in-nature and nature-in-labor, *not* with the Cartesian coupling of Nature/Society.[18] However clunky, the formulation makes a necessary point: Value relations form and re-form through the active relation of life-making—the *oikeios*. Value in motion is *value-in-nature*.

Socially necessary labor-time is determined by more than commodification. We must take care to make a part-whole distinction here. Labor-time forms *also* through the relations of power and knowledge that identify and enable unpaid work/energy to flow into the determination of value; this is the transformation of work into value. If abstract social nature's major expressions are associated with the value-facilitating praxis of mapping, quantifying, and otherwise making legible the *oikeios*, we should not conflate this collection of practices with its relational core. That relational core turns on the appropriational analogue of the capital-labor relation—the capital-unpaid work dialectic. If abstract social labor names the capital-labor relation, through which surplus value is produced,

16   Cf. T. Weis, *The Global Food Economy* (2007); J. Hribal, "Animals Are Part of the Working Class" (2003).

17   Merchant, *The Death of Nature* (1980); W. Seccombe, *A Millennium of Family Change* (1992).

18   Here I mobilize Farshad Araghi's insightful concept: labor-in-nature; see Araghi, "Accumulation by Displacement," *Review* 32, no. 1 (2009): 113–46.

abstract social nature names the relation of capital-unpaid "worker," through which rising labor productivity becomes possible over the long run.

With this working conceptualization, two major issues can be addressed.

First, abstract social labor operates solely within the confines of the commodity system; regimes of abstract social labor therefore nourish, and are in turn sustained, by relational processes of standardization, quantification, mathematization, and so forth. Without these processes, value could not exist. And without the long sixteenth century's movement towards labor productivity as the metric of wealth—breaking with feudalism's emphasis on land productivity—there could be no movement towards a regime of abstract social nature. We are looking at a conjuncture of transformations—of knowledge, production, markets, states, and classes. Dialectically speaking, the emergence of new civilizations is defined by their process of becoming. *Becoming* is not mere precondition. It is also the first moment of new historical systems, whose key patterns are at first glimpsed in episodic and "immature" form.

Our second problem is that all the standardizing, simplifying, mapping, and quantifying practices of abstract social nature—whose focus is the zone of appropriation—also pertain to similar practices within commodity production. How these two moments are similar and how they are distinct—standardization and simplification within commodity production and across the zones of socio-ecological reproduction—is a question that the present argument poses but cannot resolve. Preliminarily, I would say that something like Taylor's famous time-and-motion studies[19]—providing the basis for the "scientific management" revolution of the early twentieth century—belong to the zone of abstract social labor, reworking already-commodified relations.[20] On the other hand, something like the imposition of the metric system in Revolutionary France belongs to the zone of abstract social nature, representing the advance of capitalist power into weakly commodified relations of reproduction.[21] It is, of course, a porous distinction, not only between abstract social nature and cultural fixes, but also relative to simplifications within commodity production (e.g., scientific management). Although one must be wary of hard and fast distinctions, the "hard" transformations of material life, represented by abstract social labor are complemented and enabled by the "soft" process of symbolic practice and knowledge formation in the capitalist world-ecology. (Primitive accumulation is the necessary cyclical mediation between the two moments.) The goal of such "soft" techniques—always with the brute force of states and empires behind

---

19   F.W. Taylor, *The Principles of Scientific Management* (New York: Harper & Brothers, 1914).

20   Braverman, *Labor and Monopoly Capital* (1974).

21   Alder, "A Revolution to Measure," (1995); W. Kula, *Measures and Men* (1986).

it—is to secure access to minimally or non-commodified natures for as close to free as possible.

The mapping and quantifying practices of abstract social nature did not emerge out of the blue.[22] Taking shape across the early modern centuries, these practices reached a turning point during the eighteenth and nineteenth centuries. Perhaps most dramatic was the generalization of the metric system after 1789. Even here, the "metrical revolution"[23] found its precondition in early capitalism's new planetary consciousness, emerging from those audacious conquests and reimaginations of global space that attended colonial expansion and the cartographic revolution.[24] The meter was defined as one-ten-thousandth part of the distance from the pole to the equator," thereby combining a global imagination with "extreme unworldliness," far removed from realities of everyday life.[25] Launched by French revolutionaries towards the end of the eighteenth century, the metric system "tended to follow the barrel of a gun, only becoming instituted in Germany in 1868, Austria in 1871, Russia in 1981, China in 1947, and of course never in the United States."[26] Why was the advance of the metric system so important? Surely among the most important reasons is the "story of how a rational language—the metric system—was deliberately crafted to break the hold of the Old Regime's political economy and serve as the universal idiom of the modern mechanism of exchange."[27]

The metric system was not only a weapon of the bourgeoisie in its struggle against *ancien régimes*. It was also implicated in the class struggle in the countryside. For peasant communities across early modern Europe,

> the subjective [and localized] form of measurement . . . [was perfectly acceptable]. There were disagreements, but they could be negotiated face to face. Informal measurement was inseparable from the fabric of these relatively

---

22   "Calculation, even with decimals, and algebra have been carried on in India, where the decimal system was invented it was only made use of by developing capitalism in the West, while in India it led to no modern arithmetic or book-keeping. Neither was the origin of mathematics and mechanics determined by capitalistic interests the technical utilization of scientific knowledge, so important for the living conditions of the mass of people, was certainly encouraged by economic considerations, which were extremely favorable to it in the Occident" (M. Weber, *The Protestant Ethic and the Spirit of Capitalism* [New York: Routledge, 1992], xxxvii).

23   W. Kula, *Measures and Men* (1986).

24   M.L. Pratt, *Imperial Eyes* (1992); R.H. Grove, *Green Imperialism* (Cambridge: Cambridge University Press, 1995).

25   T.M. Porter, *Trust In Numbers* (Princeton: Princeton University Press, 1995).

26   P. Mirowski, *The Effortless Economy of Science?* (Durham, NC: Duke University Press, 2004), 150.

27   Alder, "A Revolution to Measure" (1995), 39.

autonomous communities . . . [In contrast,] the metric system was not designed for peasants. It did not bring back the true bushel [which varied by locality], but discarded the bushel in favor of a system of wholly unfamiliar quantities and names, most of them drawn from an alien dead language. The institutionalization of the metric system involved special difficulties because of the aspiration to universalism that helped to give it form. This universalism was consistent with the ideology of the revolution, and more particularly with the ideology of empire.[28]

These metrical revolutions are suggestive of broader transformations in the regime of abstract social nature. They imply, as well, state- and capital-led "simplifications . . . [that imposed a] standard grid whereby [humans and the rest of nature] could be centrally recorded and monitored";[29] they include also the "whole system of surveillance, hierarchies, inspections, bookkeeping, and reports . . . that can be described as the disciplinary technolog[ies] of labor."[30] If the hallmarks of abstract social labor are control and exploitation, the defining characteristics of abstract social nature are control and *appropriation*. We are looking at the historical processes of measurement and mapping as forms of how capitalism brings ever-wider "domains of experience under systematic" order and control.[31] These expansive (and expansionary) processes of rationalizing and controlling domains of experience clearly cut across the Cartesian binary, seeking to identify and enclose any form of life-activity—including the congealed work of extremely ancient life (fossil fuels)—that might be useful for capital accumulation.

VALUE AND ABSTRACT SOCIAL NATURE

In the English language, value signifies two things. First, it refers to those objects and relations that are valu*able*. Second, it refers to notions of morality, as in the fact/value binary that has loomed so large in modernist thought. Marx's deployment of the "law of value" was, of course, aimed at identifying the relational core of capitalism, grounded in the expanded reproduction of abstract social labor. Marxists since Marx have defended—or sometimes elided[32]—the law of value as an economic process that encompasses that first meaning of value, those objects

---

28   T.M. Porter, *Trust In Numbers* (1995), 223.

29   J. Scott, *Seeing Like a State* (New Haven: Yale University Press, 1998), 2–3.

30   Foucault, *Society Must Be Defended* (2003), 242.

31   M.N. Wise, "Introduction," in *The Values of Precision*, ed. M.N. Wise (Princeton: Princeton University Press, 1995), 3–16.

32   Wallerstein, *The Modern World-System I* (1974).

and relations that capitalist civilization deems valu*able*. And so it has been difficult indeed to suggest that the operation of the law of value—the expanded
reproduction of value-*relations*, enabling the quantitative expansion of abstract
labor—may encompass both meanings.

Difficult, but not impossible. Historically speaking, it is hard to deny that
new knowledges and symbolic practices—say, cartographies and double-entry
bookkeeping—were crucial to the formation of capitalism. That this early
capitalism might be a precocious value regime is often doubted, even dismissed.
But any casual dismissal does not seem reasonable: a new world-praxis, by
empires and capitals, premised on abstract time and space, money and nature,
should give one pause. To introduce such symbolic-cultural affairs into value
is of course to destabilize the subjective/objective binary presumed by most
political economy. The truth is that the objective world of value has been
forged through the subjectivities of "capital's imagination."[33] The calculative
character of value is not a matter of capital using an objective knowledge—
premised on dualism and quantification—but a matter of capital deploying its
symbolic power to represent the arbitrary character of value relations *as* objective.[34] This is Mitchell's point in his account of British economy-making in
colonial Egypt, centering on calculability not merely as an objective tool of
empire, but as a project immanent to imperialism's bundling of power, class,
and nature in the early twentieth century. This line of argument has, alas,
centered more on politics than on *political economy*. Attention has been
lavished on the sphere of power without sufficient attention to the value-relations that determine the decisive stakes of the game. It is not that capital
operates independently of power. Rather, systemic rules of reproduction are
not determined by power in general, or by territorial power, but by agents
unfolding through the law of value-in-nature.

This re-framing may help us to clarify the configuration of paid and unpaid
work. For a long time, the "objective" world of economic process was immu-
nized from moral critique—notwithstanding a centuries-long countercurrent of
moral economy protest and argument.[35] But was not this fact/value antinomy
itself a strategic way of making rational the essentially arbitrary boundary
between paid and unpaid work? That is to say, are not the two common usages
of value—as morality and economy—implied in capitalism's law of value?

The preceding suggests that knowledge/culture and value as abstract labor are

---

33   M. Haiven, "Finance as Capital's Imagination?" *Social Text* 29, no. 3 (2011): 93–124.

34   P. Bourdieu, "Symbolic Power," *Critique of Anthropology* 4 (1979): 77–85;
Bourdieu and Wacquant, *An Invitation to Reflexive Sociology* (1992).

35   E.P. Thompson, "The Moral Economy of the English Crowd in the Eighteenth
Century," *Past and Present* 50, no. 1 (1971): 76–136.

indeed closely linked. But how? The argument may be stated simply enough. Abstract social nature names a systemic family of processes aimed on simplifying, standardizing, and otherwise mapping the world in service to the quantitative expansion of abstract labor. In this reading, abstract social nature signifies those spatio-temporal practices that identify and facilitate the appropriation of unpaid work. These appropriations do more than supply necessary raw materials; they co-determine "socially" necessary labor-time. In this view, abstract social nature can be understood as directly constitutive of value *relations* in creating the conditions for the generalization of commodity production and exchange. This has never been a linear sequence—either with new knowledges in the lead, or as derivative of commodification. Rather, it has been a conjunctural affair, in which cascading processes of commodification, capital accumulation, and symbolic innovation have constituted a virtuous circle of modern world development. I do not propose a revision of Marx's law of value in a strict sense: the substance of capital *is* abstract social labor. But the relations that make abstract labor's growth possible cannot be reduced to the economic sphere; they must be grounded in the *technics* of capitalist power and the conditions for the expanded reproduction of capital. Neither an adequate history of capitalism, nor a sufficiently dynamic theory of capitalist limits, is possible within an economistic reading of the law of value.

Central to theorizing capitalism's limits is the law of value's drive to convert the "natural distinctness" of particular commodities into "economic equivalence,"[36] and particular labor processes into "general types of work motions."[37] We know these are value-relations in which "sociology and economics pervade each other:"[38] the "economic" relations of value imply the class struggle of bourgeois and proletarian. But what of ecology? Is this beside the point?

Capitalism, as project, seeks to create a world in the image of capital, in which all elements of human and extra-human nature are effectively interchangeable. In the fantasy of neoclassical economics, one "factor" (money, land, resources) can be substituted for another; the elements of production can be moved easily and effortlessly across global space.[39] This effort to create a world in the image of capital is capitalism's *correspondence project*, through which capital seeks to compel the rest of the world to correspond to its desire for a universe of "economic equivalence." But of course the world— extra-human natures of all kinds, but also the re/producing classes—does

36   Marx, *Grundrisse* (1973), 141.

37   Braverman, *Labor and Monopoly Capital* (1974), 125.

38   J.A. Schumpeter, *Capitalism, Socialism and Democracy* (New York: Harper & Row, 1950 [1942 orig.]), 45.

39   Perelman, "Scarcity and Environmental Disaster" (2007).

not much want a world of capitalist equivalence. At some level, all life rebels against the value/monoculture nexus of modernity, from farm to factory. No one, no being, wants to do the same thing, all day, every day. Hence, the struggle over the relation between humans and the rest of nature is necessarily a class struggle. (But not *just* a class struggle.) The struggle over the grip of commodification is, in the first instance, a contest between contending visions of life and work. Extra-human natures, too, resist the grim compulsions of economic equivalence: superweeds frustrate genetically modified agriculture; animals resist their assigned roles as objects and forces of production. In this way, capitalism's correspondence *project* meets up with all manner of contending and contentious visions and resistances to create a contradictory historical *process*.

Among these contradictions, at the top of the list we find those countervailing forces that threaten to slow down the turnover time of capital and to defy the radically simplifying disciplines of capital. Working-class struggle in the heartlands of industrial production is a good example.[40] So too is the revolt of extra-human nature in modern agriculture, where a distinctive form of struggle manifests: the "battle with weeds" and troublesome pests.[41] The pesticide/herbicide treadmill (and its cognates) is bound up with Cheap Nature strategies that hothouse evolutionary adaptation at the point of production and the scale of world accumulation. On the one hand, as the flurry of news reports on the "superweeds" sweeping across the GMO soy zones of the U.S. revealed in 2010–2011, biological natures now appear to be evolving faster than the capacity of capital to control them—resulting in a "Darwinian evolution in fast-forward."[42] On the other hand, the revolt of extra-human natures is aided by the revolutionary geography of accumulation itself: from the origins of modernity, "the accumulation of capital . . . is strongly and positively associated with the accumulation of alien invasive species."[43] In sum, capitalism's speed-up and geographical rationalizations suggest a struggle not only over the configuration of nature but equally of capitalist space. This is an ongoing contest over the systemic tendency towards "geographical inertia"[44] that extends well-beyond the

40   D. Montgomery, *Worker's Control in America* (Cambridge: Cambridge University Press, 1979); B.J. Silver, *Forces of Labor* (Cambridge: Cambridge University Press, 2003).

41   N. Clayton, "Weeds, People and Contested Places," *Environment and History* 9, no. 3 (2003): 301–331.

42   W. Neuman and A. Pollack, "Farmers Cope with Roundup-Resistant Weeds" (*New York Times*, May 3, 2010).

43   C. Perrings, "Exotic Effects of Capital Accumulation," *Proceedings of the National Academy of Sciences* 107, no. 27 (2010): 12063–4; Crosby, *The Columbian Exchange* (1972).

44   Harvey, *The Limits of Capital* (1982), 428–9.

built environment to encompass *all* environments within value's gravitational pull.

How have these spatio-temporal contradictions, of compressed time and simplified space, been resolved? By and large, through geographical expansion and restructuring. The two moments are geographically distinctive, but unified. Both turn on externalizing costs and appropriating unpaid work—inwards towards the relations of reproduction (e.g., the shift to the two-income household in the North since the 1970s) and outwards towards minimally commodified zones of Cheap Nature.

These paired movements of geographical expansion and restructuring are at the core of capitalism's successive spatial fixes, necessary to resolve successive *conjonctures* of overaccumulation. They are constituted through a double movement: 1) the widening and deepening of the zone of commodification (value production/abstract social labor); and 2) on a greater scale, the widening and deepening of the zone of appropriation. This latter movement turns on the production of abstract social nature: produced through the biopolitical, geographical, and scientific-technical knowledges and practices necessary to secure the conditions for renewing the Four Cheaps. This means that new "frontiers" of unpaid work must be identified, and pressed into the service of capital accumulation.

This reading of the law of value allows us to see the difference between capitalism as historical *project*, and capitalism as historical *process*. As project, capitalist civilization produces both symbolic forms and material relations that lend Cartesian dualism its kernel of truth. Capitalism creates the idea and even a certain reality of "the" environment as an external object. The idea of the environment as external object is not wholly false, but rather a historical creation of the capitalist world-ecology. The mistake of environmental studies has been to confuse capitalism's world-praxis—reproducing the environment as external object—with capitalism's world-process. In that historical process, environments are always inside and outside of us, material and symbolic *at once*. Capitalism, as co-produced historical reality, compels the *project* to deal with nature (as *oikeios*), no matter value's utopian fantasies and its universe of economic equivalents.

ABSTRACT SOCIAL NATURE AND THE RISE OF CAPITALISM

The long sixteenth century opened a new era of abstraction. At this time, we begin to see abstract social nature at the core of the emergent law of value, mobilizing both material and symbolic machineries of power and production.

Foremost among these symbolic revolutions—bound closely to material processes—were remarkable innovations in ways of seeing and knowing:

> The new approach was simply this: reduce what you are trying to think about to the minimum required by its definition; visualize it on paper, or at least in your mind, be it the fluctuation of wool prices . . . or the course of Mars through the heavens, and divide it . . . into equal quanta. Then you can measure, that is, count the quanta.[45]

Early modernity's epoch-making abstractions were registered through the era's new cartographies, new temporalities, new forms of surveying and property-making, schools of painting and music, accounting practices, and scientific revolutions.[46] Together, these constituted a vast but weak regime of abstract social nature. The early modern materialist revolution that dethroned medieval holism and divine teleology was implicated in an epochal shift from feudalism to capitalism. Early capitalism's scientific revolutions replaced a mode of reason favorable to feudal arrangements with a new reasoning of mathematical abstraction and cartographic perspective conducive to endless accumlation.[47] The audacity of the project can hardly be overstated, circumscribing nature "in advance, in such a way as to be determinable and accessible to inquiry as a closed system, [conceptualized] so that the entirety of [nature could . . .] be accessible to calculative knowledge."[48]

This vast but weak regime—combining abstract labor and abstract nature— reached an early tipping point towards the end of the sixteenth century. The dynamic center of abstract social nature was—not surprisingly—the Low Countries and after 1600, the Dutch Republic. Here space, time, and money were rationalized and abstracted as never before. In the northern Netherlands after 1585, we find the era's leading mapmakers, excelling both in the quantity and quality of map production.[49] So central was cartographic knowledge to the

---

45   Crosby, *The Measure of Reality* (1997), 228.

46   F. Capra, *Turning Point* (1982); D. Cosgrove, *Geography and Vision* (London: I.B. Tauris, 2008); A.W. Crosby, *The Measure of Reality* (1997); Mumford, *Technics and Civilization*; M. Postone, *Time, Labor, and Social Domination*; D. Landes, *Revolution in Time*.

47   Pickles, *A History of Spaces* (2004), 75–106; Merchant, *The Death of Nature* (1980).

48   Heidegger, quoted in S. Elden, *Speaking Against Number* (Edinburgh: Edinburgh University Press, 2006), 121.

49   R.W. Unger, "Dutch Nautical Sciences in the Golden Age," *E-Journal of Portuguese History* 9, no. 2 (2011): 68–83; C. Koeman, et al., "Commercial Cartography and Map Production in the Low Countries, 1500–ca. 1672," in *History of Cartography*, Vol. 3 (Part 2): *Cartography in the European Renaissance*, ed. D. Woodward (Chicago: University of Chicago Press, 1987), 1296–1383.

Dutch East India Company (VOC) that pilots of VOC vessels were given uniform instructions to map new territories in minute detail. By 1619, the company had created an internal mapmaking office to coordinate the flow of geographical knowledge.[50] Nor were these mapping impulses strictly colonial. Internal to the northern Netherlands, polderization, water-control, and capitalist agriculture propelled a cadastral revolution whose surveys were so detailed they would not be superseded for two centuries.[51] Work-time, too, was subjected to a "radical rationalization" after the 1574 synod of the Reformed Church, which "abolished *all* holy days," and extended the work-year by 20 percent by 1650.[52]

With space and work, so with money. Here too the VOC loomed large, its 1602 formation giving new form to world money- and credit-creation, dramatized with the foundation of the Amsterdam Bourse (stock market) that same year, and the Amsterdam Exchange Bank in 1609. As American silver flowed into Amsterdam—silver wrested from the earth with biopolitical, no less than mechanical, ingenuity[53]—it provided the conditions for the rise of fiat money.[54] World money, as Mitchell clarifies, is "always material as well as calculative"— and always world-ecological.[55] As for the Bourse, not only were shares of the Dutch East India Company traded, but also, very soon, a growing number of commodities (360 different commodities by 1639!) and even option-derivatives (futures).[56] The Bourse's material coordinations and symbolic "rationality provided the basis for a universalisation and intensification of world credit practices which served to set the Dutch[-led world's] financial order apart from pre-modern world finance."[57]

In emphasizing early modern developments once more, I wish to underscore the epochal shift of the sixteenth century, whose strongest impulses were

---

50   K. Zandvliet, "Mapping the Dutch World Overseas in the Seventeenth Century," in *History of Cartography*. Vol. 3 (Part 2), ed. D. Woodward (Chicago: University of Chicago Press, 1987), 1433–62.

51   R.J.P. Kain and E. Baigent, *The Cadastral Map in the Service of the State* (Chicago: University of Chicago Press, 1992).

52   J. de Vries, "The Labour Market," in *The Dutch Economy in the Golden Age*, ed. K. Davids and L. Panitch (Amsterdam: Nederlandsch Economisch-Historisch Archief, 1993), 60; *The Industrious Revolution* (Cambridge: Cambridge University Press, 2008), 88–9.

53   Moore, "Amsterdam Is Standing on Norway, Part II" (2010).

54   S. Quinn, Stephen, and W. Roberds, "The Bank of Amsterdam and the Leap to Central Bank Money," *American Economic Review* 97, no. 2 (2007): 262–5.

55   Mitchell, *Carbon Democracy* (2011).

56   L.O. Petram, "The World's First Stock Exchange" (PhD dissertation, University of Amsterdam, 2011).

57   P. Langley, *World Financial Orders* (New York: Routledge, 2002), 45.

renewed and amplified in the long nineteenth-century transition to fossil fuels. The rise of large-scale industry, co-produced through a new phase of appropriation (centered on fossil fuels), was unthinkable in the absence of these symbolic-material revolutions—producing abstract time, space, money, and nature. This family of abstractions was central to the revolutionary transformation of the Atlantic-centered capitalist world-ecology, three centuries before the steam engine reached maturity.

This line of thought allows us to read the history of capitalism through a succession of scientific revolutions that actively co-produced distinctive historical natures in and through successive phases of capital accumulation. These scientific revolutions not only produced new opportunities for capital and states, but transformed our understanding of nature as a whole, and perhaps most significantly, of the boundaries between humans and the rest of nature.[58] The point has been underscored by neoliberalism's systematic combination of shock doctrines with revolutions in the earth system and life sciences, tightly linked in turn to new property regimes aiming to secure not only land but life for accumulation.[59] This has unfolded at the nexus of the global and molecular scales.[60] On the one hand, the new life sciences emerging after 1973 (with the invention of recombinant DNA) became a powerful lever for producing new conditions of accumulation premised on redistribution and speculation—patenting life forms, starting with the micro-organisms recognized in 1980 by the US Supreme Court. The ambition has been to enclose "the reproduction of life itself within the promissory accumulation of the debt form."[61] On the other hand, the earth system sciences, aided considerably by the mapping sciences (e.g., remote sensing, GIS, etc.), have sought to reduce

> the Earth . . . to little more than a vast standing reserve, serving as a ready resource supply center and/or accessible waste reception site . . . [They] aspire to scan and appraise the most productive use of . . . [the] resourcified flows of energy, information, and matter as well as the sinks, dumps, and wastelands for all the by-products that commercial products leave behind.[62]

---

58   Young, "Is Nature a Labor Process?"(1985).

59   Klein, *The Shock Doctrine* (2007); M. Cooper, *Life as Surplus* (Seattle: University of Washington Press, 2008); B. Mansfield, ed., *Privatization* (New York: Routledge, 2009).

60   K. McAfee, "Neoliberalism on the Molecular Scale," *Geoforum* 34, no. 2 (2003): 203–19.

61   M. Cooper, *Life as Surplus* (2009), 31.

62   T.W. Luke, "Developing Planetarian Accountancy," 133; Costanza, et al., "The Value of the World's Ecosystem Services and Natural Capital" (1997).

From this perspective, the combinations of science, capital, and power that have loomed so large in the history of neoliberalism may be fruitfully located within a longer history. Something like "bioprospecting"[63] has deep roots in the colonializing thrust of early capitalism,[64] an era in which botany was not only "big science" but "big business."[65] (Then as now.) "From its inception [early modern] botany served the needs of transnational merchant capital."[66] But was it only *merchant* capital? Here we find a key originary moment of abstract social nature, in an era when much of the colonial project's profitability turned "on natural historical exploration and the precise identification and effective cultivation of" extra-European plants.[67] Such processes, unifying "science, capital, and power,"[68] were in motion from the earliest moments of the capitalist world-ecology. From the late fifteenth century, as sugar was remaking Madeira,[69] the Portuguese were also "developing a system of acclimatisation gardens and . . . were carrying out a complex, although not highly organised, series of plant transfers," linking the Indian Ocean with West Africa, the Caribbean, and Brazil.[70]

Such movements represented early capitalism's audacious global project to produce abstract social nature. These would culminate in "massive taxonomical exercise[s]" with Linnaeus in the eighteenth century:[71]

> When Linnaeus returned to Sweden [in 1738], he fulfilled numerous commissions for industrial and pharmaceutical uses of plants . . . and as superintendent of the botanical garden of the University of Uppsala devoted himself to raising seeds and cultivating plant transfers from colonial satellites. Like other botanists of the period, he explored the possibilities of plant cultivation in area where cheap colonial labor was available, and studied economic plants to determine whether native-grown might substitute for imported.[72]

---

63   K. McAfee, "Selling Nature to Save it?" *Society and Space* 17, no. 2 (1999): 133–54.

64   L.L. Schiebinger, *Plants and Empire* (Cambridge: Harvard University Press), 2004.

65   L.L. Schiebinger and C. Swan, "Introduction," in *Colonial Botany*, ed. by authors (Philadelphia: University of Pennsylvania Press, 2005), 3.

66   Cañizares-Esguerra, "Iberian Science in the Renaissance" (2004): 99.

67   L.L. Schiebinger and C. Swan, "Introduction," *Colonial Botany* (2005), 3.

68   Brockway, *Science and Colonial Expansion* (1978), 461.

69   Moore, "Madeira, Sugar, and the Conquest of Nature, Part I" (2009); "Madeira, Sugar, and the Conquest of Nature, Part II" (2010).

70   Grove, *Green Imperialism* (1995), 73–4.

71   Richards, *The Unending Frontier* (2003), 19.

72   A. Boime, *A Social History of Modern Art*, Vol. 2 (Chicago: University of Chicago Press, 1990).

The Linnaean revolution, building on earlier Iberian and Dutch botanical initiatives, set in motion a process that would be elaborated and extended: first by the Kew Gardens of the British Empire in the later nineteenth century, and then with the International Agricultural Research Centers of the American empire after World War II.[73] Each implied a new historical nature, emerging from the innovations of capitalist production, science, and power in forging new combinations of paid and unpaid work across the world.

The new law of value—as a way of organizing nature—manifested earliest, and most spectacularly, in two domains. The first could be found in an extraordinary, cascading series of landscape and bodily transformations across the Atlantic world and beyond (see Chapter Seven); the second, in an emergent set of perspectives that allowed European states and capitals to see time, space, and nature as external to human relations. The conceit of capital, from its very origins, was to represent the world through the God trick: to treat the specifically capitalist ordering of the world as "natural," claiming to mirror the world it was seeking to re-construct.[74]

These remarkable innovations in ways of seeing and knowing were, in the first instance, premised on a new quantitativism whose motto was: reduce reality to what can be counted, and then "count the quanta."[75] Such quantitative reductionism was paired closely with transforming space into something that could be viewed from outside. Here the emergence of perspective in Renaissance painting—linked tightly with the renaissance of Euclidean geometry in northern Italy[76] —was important far beyond the aesthetic realm. Renaissance perspective "turned the symbolic relation of objects into a visual relation: the visual in turn became a quantitative relation. In the new picture of the world, size meant not human or divine importance, but distance."[77] In this quantitative reductionism, "space was robbed of its substantive meaningfulness to become an ordered, uniform system of abstract linear coordinates."[78] This was crucial to a new mapping of the world, without which a modern world-market, modern state-formation, and modern property-making was impossible. The early

---

73   Brockway, *Science and Colonial Expansion* (1978); R. Drayton, *Nature's Government* (New Haven: Yale University Press, 2001); Kloppenburg, *First the Seed* (1988).

74   B. Warf, *Time-Space Compression* (New York: Routledge, 2008), 40–77.

75   Crosby, *The Measure of Reality* (1997), 228.

76   "The critical advance came from the re-evaluation of Euclid and the elevation of geometry to the keystone of human knowledge, specifically its application to three-dimensional space representation through single-point perspective theory and technique" (D. Cosgrove, "Prospect, Perspective and the Evolution of the Landscape Idea," *Transactions of the Institute of British Geographers* 10, no. 1 [1985]: 47).

77   Mumford, *Technics and Civilization* (1934), 20.

78   J. Martin, *Downcast Eyes* (Berkeley: University of California Press, 1994), 52.

modern transition in mapping practices, Pickles observes,[79] took shape out of a "series of concrete concerns about property and identity emerging" during the rise of capitalism. "First, there was a need for maps to envision and consolidate new communities, increasingly imagined as territorially bounded states and discrete unities of people." Second, surveys became central to bourgeois property rights, as "capitalist practices of land alienation and sale increasingly became the norm."

Here we see abstract social nature in its earliest formation. Especially in relation to bourgeois property—as in seventeenth-century England—it is difficult to exaggerate this new way of seeing and mapping. The new survey practices helped to "reformat property" by reimagining such spaces as "geometric" and "calculable."[80] Land ownership, especially (but not only) in England, was reduced to "facts and figures, a conception which inevitably undermines the matrix of duties and responsibilities which had previously been seen to define the manorial community."[81] Not for nothing, the modern map "was effectively an invention of the sixteenth century."[82] Far from derivative of political economy and empire— but unthinkable except in relation to capital and power—these new ways of seeing were co-constitutive of the historical natures that simultaneously limited and enabled successive bursts of commodification and appropriation inside and outside Europe.[83] Mapping space was constitutive of global conquest, not merely representative of it. Both global commodification and the global appropriation of unpaid work/energy turned on *representing* the "practical activities" of astronomical observation in a manner that was abstract and yet useful for capital and empires.[84] The great breakthrough of Mercator, who was as much capitalist as cartographer, was to construct

a plane representation which depicted the meridians as parallel to each other rather than, as is the case with the true representation of the globe, converging on the north and south poles . . . The importance of Mercator's innovation in terms of accurate navigational practice and commercial profit was quite clear. Instead of taking awkward and imprecise bearings on board ship across the surface of a globe or a portolan chart, his new projection allowed for a line of bearing to be drawn accurately across the surface of a plane map, explicitly

---

79   Pickles, *A History of Spaces* (2004), 99.

80   N. Blomley, "Disentangling Property, Making Space," in *Performativity, Space and Politics*, ed. R. Rose-Redwood and M. Glass (New York: Routledge [forthcoming]).

81   A. McRae, "To Know One's Own: Estate Surveying and the Representation of the Land in Early Modern England," *Huntington Library Quarterly* 56, no. 4 (1993): 341.

82   Harvey, *Maps in Tudor England* (1993), 8.

83   Moore, "Ecology and the Rise of Capitalism" (2007).

84   D. Cosgrove, *Geography and Vision* (London: I.B. Tauris, 2008), 21.

foregrounding ... its usefulness to the art of navigation ... With pilots and navigators in mind, Mercator went on to outline the mathematical procedure which allowed him to employ an accurate grid of straight lines across his map.[85]

Nor was this early modern revolution—the birth of abstract social nature—confined to space and extra-human nature. We can also see abstract social nature at work in the slave trade. Much as a meatpacker today demands a "standard hog" from suppliers,[86] so the slave market of the seventeenth-century Caribbean was measured in terms of the "standard" slave: male, thirty-to-thirty-five years old, between five and six feet tall. This standard slave was a full *pieza de India* (piece of the Indies). Individuals who did not measure up were reduced to—and reckoned as—some fraction.[87] It was a small step to move from considering extra-human natures, local property, or global space, in terms of equivalents and interchangeability, to considering human natures in the same fashion. While the *pieza de India* is often considered as merely a measurement for taxation,[88] it was widely used in the seventeenth century as a unit of measuring labor-power, from Angola to the Caribbean.[89] The *pieza de India*

> was a measure of potential labor [labor-power], *not of individuals*. For a slave to qualify as a *pieza*, he had to be a young adult male meeting certain specifications as to size, physical condition, and health. The very young, the old, and females were defined for commercial purposes *as fractional parts of a* pieza de India. *The measure was convenient for Spanish imperial economic planning, where the need was a given amount of labor power, not a given number of individuals.*[90]

These developments reveal early capitalism as very real and modern indeed. The shift from land productivity to labor productivity revealed a new law of value. But this new law was more than a valuation premised on abstract social labor. It implied a second dialectical moment: abstract social nature. For humans are

85   J. Brotton, *Trading Territories: Mapping the Early Modern World* (Ithaca: Cornell University Press, 1997), 166.

86   F. Ufkes, "Lean and Mean: US Meat-Packing in an Era of Agro-Industrial Restructuring," *Environment and Planning D: Society and Space* 13, no. 1 (1995): 683–705.

87   E. Williams, *From Columbus to Castro* (New York: Harper and Row, 1970), 139.

88   J.F. King, "Evolution of the Free Slave Trade Principle in Spanish Colonial Administration," *Hispanic American Historical Review* 22, no. 1 (1942): 34–56.

89   P.C. Emmer, "The History of the Dutch Slave Trade: A Bibliographical Survey," *Journal of Economic History* 32, no. 3 (1972): 736.

90   P.D. Curtin, *The Atlantic Slave Trade* (Madison: University of Wisconsin Press, 1969), 22. Emphases added.

unevenly exploited by, and appropriated for, capital. The valuation of labor-power inside commodity production implied and necessitated the *de*valuation of labor-power outside commodity production. This dialectic of paid and unpaid work has given rise to multiple misrecognitions in Marxist political economy because human work is exploited (e.g., wage-work) and appropriated (e.g., unpaid household labor). Thus humans, alone among species, have found themselves unevenly exploited *and* appropriated by capital. All manner of racialized and gendered mediations—suggestive of Shapiro's cultural fixes—have served to normalize the appropriation of humanity's free gifts over the past five centuries. It turns out that capitalism itself practiced a form of human exceptionalism—internalized even by many radical political economists—that restricted our attention to labor-power within the circuit of capital. This is a pillar of any analysis of capital accumulation. But taken too far, the framing of capitalist development in these terms alone produces an unduly narrow basis for understanding the combined and uneven geographies of accumulation. Every act of exploitation implies an even greater act of appropriation.

What we see, from the earliest moments of the capitalist world-ecology, is a law of value emerging through a double dialectic. The first is premised on exploitation: abstract social labor/capital and wage-labor. The second is premised on appropriation: abstract social nature/capital and unpaid work/energy. This allowed for the historical combination of accumulation strategies—capitalization and appropriation. Through capitalization, labor productivity is advanced through the rising value composition of production; through appropriation, labor productivity is advanced by seizing upon Cheap Natures, thereby reducing the value composition of production.

The systemic formation of value relations occurred through a cascading series of small and large shifts in the Atlantic world after 1450. These shifts transcended the convenient boundaries of economy, culture, politics, and so forth; they favored a view of reality and a practice of material transformation that encouraged a mathematized and mechanical world-praxis. At the same time, the emergence of a capitalist world-praxis depended upon the explosive growth of commodity production and exchange after 1450, an expansion which was, nevertheless, quantitatively modest in the overall weight of the Atlantic world-ecology for some time, and insufficient *on its own* to effect the rise of capitalism. The genius of early modern commodification—in contrast to feudal Europe—was its articulation with the appropriation of Cheap Natures, such that the scale and speed of landscape transformations outpaced the quantitative growth of commodification as such. This allowed labor productivity within a narrow sphere to rise—dramatically. For it was on early capitalism's frontiers that the greatest combinations of mechanization and appropriation occurred. Was it so different later, with the arrival of the steam engine and coal's "vertical" frontier? What we are looking at, after 1450, is a process of transition through which new rules of reproduction emerged, and new stakes of the game were established, creating new logics of power and production. That is the magic of great historical transitions. These new rules and stakes of the game turned on commodification, whose radical expansions after 1450 turned on the symbolic and material abstractions of concrete labors into money-capital and abstract labor. This was necessary for the transition from the appropriation of surplus-product to the accumulation of surplus-value.

Necessary, but not sufficient. That this transition involved more than abstract social labor has long been recognized. There is a considerable literature—much of it written over the past decade—on primitive accumulation and the role of state power to secure the necessary conditions of the accumulation of capital.[91] But no combination of state violence and capitalist innovation in commodity production could produce the knowledges necessary to map, navigate, survey, and calculate the world. By calling this family of processes abstract social nature, we should not exaggerate. The Iberian pioneers excelled at cartography, natural history, and navigation in ways clearly different from the mathematizing and mechanizing procedures of seventeenth-century science in northern Europe.[92] We should be under no illusions that this initial phase of producing new knowledges resembles ideo-typical models that conform to subsequent eras. But we might also take care not to *under*state the efficacy of Iberian empire-building overseas, made possible through the new technics of "long-distance control."[93] These *technics* made possible durable trans-oceanic empires heretofore unknown in world history. None of which suggests the autonomy of the intellectual sphere, but rather its constitutive role in forming a weak, *but vast*, law of value that took the globe as its theater.

And for the value added of calling these processes abstract social nature? Three reasons stand out. In the first instance, any conception of value as economically reductionist undermines our capacity to explain the rise of capitalism as a unity of power, capital, and nature. Second, historically speaking, it is difficult to sustain, on any consistent empirical basis, the *a priori* assertion of economic processes propelling the transition to capitalism. It seems to me that this is the inverse of Weberian approaches that insist on the capitalist spirit and its fondness for rationalization. Instead, we see in the sixteenth century a family of processes—quasi-dependent on, and quasi-independent from each other—that

---

91   Cf. M. Perelman, *The Invention of Capitalism* (2000); Harvey, *The New Imperialism* (2003); M. de Angelis, *The Beginning of History* (2007).

92   Cañizares-Esguerra, "Iberian Science in the Renaissance" (2004).

93   J. Law, "On the Methods of Long Distance Control," in *Power, Action and Belief*, ed. J. Law (New York: Routledge, 1986), 234–63.

enabled a revolutionary configuration of commodification and appropriation. It is difficult for me to see the new "measures of reality"—in accounting, timekeeping, mapping space, and externalizing nature—as any less definitive in the process of transition than the new mechanizations of key commodity sectors. Rather, the cascading processes that facilitated—but did not ensure—the triumph of capitalism emerged sometimes from commodification, sometimes from imperial and state machineries, and sometimes from new modes of knowledge production (abstract social nature). As so we are back to the world-historical trinity of the rise of capitalism: abstract social labor, primitive accumulation, abstract social nature. Of course, each was implied in the others, and the world-historical weight of each varied as this new world-praxis formed in the sixteenth century.

Finally, with abstract social nature we find a way out of the state-centric rendering of this process, brilliantly crystallized in Scott's[94] arguments on "state simplifications" and Foucault's wide-ranging discussions on governmentality and biopower.[95] If the production of abstract social natures has often been closely bound to imperial and state power, such political structures have hardly been independent of world accumulation. State- and market-led simplifications reveal a process of remaking life-activity—entraining a range of processes aimed at standardizing and geometrically encoding and mapping natures in the interests of facilitating capital accumulation. The unpaid work of "women, nature, and colonies," in this perspective, are not merely plundered but *actively created* through symbolic praxis, political power, and capital accumulation. This process of active creation is signaled by the nexus: historical nature/abstract social nature/abstract social labor. In this sense, our reading of value establishes an interpretive basis for what we have seen in modern world history—worlds of landscapes, cultures, markets, states, and re/production (and so much more) that resemble and reproduce (even as they contest or condition) the radical simplifications immanent in the law of value.

The law of value allows us to explain precisely what has been hidden in plain sight: the epoch-making transition in humanity's environment-making relations that began in the sixteenth century, and which have reached a limit today. A world-ecological reading of value-relations illuminates these limits as relationally constituted through capitalism, itself producer/product in the web of life. The law of value, in this approach, becomes a methodological premise that permits the excavation of capitalism's foundational logic. This logic encodes labor productivity as the overarching metric of wealth—inverting the long-standing primacy of land productivity in premodern civilizations—and

---

94   Scott, *Seeing Like a State* (1998).
95   Foucault, *Society Must Be Defended* (2003).

mobilizes the rest of nature in the service of labor productivity. Value relations, understood solely in terms of abstract social labor, cannot explain this long-run mobilization of unpaid work/energy outside the circuit of capital. Nor do the state and science work as external factors, practically independent of capital accumulation. State, science, and capital constitute a singular process, shaped by a double imperative: to simplify natures, and to extend the domain of appropriation faster than the zone of exploitation. Marx's insight that soil fertility could act like fixed capital was no throwaway comment; it is an observation that speaks to capitalism's voracious appetite for non-capitalized natures, without which capital's labor productivity revolutions are unthinkable.

Part IV

THE RISE AND DEMISE OF CHEAP NATURE

Cheap Labor?: Time, Capital and the Reproduction of Human Nature

By this policy of the squandering and destruction of man's productive forces capitalism condemns itself... Deprived of the historical intake of labor-value produced outside its sphere and of the principal brake on falling rates of profit, capitalism may well show itself to be too costly a mode of production to success-fully mobilize, as it did at the outset, the productive forces, and therefore to guarantee progress. The coming "final" crisis would then be foreshadowed by the present situation. (Meillasoux, 1981)

The dialectic of capitalization and appropriation turns, fundamentally, on the relations through which humans are re/produced. Thus the centrality of Cheap Labor-Power. Without it, accumulation breaks down. For Marx,

> The reproduction of labour power, which must incessantly be re-incorpo-rated into capital as its means of valorization [capital's self-expansion], which cannot get free from capital, and whose enslavement to capital is only concealed by the variety of individual capitalists to whom it sells itself, forms, in fact, a[n] [*essential*] factor in the reproduction of capital itself. Accumulation of capital is therefore multiplication of the proletariat.[1]

To Marx's famous observation we may now add: the accumulation of capital is the multiplication of the proletariat is the appropriation of unpaid work/energy. In turning "blood into capital,"[2] the capital relation unfolds the production of wealth as value, and the appropriation of unpaid work (the re/production of life) as the condition of value. Capitalism does this under definite geographical conditions. The regime of abstract social labor emerged—even before large-scale industry—under conditions of rapid geographical expansion.[3] But the implications of this relation go deeper than arguments about global expansion

---

1 Marx, *Capital*, Vol. I (1977), 763–4; Bracketed words from Marx, *Capital*, Vol. I (1967), 575–6. Emphasis added.

2 Marx, *Capital*, Vol. I (1977), 382.

3 Moore, "Ecology and the Rise of Capitalism" (2007); C. Tilly, "Demographic Origins of the European Proletariat" (CRSO Working Paper No. 207, Center for Research on Social Organization, University of Michigan, 1979).

as pivotal to the rise of capitalism.[4] Abstract social labor does not *create* frontiers so much as it *is* a frontier process itself. That frontier is the boundary between commodified and uncommodified life, and capital moves across that boundary through the mapping and quantifying technics of abstract social nature. For all the "self-contained" character of *Capital*, the production of surplus value is not only the proletarianization of labor and the accumulation of capital, but the production of global spaces of appropriation.

Marx has been frequently criticized for reducing the reproduction of labor-power into the consumption of commodities. In the process, we are told, he ignored the contributions of unpaid work (especially domestic work).[5] This does not seem to be entirely correct. In his classic discussion of "The Working Day," Marx makes clear that any containment of the reproduction of labor-power within the commodity system would quickly lead to rising labor costs and faltering accumulation. "It would *seem* that the interest of capital itself points in the direction of a normal working day."[6] The longer the working day, and the more intensive the work, the greater the "deterioration of human labor-power."[7] Not for nothing is capitalism—*even before the era of large-scale industry*—"the first system . . . to provide . . . the impetus for industrial pathology."[8] At first glance, such deterioration of labor-power seems to run contrary to capital's self-interest, since "used up" labor-power must be replaced, an "expensive" proposition.[9] But, while the "value of labor-power *includes* the value of the commodities necessary for the reproduction of the worker," the value of these commodities is determined by a *combination* of capitalized and appropriated work—of paid and unpaid work. Valorized labor-power directly determines the value of the commodities necessary for the reproduction of the worker. *At the same time*, unpaid work in reproduction co-determines the socially necessary labor-time that establishes the value of those commodities. This unpaid work/energy, as we have seen, is not limited to the household, but extends to the whole system of Cheap Nature. Necessary labor-time is *co-produced* through capitalization *and* appropriation.

Why *co*-produced? Because capital necessarily draws on zones of uncommodified work (unpaid work); the reproduction of labor-power occurs only *partly* within the zone of commodity production and exchange. To sustain the full costs of household reproduction within the commodity system would

4   Cf. Wallerstein, *The Modern World-System I* (1974).

5   C. Meillassoux, *Maidens, Meal and Money* (Cambridge: Cambridge University Press, 1981); S. Federici, *Revolution at Point Zero* (Oakland: PM Press, 2012).

6   Marx, *Capital*, Vol. I (1977), 377. Emphasis added.

7   Ibid., 376.

8   Ibid., 484.

9   Ibid., 377.

quickly bring the accumulation process to a halt. Fully proletarian households are therefore quite rare in capitalism even today, limited almost entirely to well-paid professional workers (lawyers, doctors, professors, etc.). Historically, even in the heartlands of proletarianization, the reproduction of labor-power has depended on all manner of unpaid work, or work remunerated at a level insufficient to reproduce labor-power *on its own*. The last point is important, because we are dealing with relative *degrees* of unpaid work, shifting configurations of paid and unpaid work in the "semi-proletarian household."[10] In early twentieth-century America, for example, half of all immigrant women in American cities—at a time when immigrants were the majority in large cities—took in paying boarders, an activity that included all manner of cleaning, cooking, and emotional labor. Indeed, even in mid-sized industrial towns—such as Muncie, Indiana—about half of all working-class families cultivated small vegetable gardens as late as the 1920s.[11]

There is a temptation to acknowledge this reality of abstract social labor as co-produced through capitalization and appropriation, and at the same time to deny that Marx recognized the problem.[12] And if it were entirely a matter of whether Marx was right—or wrong—it would hardly be worth quibbling about. We would do well to attend to how Marx constructed the argument about the reproduction of labor-power. For Marx consistently moves from *general* abstractions, such as production or population or exchange in general, towards successively more specific, or *determinate*, abstractions.[13] In an illuminating passage, Marx offers both a general and a determinate abstraction of labor, moving from the former to the latter:

As useful activity directed to the appropriation of natural factors in one form or another, labour is a natural condition of human existence, a condition of material interchange between man and nature, quite independent of the form of society. On the other hand, the labour which posits exchange-value [commodified labor-power] is a specific social form of labour.[14]

In *Capital*, we find Marx consistently moving from a "pure" model of capital

---

10   J. Smith and I. Wallerstein, *Creating and Transforming Households* (Cambridge: Cambridge University Press, 1992).

11   L. Gordon, "US Women's History," in *The New American History*, ed. E. Foner (Philadelphia: Temple University Press, 1990), 271.

12   Cf. S. Federici, *Revolution at Point Zero* (2012).

13   Marx, *Grundrisse* (1973); P. Murray, *Marx's Theory of Scientific Knowledge* (Atlantic Highlands, NJ: Humanities Press, 1988).

14   K. Marx, *A Contribution to the Critique of Political Economy*, trans. N.I. Stone (Chicago: Charles H. Kerr & Co., 1904 [orig. 1859]), 33.

accumulation towards more determinate abstractions. The argument in "The Working Day" offers an implicit theory of capitalism's tendency towards the underproduction of labor-power and the non-market mechanisms for attenuating this contradiction. This is especially evident in his treatment of the reproduction of labor-power. Marx's initial abstraction of labor-power's value as defined by the value of commodities is subsequently modified by a new, historically determinate abstraction in which the zone of appropriation is central.[15] Here, "latent" layers of the reserve army of labor are crucial.[16] Having "seized the vital forces of the people at their very roots . . . the degeneration of the industrial population is *retarded only by the constant absorption of primitive and natural* ['physically uncorrupted' human] elements from the countryside,"[17] a movement later examined in Marx's famous discussion of primitive accumulation. Quoting Cairnes with approval, Marx observes that if labor-power can be

> *supplied from foreign preserves* . . . the duration of [the worker's] life becomes a matter of less moment than its productiveness while it lasts. It is accordingly a maxim of slave management, in slave importing countries, that the most effective economy is that which takes out of the human chattel in the shortest space of time the utmost of exertion that it is capable of putting forth.[18]

To which Marx adds: "*Mutato nomine te fabula narratur* [The name is changed but the tale is told of you!]. For slave trade, read labor-market, for Kentucky and Virginia [in the slave trade], Ireland and the agricultural districts of England, Scotland, and Wales, for Africa, Germany.[19] For labor-power, read nature. Marx makes the connection directly:

> Capital asks no questions about the length of life of labour-power. What interests it is purely and simply the maximum of labour-power that can be set in motion in a working day. It attains this objective by shortening the life of labour-power, *in the same way* as a greedy farmer snatches more produce from the soil by robbing it of its fertility.[20]

In the same way . . . Here is an insightful dialectical statement about how the capital relation unfolds through the *oikeios*. As we saw in Chapter Three, the

---

15   Marx, *Capital*, Vol. I (1977), 276–7.
16   Ibid., 796.
17   Ibid., 380.
18   J. Cairnes, *The Slave Power* (London: Parker, Son and Bourn, 1862); Marx, *Capital, Vol. I* (1977), 377.
19   Marx, *Capital*, Vol. I (1977), 376. Emphasis added.
20   Ibid., 378. Emphasis added.

"interdependent process of social metabolism" turns on a singular—but histori-cally differentiated—metabolism of human and extra-human natures. Here we can illuminate the symbolic violence of the Cartesian binary, obscuring the connective tissues between the "shortening of the life" of the worker, and the "robbery" of the soil.

It is difficult to see these connective tissues in most Green Thought. Wake up any environmentalist in the middle of the night and ask: "Where do we see exhaustion and depletion?" The answer is ready-made: in flora and fauna, in soils and resources. But what happens if we invert that answer, and begin from the standpoint of the worker's exhaustion, and the exhaustion of work-systems? Such an inversion need not be anthropocentric; through it, we may illuminate the unifying relations exhausting human and extra-human natures in the capi-talist world-ecology.

If the exhaustion of the worker is paramount, we must ask a crucial question: *Who* is the worker? Not just the wage-worker, to be sure, but all life-activity that "works" within capitalism's value-relations. As we have seen, some of this work is formal, but much of it is not. A small share of it occurs within factories, offices, and stores, but most of it does not. We may revisit our two major forms of exhaustion—"maxed out" and "wiped out"—first encoun-tered in Chapter Five. Most typical is the former: a given working population becomes *maxed out* when it can no longer deliver a rising stream of work/energy into—or in support of—the circuit of capital. The American working class today is not exhausted in the sense of imminent physical breakdown; it *is* exhausted in its capacity to deliver a rising volume of unpaid work to capi-tal. Its potential for delivering unpaid work is maxed out. The proliferation of "shifts"—a second and third shift in paid and unpaid work—and the neoliberal extension of the workweek give us reason to think that American workers cannot work much more, or much harder.[21] (On the margins, perhaps, but not more than this.)

Such exhaustion also implicates our second, "wiped out," moment. This is the specter of an absolute—not just relative—decline in work/energy flows. It can be seen in the sharp rise of mental health problems across the Global North since the 1980s,[22] and a cancer epidemic even after the major decline in cigarette smoking, and out of proportion to diagnostic advances.[23] What this means is straightforward: exhaustion takes many forms and cannot be reduced to

21   Cf. Hochschild, *The Second Shift* (1989).

22   HHS [U.S. Department of Health and Human Services], *Health United States 2010* (Washington, D.C.: U.S. Government Printing Office, 2010).

23   M. Davis, *Planet of Slums* (London: Verso, 2006).

biophysical breakdown. Beyond mounting health problems, one could also look at declining fertility—a "baby strike" of proletarian women across the North Atlantic in recent decades, and now extending to industrialized East Asia.[24] This suggests that over the course of an accumulation cycle, the relations of reproduction, which were once outside the cash nexus, become progressively monetized. Reproduction becomes channeled through commodity relations, and the share—but not necessarily the mass—of *un*paid work declines or stagnates. Human nature becomes increasingly capitalized in the old centers of production. That capitalization is hardly without its class politics: the struggle over the terms of the reproduction of labor-power assumes increased salience. Capital becomes increasingly dependent on the *commodified*, rather than the uncommodified, reproduction of life.

Once again we see the tendency of the ecological surplus to fall. Its most obvious indicator is the rising price of the Big Four inputs. Labor, food, energy, and raw materials become more and more expensive.[25] The Four Cheaps stop being cheap. This usually does not happen all at once, although this is what we have seen since 2003. The point at which the Four Cheaps stop becoming cheaper and start becoming dear is the *signal* crisis of a phase of capitalism: such crises "signal" the exhaustion of an accumulation regime. For neoliberal capitalism, this signal crisis—far more important than the near-meltdown of the financial system in 2008—began around 2003. Since then, the ecological surplus has been falling, with few signs of an impending reversal. The greatest commodity frontiers have already been exhausted, while the mass of capital continues to rise.

The cyclical resolution of such overaccumulation crises—crises defined by a rising mass of "surplus" capital that cannot be reinvested profitably—has depended upon the cyclical restoration of the Four Cheaps. The falling ecological surplus is therefore closely linked to the contraction of profitable opportunities for investment in the real economy (M-C-M'). Cheap oil, or Cheap labor, or Cheap metals, *make possible* new innovations—such as the railroad and steam engine, or the automobile in their respective eras. (The process is of course cascading, and not a linear process of *first* Cheap Nature, *then* epochal innovation.) The production systems, urban spaces, and infrastructural development implied by these new machines absorbed gigantic volumes of surplus capital. Indeed, the extraordinary history of successive industrializations in the North

---

24   G. Livingston, and D. Cohn, "The New Demography of American Motherhood," (Pew Research, 2010), www.pewsocialtrends; *Economist*, "Women in South Korea: A Pram Too Far," *Economist*, (October 26, 2013).

25   There is, of course, always unevenness between each input, and always geographical variation.

Atlantic between 1790 and 1960—spanning the first, second, and Fordist industrial revolutions—can be told through the ways these epochal inventions (coal/steam, auto/oil) reworked the global *oikeios* and enabled rising contribution of unpaid work/energy. Intriguingly, the information technology "revolution" of the past forty years has been manifestly inadequate in delivering new stream of work/energy, absorbing surplus capital, or advancing labor productivity.[26] In making possible those great waves of industrialization, the Four Cheaps are central to the resolution of recurrent overaccumulation crises in historical capitalism. Consequently, the cyclical "end" of the Four Cheaps, in successive accumulation cycles, corresponds to a growing mass of surplus capital with no place to go. The exhaustion of commodity frontiers—and the slowed growth of system-wide unpaid work—is consequently linked strongly to the peculiar forms of financialization that have emerged since the 1970s. As accumulation in the real economy falters, a rising share of capital gravitates towards financial rather than productive activities (M-M′ rather than M-C-M′).[27] At some point, of course, these financialized bets on the future must pay off—or the player must go broke.

The ecological surplus—the declining relative contribution of unpaid work to capital accumulation—can decline for several reasons. Among these, five are especially salient. One is that the cash nexus, under conditions of modern territorialism and the extension of abstract social nature, tends to disorganize pre-capitalist arrangements of power and production. Sometimes this dis-organization comes in the form of colonialism, as when the Spanish colonial restructuring of seventeenth-century Peru disorganized village life.[28] Such dis-organizations are a cyclical phenomena of the capitalist world-ecology. They were still in play three centuries later, in colonial Africa as capitalist development induced a shift from "rotating" to "irreversible" migration.[29] The class struggle itself is a second vector of the falling ecological surplus. Working classes have tended to demand a "family wage"—along with demands for socializing the costs of reproduction, in health care, old age pensions, and education especially.[30] This had the effect of "locking in" capital to higher reproduction costs,

---

26   Foster and McChesney, *The Endless Crisis* (2012); Gordon, "Is US Economic Growth Over?" (2012).

27   M-M′ comes into play during capitalism's successive financial expansions (see Chapter Six). See Arrighi, *The Long Twentieth Century* (1994); A. Leyshon and N. Thrift (2007), "The Capitalization of Almost Everything," *Theory, Culture and Society* 24, nos. 7–8 (2007): 97–115.

28   Moore, "Amsterdam Is Standing on Noway, Part I" (2010).

29   Meillassoux, *Maidens, Meal and Money* (1981), 110.

30   Wallerstein, *Historical Capitalism* (1983).

especially in the Global North since the 1970s.[31] (South-North emigration has been a powerful check on this tendency.) Since then, we have also seen the rise of environmental movements across the world—our third vector. These movements have pushed states to limit pollution, and to clean up the costs of previous pollution. This is the weakest of our vectors until now, because it has been possible—until now—to defer costs in time, to the next generation, and to displace costs over space, from North to South. It is arguably the strongest vector of rising costs in the decades ahead, an issue we explore in the next chapter. A fourth factor is the tendency of radical simplification strategies, such as monoculture, to remove nutrients from agro-ecosystems, and to produce pest- and weed-friendly environments. This tends towards rising energy and toxic inputs, which are themselves increasingly costly. Finally, the falling ecological surplus also implicates the depletion of energy and mineral sources, which, as in agriculture, tend to call forth increasingly costly—and toxic—inputs (e.g., cyanide gold mining, hydraulic fracturing, offshore drilling).

If the declining relative contribution of unpaid work is such a problem, why then does capital tolerate, and at times strongly encourage, the capitalization of reproduction? On balance, capital does so for two big reasons. First, to bring reproduction processes into the circuit of capital allows for particular capitalist agencies (firms) to gain short-run gains in the competitive struggle for shares of world surplus value. A firm needs a regular supply of labor-power no less than raw materials. Second, at a systemic level, the commodification of labor-power, especially during periods of stagnation, increases the consumption of commodities.[32] The commodification of food is obviously central here, and the neoliberal experience of "forced underconsumption" (hunger) is scarcely at odds with food's marketization.

Labor-power is instructive, because it challenges us to think through the differentiated unities of capitalism-in-nature. Capitalism, as Marx suggests, exhausts the soil and the worker through a singular, if uneven, relation. While such exhaustion is absurd, it is not irrational. Over the middle run of a half-century, capitalizing reproduction costs tends to maximize unpaid work. Beyond a half-century, the relative share of unpaid work begins to stagnate, then declines. The capitalized composition of nature rises. The ecological surplus falls. Two consequences ensue: the reproduction costs for capital rise, and capital flows

---

31   J. Smith, "Transforming Households," *Social Problems* 34, no. 5 (1987): 416–436.

32   "One of the major forces behind proletarianization has been the world's workforces themselves. They have understood, often better than their self-proclaimed intellectual spokesmen, how much greater the exploitation [I would say *appropriation*] is in semi-proletarian than in more fully proletarianized households" (Wallerstein, *Historical Capitalism* [1983], 36–37).

towards new labor frontiers. (And often—this is the history of American capitalism especially—labor has moved *towards* the dynamic capitalist centers.) While it would *seem* that the interest of capital itself points in the direction of "sustainable" reproduction regimes, capital's short-termism and the flexibility of socio-ecological reproduction propel serialized boom/bust sequences in capitalist history—premised on the exhaustive tendencies of capitalization and appropriation. These contradictions are attenuated through the distinctive temporal rhythms of commodity production and socio-ecological reproduction. While the time of paid work is "linear and clock-oriented," the unpaid work of household reproduction "is grounded in recurring rhythms and patterns of activities that are often cyclical rather than linear, task-based instead of clock-based, and embedded in meaning."[33] Capital seizes upon the flexibility of reproductive work—up to a point, it can be molded around the disciplines of abstract time—as it invades everyday life, and encompasses more and more work within the logic of abstract social labor. But such flexibility is not infinite. The *real* working day—of paid and unpaid work—cannot be extended without limit.

Commodity production works on a very short time frame. At its longest, this is the business cycle (seven-to-twelve years). Of course, production cycles are even shorter, and have become more so in recent decades, manifested in a profusion of "flexible" forms of capitalist production.[34] As Melissa Wright has shown,[35] such flexibilization was premised on the rapid appropriation and subsequent exhaustion of women workers across the Global South. The "disposable third world woman worker" became a pillar of Cheap Labor in the neoliberal era.[36] As early as the 1970s, 30 percent of South Korean women workers had "a 15-hour or even longer day, [and] disablement as a result of work-accidents . . . increased by an annual average of 17 percent."[37] This was not, of course, a novel development. Seccombe charts a similar trajectory for women and children in the industrializing regions of nineteenth-century England and France.[38] What Wright and Seccombe highlight is the historically transient character of cheap labor commodity frontiers. At some point, the

---

33 M. Hilbrecht, et al., "'I'm Home for the Kids': Contradictory Implications for Work-Life Balance of Teleworking Mothers," *Gender, Work and Organization* 15, no. 5 (2008): 456–7.

34 Harvey, *The Condition of Postmodernity* (1989).

35 M.W. Wright, *Disposable Women and Other Myths of Global Capitalism* (New York: Routledge, 2006).

36 Ibid., 29.

37 A. Lipietz, "Towards Global Fordism," *New Left Review* I, no. 132 (1982): 33–47.

38 W. Seccombe, *Weathering the Storm* (London: Verso, 1995), 71–80.

flexibility of unpaid reproductive work no longer suffices to sustain a rising ecological surplus.

The implication is banal, but bears emphasis after the "great doubling" of the world's workforce (actual and potential) since 1990.[39] Cheap labor-power is not an eternal condition of capitalist civilization. The provision of labor-power and unpaid work is not merely a "social" question, but a world-ecological question: the value (or cheapness) of labor-power is directly bound up with the unpaid work of humans and the rest of nature. The connection between human labor-power and extra-human work is not distant but intimate, dialectical, immediate.[40]

In place of a Cartesian optic—the "exploitation of labor *and* nature"[41]—I would begin with two forms of labor-*in*-nature. One is paid work within the commodity system. The other is unpaid work outside direct commodity production but within the capitalist division of labor. A method premised on the double internality allows us to unify these distinctive moments: whenever we consider labor (labor-in-nature) we do best to move immediately to consider nature-in-labor, and back again. Labor-in-nature is nature-in-labor. Work is a co-production of the human and the rest of nature; it is indeed a metabolism, as Marx suggests. And this metabolism takes the form of the law of value—as *connective historical process*—sustained through regimes of abstract social labor and abstract social nature, reproduced through relations of capitalization and appropriation.

This contradictory relation has been one of burning the candle at both ends. On one side we find the production time of capital; on the other side, the reproduction time of life. This strategy works so long as there are plenty of candles to burn, and so long as making new candles is easy. For the lifeblood of capitalism is the life-activity of reproducing human beings who can become workers. If this does not occur "cheaply," but instead becomes more expensive, the very basis of value—commodified labor-power—becomes a problem. Here the intergenerational reproduction of labor-power enters the stage. Considering the era of the Industrial Revolution, Seccombe observes how

> Industrial capitalism in the moment of its triumphant breakthrough here revealed its darker side. Private capitalists, under the whip of competition, displayed a ruinous indifference to the most elementary preconditions of the

39   R. Freeman, "What Really Ails Europe (and America)," *The Globalist* (June 3, 2005).

40   Although Green critics have emphasized problems with food, energy and raw materials, labor remains epiphenomenal in their analyses. See, e.g., Heinberg, *Peak Everything* (2007); Foster, *The Ecological Revolution* (2009); J.G. Speth, *The Bridge at the End of the World* (New Haven: Yale University Press, 2008).

41   Foster, et al., *The Ecological Rift* (2010), 80. Emphasis added.

proletariat's life-reproduction, and above all, to women, forced to try to reconcile the antagonistic demands of the daily and generational cycles of labour-power.[42]

Has it been so different in the long twentieth century?

This "whip of competition" occurs both in production and in the market. It imposes a time-discipline on all capitalist production, but extends far beyond production. Capital's commitment to labor productivity as the metric of wealth reveals capitalism as a *temporal* regime: a system committed to the "annihilation of space by time."[43] The annihilation of space, to be sure, but also the annihilation of life-activity by abstract time: the drive to compel all life-activity to work on the rhythms of capital. The advent of what Thompson calls "industrial time"[44]—which precedes the Industrial Revolution by several centuries—was not just a factory-based phenomenon. It was equally a family phenomenon, and both factory and family transformations were linked tightly with the sugar plantation system, itself organized on industrial time. In nineteenth-century Britain,

> food choices were reckoned partly in terms of available time, and not solely in terms of relative cost. [T]he division of labor within the family shaped the evolution of British food preferences; a wife's leaving the house to earn a wage had a restrictive effect on the family diet, even though her work might increase the family income . . . There seems no doubt that [the factory system provided unusual access] to sugar and its by-products [for industrial workers, because these foods allowed] the saving of time, [and therefore partially compensated for the] exhausting jobs it offered women and children. The decline of bread-baking at home was representative of the shift from a traditional cooking system, costly in fuels and in time, toward 'convenience eating.' Sweetened preserves [jam], which could be left standing indefinitely without spoiling and without refrigeration, which were cheap and appealing to children, and which tasted better than more costly butter with store-purchased bread, outstripped or replaced porridge, much as tea had replaced milk . . . In practice, the convenience foods freed the wage-earning wife from one or even two meal preparations per day, meanwhile providing large numbers of calories to all her family.[45]

Feminist scholars have frequently suggested the centrality of the contradiction between the reproduction time of life and the reproduction time of capital. But

---

42 W. Seccombe, "Marxism and Demography," *New Left Review* I, no. 137 (1983): 44.
43 Marx, *Grundrisse* (1973), 524.
44 E.P. Thompson, "Time, Work-Discipline, and Industrial Capitalism," (1967): 56–97.
45 Mintz, *Sweetness and Power* (1985), 130.

its implications have yet to be extended to capitalism in the web of life. If we are to grasp the temporal contradiction between life and capital as a limit of capitalist civilization, then we can no longer stay within the Nature/Society binary. It becomes impossible to say that *external* Nature is the limit of civilization—for the very good reason that such limits are co-produced by humans within nature as a whole. Nature is co-produced. Capitalism is co-produced. Limits are co-produced.

If the great concern of environmental historians has, to this point, been space,[46] it is now possible to consider space-in-time (and time-in-space). Hence, the centrality of work. Central to the law of value is the drive is to reduce socially necessary turnover time of capital to zero—an ambition that comes closest to reality in the high-frequency currency trading of the twenty-first century. This drive to reduce the turnover time of capital to zero is, in fact, a pivotal moment in the environmental history of capitalism, reaching beyond the domains of production, exchange, transportation, and communication.[47] The annihilation of space by time transforms all life and space within the law of value's gravitational pull. Consider, for instance, the "factory farming" revolution in meat production. This revolution effected the transition from the 73-day chicken in 1955 to the 42-day chicken in 1995 in North America.[48] Perhaps even more dramatically, we can see this revolution in the transformation of pork production in China, where the 12-month pig in 1978 had become a 6-month pig by 2011.[49] Here the "factory *as* environment" is on full display.[50]

Is it so different for human workers? The danger is to see "factory farming" as an environmental question and "factory production" as a social question. But such dualism simply obscures too many questions in capitalism's production of time, space, and nature. The transition from Fordist to neoliberal meatpacking in the United States—we may recall the nineteenth-century origins of the modern assembly line in American meatpacking[51]—was a transition from well-paid and reasonably safe work to low-paid and highly dangerous work after 1980. This transformation not only rendered meatpacking the most dangerous industrial job in America, but radically undermined food safety, as outbreaks of

---

46   But see Cronon, *Nature's Metropolis* (1991).

47   Harvey, *The Condition of Postmodernity* (1989); Warf, *Time-Space Compression* (2008).

48   W. Boyd, "Making Meat," *Technology and Culture* 42, no. 4 (2002): 631–64.

49   M. Schneider, *Feeding China's Pigs* (Minneapolis: Institute for Agriculture and Trade Policy, 2011); M. MacDonald and S. Iyer, *Skillful Means: The Challenges of China's Encounter with Factory Farming* (New York: BrighterGreen, 2011).

50   C. Sellers, "Factory as Environment," *Environmental History Review* 18, no. 1 (1994): 55–83.

51   Cronon, *Nature's Metropolis* (1991).

bacterial contamination proliferated.[52] Given the centrality of Cheap labor-power, we might also point out the centrality of Latino immigrants in the neoliberal meatpacking sector. The delivery of this Cheap Labor was made possible by a two-pronged class offensive. One was carried out within national boundaries, resulting in the simultaneous destruction of the agrarian petite bourgeoisie and industrial working-class power[53]—in this case, the medium-sized family pork farmers and highly-organized meatpacking workers.[54] The other movement of class struggle assumed a neocolonial and neoliberal character, as Mexico's agrarian order was progressively destabilized, especially after 1994. The annihilation of space by time—and its coordinates in the new configuration of space-time and time-space—signals the accumulation of capital, the pursuit of power, and the co-production of nature . . . *all at the same time*!

This acceleration of historical change—the time-space compression of life and space[55]—is hardly of recent vintage. It was part and parcel of the rise of capitalism.[56] The rise of "abstract time" was central; the annihilation of space by time could occur only when temporality could be grasped as an "independent" variable.[57] Independent of what? In the first instance, independent of land productivity as the basis of civilization. When power resided in the control of land, as in feudal Europe or Song China, civilizational time was the time of the seasons, of sowings and harvests, births and deaths, of "cataclysms and festivals."[58] It was an irregular sort of time. Even here, we should remember that women and men, in power and in everyday life, actively co-produced time; they were not passive subjects of "natural" cycles. Nevertheless, the influence of the latter was strong, and in such civilizations, either the capacity or the motivation (or both) to create abstract time was lacking. Those capacities and motivations would begin to shift in fourteenth-century Europe. The first mechanical clocks appeared at the end of the thirteenth century, and over the long

---

52   L. Gouveia and A. Juska, "Taming Nature, Taming Workers," *Sociologia Ruralis* 42, no. 4 (2002): 370–90.

53   K. Moody, *An Injury to All* (London: Verso, 1988); C. MacLennan and R. Walker, "Crisis and Change in U.S. Agriculture," in *Agribusiness in the Americas*, ed. R. Burbach and P. Flynn (New York: Monthly Review Press, 1980), 21–40.

54   Food and Water Watch, *The Economic Cost of Food Monopolies*, (Washington, D.C.: Food and Water Watch), 2012; P.J. Rachleff, *Hard-Pressed in the Heartland* (Boston: South End Press, 1993).

55   Harvey, *The Condition of Postmodernity* (1989).

56   Moore, "Ecology and the Rise of Capitalism" (2007); Warf, *Time-Space Compression* (2008), 40–77.

57   Postone, *Time, Labor, and Social Domination* (1993).

58   G.J. Whitrow, *Time in History* (Oxford: Oxford University Press, 1989), 110.

fourteenth-century crisis, clocks would become a feature of everyday life in urban-industrial Europe. This transition from clocks to clock-*time* was indeed novel. This was less a matter of technology than of *technics*—a clock is clock. It becomes clock-*time*, converging technology, power, and nature, only under definite circumstances.[59]

A civilization premised on money and labor-time called forth a very different kind of time. On balance, European feudalism remained in the pre-modern pattern of boom and bust, premised on dynamics of land productivity, frontier expansion, and lord-peasant relations. But it was also a civilization premised on an extraordinary fragmentation of power and wealth. This allowed for new concentrations of proletarianization and manufacturing, especially from the later thirteenth century, that prefigured the rise of capitalism. "Great clothing towns such as Douai, Ypres or Brussels . . . [could be compared to] one vast factory," with bells regulating the start and end of the working day.[60] By the early fourteenth century, bell-time would retreat before the rapid advance of clock-time; this was still something short of abstract time, but it was also something increasingly removed from the agrarian-time of the tenth century. By the middle of the fourteenth century, "the uniform hour of sixty minutes soon . . . [replaced] the day as the fundamental unit of labour time in the textile industry." The new, time-segmented working day became the object of intense class struggles during the protracted feudal crisis.[61] Indeed, it is in this era of epochal crisis that we find the origins of the idea of labor *productivity* with its sensibility that "time is money."[62]

By the end of the fourteenth century, clock-time, with its 60-minute hours, "was firmly established in the major urbanized areas of western Europe, replacing the day as the basic unit of time."[63] And if the first stirrings of abstract time had originated in monasteries, by 1370—at least in France—clock-time was

---

59   And so, for example, Su Sung, in eleventh-century China, had invented a mechanical clock, but one designed for the Emperor, not for everyday life. J. Needham, et al., *Heavenly Clockwork: The Great Astronomical Clocks of Medieval China*, 2nd ed. (Cambridge: Cambridge University Press, 1986 [1960 orig.]).

60   E.M. Carus-Wilson, "The Woolens Industry," in *The Cambridge Economic History of Europe*, Vol. 2, eds. M. Postan and E.E. Rich (Cambridge: Cambridge University Press, 1952), 644.

61   G.J. Whitrow, *Time in History* (Oxford: Oxford University Press, 1989), 108; J. Le Goff, *Time, Work and Culture in the Middle Ages* (Chicago: University of Chicago Press, 1980), 43–52.

62   D. Landes, *The Wealth and Poverty of Nations* (New York: W.W. Norton, 1998), 49–50.

63   J. Le Goff, *Time, Work and Culture in the Middle Ages* (Chicago: University of Chicago Press, 1980), 49.

relentlessly secularized: "the new time . . . [had become] the time of the state."[64] What distinguished this new time was not simply its linearity and regularity, but the ways in which time was represented as "exterior to life."[65] The clock (as *technics*) did for time what Renaissance perspective did for space. It "dissociate[d] time from human events and . . . create[d] the belief in an independent world of mathematically measurable sequences."[66]

By the advent of the long sixteenth century, the outward thrust of European capitalists and states fused clock-time with "merchant's time" in its broader sense.[67] We began to see new forms of world-time—abstract time—that were more than "merely a means of keeping track of the hours." Abstract time became a means of "synchronizing the actions of men" and nature,[68] in a new tapestry of money, commodity production, and state power.

This "revolution in time"[69] underpinned early capitalism's revolution in space, and the sharp acceleration of landscape change that occurred after 1450 (see Chapter Seven). This acceleration is rooted in the historical relation of value as a utopian project, which has real-world correspondence in the acceleration of environmental change: hence the importance of capital's correspondence project. This project, as we have seen, seeks to reduce the time of life to the time of accumulation. This is obviously impossible. Nevertheless, the desire for instantaneous capitalism animates the grim compulsions of world accumulation. It is, then, not only the "radical simplification" of landscapes and other natures that reveals the law of value at work; it is also the drive to make the "time of nature" ever closer to the "time of capital."

This is capitalism's *correspondence project*, through which capital seeks to remake reality in its own image, and according to its own rhythms. Agricultural landscapes become exhausted because capital must extract unpaid work faster than agro-ecological relations can reproduce themselves. Working classes become exhausted because capital must extract surplus labor as fast as possible. Particular capitalists might gain in the process, but over time, *capital as a whole suffers* because the system-wide capitalization of reproduction costs proceeds apace. The share of unpaid work declines. The ecological surplus falls.

---

64   Ibid., 50.

65   A.J. Gurevich, "Time as a Problem of Cultural History," in *Cultures and Time,* ed. L. Gardet, et al. (Paris: UNESCO Press, 1976), 241.

66   Mumford, *Technics and Civilization* (1934), 15.

67   Le Goff, *Time, Work and Culture in the Middle Ages* (1980).

68   Mumford, *Technics and Civilization* (1934), 14.

69   Landes, *Revolution in Time* (1983).

THE RISE AND DEMISE OF CHEAP NATURE: THE NEOLIBERAL MOMENT

Can the tendency of the ecological surplus to fall be seen during the neoliberal era? We may recall that a high world-ecological surplus represents a ratio of low capitalization to high appropriation. This is a necessary condition for the revival of accumulation. The neoliberal "boom" that commenced after 1983 was accompanied—or preceded—by a significant cyclical decline in food, energy, and resource prices. Commodity prices for food declined 39 percent— and metals by half—between 1975 and 1989. Meanwhile, oil stabilized by 1983, for the next twenty years, at a price per barrel about twice that of the postwar era.[70]

But it was not only extra-human natures that became Cheap.

The 1980s revival of accumulation also turned on Cheap Labor. This entailed an accumulation regime that could supply both paid and unpaid work in sufficient volumes to restore accumulation. In formal terms, re-establishing Cheap Labor meant reducing the value of labor-power. This was not easy to accomplish. There were five key dimensions of the neoliberal project to restore Cheap Labor after 1973. The first was wage repression. Bourgeoisies across the Global North began to organize as a class, and moved aggressively against trade unions following the 1974–1975 recession.[71] Wage repression was especially important as labor productivity growth sagged in the 1970s, a deceleration that increasingly looks permanent.[72] Second, the falling rate of profit in American industry—induced both by labor's class power and the rising organic composition of capital—led American and other capitalists to move rapidly towards the "global factory" in the 1970s.[73] This was a tectonic shift in world history that entailed the simultaneous de-industrialization of core zones and

---

70   P. McMichael, "Global Development and the Corporate Food Regime," in *New Directions in the Sociology of Global Development*, ed. F.Htel and P. McMichael (Oxford: Elsevier, 2005). M. Radetzki, "The Anatomy of Three Commodity Booms," *Resources Policy* 31 (2006): 56–64. D. van der Mensbrugghe, et al., "Macroeconomic Environment and Commodity Markets," in *Looking Ahead in World Food and Agriculture*, ed. P. Conforti (Rome: FAO, 2011). MGI [McKinsey Global Institute], "MGI's Commodity Price Index—an Interactive Tool," (2014), www.mckinsey.com.

71   Moody, *An Injury to All* (1988).

72   R.J. Gordon, "Revisiting U.S. Productivity Growth over the Past Century with a View of the Future" (Working Paper 15834, Cambridge: National Bureau Of Economics Research, 2010); R.J. Gordon, "Is U.S. Economic Growth Over?" (2012).

73   R. Barnet, *The Lean Years* (New York: Simon and Schuster, 1980); D.M. Gordon, et al., *Segmented Work, Divided Workers* (Cambridge: Cambridge University Press, 1982).

the rapid industrialization of the Global South.[74] Third, the global factory depended upon the "great global enclosure" that commenced in the early 1980s.[75] These global enclosures, realized through structural adjustment programs and market liberalization, restructured agrarian class relations worldwide, dispossessing hundreds of millions of peasants worldwide. In China alone, some 200–300 million migrants moved from countryside to city.[76] This new global proletariat dwarfed any that had come before it. In concert with the opening of Russia, China, and India to the world market, the world proletariat doubled after 1989.[77] Fourth, this "great doubling" represented an even greater expansion of the female proletariat, adding paid work on top of unpaid work on an unprecedented scale. Neoliberal proletarianization was, in this reckoning, an unprecedented global expansion of Hochschild's "second shift".[78] Finally—and almost universally ignored by environmentalists—Cheap Labor was made possible through a new regime of "forced underconsumption," manifested in wage repression in the North and declining well-being across the South (China excepted).[79]

By 2003, the world-ecological surplus stopped rising, and began to decline. Registered by the slow-, then fast-moving, commodity boom, this was the signal crisis of neoliberalism as a way of organizing nature. This expression of crisis signals the beginning of a cyclical contraction of the ecological surplus; its clearest indicator was the rising price of metals, energy, and food commodity prices. But this was not just any commodity boom, not least because of its unusual durability—although past its peak in terms of prices (at least for now), it remains a "boom" in the sense that prices remain considerably above their 1980–2000 averages. What does this seemingly endless commodity boom indicate? At a minimum, the peculiar character of this boom—which included more primary commodities, lasted longer, and saw more price volatility than any previous commodity boom in modern world history[80]—indicates an exhaustion of neoliberalism's Cheap Nature strategy. Notably, neoliberalism's strategies for reducing the Big Four input prices began to falter at least five years prior to the financial events of 2008. Economists talk of this very long commodity boom as a "supercycle"—a decades-long increase

---

74   G. Arrighi, et al., "Industrial Convergence, Globalization, and the Persistence of the North-South Divide," *Studies in Comparative International Development* 38, no. 1 (2003): 3–31.

75   F. Araghi, "The Great Global Enclosure of Our Times" (2000).

76   M. Webber, "The Dynamics of Primitive Accumulation," *Environment and Planning A* 44, no. 3 (2012): 560–579.

77   Freeman, "What Really Ails Europe (and America)" (2005).

78   Hochschild, *The Second Shift* (1989).

79   Araghi, "Accumulation by Displacement" (2009).

80   World Bank, *Global Economic Prospects 2009* (2009).

in basic commodity prices. But so far, they have invoked an abstract "world of scarcity"[81] rather than consider the possibility that today's supercycle represents a historical limit to capitalism's *longue durée* regime of Cheap Nature.

Suggestive of such co-produced limits is the erosion of Cheap Labor. In other words, the signal crisis of neoliberalism is not merely a question of extra-human natures—reflected in the commodity boom—but of human nature too. In China, real wages increased 300 percent between 1990 and 2005.[82] Manufacturing wages grew six times faster than the rate of inflation, and unit labor costs rose 85 percent between 2000 and 2011.[83] Rising unit labor costs are all the more peculiar given the spectacular increase in labor productivity: output per Chinese worker grew 7.2 percent annually between 1993 and 2013.[84]

Meanwhile, the usual strategy of moving to Cheap Labor frontiers—seeking new streams of unpaid work in support of low-wage workers—is in motion, but with diminishing returns. Within China, the government's "Go West" policy, which aimed to attract industry to the interior, has narrowed labor costs between interior and coastal regions to a "surprisingly . . . paltry wage differential."[85] Rural-to-urban migration has slowed considerably in recent years.[86] By 2012, per capita foreign investment in Cambodia moved ahead of China.[87] But Cambodia is much smaller than China, which is part of the broader problem: the frontiers are shrinking at the very moment when capital needs ever-greater commodity frontiers to resolve the overaccumulation problem. Meanwhile, the very information and communication technologies that have made possible global production are now also being used in the class struggle:

> Workers in Cambodia today have begun syndical action after only a few years, not after twenty-five. There are strikes and pressure for higher wages and benefits, which they are receiving. This of course reduces the value for the multinationals of moving to Cambodia, or Myanmar, or Vietnam, or the

81   Jacks, "From Boom to Bust?" (2013).

82   Midnightnotes.org, "Promissory Notes. From Crisis to Commons" (2009).

83   USDC [United States Department of Commerce], "Assess Costs Everywhere" (2013). Accessed April 24, 2013, acetool.commerce.gov/labor-costs.

84   ILO [International Labour Office], *Global Employment Trends 2014: Risk of a Jobless Recovery?* (Geneva: International Labour Office, 2014), 52.

85   J. Scott, "Who Will Take Over China's Role as the World's Factory Floor?" *Saturna Sextant Newsletter* (August 2011), 1.

86   B. Fegley, "30 Years of Double-Digit Chinese Growth," *From the Yardarm* 7, no. 1 (2013).

87   K. Bradsher, "Wary of China, Companies Head to Cambodia," *New York Times* (April 8, 2013).

Philippines. It now turns out that the savings of moving from China are not all that great.[88]

The ongoing erosion of Cheap Labor is not exclusively an East Asian story. Less well understood, but no less significant, is the transition across the Global North to a "second (and third) shift"—wage work plus unpaid reproductive labor. This transition enacted and embodied one of the last great commodity frontiers of historical capitalism. Unpaid household work has been a pillar of endless commodification since the sixteenth century.[89] In the Global North, and especially in North America, after 1970 we witnessed the accelerated proletarianization of women. This marked the demise of the Fordist one-income family and the rise of the "flexible" two-income household. This 1970s acceleration had been prefigured by Soviet developmentalism,[90] and also by the fast entry of American women into paid work since the 1930s.[91] These, too, were commodity frontiers, marked by the progressive commodification of work-potential and the progressive appropriation of (human) nature's "free gifts." Hence the imposition of multiple "shifts," and the double squeeze on women's time via the simultaneously operating pressures of capitalization and appropriation; even as early as the mid-1960s a growing number of married American women had traded in their 55-hour work week at home for the 76-hour work week at home and (paid) work.[92] If this were all—as in Hochschild's[93] rendering of the commodity frontier—there would be little to add. What the theory of the commodity frontier illuminates is not only the pattern of successively paired commodifying/appropriating movements, but the finite opportunities inscribed in each such movement. In the United States, the extraordinarily rapid increase in mothers' labor force participation—50 percent between 1975 and 1995[94]—was not only a

88   I. Wallerstein, "End of the Road for Runaway Factories?" Commentary 351 (April 15, 2013). Accessed November 14, 2013), www2.binghamton.edu/fbc/commentaries/archive-2013/351en.htm.

89   M. Mies, *Patriarchy and Accumulation* (1986).

90   M. Sacks, "Unchanging Times," *Journal of Marriage and Family* 39, no. 4 (1977): 793–805.

91   C. Goldin, "Gender Gap," in *The Concise Encyclopedia of Economics,* ed. D.R. Henderson (2008). Accessed May 1, 2013, www.econlib.org/library/Enc/GenderGap.html.

92   H.I. Hartmann, "The Family as the Locus of Gender, Class, and Political Struggle," *Signs* 6, no. 3 (1981): 366–94.

93   A. Hochschild, "The Commodity Frontier," (Working Paper No. 1, Center for Working Families, University of California, Berkeley, 2002).

94   BLS (Bureau of Labor Statistics), "Labor Force Participation Rate of Mothers, 1975–2007," *The Editor's Desk,* (January 8, 2009). Accessed May 1, 2013, www.bls.gov/opub/ted/2009/jan/wk1/art04.htm.

powerful moment of neoliberal wage repression while maintaining effective (consumer) demand; it was also a one-shot deal. The commodity frontier is a one-way ticket. Frontiers, once appropriated and commodified, are no longer frontiers. They do, however, move on, as we have seen in the rollout of the proletarian relation for women across the Global South since the 1980s.[95]

CONCLUSION

The appropriation of unpaid domestic labor and extra-human nature's bounty—*both* unpaid work—is not a residual of real production in capitalism. Rather the cyclical and relentless expansion of the zone of appropriation of unpaid work is, along with the revolutionizing of commodity production, the decisive requirement of accumulation. The imperative faced by capital to expand the zone of unpaid work faster than the capitalization of the *oikeios* is the historical basis through which capitalist power lumped together the epoch-making appropriations of "women, nature, and colonies."[96] Without women, nature, and colonies—a stylized list, to be sure—accumulation falters. The appropriation of de-valued work must necessarily outweigh the capitalization of work, lest the costs of the Big Four inputs (labor-power, food, energy, raw materials) begin to rise, and opportunities for accumulation through commodity production and exchange (M-C-M´) begin to decline.

The possibility of the "end" of Cheap Labor can only be adequately understood through the central systemic nexus of the capitalist division of labor: the relation between food and labor-power. To this we now turn.

---

95   N. Kabeer, *Marriage, Motherhood and Masculinity in the Global Economy* (IDS Working Paper 290, Institute for Development Studies, University of Sussex, 2007); McMichael, *Development and Social Change*, 5th ed. (2012).

96   M. Mies, *Patriarchy and Accumulation* (1986).

CHAPTER 10

The Long Green Revolution: The Life and Times of Cheap Food in the Long Twentieth Century

The road to the modern world has been paved with Cheap Food. Cheap Food was, of course, always cheap food *for some*. Even during neoliberalism's era of low commodity prices, close to one-third of humanity suffered from some form of malnutrition.[1] As Araghi quips, there has been only *one* "food" regime. The others? *Hunger* regimes.[2]

Cheap Food has been a recurrent condition for the revival of accumulation in successive eras of capitalism. Neoliberalism was no exception. The cheapest food in world history was realized after the crises of the 1970s. Cheap Food, in concert with strategies that re-stabilized energy, raw materials, and labor-power, enabled the revival of accumulation that began in the early 1980s. The commodity boom of 2003–2012—led by a tightly linked food/fuel nexus[3]—signaled the erosion of these Four Cheaps and the ensuing collapse of investment opportunities. For this reason, the commodity boom represents the *signal crisis* of neoliberalism. A signal crisis announces the tipping point in the regime's capacity to appropriate unpaid work/energy: in other words, to deliver strategic inputs in a way that reduces, rather than increases, the system-wide costs of production. What remains to be seen is whether the present *conjoncture* is exclusively a tipping point of neoliberal capitalism, or if the exhaustion of the Four Cheaps also signals the exhaustion of the *longue durée* regime of Cheap Nature.

What is Cheap Food? More calories produced with less average labor-time in the commodity system. In this context, "more calories" and "less labor-time" refers to the long-run trend: more and more calories, less and less socially necessary labor-time. The price of food is so important because it conditions the value of labor-power. Capitalist agriculture has not only increased productivity and reduced the wage-bill, but made possible the dynamic pairing of

---

1   T. Weis, *The Global Food Economy* (London: Zed, 2007).

2   F. Araghi, "The End of Cheap Ecology and the Future of 'Cheap Capital'" (Paper presented to the Annual Meeting of the Political Economy of World-Systems Section of the American Sociological Association, University of California-Riverside, April 11–13, 2013).

3   J. Baffes, "A Framework for Analyzing the Interplay Among Food, Fuels, and Biofuels," *Global Food Security* 2, no. 2 (2013): 110–16.

proletarianization and rising productivity. It has done so by setting "free" peasants and others once tied to the land, at the same time as it has reduced the cost (value composition) of labor-power, which facilitates a rising rate of exploitation even in the absence of significant technical advance.

Capitalism and the centrality of cheap food

The relation between capitalism and agriculture has been a remarkable one. Unlike previous civilizations, capitalism organized a series of extraordinary expansions of the food surplus premised on rising labor productivity. We call these expansions agricultural revolutions. Pre-capitalist civilizations could and did effect significant expansions of the food surplus. But they were not premised on a state- and market-enforced productivity model. Consequently, the "golden ages" of these civilizations invariably turned to crisis so long as cultivation remained in the hands of peasants, who could not be dispossessed for their low productivity. In contrast, capitalism achieved its long-run expansion by imposing bourgeois property relations on the countryside, compelling the transition from peasant producer to capitalist farmer. With the transition to capitalism, the new property relations propelled a process of dispossession and differentiation that enabled rising labor productivity in agriculture and a rising food surplus.

There have certainly been non-capitalist modes of cultivation that have achieved very high levels of food production with very modest effort. Where an average "worker-hour" in English agriculture around 1800 yielded about 2,600 calories, dominated by milk and wheat, around the same time, the average "worker-hour" in Brazilian swidden agriculture, centered on manioc, maize, and sweet potatoes, yielded 7,000–17,600 calories.[4] But nowhere was rising labor productivity in agriculture realized over such a *longue durée*, and over such vast geographies, until the rise of capitalism.[5] This rising agricultural productivity was shaped and reinforced by agrarian class structures that expelled "superfluous" populations from the land. It was the essential condition for creating vast reservoirs of Cheap labor-power, and vast agricultural surpluses to keep this labor fed, and relatively cheap. From the Dutch and English agricultural revolutions of the early modern era, to the family farm and Green Revolutions of the nineteenth and twentieth centuries, the bloody expropriations of capital have justified themselves on the basis of this signal achievement.

---

4   G. Clark, *Farewell to Alms* (Princeton: Princeton University Press, 2007), 67–8.

5   Moore, "Ecology and the Rise of Capitalism" (2007); R. Brenner, "Agrarian Class Structure and Economic Development" (1976); R. Brenner, "The Low Countries in the Transition to Capitalism," *Journal of Agrarian Change* 1, no. 2 (2001): 169–241.

Agricultural revolutions accomplished two big things. First, they yielded a quantum leap in the food surplus—a "surplus" because the expanded body of use-values is sufficiently large to drive down the *system-wide* costs of reproducing labor-power. The connection with the world proletariat is crucial. The cost of working-class reproduction is strongly conditioned by the price of food. One means of extracting surplus value more effectively is therefore the reduction of the value of food, and reducing the value composition of food works not only through the exploitation of labor-power, but also through the appropriation of unpaid work/energy. This is the real historical specificity of Cheap Food.

Second, agricultural revolutions have been central to the successive rise of the Dutch, British, and American hegemonies in capitalism. Food and agriculture is about world power no less than world accumulation. Hegemonies are ecological projects, and each great power wove together internal *and* external agricultural revolutions in the drive to world primacy.

It is difficult to see these two accomplishments in the history of neoliberalism. Historically, ascendant hegemonic powers have led an agricultural revolution that yielded a quantum leap in the delivery of Cheap Food to a critical mass of the world proletariat—the Dutch in the sixteenth and seventeenth centuries, the English in the seventeenth and eighteenth centuries, the Americans in the nineteenth and twentieth centuries.[6] These revolutions were, in Arrighi's sense of the term, 'organizational revolutions',[7] unfolding at multiple scales and extending from innovations in the forces of production to class formation to new forms of credit and transport.

Not only has the neoliberal era been characterized by a progressive slowing of agricultural productivity growth, we can see on the horizon signs of an unprecedented reversal. Is the neoliberal world order—in the midst of a signal but not yet terminal crisis—leading capitalism towards what Braudel once called an "agricultural revolution in reverse"?[8] In this, the longest chapter of this book, we will chart the rise—and systemic unraveling today—of the Cheap Food model that has made the modern world possible.

Until the late twentieth century, every epoch-making "economic miracle" rested upon an epoch-making agricultural revolution sufficient not merely to feed itself, but also to lead the world. Each world hegemony provided a new model of

---

6   R. Brenner, "The Low Countries in the Transition to Capitalism" (2001); H. Friedmann, "World Market, State, and Family Farm", *Comparative Studies in Society and History* 20, no. 4 (1978): 545–586; R.A. Walker, *The Conquest of Bread* (New York: New Press, 2004).

7   Arrighi, *The Long Twentieth Century* (1994).

8   F. Braudel, *The Mediterranean and the Mediterranean World in the Age of Philip II*, Vol. I (1972), 427.

agricultural development: the Dutch Republic was the 'mecca' of agricultural knowledge for Europe in the seventeenth century.[9] Later, the English and then the Americans would dispense, by means fair and foul, their agronomic wisdom to the rest of the world in the nineteenth and twentieth centuries.[10] If we are indeed confronting a crisis of the American model of global agriculture—the successive transformations of the "long" Green Revolution that began in the 1930s[11]—then the crisis of American hegemony and crisis of world agriculture may be much more tightly connected than usually supposed.

THE TWO REVOLUTIONS OF INDUSTRIAL AGRICULTURE:
FROM THE AMERICAN WEST TO THE LONG GREEN REVOLUTION

We may recall from Chapter Five the developmental crisis of the long eighteenth century. The whole of Europe—and England especially—saw food prices rise and real wages fall sharply between the 1740s and the end of the Napoleonic Wars in 1815.[12] From this developmental crisis emerged a new way of organizing capitalist agriculture: *industrial agriculture.*

England's seventeenth-century agricultural revolution—our classic frame of reference—was not 'simply' the expression of convertible husbandry, new drainage systems, new class structures, new property relations, and so forth. These could do their epochal work only on the basis of a double movement of geographical expansion. The first was an "inner" conversion of nitrogen-rich pasture into arable land, opening a nitrogen frontier internal to England.[13] The second was an "outer" conversion of the English Caribbean into sugar plantation monocultures. English, then British, capitalism thrived on the basis of this double movement. The industrial revolution took shape on its basis, the first movement issuing labor surpluses;[14] the second, capital surpluses.[15]

By   1760,   this   agricultural   revolution   was   showing   signs   of

9   D.B. Grigg, *The Agricultural Systems of the World* (Cambridge: Cambridge University Press, 1974) 165.

10   R. Drayton, *Nature's Government* (New Haven: Yale University Press, 2001); J.R. Kloppenburg, Jr., *First the Seed* (1988).

11   R. Patel, "The Long Green Revolution," *Journal of Peasant Studies* 40, no. 1 (2013): 1–63.

12   B.H. Slicher van Bath, *The Agrarian History of Western Europe* (1963), 222–36.

13   M. Overton, *Agricultural Revolution in England* (Cambridge: Cambridge University Press, 1996).

14   Brenner, "Agrarian Class Structure and Economic Development in Pre-Industrial Europe" (1976).

15   R. Blackburn, *The Making of New World Slavery* (London: Verso, 1997).

exhaustion—especially within England. Per-acre yield growth stagnated after mid-century. Most European agriculture experienced the same. Was this a case of "soil exhaustion"—not enough nutrients to sustain rising productivity? Yes and no. Capitalist agriculture tends to exhaust the soil, though this varies enormously by crop and soil type. So soil structure and nutrient composition is always in play whenever we see a faltering agricultural model. At the same time, our best guide to interpreting the late eighteenth-century agricultural impasse—one with striking parallels to our present conjuncture—is to examine the exhaustion of the English agricultural revolution as a double internality. For Pomeranz, the impasse is best understood as one of socio-ecological organization rather than a narrow problem of resource depletion:

> Per-acre and total yields from arable land remain[ed] flat and the threat of decline constant, until Britain began mining, importing, and later synthesizing fertilizer mostly after 1850 . . . [A]lthough the English studied continental practices, classical agricultural manuals, and their own experiments very intently, much of what they learned about how best to maintain soil fertility while increasing yields was not actually applied in England, because it involved highly labour-intensive methods and English capitalist farmers . . . were intent on labour-cost minimization and profit maximization. The methods they adopted instead, which raised labour productivity, represented a *fundamental break with much of the literature on best farming practices and actually interfered with preserving soil fertility in many cases.*[16]

This was no case of "natural limits." Rather, what appeared as a biophysical impasse was itself a co-produced limit of capitalist relations. Pomeranz's explanation focuses on the calculations of capitalist farmers, but may be reinterpreted from the standpoint of capital as a whole. Until off-farm phosphates became available after the Napoleonic wars,[17] the only way to significantly raise land yields was through labor-intensification. To some degree, this course was followed, as work hours increased sharply—in both countryside and city—during the second half of the eighteenth century.[18] What is most striking about the general pattern—more hours worked with no change in per capita consumption—is that it was most pronounced in agriculture, where hours during the labor-intensive planting and harvest seasons were already long.[19] The solution

---

16 Pomeranz, *The Great Divergence* (2000), 216–17. Emphasis added.

17 F.M.L. Thompson, "The Second Agricultural Revolution, 1815–1880", *Economic History Review* 21, no. 1 (1968): 62–77.

18 H-J. Voth, "The Longest Years: New Estimates of Labor Input in England, 1760–1830," *Journal of Economic History* 61, no. 4 (2001): 1065–82.

19 R.C. Allen and J. L. Weisdorf. "Was There an 'Industrious Revolution' Before the

highlighted by Pomeranz—one that would have gone against the grain of "labor-cost minimization"—was the one thing on which British capitalism could not compromise. For such a turn would have moved labor back into agriculture at the moment such labor supplies were most needed, to propel both the industrialization drive and to meet the manpower demands of the war.

How, then, was Cheap Food restored after 1815? In a word, America.

The "first" industrial agriculture

The nineteenth century restoration of Cheap Food occurred through a combination of "productivity and plunder": new technical innovations, such as the steamship, railroads, and mechanization, combined with an extraordinary frontier movement across North America.[20] The breadbasket of capitalism would migrate, from Europe to the United States. This was an extraordinary development in human history; no civilization had relocated its agro-ecological heartland from one continent to another. This transition was the work of the "first" nineteenth century (c. 1763–1830s), an era of profound chaos and restructuring during which a new configuration of town and country emerged, "dripping with blood and dirt" (as Marx would say).[21] Peasants across the Atlantic world revolted against a worldwide surge of primitive accumulation—from Pugachev's revolt in Russia to a series of "back country" rebellions in North America[22]—aimed at deepening capital's hegemony over transatlantic agricultures. Nowhere was this more significant than in the nascent United States, whose modern political form takes shape through the Constitutional settlement of 1789, prompted by Shay's Rebellion (1786). For the creation of a strong centralized state was fundamental to the creation of a regime of abstract social nature—codified through successive Northwest Ordinances in the 1780s—that ensured the expanded reproduction of bourgeois property across the continent.[23] Thus do the class struggle, political geography, and agricultural revolution form an organic whole in successive eras of capitalist development.

Industrial and agricultural revolutions therefore unfold together, however unevenly. The full flower of English industrialization (1840s–1870s) occurred

---

Industrial Revolution? An Empirical Exercise for England, c. 1300–1830," *Economic History Review* 64, no. 3 (2011): 715–29.

20   Centrally, but also comprising cash-crop expansions via white settler colonialism worldwide (cf. P. McMichael, *Settlers and the Agrarian Question* [1984]).

21   Marx, *Capital*, Vol. I (1977), 926.

22   Wallerstein, *The Modern World-System III* (1989); T.P. Slaughter, *The Whiskey Rebellion* (1986).

23   C. Parenti, "The *Inherently* Environmental State: Nature, Territory, and Value" (Unpublished paper, Department of Global Liberal Arts, New York University, 2014).

just as the American Midwest became capitalism's newest breadbasket. There was a distinctive vortex of nature, capital, and cultivation at the dawn of this new, American-led, agricultural revolution. By the 1840s,

> European settlers finally broke the matted grasses with a steel plow, invented and manufactured by John Deere . . . The plow was drawn by animals, more like European farming than that of indigenous people. The draft animals of settlers and, the cattle herded by cowboys, filled the niche of the slaughtered native buffalo. Both exotic crops and animals had to be fenced. Lacking wood in the treeless plains, fencing awaited the invention of barbed wire. Dwellings . . . required the import of lumber. Plows, land, animals, materials to construct and enclose farms, all came from outside the farm and even the region. Cash was therefore scarcer and more pressing than natural fertility. Transplanted exotic humans were compelled from the beginning to grow and sell as much as possible. Mining the nutrients accumulated by nature over thousands of years, settler farmers, cowboys and ranchers could sell the products of transplanted species back to the Old World at cut-rate prices. However, soil that is not renewed is depleted. Settlers were more deeply embedded in markets than in the earthly cycles of the Great Plains.[24]

These earthly cycles were, however, not abolished but joined in a new synthesis. The history of agriculture is a co-productive, world-ecological affair: a history of how humans make the rest of nature, and of how nature makes human organization. That such co-production is regularly *forgotten*, in the myth of humanity's separation from nature, is an accomplishment of the Cheap Food regime: "by linking and integrating the products [and relations] of so many ecosystems and communities, [this regime] obscured the very connections it helped create."[25] The new synthesis, specific to the era of large-scale industry and its heirs, was agro-industrialization, or simply "industrial agriculture"—assuming both symbolic and material forms.[26] The first of two great phases of agro-industrialization began in the decades before the Civil War, not only feeding England but propelling American industrialization—beyond textiles, and in the capital-goods sector—after 1840.[27]

Agro-industrialization was, however, more than a mechanical affair. It was,

---

24 Friedmann, "What on Earth is the Modern World-System?" (2000): 491–2.

25 Cronon, *Nature's Metropolis* (1991), 256–7.

26 Weis, *The Global Food Economy* (2007); Weis, *Ecological Hoofprint* (2013).

27 C. Post, *The American Road to Capitalism* (Leiden: Brill, 2011); B. Page and R. Walker, "From Settlement to Fordism," *Economic Geography* 67, no. 4 (1991): 281–315.

pivotally, about deploying power, capital, and science to appropriate the wealth of a continent. American agriculture's extraordinary accomplishment in the nineteenth century was its capacity to harness continental space as central to rising labor productivity. Here was an agricultural revolution with little or no gains in land productivity: yields per hectare were the same for maize and wheat in 1930 as they had been in 1870.[28] Labor productivity, however, surged, especially for the big cereal crops. Labor-time in maize cultivation fell by nearly two-thirds in pre-harvest work, and one-half in harvesting, between 1840 and 1900.[29] It tumbled still further in the next three decades.[30] Off-farm revolutions in transport magnified productivity gains yet again, sharply reducing food prices before the Civil War.[31]

Although "biological innovation" and mechanization were responsible for a considerable measure of this advance, the decisive variable was the blood and dirt of the frontier. On the one hand, this was the frontier made possible through an extraordinary mix of violence and spatial rationalization. Yes, the land was cleared of troublesome natives. More significant over the long run, however, was the innovative production of new abstract social natures, above all, a new spatial grid and geological surveys that made the continent legible for capital accumulation. Thus the centrality of the American state in making this agricultural revolution possible. On the other hand, the Midwestern and Great Plains frontiers offered up millennia of accumulated nutrients (and water), which sustained industrial agriculture's rapid advance in the closing decades of the nineteenth century. Western Kansas wheat farmers in the 1870s enjoyed labor productivity that outstripped some European cultivators by an order of magnitude.[32] But within two decades, land productivity began to decline in western Kansas. In the 1920s, yields per acre were between one-quarter and one-half of the 1890s peak.[33] The "first" industrial agricultural model had exhausted itself by the early decades of the twentieth century, in large measure because the "soil mining" strategy—combined with rapid mechanization—became increasingly counterproductive as the frontier closed. If the first agro-industrial model consolidated

---

28   Kloppenburg, *First the Seed* (1988), 89.

29   W.N. Parker, *Europe, America, and the Wider World* (Cambridge: Cambridge University Press, 1991), 160, 174.

30   G. Smiley, "US Economy in the 1920s," in *EH.Net Encyclopedia*, ed. R. Whaples (2004). Accessed June 3, 2014, eh.net/encyclopedia/the-u-s-economy-in-the-1920s.

31   D.C. North, *The Economic Growth of the United States, 1790–1860* (New York: W.W. Norton, 1966).

32   G. Cunfer and F. Krausmann, "Sustaining Durée Fertility: Agricultural Practice in the Old and New Worlds," *Global Environment* 4 (2009): 29–30.

33   Ibid.; G. Cunfer, "Manure Matters on the Great Plains Frontier," *Journal of Interdisciplinary History* 34, no. 4 (2004): 539–67.

England as the workshop of the world, a new agro-industrial model would have to be found before America became the world's assembly line.

The "Long" Green Revolution

Often regarded as a Cold War project, the Green Revolution emerged first in the United States during the 1930s. Here was an agricultural revolution on the classic model: a series of interconnected organizational, technical, and agronomic innovations. These went beyond a series of modest technical adjustments to realize a *great* leap forward in the provision of Cheap Food. In so doing, such agricultural revolutions have enabled the revolutionary expansion of the world proletariat—and its subsequent low-cost reproduction—that accompanies a new long wave of accumulation.

It is difficult to overstate the success, in capitalist terms, of this long Green Revolution. Its global moment blossomed in the mid-1950s, with the U.S. Public Law 480 (1954) and Khrushchev's push to expand Soviet cereal output (1953). (Let us not forget that the Soviets learned industrial agriculture from the Americans![34]) Global cereal output more than doubled (126 percent) between 1950 and 1980.[35] Worldwide, grain yields per hectare grew 60 percent between 1960 and 1980, but much faster in the hot zones of the Green Revolution: 87 percent in India (for wheat), essentially the same yield growth for the U.S. in the midst of the hybrid corn revolution.[36] The world cereal trade expanded even faster. At the apex of "national" agricultures,[37] the cereal trade grew rapidly: more than tripling between 1952 and 1972, between the peak of food prices resulting from postwar reconstruction and the eve of the 1972–75 commodity boom.[38]

Cheap Food was produced, produced, and even "over"-produced: although for capital as a whole, food can never be too cheap. Food commodity prices

---

34   D.K. Fitzgerald, *Every Farm a Factory* (New Haven: Yale University Press, 2003).

35   Calculated from EPI [Earth Policy Institute], "Fertilizer Consumption and Grain Production for the World, 1950–2013" (2014). Accessed July 10, 2014, www.earth-policy.org/data_center/C24 .

36   Calculated from, respectively, EPI, "World Average Corn, Wheat, and Rice Yields, 1960–2012" (2013). Accessed July 10, 2014, www.earth-policy.org/data_center/C24; EPI, "Wheat Production, Area, and Yield in India 1960–2011" (2012). Accessed July 10, 2014, www.earth-policy.org/data_center/C24; W.W. Cochrane, *The Development of American Agriculture* (1979), 128.

37   H. Friedmann and P. McMichael, "Agriculture and the State System," *Sociologia Ruralis* 29, no. 2 (1989): 93–117.

38   A. Warman, *Corn and Capitalism* (Chapel Hill, NC: University of North Carolina Press, 2003).

declined 3 percent annually in the two decades after 1952—three times faster than the twentieth century average.[39] The real price of rice, maize, and wheat dropped 60 percent between 1960 and the end of the last century.[40] World market prices for staple foods fell steadily even as world urbanization—a rough-and-ready index of proletarianization—proceeded at breakneck speed.[41] Even after the crises of the early 1970s, the vitality of national farm sectors created through the Green Revolution provided strong yield growth for another decade. After 1982, they offered fertile terrain for conversion into neoliberal agro-export zones.[42] This postwar agricultural revolution ably meets our litmus test: a revolutionary expansion of the food surplus during a revolutionary expansion of the world proletariat.

We have sketched the accomplishments of the long Green Revolution. But how did this revolution work its magic?

The Green Revolution's core synthesis brought together the nineteenth century's dynamic family farm model with hybrid corn (maize), the biological pivot of a new property regime. The commercial introduction of hybrid maize in the U.S. in the mid-1930s produced rising yields per acre, and rising capitalization through mechanization and skyrocketing fertilizer (and then pesticide) use. Hybrid maize marked an early turning point in capital-oriented biological innovation. By crossing inbred lines of maize whose seed produced high yields but could not be reproduced, American seed companies severed the age-old connection between seed and grain.[43] Hybridization thus married bio-technical control to the coercive dispositions of market competition, chaining metropolitan farmers to the "vicious cycle . . . [of a] technological treadmill" and accelerated class differentiation.[44]

The "magic" of this Green Revolution was found in an old script with a new twist. The new model reshaped world power, accumulation, and nature through a new configuration of capitalization and appropriation, taking shape in the 1930s with the introduction of hybrid corn and new, higher-yielding strains of wheat.[45] The potential of the hybrid revolution was amplified by massive state funding of university-led

---

39   Calculated from K.O. Fuglie and S.L. Wang, "New Evidence Points to Robust but Uneven Productivity Growth in Global Agriculture," *Amber Waves* 10, no. 3 (2012): 2.

40   FAO, *World Agriculture Towards 2015/2030* (Rome: FAO, 2002).

41   J.A. Davis, "The European Economies in the Eighteenth century," in *An Economic History of Europe,* ed. A. Di Vittorio (New York: Routledge, 2006), 92–134.

42   P. McMichael, "Rethinking Globalization," *Review of International Political Economy* 4, no. 4 (1997): 630–62; D. Tilman, et al., "Agricultural Sustainability and Intensive Production Practices," *Nature* 418, no. 6898 (2002): 671–7.

43   Kloppenburg, *First the Seed* (1988), 91–129.

44   Ibid., 119.

45   Ibid.

agricultural research, with origins in the late nineteenth century, and a new phase of capitalization that included mechanization but went far beyond. Labor inputs fell by more than two-thirds, and mechanization rose 213 percent, between 1935 and 1970. Meanwhile fertilizer and pesticide inputs increased by an extraordinary 1,338 percent.[46] This was the "petrochemical-hybrid complex," systematically combining "new plants, fertilizers, pesticides, and irrigation schemes."[47]

The new hybrid corn raised yields more than fourfold between 1935 and 1980.[48] Labor productivity in American agriculture surged to 3.8 percent per year between 1929 and 1964, outpacing industry by more than 50 percent.[49] The hybrid revolution was, however, won at a heavy cost to farmer autonomy. Because hybrid crops, in contrast to open-pollinated ones, produce seed of inferior quality, hybridization "uncouples" seed from grain. This compelled farmers to make an annual pilgrimage to seed stores to purchase new seeds.[50] Hybridization was therefore a powerful strategic wedge, opening new opportunities for the capitalization of farming. American agriculture was radically—and rapidly—extroverted. The relation of market and non-market inputs in agricultural production inverted almost overnight. The share of purchased inputs more than doubled, while non-market inputs declined by over half, in the decades after 1935.[51] The immediate result was a rapid shake-out of uncompetitive farmers. Nearly four million *farms* disappeared between 1935 and 1970. By 1969, 219,000 farms—the top 7 percent—produced nearly 53 percent of total output.[52] Meanwhile, as non-agricultural employment skyrocketed—reaching 95 percent of the total by 1970[53]—spending on food dropped from 24 percent to 14 percent of average household income.[54] Here was the capitalization of nature at full throttle—and the even-faster appropriation of nature.

This rapid capitalization was made possible by an extraordinary alchemy: turning oil and natural gas into food. After 1935, farming was no longer just

---

46   Calculated from W.W. Cochrane, *The Development of American Agriculture* (1979), 130–1.

47   Walker, *The Conquest of Bread* (2004), 150–51.

48   Kloppenburg, *First the Seed* (1988), 89.

49   Calculated from Mandel, *Late Capitalism* (1975), 191.

50   Kloppenburg, *First the Seed* (1988), 93.

51   Kloppenburg, *First the Seed* (1988), 33; W.W. Cochrane, *The Development of American Agriculture* (1979), 129–32.

52   Cochrane (1979), 133–4.

53   G. Jacobs and I. Šlaus, "Global Prospects for Full Employment," *The Cadmus Journal* 1, no. 2 (2011): 61.

54   H. Elitzak, "Food Cost Review, 1950–97," *Agricultural Economic Report No. 780* (Food and Rural Economics Division, Economic Research Service, U.S. Department of Agriculture, 1999), 20.

farming. It was *petro*-farming.[55] The epoch-making geographical shift after the 1930s was, consequently, distinctive. Petro-farming allowed for a combination of frontiers—global and subterranean—to come into play. This was a quantum expansion in the repertoire of strategies associated with accumulation by appropriation. It multiplied the sources of potential unpaid work/energy as never before. The major transition was from inputs drawn primarily within farming regions to energy- and chemical-intensive inputs drawn from outside. This marked the great fertilizer and pesticide-herbicide revolution.

Two important transitions in capitalist agriculture followed. First, capitalist agriculture became massively *in*efficient in its energy use. Although long implicit in capitalist agriculture, the "second" American agricultural revolution after 1935—Year Zero of the long Green Revolution—exploded the labor/land energy budgets of the previous four centuries. Energy—*cheap* energy—was pivotal. This was the condition for the rapid advance of labor productivity. It took about 2.5 calories of energy to deliver a calorie of food in the 1930s. The ratio then moved sharply upwards, to 7.5:1 in the 1950s, and 10:1 by the early 1970s.[56] By the twenty-first century, fifteen-to-twenty calories were needed to deliver one calorie of food from farm to table, considerably more for globally sourced fruit.[57]

The second great transition inaugurated by the long Green Revolution was toxification. For the first time, agriculture became a leading agent of toxification. Pesticide and herbicide production increased by an order of magnitude between 1950 and 1980.[58] For many years, the poster child for this toxification was DDT (Dichloro-diphenyl-trichloroethane). Some 1.3 billion pounds of this pesticide—and powerful carcinogen—were used in the U.S. alone between 1945 and 1972.[59] Today, a billion pounds of pesticides and herbicides are used each year in American agriculture.[60] The long-recognized health impacts have been widely

---

55   Walker, *The Conquest of Bread* (2004).

56   J.S. Steinhart and C.E. Steinhart, "Energy Use in the U.S. Food System," *Science* 184, no. 4134 (1974): 307–16; D. Pimentel, et al., "Food Production and the Energy Crisis," *Science* 182 (1973), 443–9.

57   P. Canning, et al., "Energy Use in the U.S. Food System" (Economic Research Report Number 94, Washington: United States Department of Agriculture, 2010); T.L. Acker, et al., "Energy Inefficiency in Industrial Agriculture," *Energy Sources, Part B* 8, no. 4 (2013): 420–30.

58   D. Tilman, et al., "Agricultural Sustainability and Intensive Production Practices," *Nature* 418, no. 6898 (2002): 671–7.

59   EPA.gov, "DDT: A Review of Scientific and Economic Aspects of the Decision to Ban Its Use as a Pesticide" (Washington, D.C: United States Department of Commerce, 1975).

60   C. Cook, "The Spraying of America" (2005).

studied.[61] Although the translation of such "externalities" into the register of accumulation is imprecise, their scale is impressive, totaling nearly $17 billion in unpaid costs for American agriculture in the early twenty-first century.[62] This is a kind of "ecosystem services" *in reverse*. The capitalist mode of calculation favors, however, yet more toxification, barring a political response: $17 billion in health care costs, reckoned as externalities, is a paper tiger in the face of preventing an estimated $33 billion in annual weed-mediated losses[63]—losses that promise to increase rapidly apace with galloping climate change, as we will see later in this chapter.

The globalization of petro-farming—from Mexico to the Punjab—closely followed the American agricultural path, a crucial moment in the agrarian class struggles and geopolitics of the Cold War.[64] And yet, in this long Green Revolution, the decisive geographical shift was only secondarily global—if by global we implicate the *surface* of the earth. There *was* significant expansion of cropland, but this was not unprecedented: the pace of agricultural expansion between 1950 and 1980 was noticeably slower (.83 percent per annum) than it was between 1840 and 1880 (1.03 percent).[65] The really revolutionary act of the long Green Revolution was its subterranean thrust, sucking down prodigious volumes of cheap energy and cheap water. World agriculture appropriated water as nearly three times the pace of cropland expansion between 1950 and 1980.[66] In the U.S., the area planted in cereals actually declined while agriculture's water

61   Cf. R. Carson, *Silent Spring* (New York: Houghton Mifflin, 1962); A. Wright, *The Death of Ramón González* (Austin: University of Texas Press, 1990); D. Steingraber, *Living Downstream* (New York: Vintage, 1997).

62   E.M. Tegtmeier and M.D. Duffy, "External Costs of Agricultural Production in the United States," *International Journal of Agricultural Sustainability* 2, no. 1 (2004): 1–20.

63   T. Christopher, "Can Weeds Help Solve the Climate Crisis?" *New York Times* (June 29, 2008).

64   D.A. Sonnenfeld, "Mexico's 'Green Revolution,' 1940–1980," *Environmental History Review* 16, no. 4 (1992): 28–52; J.H. Perkins, *Geopolitics and the Green Revolution* (Oxford: Oxford University Press, 1997).

65   The FAO's estimate of cropland expansion between 1955 and 1995 is more modest, suggesting a rate of cropland expansion just half (.36 percent per annum) of Richards' estimate (calculated from FAO, 2000: 125). Calculated, respectively, from J.F. Richards, "Land Transformation," in *The Earth as Transformed by Human Action*, ed. B.L. Turner II, et al., (Cambridge: Cambridge University Press, 1990), 164; M.G. Mulhall, *The Dictionary of Statistics*, 4th ed. (London: Routledge, 1899), 7.

66   Calculated from above, and R.S. Chen, "Global Agriculture, Environment, and Hunger," *Environmental Impact Assessment Review* 10, no. 4 (1990): 335–38; USGS [United States Geological Survey], "Irrigation Water Use," (2014), Accessed July 18, 2014, water.usgs.gov/edu/wuir.html.

consumption increased 80 percent.[67] The appropriation of energy increased even faster. World fertilizer use rose 729 percent between 1950 and 1980, nearly nine times the rate of cropland expansion.[68] This was a geographical shift from the primarily horizontal to the primarily vertical: not from one continent to another, although the Green Revolution model *was* globalized, but—*primarily*—from one geological layer to another.

How did the long Green Revolution differ from previous agricultural revolutions? Like every agricultural revolution before it, the Green Revolution increased the world-ecological surplus, through the judicious (if brutal) reconfiguration of peasant ecologies, especially in South and Southeast Asia. In one sense, this had long been the pattern, as agricultural revolutions had always increased the ecological surplus through the appropriation of Cheap Nature. This was, as we have seen, the case with the "first" industrial agricultural revolution in the mid-nineteenth-century Midwest. And it was the case with the English and Dutch agricultural revolutions of the seventeenth and sixteenth centuries, alongside (neo)colonial revolutions in American sugar and Polish grain especially. In another sense, however, the Green Revolution did not fit the pattern, prefiguring the neoliberal agro-ecological impasse in the twenty-first century. For this revolution enjoyed lower biophysical 'rent' than its forerunners, and this goes far to explaining the high rate of investment and technical change in the later period. Relative to "first" industrial agriculture of the 1840s, the long Green Revolution set in motion during the 1930s represented a (modestly) less dramatic expansion of the ecological surplus. Capitalization increased much faster, and appropriation relatively slower, than in previous eras. Nevertheless, the mass of appropriated unpaid work/energy continued to rise relative to the mass of capital, because nature is very, *very* big and capital only began to deepen its global reach after 1945.

A big part of the Green Revolution's success—*where and when* it was successful on its own terms—was its combination of cutting-edge technology with low-cost land and labor. This drove down food prices and therefore, all things being equal, the cost of labor-power. In other words, Cheap Food relieved pressure on capital's wage bill, attenuating the falling rate of profit. Across the South, agriculture was subordinated to the industrialization drive, a hallmark of the American postwar development project.[69] At the level of appearances, we are treated, then, to something of an optical illusion—a new stream of capital inputs leads one to think of the Green Revolution in terms of capital-intensity. But

67   Ibid.

68   EPI, "Fertilizer Consumption and Grain Production for the World, 1950–2013," (2014). Accessed July 10, 2014, www.earth-policy.org/data_center/C24.

69   McMichael, *Development and Social Change*, 5th ed. (2012).

insofar as this "revolutionary" project appropriated, *at little or no cost to capital*, quality land, water access, and labor-power, the value composition of yields was in fact very low. Thus, Cheap Food. The long Green Revolution owed its revolutionary achievements to plunder as much as productivity.

FEEDING NEOLIBERALISM: AN UN-REVOLUTIONARY AGRICULTURAL REVOLUTION

The long Green Revolution sustained rising productivity at least a decade after the accumulation crisis of the 1970s. Because the historical geography of the long Green Revolution played out in successive phases on a planetary scale—tearing through successive "frontier" zones of uncapitalized nature—world agriculture continued to deliver significant food surpluses into the 1980s. This explains some measure of the rapid decline in food prices after 1975 that underwrote the initial phases of neoliberal restructuring. Between 1975 and 1989, world food prices declined 39 percent, and still further in the decade that followed.[70] As we know, the era of Cheap Food inaugurated in the mid-1970s came unraveled after 2002, a story we will pick up in the next section. For the moment, let us consider how Cheap Food was sustained after the 1970s, as agricultural productivity growth began to slow.

The sharp fall in food prices after 1975 reflected a peculiar sort of agricultural revolution. It *was* a revolution in the sense that more food was delivered for lower prices. In terms of productivity, however, it was most unrevolutionary. In contrast to previous agricultural revolutions, there has been no epoch-making advance in productivity since the 1970s. Indeed, quite the opposite. Yield growth has progressively slowed, despite the introduction of agro-biotechnology and the generalized deployment of fertilizers and other inputs.

Signs of productivity slowdown were evident from the mid-1980s.[71] Yield growth in American grain farming slowed after 1982, as did total output growth. This decline was modest—on the range of 10–15 percent between 1981 and 2004.[72] *Labor* productivity growth, however, slowed by more than a third in the period 1981–2004, relative to the previous four decades.[73] American cereal agriculture

---

70 McMichael, "Global Development and the Corporate Food Regime" (2005), 279; FAO, "FAO Food Price Index," (2009).

71 F.H Buttel, M. Kenney, and J.R Kloppenburg Jr., "From Green Revolution to Biorevolution," *Economic Development and Cultural Change* 34, no. 1 (1985): 31–55.

72 K.O. Fuglie, et al., "Productivity Growth in U.S. Agriculture," *Economic Brief* 9 (Washington, D.C.: US Department of Agriculture, Sep. 2007), 5; Calculations from EPI, "U.S. Grain Production, Area, Yield, and Stocks, 1960–2012," (2013). Accessed July 10, 2014, www.earth-policy.org/data_center/C24.

73 K.O. Fuglie, et al., "Productivity Growth in U.S. Agriculture", 5.

remained ahead of the curve relative to the North as a whole, where yield growth slowed a startling 79 percent between 1970–90 and 1990–2010.[74] Across the Global South, yield growth slowed by one-third in the decade after 1982, relative to the period 1967–82.[75] The decline was delayed in the case of wheat, but the fall was much more rapid. For Indian wheat, per hectare yield growth averaged 3.4 percent annually between 1982 and 1992, but fell to a paltry 0.6 percent over the next decade.[76] Indeed, per capita foodgrain consumption *declined* in India after 2002.[77] Rice's decline was slower but more significant, given its salience in South and East Asia's food supply. Wet rice cultivation saw its yield growth fall from 2.5 percent a year between 1962 and 1982, to just, 0.8 percent annually in the next three decades.[78] In spite of all this, and rising demand from an expanding world proletariat food prices continued to fall until 2002.[79]

Given the progressive slowdown in agricultural productivity, we should rightly ask: How was Cheap Food restored after 1975? To answer this question we must move from agro-ecology into the core concerns of political economy.

The cumulative woes of Pax Americana reached a tipping point in the early 1970s. Nixon closed the Federal Reserve's Gold Window in 1971. A commodity boom in metals and food began in 1972, joined by a massive oil price spike in late 1973. "Raw materials prices rose more sharply during an eighteen-month period between 1972 and 1974 than during any previous time of such duration over" the previous two centuries.[80] Prefiguring early twenty-first century developments, the commodity boom quickly pushed the world-economy into recession, its most serious since the 1930s. The 1974–75 downturn stood in stark contrast to the expansion of the previous three decades: "industrial output dropped 10 percent in the Global North. The American stock market lost half its value and the world system was rocked by the two biggest bank failures since the Depression, as Franklin National in the U.S. and Bankhaus Herstatt in Germany both collapsed."[81]

74   FAO, *FAO Statistical Yearbook 2012* (Rome: FAO, 2012).

75   Calculated from M. Strauss, "When Malthus Meets Mendel," *Foreign Policy* 119 (2000): 107.

76   I. Matuschke and M. Qaim, "Adoption and Impact of Hybrid Wheat in India" (Paper presented to the International Association of Agricultural Economists Conference, Gold Coast, Australia, August 12–18, 2006), 2.

77   P. Patnaik, "The World Food Crisis," *People's Democracy*, 35, no. 9 (2011), pd.cpim.org/2011/0227_pd/02272011_10.html. Accessed March 18, 2011.

78   The Economist, "Antibiotic Resistance: The Drugs Don't Work," *Economist* (May 3, 2014).

79   Freeman, "What Really Ails Europe (and America)" (2005).

80   J. Kolko, *Restructuring the World Economy* (New York: Pantheon, 1988), 22.

81   McNally, *Global Slump* (2011), 31.

In 1975, New York City declared bankruptcy, and the next year the British Labour government turned to the IMF for emergency loans, and imposed an early form of structural adjustment.[82] In the five years after 1973, the manufacturing rate of profit fell by a quarter in the G-7 economies, and would not revive until 1983—and even then, at a much lower rate than that of the postwar golden age.[83]

In this conjuncture, Cheap Food became more important than ever. As accumulation slowed in the 1970s, so did labor productivity growth. In the OECD zone, productivity tumbled 61 percent in 1973–1979 relative to the 1960s.[84] Although G-7 profitability revived after 1983, labor productivity did not. How could profitability revive, and productivity growth stagnate? In part, because of the wage freeze across the Global North after 1974. Speaking to the U.S. context, Brenner observes a "repression of wages without precedent during the last century, and perhaps since the Civil War."[85] Nevertheless, food expenses as a share of income continued to fall. Between 1980 and the end of the century, food expenses declined from 13.4 percent to 10.7 percent of household income[86]—a figure that scarcely changed by 2011, even with food commodity prices at very high levels.[87]

The novelty of neoliberalism's peculiar agricultural revolution is found in a strange mix of finance and empire, combined with coercive overproduction and forced underconsumption—*without a productivity revolution*. We can consider these moments in their respective turns.

First, for neoliberalism to succeed, there had to be a way to keep cultivators running on a treadmill that ramped up commodity production despite falling world market prices. There were two great waves of agricultural export expansion in this period. One occurred in the 1970s, anticipating and reinforced by the food price spike of 1972–1974, but continuing until 1980, as the dollar value of world

---

82   Ibid.; D. Harvey, *A Brief History of Neoliberalism* (2005).

83   Brenner, *The Economics of Global Turbulence* (2006), 145; McNally, *Global Slump* (2011); R. Went, *The Engima of Globalization* (New York: Routledge, 2002).

84   Calculated from J. Crotty, "Slow Growth, Destructive Competition, and Low Road Labor Relations," *Working Paper Series* 6 (Political Economy Research Institute, University of Massachusetts, Amherst, 2000), 6.

85   Brenner, *The Economics of Global Turbulence* (2006), 3.

86   H. Elitzak, "Food Cost Review, 1950–97," *Agricultural Economic Report No. 780* (Food and Rural Economics Division, Economic Research Service, U.S. Department of Agriculture, 1999).

87   Food prices for the poorest 20 percent are about 50 percent higher than for the middle 20 percent. "Cheap Food" is clearly not cheap for all. D. Thompson, "How America Spends Money on Food," *Atlantic* (March 8, 2013). Accessed February 12, 2014, www.theatlantic.com/business/archive/2013/03/cheap-eats-how-america-spends-money-on-food/273811; D. Gambrell, "America's Shrinking Grocery Bill," *Business Week* (February 28, 2013).

agricultural exports grew fourfold. Through the 1970s, agricultural trade grew faster than output, and by 1980 the two growth curves moved in tandem,[88] a crucial turning point in the consolidation of the neoliberal food regime. By 1985, another export wave began, as exports doubled over the following decade.[89]

Both waves were debt-driven, but in distinctive ways. In the 1970s, Cheap Money flooded the South. Between 1974 and 1978 "the international exposure of the major Western banks rose from $280 billion to $900 billion."[90] This was spearheaded by New York banks, (in a shift from the older dominance of multilateral loans). Although some measure of borrowing was devoted to unproductive purposes, much of it, especially in Latin America, was committed to extending the agro-industrialization of the Fordist era.[91] Cheap Money afforded by the combination of overaccumulated capital in the North and petro-dollars from the OPEC zone, therefore helped to establish the conditions for sustained overcapacity in agricultural and raw materials sectors in the neoliberal era.[92] These conditions were partly realized through infrastructure projects—such as the trans-Amazonian highway expansion—and partly through capital goods imports. But the tendency was not limited to the South. Indeed, the South's agro-extractive overcapacities were sustained in the 1980s and '90s by grain farmers in the North. Their relations were joined through the debt regime. American farmers saw their debt burden triple in the 1970s.[93] Breaking with the postwar pattern, U.S. farmers financed expansion largely through "outside debt capital," fueling an asset boom that reinforced overproduction tendencies in the early 1980s.[94] By 2004, just 3.4 percent of U.S. farms produced over 45 percent of output by value, close to doubling the output share of the largest farms in the 1970s.[95]

88   FAO, *The State of Food and Agriculture 1995. Agricultural Trade: Entering a New Era?* (Rome: FAO, 1995).

89   FAO, *The State of Food and Agriculture. Agricultural Trade and Poverty: Can Trade Work for the Poor?* (Rome: FAO, 2005).

90   A. Lipietz, "How Monetarism Has Choked Third World Industrialization," *New Left Review* I, no. 145 (1984): 77.

91   R.J. Ortiz, "Latin American Agro-Industrialization, Petrodollar Recycling, and the Transformation of World Capitalism in the Long 1970s," *Critical Sociology* (online, 2014).

92   Ibid.

93   M. Strange, *Family Farming* (Omaha: University of Nebraska Press, 1988), 21–22.

94   B.J. Barnett, "The U.S. Farm Financial Crisis of the 1980s," *Agricultural History* 74, no. 2 (2000): 371; M. Kenney, et al., "Midwestern Agriculture in US Fordism," *Sociologia Ruralis* 29, no. 2 (1989): 131–148.

95   C. MacLennan and R. Walker, "Crisis and Change in U.S. Agriculture"; M.K. Hendrickson, et al., "Does the World Need U.S. Farmers Even if Americans Don't?" *Journal of Agricultural and Environmental Ethics* 21 (2008): 311.

By 2010, 12 percent of American farmers were responsible for 88 percent of farm value.[96]

Some share of this concentration was driven by the success of the American "development project" across the South, where dynamic national capitalisms had taken shape. By the 1970s, more than American *industry* was challenged by international competitors. American farmers' export-dependence deepened over the next four decades, even as they were subjected to new competitive pressures. The "new agricultural countries" that emerged in the 1970s and '80s—such as Thailand, Brazil, Mexico, and Chile—"revived the intense export competition on world markets that" characterized the period 1846–1929, threatening American dominance in such key export sectors as oilseeds and meals.[97] Meanwhile, Europe became a wheat exporter, complementing Argentina's resurgence. Together, the two zones nearly doubled their world market share between 1975 and 1985. American wheat's share of the world market, 30 to 40 percent in the 1980s and early '90s, tumbled after 1995, falling to 20 to 30 percent in the following decade.[98]

A deepening of these competitive dynamics occurred in the 1980s. The turning point was the conjuncture of Third World debt crisis and world recession in 1981–82. The contradictions that had come to the fore during the 1974–75 downturn were now reinforced by those of the emergent debt regime. The stage for world recession was set by the "Volcker shock" in October 1979, as the U.S. Federal Reserve suppressed inflation—finance capital's greatest fear—by nearly tripling the real interest rate over the next two years, relative to the 1965–79 average.[99]

---

96   W. Hauter, *Foodopoly* (New York: The New Press, 2012), 13.

97   The greatest role of the new agricultural countries, as they developed after 1980, was in the provisioning of so-called "high value foods . . . such as fruits and vegetables, poultry, seeds, dairy products and shellfish." As the world cereal trade declined in the 1980s, trade in high-value foods rose eight percent annually (P. Rosset, et al., "Thailand and the World Tomato," *International Journal of Sociology of Agriculture and Food* 8 (1999): 72); Harriet Friedmann, "The Political Economy of Food," *New Left Review* I/197 (1993): 29–57.

98   USDA, "U.S. Wheat Trade" (2013). Accessed July 22, 2014, www.ers.usda.gov/topics/crops/wheat/trade.aspx#.U_oeOPldXvQ; T. Darr and G. Gribbons. "How US Exports Are Faring in the World Wheat Market," *Monthly Labor Review* 108 (1985): 10–24.

99   "The interests of capitalists who deal in money to make profit have always been substantially different from the interests of capitalists who are engaged in material production for profit on the basis of borrowed money. Financiers are creditors, and creditors wish, above all, to prevent inflation, which erodes their returns, to maintain high real interest rates, and to have complete freedom to move their finance in and out of countries in search of the highest profits, which are mainly speculative in nature. Further, rather than accumulation through the route of productive investment, the rapid

Personal, corporate, and government debt in the North—and as we have seen, in the South too—had all been rising fast after 1973, with the jobless multiplying, growth faltering, and the rate of profit slowing.[100] The world recession of 1981–82 at once consolidated the new contradictions—those swirling around new configuration of debt and finance—and moved to resolve the older problems: an assertive Third World abroad, and restive working classes at home. While economically speaking, the 1981–82 recession was worse than that of 1974–75,[101] its qualitative dimensions were even more significant.

When Mexico's finance minister arrived in Washington, D.C. in August 1982 with news that his country could no longer service its debt, this presented a significant problem for world accumulation. Mexico's interest bill had tripled between 1979 and 1982. By the latter date, Latin American debtors, with Mexico and Brazil in the van, found debt service eating up 60 percent of export revenues: three times the average for the South.[102] It got more problematic, fast. The Portillo government "nationalized Mexico's private banks, declaring that they had 'looted the nation far more than had any colonialist power.'"[103] The 1982 debt crisis threatened to fracture the neoliberal order just as it had consolidated power in the North and realized counter-revolution in key zones of the South. The debt of the "extended" Third World—including eastern Europe—had grown twelvefold since 1970.[104] American banks were especially vulnerable. By 1981, the largest U.S. banks had extended loans to Third World states—Mexico and Brazil above all—whose face value came to a stunning 233 percent of total capital and reserves.[105]

---

centralization of capital via takeovers and acquisition of cheapened foreign assets is the preferred route for finance capital, which is achieved through periodic asset-deflation along with income deflation in those developing countries that have opened themselves fully to the destabilizing effects of these flows." (U. Patnaik, "Global Capitalism, Deflation and Agrarian Crisis in Developing Countries," *Journal of Agrarian Change* 3, nos. 1–2 [2003]: 34); J. Kolko, *Restructuring the World Economy* (1988), 41–2; F.W. Engdahl, "The Financial Tsunami: The Financial Foundations of the American Century, Part II" (Centre for Research on Globalization, 2008). Accessed January 18, 2011, www.globalresearch.ca/index.php?context=va&aid=7813.

100   Harvey, *The Condition of Postmodernity* (1989); A. Kliman, *The Failure of Capitalist Production* (London: Pluto Press, 2012); McNally, *Global Slump* (2011).

101   Kolko, *Restructuring the World Economy* (1988).

102   R.K. Schaeffer, *Understanding Globalization* (Lanham, MD: Rowman & Littlefield, 2003), 101; S. Gindin and L. Panitch, *The Making of Global Capitalism* (London: Verso, 2012), 214.

103   Gindin and Panitch, *The Making of Global Capitalism*.

104   Schaeffer, *Understanding Globalization* (2003), 95.

105   Gindin and Panitch, *The Making of Global Capitalism*; McNally, *Global Slump* (2011), 98.

There were two possible outcomes to crisis. The danger was that Mexico, Brazil, and other heavily indebted states would default, refusing to pay their debts without significant restructuring. This would have devalorized loan-capital on a massive scale and reflated primary commodity prices, transforming the severe recession of the early 1980s into a prolonged depression for the North. As we know, this did not happen.

The other possibility—which *did* happen—was an expansion of the debt regime. Latin American debt tripled during the 1980s.[106] The debtor states of the South acceded to the new debt regime—which included the rapid liberalization of domestic financial and agricultural sectors—following the fiscal turbulence of 1982. Among the most important consequences was a new system of international debt peonage that reinforced the "export glut" of primary commodities.[107] The new regime "exerted pressure on states to intensify the commodification of land and labor. Land and natural resources in general [became] the objects of enhanced export strategies to generate foreign exchange, often to service debt."[108] Far-reaching transformations of earth and bodies ensued throughout the South, as deforestation advanced, toxification intensified, and diets suffered.[109] For the moment—*but just for the moment*—these environmental transformations scarcely registered in the ledgers of world accumulation.

The consequences were immediate. In the periphery, the number of negative "price shocks"—defined as any year-on-year decline in real prices by 10 percent or greater—grew from 25 to 90 between 1981–83 and 1984–86; their severity was 25 to 50 percent greater.[110] Worldwide, non-energy raw materials prices fell by nearly half between 1980 and 1992.[111] As Gowan wryly observes, within the North, the new debt regime worked for rentiers, who "[got] their debts paid," and for industrial capital, who got "cheaper imports for the inputs needed for production"[112]—not to mention cheaper food for workers.

The debt regime that emerged after 1982 compelled the radical extroversion

---

106   Schaeffer, *Understanding Globalization* (2003), 96.

107   P. McMichael, *Development and Social Change*, 4th ed. (Thousand Oaks, CA: Sage, 2008), 130.

108   P. McMichael, "The Global Crisis of Wage-Labour," *Studies in Political Economy* 58 (1999): 26–27.

109   Ibid., 11–40; F. Araghi, "The Great Global Enclosure of Our Times," in *Hungry for Profit*, eds. F. Magdoff, et al., (New York: Monthly Review Press, 2000), 145–60; W.F. Bello, *Dark Victory* (London: Pluto Press, 1994); S. George, *The Debt Boomerang* (Boulder: Westview Press, 1993); M.W. Wright, *Disposable Women* (2006).

110   IMF, *Fund Assistance for Countries Facing Exogenous Shocks* (2003), 37. Accessed March 11, 2011. www.imf.org/external/np/pdr/sustain/2003/080803.pdf.

111   Schaeffer, *Understanding Globalization*, 103.

112   P. Gowan, *The Global Gamble* (London: Verso, 1999), 103.

of the South's tenuous national farm sectors that had taken shape after World War II. As in previous agricultural revolutions, the new debt-driven agro-food regime effectively expelled cultivators from the land.[113] By 1980 there had begun a momentous transition from the *relative* to the absolute decline of Third World peasantries. A decade later, 20 to 30 million people were moving from rural villages to the cities of the South every year.[114] But, absent a significant revolution in agricultural productivity, this movement of deruralization was both enabled by, and compelled, a declining food "self-sufficiency ratio." A declining ratio is by no means a *necessary* sign of weakness, as we have seen with British food imports during the nineteenth century. In Africa, food imports grew three times faster than population during the 1960s and '70s, while maintaining strong economic growth until 1974.[115] But absent an agricultural revolution— *somewhere*—declining food self-sufficiency is much riskier. Food dependence increased over most of the Global South in the 1970s and '80s.[116] Among the consequences was an increasing frequency of famine and hunger, along with a decades-long economic stagnation.

But Cheap Food after the 1970s was also realized by the rapid capitalization of agro-food complexes in the North. The neoliberal project turned the competitive advantage of Northern agriculture into a means of restoring Cheap Food. Industrial agriculture's labor productivity growth more than doubled that of the wider national economy in the U.S.[117] Indeed, the gap between the productivity of industrial agriculture, mostly but not entirely concentrated in the North, and low-input ("peasant") cultivation widened sharply during the globalization of the Green Revolution and from there, across the neoliberal era.[118] By 2010, the North was producing an impressive 11,741 calories per capita per day, more than twice as much as East Asia and nearly four times that of South Asia[119]—an achievement that owed much to rapid concentration of farm output in the hands

---

113   F. Araghi, "Global Depeasantization, 1945–1990," *The Sociological Quarterly* 36, no. 2 (1995): 337–68; F. Araghi, "The Great Global Enclosure of Our Times" (2000).

114   Ibid.

115   C.K. Eicher, "Facing up to Africa's Food Crisis," *Foreign Affairs* 61, no. 1 (1982): 156; G. Arrighi, "The African Crisis," *New Left Review* II, no. 15 (2002): 5–36.

116   P. Uvin, "The State of World Hunger," *Nutrition Reviews* 52, no. 5 (1994): 3.

117   Fuglie and Wang, "New Evidence Points to Robust but Uneven Productivity Growth" (2012): 1–6; R.J. Gordon, "Is US Economic Growth Over?" (Working Paper 18315, National Bureau of Economic Research, 2012).

118   S. Amin, "World Poverty, Pauperization, and Capital Accumulation," *Monthly Review* 55, no. 5 (2003): 1–9; D.F. Bryceson, "Sub-Saharan Africa's Vanishing Peasantries and the Specter of a Global Food Crisis," *Monthly Review* 61, no. 3 (2009): 48–62; T. Kastner, et al., "Rapid Growth in Agricultural Trade: Effects on Global Area Efficiency and the Role of Management," *Environmental Research Letters* 9 (2014): 1–10.

119   FAO, *FAO Statistical Yearbook 2012* (Rome: FAO, 2012), 35.

of big farms across the world, but especially in the Euro-American core.[120] The result? Combined with selective agricultural liberalization, and mediated by the structural adjustments after 1982, Northern Cheap Food flowed into the South, displacing millions of peasants. Voilà! Cheap Food plus liberalization produces Cheap Labor.

The neoliberal debt regime worked so well because it prevented the kind of de-linking that had occurred in previous crises. The dietary moment of combined and uneven development experienced by Africa in the 1980s was hardly novel. Baltic grain flowed out of Poland and into Amsterdam during the mid-seventeenth century as Polish peasant diets were squeezed—and soil fertility exhausted—under the Dutch-led "system of international debt peonage."[121] However, Poland's crises led to its relative de-linking from world trade by the eighteenth century; although hardly prosperous, its exposure to agro-extractive dispossession, dietary immiseration, and resource exhaustion was greatly relaxed.

No such relaxation could occur at the dawn of the neoliberal era. The financial-imperial power that fused in the early 1980s as the "Washington Consensus" was directed at preventing the South's relative withdrawal from the world market. Such withdrawal had long been the pattern, as world-economic contractions provided room for peripheral and semi-peripheral zones to develop home markets and pursue "core-like" capitalist development—Mexico during the seventeenth century, British North America after 1763, or Latin America in the 1930s. But relative withdrawal was precisely what could not be tolerated by an emergent accumulation regime that was *not* in the midst of a new productivity revolution. This was all the more crucial at the dawn of the 1980s, after a decade of very low productivity growth. For neoliberalism to succeed there had to be a way to keep the Southern producers locked into producing for the world market—even at the cost of the forced "under-reproduction" of human and extra-human nature.

Under these conditions, the new debt regime made "global distress-sellers" of that growing share of the world's cultivators who were subject to market discipline: especially but not only within the South.[122] Since the 1980s, producers of such "high value" products as coffee, bananas, or seafood, each with its own temporality, found few alternatives to increasing production even as market

---

120   J.C. Franco and S.M. Borras Jr., eds. *Land Concentration, Land Grabbing and People's Struggles in Europe.* (Amsterdam: Transnational Institute, 2013). Accessed June 13, 2014, www.eurovia.org/IMG/pdf/Land_in_Europe.pdf. GRAIN, "2,4-D Soy: Waging War on Peasants," *GRAIN Report* (2014). Accessed 4 June, 2014, www.grain.org/article/entries/4945-2-4-d-soy-waging-war-on-peasants.

121   Wallerstein, *The Modern World-System I* (1974), 121–2.

122   Patsaik, "Global Capitalism, Deflation and Agrarian Crisis" (2003), 3.

prices fell.[123] The important shift was not achieved through the conversion of peasant smallholders—who were pushed onto smaller and smaller plots, such that 90 percent of the world's "farms" today are less than 2.2 hectares—but rather through the global extension of industrial agriculture.[124] Stunningly, virtually all cropland expansion since 1990 has been export-oriented[125]—a starker contrast with the era of "national agricultures" is hard to imagine.

THE CONTRADICTIONS OF NEOLIBERAL AGRICULTURE

The neoliberal agro-food model was remarkably successful. By 2000, the FAO's food price index stood at 92. It had oscillated around 100 since 1983. The timing wasn't accidental. Accumulation across the North revived just at this time. And oil prices, too, embarked on two decades of relative stability. For food, the 2000 index figure was nearly a third lower than the average for the 1960s, at the height of the global phase of the long Green Revolution.[126] As a share of household income for the North's working classes—an admittedly selective measure, but one central to the maintenance of wage repression—food had never been so cheap.[127]

By 2003, food prices were ticking upwards. Slowly at first. Then rapidly. By 2008, commodity food prices were 62 percent higher than in 2002. By 2011, they were 77 percent higher.[128] While the food price index never reached the unusual heights of 1974–75, prices were nevertheless lower in the 1970s (c.

123   MGI [McKinsey Global Institute], "MGI's Commodity Price Index—an Interactive Tool," (2014); F. Asche, "Global Seafood Markets in 2030." (Presentation to the Institute for Social and Economic Research, University of Alaska, October 24, 2012). Accessed July 12, 2014, greenandgold.uaa.alaska.edu/media/AscheAlaskaAnchorage.pdf; FAO, *The World Banana Economy, 1985–2002.* (Rome: FAO, 2003). Accessed June 29, 2014, www.fao.org/docrep/007/y5102e/y5102e00.htm.

124   GRAIN, *Hungry for Land* (2014), report. Accessed June 18, 2014, www.grain.org/article/entries/4929=hungry-for-land-small-farmers-feed-the-world-with-less-than-a-quarter-of-all-farmland.pdf

125   Kastner, et al., "Rapid Growth in Agricultural Trade" (2014).

126   FAO, "World Food Situation: FAO Food Price Index," (2014). Accessed May 16, 2014, www.fao.org/worldfoodsituation/foodpricesindex/en/; Calculated from FAO, "Food Price Index: Nominal and Real," (2014). Accessed August 18, 2014, www.fao.org/fileadmin/templates/worldfood/Reports_and_docs/food_price_index_nominal_real.xls.

127   Thompson, "How America Spends Money on Food" (2013); Elitzak, "Food Cost Review, 1950–97 (1999); R. Schnepf, *Consumers and Food Price Inflation* (Washington, D.C.: Congressional Research Service, 2013).

128   Calculated from FAO, "Food Price Index: Nominal and Real," (2014).

1973–1981) than in the recent period (2007–2014). The difference between the "normal" prices of the 1960s and the "high" prices of the 1970s was, moreover, considerably smaller than what we've seen since 2000. Indeed, the food price index for the 1970s was just 7.6 percent higher than the average for the 1960s.[129] In contrast, the past decade's food inflation has seen prices rise 50 percent relative to the cheap food of the 1990s.[130] And they show few signs of returning from orbit. Capitalism appears to have swept Cheap Food into the dustbin of history.

Recent years have seen the widest range of explanations for high food prices: the meat-industrial complex, financial speculation, the agro-fuel expansion, the rise of "new middle classes" across the South, accelerating climate change, rising energy prices, growing population and urbanization, the dispossession of smallholders who grow much of the world's food, and much beyond. Of course, many of these explanations overlap. All, and surely more, are implicated in the present conjuncture. In this section, my concern is not to reconstruct the history of the food price hike, but rather to ask: Can Cheap Food be restored?

I am not sure that the old answers to this question apply. The frontiers that sustained agricultural revolutions over the past five centuries have largely vanished. The sixteenth-century Dutch grew rich thanks to cheap grain from Poland's Vistula Basin; the nineteenth-century British had Ireland, the Caribbean, and the American Midwest. When the U.S. came to world power, it had the Midwest, plus the American South and California, *and* Latin America. Major food surpluses were won in all cases from untapped frontier zones combined with new technical regimes and labor organization. And, as we have seen, South Asia's Green Revolution owed much to the appropriation of 'vertical' frontiers: plentiful aquifers at home and relatively cheap energy supplies (for fertilizer) abroad. Cheap water and cheap energy *qua* fertilizer are rapidly disappearing today.[131] And, while biotechnology and biopiracy through the "new" enclosures have made some capitalists very rich, they have done little to achieve what all previous agricultural revolutions had done: restore Cheap Food.

Do the deepening contradictions of today's Cheap Food model imply a *developmental crisis*, one open to resolution within capitalism? If it does, we would expect to see an agricultural revolution taking shape in China, the most dynamic new

---

129   Calculated for the period 1962–72 (133.6) relative to 1973–81 (143.7) (calculated from FAO, ibid.).

130   Calculated for the period 1993–2002 (101.6) relative to 2007–14 (152.6).

131   M. Palaniappan and P.H. Gleick, "Peak Water," in *The World's Water 2008–2009*, ed. P.H. Gleick (Washington, D.C.: Island Press, 2008); Index Mundi, "DAP fertilizer Monthly Price–US Dollars per Metric Ton," *Index Mundi* (2014). Accessed August 13, 2014, www.indexmundi.com/commodities/?commodity=dap-fertilizer&months=360.

center of accumulation. China's post-1979 *"de facto* privatization of agriculture,"
accompanied by skyrocketing fertilizer use, boosted yields and output considerably—although not more than in the 1960s and '70s.[132] Following an initial burst of
productivity and output in the 1980s, however, Chinese agriculture has not been
particularly revolutionary. Cereal production rose from 300 to 500 million tons a
year between 1979 and 1996.[133] But yield growth in wheat—China is the world's
largest producer—has stagnated, and output along with it, since 1998.[134] In rice, by
the 1990s yield growth had slowed to less than half the pace of the 1960s, and
output declined by 4 percent. China's soy imports exceeded domestic production
for the first time in 2003.[135] For all the remarkable accomplishments of the Chinese
"miracle," labor productivity in industry and agriculture both remain at one-quarter (or less) than the average obtaining within the Global North.[136] In sum, there is
little to suggest that China is on the brink of an agricultural revolution that will not
only feed the world, but *lead* capitalism into a new golden age.[137] Nor does China
appear to be initiating the kind of "external" agricultural revolution that characterized Dutch power in the Baltic, or British power in the Caribbean.[138]

The unraveling of neoliberalism's Cheap Food regime has not, of course,
occurred in isolation, either from other primary commodities, or from the wider

---

132   D. Wen and M. Li, "China: Hyper-Development and Environmental Crisis," in
Socialist Register 2007: Coming to Terms with Nature, ed. L. Panitch and C. Leys (London:
Merlin, 2006), 130–146; J.Y. Lin, "Rural Reforms and Agricultural Growth in China,"
American Economic Review 82, no. 1 (1992): 34–51.

133   Wen and Li, "China: Hyper-Development and Environmental Crisis" (2007).

134   B. Lohmar, *China's Wheat Economy: Current Trends and Prospects for Imports*
(Economic Research Service, United States Department of Agriculture, 2004); W. Zhang,
et al., "Global Pesticide Consumption and Pollution: With China as a Focus," *Proceedings of
the International Academy of Ecology and Environmental Sciences* 1, no. 2 (2011): 125–44.

135   Z. Defeng, "Bridging the Rice Yield Gap in China," in *Bridging the Rice Gap in
the Asia-Pacific Region*, ed. M.K. Papademetriou, et al. (Bangkok: FAO, 2000): 69–83;
People's Daily Online, "Last Year Saw China's Soybean Import Hit a Record High in
History," *People's Daily Online* (February 14, 2004). Accessed November 12, 2009,
english.peopledaily.com.cn/200402/14/eng20040214_134838.shtml; L. Brown, "Could
Food Shortages Bring Down Civilization?" *Scientific American* (April, 2009).

136   G. Jefferson, et al., "The Sources and Sustainability of China's Economic Growth,"
Brookings Papers on Economic Activity II (2006): 1–47; S. Jin, et al., "Agricultural
Productivity in China," in *The Shifting Patterns of Agricultural Production and Productivity
Worldwide*, ed. J.M. Alston, et al. (Ames, IA: The Midwest Agribusiness Trade Research
and Information Center, 2010), 229–277.

137   V. Smil, *China's Past, China's Future* (New York: Routledge, 2004); A. Camba,
"Karl Marx in Beijing" (Paper presented to conference: From *The Long Twentieth Century*
to the Twenty-First, Binghamton University, October 11–12, 2014).

138   Moore, "Ecology and the Rise of Capitalism"; "'Amsterdam Is Standing on Norway'
Part II."

processes of accumulation. Since 2003, rising food prices have been bound up with rising energy and metal prices in what economists call a "commodity boom." The *boom* part of the concept refers to *rising* prices; in the conventional definition, once commodity prices peak, the boom is over, and prices return to "normal." In the conventional expectation, high prices during the boom years set in motion new investment that leads to new production capacities. The magic of capitalist investment then takes over, and commodity prices fall. The whole imaginary of neoclassical economic thinking is built around this assumption, which can point to a very strong historical record. Each peak in *The Economist's* food price index—between 1846 and 1972—was significantly lower, or no higher, than the one previous.[139] (World War I was the only exception, and very short-lived.) Over the twentieth century, commodity prices fell by as much as one percent a year.[140] Today, the assumption is that this "old normal" will return. But this is unlikely, especially but not only for food. Even the more optimistic predictions of the "end" of the commodity boom—remember that "*end*" means that prices stop rising—do not predict a return to cheap energy or raw materials. The old normal is assumed even while the *new normal* is glimpsed, as when a major Swedish bank qualifies a recent report on global commodities as a "commodity bust *in slow motion*."[141]

Very slow motion, indeed. The most recent commodity boom may warrant a reconceptualization. Is it possible that prices will *not* induce new efficiencies that will reduce production costs and commodity prices? Over the past century, commodity booms occurred in relation to wars and their aftermaths—or, as in the 1972–75 boom, a combination of OPEC-initiated oil tax hikes and the U.S.-Soviet grain deal. They tended to be short-lived: three years in the 1970s, two years in 1915–17, or longer but relatively mild in the 1950s (1950–57). And they involved just one or two commodity groups: metals and agriculture (1915–17, 1950–57), or oil and agriculture (1972–75). The commodity boom that began in 2003 was different. First, it included all three commodity groups—three of our Four Cheaps. Second, the prices for each group began to move in tandem with each other, especially by 2008. This had not happened before. Third, the "price increases [were] unprecedented . . . The real U.S. dollar price of commodities . . . increased by some 109 percent" between 2003 and 2008. "By contrast, the increase in earlier major booms never exceeded 60 percent."[142] And though the

---

139   J. Baines, "Food Price Inflation as Redistribution," *New Political Economy* 19, no. 1 (2014): 79–112.

140   Fuglie and Wang, "New Evidence Points to Robust but Uneven Productivity Growth" (2012).

141   Handelsbanken, *A Commodity Bust in Slow Motion* (Stockholm: Handelsbanken, 2014). Emphasis added.

142   World Bank, *Global Economic Prospects 2009* (Washington, D.C.: World Bank, 2009).

commodity price index quickly moved off its summer 2008 peak, the fall in prices during 2009 was temporary and mild. The commodity boom continued. From January 2011 into mid-2014, the commodity price index remained 80–90 percent higher than its already-lofty 2005 level.[143] New investment, as in previous cycles, has poured into energy and raw materials sectors.[144] But far from *reducing* the costs of production, the opposite has occurred:

> Deeper mines, lower-grade minerals, more remote and challenging locations and shortages of both labor and equipment have pushed up costs . . . While prices may well have peaked, this doesn't mean they will soon revert back to their pre-2002 levels. Costs have risen and are unlikely to fall rapidly, supporting prices well above earlier levels. In fact, cost pressures continue to intensify for some commodities as production increases.[145]

Nor have rising production costs been limited to extraction. American grain farmers saw their costs rise 15 to 20 percent between 2002 and 2007 on the back of rising energy prices[146]—which were as high in 2014 as they were in 2007.[147] For soy, neoliberalism's paradigm "growth crop,"[148] the trajectory is troubling for any defender of the productivist model. Worldwide, production costs for soybeans tripled in the decade after 2002.[149] And Brazil, which now threatens to "outfarm" the Americans for global preeminence, has seen soybean production costs rise by 5 percent annually since 2009.[150] Surveying the past decade of rising

---

143   Index Mundi, "Commodity Price Index Monthly Price—Index Number," *Index Mundi* (2014). Accessed August 14, 2014, www.indexmundi.com/commodities/?commodity=commodity-price-index&months=360.

144   Handelsbanken, *A Commodity Bust in Slow Motion* (2014); S. Kopits, "Oil and Economic Growth: A Supply-Constrained View" (Presentation to the Center on Global Energy Policy, Columbia University, February 11, 2014).

145   M. Rider, "The Other Side of the Super Cycle," in *Investing in 2013* (Geneva: UBS Global Asset Management, 2012), 14–15.

146   D. Mitchell, "A Note on Rising Food Prices" *Policy Research Working Paper 4682* (Development Prospects Group, The World Bank, 2008).

147   Index Mundi, "DAP Fertilizer Monthly Price" (2014); Index Mundi, "Crude Oil (Petroleum), Price Index Monthly Price–Index Number," *Index Mundi*, 2014. Accessed August 14, 2014, www.indexmundi.com/commodities/?commodity=petroleum-price-index&months=180.

148   USDA, "USDA Agricultural Projections to 2017" (2008). Accessed October 13, 2013, www.ers.usda.gov/media/274754/oce20081_1_.pdf.

149   Rider, "The Other Side of the Super Cycle" (2012).

150   AgroSouth News, "Soybean Production Costs Rise 5% Annually in Brazil", *AgroSouth News* (July 21, 2014); S.B. Hecht and C.C. Mann, "How Brazil Outfarmed the American Farmer," *Fortune* (January 10, 2008).

commodity prices, the World Bank economist John Baffes coolly observes that it "is becoming increasingly apparent that the post-2004 commodity price increases, which *initially* appeared to be a spike similar to the ones experienced during the early 1950s (Korean war) and the 1970s (oil crises), *have a more permanent character.*"[151]

The commodity boom that began in 2003 may therefore defy the economists'—and some radicals'—cornucopian presumptions. While attention has been lavished on financialization and its deepening contradictions over the past decade, the radical critique has been nearly silent on the rising costs of food, energy, and raw materials *as they relate to the central mechanisms of world accumulation.* Here we revisit the extraordinary power of the Cartesian binary in shaping our intellectual vistas, fragmenting our view of reality before we get a chance to (re)construct the really decisive connections. Of these latter, two major developmental shifts in world accumulation present themselves. One is the ongoing collapse of the mechanisms through which commodity price spikes have been fixed, historically. This mechanism says, in effect: more investment plus more state-led restructuring equals Cheap Nature. Another is the ongoing "squeeze" on world accumulation represented by this seemingly endless commodity boom: the resurgence of underproduction as a dynamic contradiction within the accumulation process.

The behavior of this recent commodity boom—in which the food/energy nexus figures so prominently—offers a useful clue to understanding the crisis of neoliberal capitalism. It is closely connected with ongoing financial expansion: indeed, food and finance have so closely intertwined over the past decade that it makes sense to speak of a singular process.[152] If neoliberalism is a phase of capitalism—distinct from neoliberalization as class project or "market-disciplinary" policies[153]—then the crisis announced by the recent commodity boom is of a specific kind: a *signal* crisis. Such crises occur when a given accumulation regime can no longer appropriate unpaid work/energy faster than the rising mass of surplus accumulated. As the global share of appropriated work/energy falls, the costs of the Four Cheaps (unevenly, as ever) tend to rise, and accumulation falters. Since 2003, we can see this signal crisis at work as strategic commodities became more—not less—costly.

---

151   J. Baffes, "A Framework for Analyzing the Interplay Among Food, Fuels, and Biofuels," *Global Food Security* 2, no. 2 (2013): 116. Emphasis added.

152   F. Kaufmann, *Bet the Farm* (Hoboken: John Wiley & Sons, 2012); J. Clapp, *Food* (Cambridge: Polity, 2012).

153   Cf. Harvey, *A Brief History of Neoliberalism* (2005); N. Brenner, et al., "After neoliberalization?" *Globalizations* 7, no. 3 (2010): 327–45.

BIOTECH: AGRICULTURAL REVOLUTION OR GÖTTERDÄMMERUNG?

Where will capital today find the conditions for new era of Cheap Food? Neoliberalism pins its hopes for agricultural revolution on biotechnology, associated with all manner of the "new enclosures."[154] It fits the classic model of agricultural revolution, insofar as it effects a redistribution of income (further differentiating classes of farmers), is enabled by the property-making and -securing capacities of states and state-like institutions, and constitutes a promising opportunity for accumulation by some sectors of capital. It *does not* fit the model, insofar as it has yet to deliver a yield boom sufficiently large to create (in concert with cheap energy and cheap inputs) the conditions for a new systemic cycle of accumulation. The biotech regime has redistributed wealth and power from cultivators to capital, but has not realized the kind of yield boom that facilitates a dramatic expansion of the world proletariat and a significant cheapening of food for these workers.

By 2011, GMO crops had grown from virtually nothing in 1996 to 10 percent of global cropland, cultivated by 16.7 million farmers in 29 countries. The United States is unquestionably the heartland of this transition with 43 percent (69 million hectares) of GMO cropland.[155] Ninety-four percent of American soybeans and 88 percent of maize are grown with GM seeds, especially but not only RoundUp Ready seeds.[156] (About which, more presently.) Half of GMO cropland is in the Global South.[157]

Agricultural biotech has done little to improve intrinsic yields. World agricultural productivity growth slowed from 3 percent a year in the 1960s to just 1.1 percent in the 1990s.[158] Gurian-Sherman,[159] in the first comprehensive survey of biotechnology's aggregate yield effect, finds almost all gains in operational, not intrinsic, yields (which "may also be thought of as potential yield"). Such reports even prompted Monsanto to announce—plaintively—that "the main uses of GM crops are to make them insecticide- and herbicide tolerant. *They don't inherently increase the yield. They protect the yield.*"[160] But it turns out that RoundUp Ready

154   J. Rifkin, *The Biotech Century* (New York: Putnam, 1998); V. Shiva, *Biopiracy* (Boston: South End Press, 1997).

155   C. James, "Global Status of Commercialized Biotech/GM Crops: 2011" (Brief 43, International Service for the Acquisition of Agri-Biotech Applications, 2011); Hauter, *Foodopoly* (2012), 243; FAO, *FAO Statistical Yearbook 2012* (Rome: FAO, 2012), 312–14.

156   Hauter, *Foodopoly* (2012), 243.

157   James, "Global Status of Commercialized Biotech/GM Crops" (2011).

158   R. Dobbs, et al., *Resource Revolution* (New York: McKinsey Global Institute, 2011).

159   D. Gurian-Sherman, *Failure to Yield* (Cambridge, MA: Union of Concerned Scientists, 2009).

160   Quoted in E. Ritch, "Monsanto Strikes Back at Germany, UCS," *Cleantech.com* (April 17, 2009). Accessed July 18 2009. Even if water and land constraints could be overcome through new genetic-chemical combinations, this would hardly clear the way

crops are not protecting yield so well, either. "Superweeds," especially but not only in GMO soy, have evolved to survive the onslaught of the famed herbicide.[161] These superweeds stand in for a much more radical shift—the transition from surplus value to negative-value—that we explore in the next section. What became clear, by the late 2000s, was that the agro-biotech expansion was actively *limiting* the space for a new agricultural revolution.

The superweeds' dramatic, if still-regional, negative impact on labor productivity points towards a broader set of forces undermining neoliberalism's Cheap Food regime. The potential for superweeds arising from GMO crops was glimpsed early on.[162] By 2005, superweeds had evolved on a large enough scale to attract popular attention.[163] Soy is a particularly revealing case. Considering that GMO soybeans already constitute 57 percent of world output, and that the United States remains the leading soy producer (37 percent), the rise of the superweed is something of a world-historical event.[164] In the U.S., concentrated in soy regions, 13 weed species (21 globally), on millions of acres in 22 states, are now immune to Round Up Ready.[165] The American superweed frontier expanded fourfold between 2008 and 2011, to 10 million acres.[166] Syngenta, the seed and agrochemical firm, projected in 2009 a superweed explosion that would engross 38 million acres by 2013.[167] At

---

towards a new productivity revolution. First, the "water question" may well be more serious than commonly recognized (Palaniappan and Gleick, "Peak Water" [2008]). Second the very capital- and energy-intensive basis of late capitalist agriculture creates an even more serious constraint on its capacity to raise yields significantly. The technical control regime—in this instance, weed and pest control—promises to induce the evolution of more resistant pests and pathogens (V. Ruttan, "Productive Growth in World Agriculture," *Journal of Economic Perspectives* 16, no. 4 [2002]: 173).

161   C.M. Benbrook, "Impacts of Genetically Engineered Crops on Pesticide Use in the United States" (The Organic Center, 2009), www.organic-center.org.

162   J. Kling, "Could Transgenic Supercrops One Day Breed Superweeds?" *Science* 274, no. 5285 (1996): 180–1.

163   C.M. Benbrook, "Impacts of Genetically Engineered Crops" (2009); cf. P. Brown, "GM Crops Created Superweeds" (2005).

164   G. Pechlaner and G. Otero, "The Third Food Regime," *Sociologia Ruralis* 48, no. 4 (2008): 351–371; T. Masuda and P. Goldsmith, "World Soybean Production: Area Harvested, Yield, and Long-Term Projections" (Working paper, National Soybean Research Laboratory, University of Illinois at Urbana-Champaign, 2008).

165   MCT News Service. "Roundup-Resistant Weeds Gain Strength," *MCT News Service* (May 13, 2010); J. Pocock, "Weed Revolt Marches On," *Corn and Soybean Digest* (January 17, 2012).

166   CFS, "Farmers and Consumer Groups File Lawsuit Challenging Genetically Engineered Alfalfa Approval." Accessed March 27, 2011, www.centerforfoodsafety. org/2011/03/18/farmers-and-consumer-groups-file-lawsuit-challenging-genetically-engineered-alfalfa-approval.

167   Syngenta, "Leading the Fight Against Glyphosate Resistance." (2009). Accessed

the end of 2013, the Union of Concerned Scientists—a somewhat more disinterested party—found an extraordinary *sixty million* acres affected by superweeds.[168] This amounts to one of "every four row crop acres" in U.S. agriculture.[169]

The superweed frontier has also advanced rapidly in the GMO soy zones of Argentina and Brazil.[170] The Latin American dimension is all the more suggestive, as the soy revolution has been realized not only through conversion of existing arable land, but also through massive forest clearing and other forms of agricultural expansion.[171] This is the classic model of the commodity frontier, which has always served to attenuate agro-ecological contradictions within cash-crop agriculture. When weeding became too great a drag on productivity in seventeenth-century Barbados, for instance, the sugar frontier moved to bigger islands such as Jamaica.[172] But the soy commodity frontier in Latin America has enjoyed only modest "yield honeymoons" relative to earlier eras; the superweeds are advancing faster than agro-capitalism can run.

Monsanto's vaunted RoundUp Ready crops are at the center of this socio-ecological fast-forward. While it would be unwise to give Monsanto too much credit, the underlying superweed tendency is nevertheless crystallized nicely by the firm's GMO soy.[173] GMO crops promised to reduce herbicide and pesticide use and to increase operational yields. That promise has quickly turned sour, with rising toxicity and diminishing returns.[174] Notwithstanding the claims of Monsanto and other Big Ag boosters,[175] it appears that glyphosate-resistant

March 11, 2011, www.syngentaebiz.com/DotNetEBiz/ImageLIbrary/WR%203%20 Leading%twentiethe%20Fight.pdf.

168   UCS, "The Rise of Superweeds—and What to Do About It," *Policy Brief* (December 2013). Accessed May 22, 2014, www.ucsusa.org/assets/documents/food_ and_agriculture/rise-of-superweeds.pdf.

169   W. Freese, "Testimony Before the Domestic Policy Subcommittee of the House Oversight and Government Reform Committee" (U.S. House of Representatives, Sept. 30 2010). Accessed February 28, 2011, truefoodnow.files.wordpress.com/2010/09/over-sight-hearing-9-30–2010-freese-oral-final.pdf.

170   J.L. Villar and W. Freese, Who Benefits from GM Crops? (Amsterdam: Friends of the Earth International, 2008); Agrolink, "Cultivo da soja deixou de ser fácil, diz agrônomo," (June 6, 2014), www.agrolink.com.br/noticias/NoticiaDetalhe.aspx?codNo-ticia=197813, accessed July 19, 2014.

171   M.A. Altieri and W.A. Pengue. "Roundup Ready Soybean in Latin America" (2006), accessed March 24, 2011, www.rapaluruguay.org/transgenicos/Prensa/ Roundupready.html; P. Cremaq, "Brazilian Agriculture: The Miracle of the Cerrado," *Economist* (August 26, 2010), ww.economist.com/node/16886442.

172   Moore, "Ecology and the Rise of Capitalism" (2007).

173   Gurian-Sherman, *Failure to Yield* (2009).

174   Benbrook, "Impacts of Genetically Engineered Crops" (2009).

175   Cf. Monsanto, "Monsanto, Dow AgroSciences Complete U.S. and Canadian

crops such as RoundUp Ready Soy are bound up with uncertain implications for human health and that GR root systems are susceptible to fungal invasions.[176] Add to this an apparent exhaustion of operational yield gains and we have a real problem for capital: "We're back to where we were 20 years ago," Tennessee soy farmer Eddie Anderson told *The New York Times* in 2010, as he prepared to revert to older plowing techniques and chemical regimes.[177] But these older techniques are not only more toxic—such as 2,4-D. They are also more costly.[178] By 2012–14, soy farmers in Indiana faced herbicide costs 3–5 times higher than in previous years.[179] Such reports can be found across the North American agricultural zone, from Manitoba to Georgia.[180] They point to a future of sharply rising production costs, as superweeds spread like wildfire: just 12 percent of U.S. farmers reported multiple glyphosate-resistant weeds on the farm in 2010, rising to 15 percent in 2011, and 27 percent in 2012.[181]

This accelerated evolution of herbicide-resistant weeds is the cutting edge of the superweed effect. At its core is the tension between capital's efforts to control and commensurate extra-human nature, and the latter's co-evolutionary capacity to elude and resist that control. This is the taming cycle: "the more [capital] 'tames' natural processes, the more they spin out of control, provoking new and more aggressive taming measures with increasingly disastrous outcomes."[182] The crucial issue of this taming cycle is its relation to the "time-space compression" central to the accumulation of capital: those compressions both depend upon, and drive ever faster, the time-space compression of biophysical natures. As with toxification, we have a temporal lag. In historical capitalism, extra-human nature *initially* moved much slower than the human-initiated control strategies that seek to govern it.

Regulatory Authorizations for SmartStax Corn; Plans Set to Launch Seed Platform on 3 Million to 4 Million-Plus Acres" (2009). Accessed October 11, 2010, monsanto.mediaroom.com/index.php?s=43&item=729.

176   R.J. Kremer and N.E. Means, "Glyphosate and Glyphosate-Resistant Crop Interactions with Rhizosphere Microorganisms," *European Journal of Agronomy* 31 (2009): 153–61.

177   W. Neuman and A. Pollack, "Farmers Cope with Roundup-Resistant Weeds," *New York Times* (May 3, 2010).

178   Price, Andrew J., et al., "Glyphosate-Resistant Palmer Amaranth," *Journal of Durée and Water Conservation* 66, no. 4 (2011): 265–275; GRAIN, "2,4-D Soy Waging War on Peasants," *GRAIN Report* (2014).

179   M. Wines, "Invader Batters Rural America, Shrugging Off Herbicides," *New York Times* (August 11, 2014).

180   Farm Industry News, "Glyphosate-Resistant Weed Problem Extends to More Species, More Farms," *Farm Industry News* (January 29, 2013); L. Rance, "Finding Better Ways to Fight Superweeds," *Winnipeg Free Press* (August 9, 2014).

181   Food and Water Watch, *Superweeds* (Washington, D.C.: Food and Water Watch, 2013); Farm Industry News, "Glyphosate-Resistant Weed Problem" (2013).

182   V. Wallis, "Species Questions," *Organization and Environment* 13, no. 4 (2000): 505.

This masked, but did not abolish, the ongoing evolution of extra-human natures that contest capital's radical simplification strategies. For centuries, the possibility of moving to new frontiers created the mirage of suspending the most problematic aspects of the taming cycle. But as frontiers of appropriation close, the very dynamism of the system—based on capitalization and innovating control strategies through it—intensifies the evolutionary response. Now extra-human natures are evolving faster than the controls imposed upon them.

The superweed effect speaks to the wildly proliferating and increasingly unpredictable responses of extra-human nature to the disciplines of capital today. The short-run promise of RoundUp Ready crops was to maximize operational yield by reducing costs and weeds simultaneously. The middle-run yields not only more weeds, more herbicide, and higher costs—but also more toxification, as glyphosates are combined with "more toxic weedkillers" such as atrazine, an endocrine disrupter, and 2, 4-D, a powerful carcinogen. Perversely enough, all of it would be acceptable (to capital) if the new model produced a new yield boom, producing more food with less labor. But this boom has not materialized.

The superweed effect marks a quantity-quality shift in the history of an enduring contradiction. Capitalism's long history of agro-ecological control regimes began with the monocultures and highly regimented work disciplines of early modern plantations. Today, it has crossed a world-historical threshold with molecular and other disciplinary projects. The functionality of abstract social nature is breaking down. This shift is a new era of extra-human nature's resistance, in which the short-run fixes not only become progressively shorter-run, but progressively more toxic. In previous eras, capital's need for totalizing control, however significant, was less extensive, for the sound reason that faltering labor productivity in one zone could be "fixed" through a new round of global expansion. Problems with English agricultural productivity in the eighteenth century, for example, were never resolved within England, but rather through successive frontier movements, especially in North America. The accessibility of sizeable frontiers of appropriation in previous eras that capital's pursuit of control was more relaxed, its capacity to achieve rising productivity greater, its toxification tendencies weaker.

This suggests that twenty-first century capitalism confronts a historical nature very different from earlier centuries.

CHEAP FOOD, BAD CLIMATE: FROM SURPLUS VALUE TO NEGATIVE-VALUE

This evolutionary response—the superweed effect—is bound up with a profound shift in the history of capitalism: the transition from surplus value to negative-value. In this transition, the "old" contradictions of depletion are meeting up with the "new" contradictions of waste and toxification. The old productivist model—the law of Cheap Nature—has been adept at finding fixes to resource depletion. But it is ill suited to dealing with negative-value, those forms of nature that elude and frustrate Cheap Nature "fixes." Superweeds are clearly expressive of this tendency. They can now be controlled only with great toxification and greater cost. Meanwhile both direct and indirect toxification from capitalist agriculture feeds, with increasing force, into new forms of negative-value: climate change, cancer epidemics, and so forth.

The barriers to a new agricultural revolution are, consequently, extraordinary. This is true even if we bracket the geopolitical tensions that have stalled agro-food liberalization, and the class struggles from below that have challenged market-dependent "food security" in the name of food sovereignty.[183] The list of prominent biophysical challenges surely begins with climate change, which is *already* suppressing work/energy potential. The UN sees "an absolute decline" in net primary productivity for 12 percent of the planet[184] by 2050, but the problem is even more immediate. While global NPP increased between 1982 and 1999—was this merely coincident with the neoliberal golden age?—it declined between 2000 and 2009.[185] With global impacts concentrated in the South (Indonesia's NPP declined nearly 20 percent), the decade was punctuated by a series of severe droughts.[186] These have continued, with Russia's in 2010 followed by severe drought in the North China Plain in 2010–11, and in North America in 2012. To climate change we can add rising energy costs; escalating competition for arable land from agro-fuels; the proliferation of invasive species; the superweed effect; the end of Cheap water, as global warming melts glaciers, rearranges precipitation patterns, and drives aquifer depletion; and the declining effectiveness of fertilizers on yield growth.

But climate change is not simply one more "environmental" issue to add to capitalism's cumulative woes. The nineteenth-century opening of the atmosphere as a planetary waste dump for capital's pollution has now reached a critical moment. This holds for ongoing biospheric "state shifts,"[187] and also for how waste is feeding back into the ledger of world accumulation. Here again is our double internality, as the biosphere internalizes capitalism's contradictions, and now, as capitalism internalizes biospheric change.

---

183   Weis, *The Global Food Economy* (2007); McMichael, *Food Regimes* (2013).

184   C. Nellemann, et al., eds., *The Environmental Food Crisis* (Oslo: United Nations Environment Programme, 2009).

185   M. Zhao and S.W. Running, "Drought-Induced Reduction in Global Terrestrial Net Primary Production from 2000 Through 2009," *Science* 329 (2010): 940–943.

186   Ibid.

187   A.D. Barnosky, et al., "Approaching a State Shift in Earth's Biosphere," *Nature* 486 (2012): 52–58.

Climate change is the paradigm moment of the transition to negative-value. There is no conceivable way that capitalism can address climate change in any meaningful way, because climate change poses a fundamental challenge to the old productivist model. That challenge has two major expressions. The first says that production systems must internalize waste costs, including of course greenhouse emissions. The second says that the internalization of waste costs cannot be offset through new Cheap Nature strategies that are themselves highly polluting. In other words, any effective response to climate change will have to go forward without the myth—and practice—of unpaid work and unpaid waste.

The paired, but spatially and temporally uneven, processes of appropriating unpaid work/energy and toxifying the biosphere have reached a breaking point. The accumulation of negative-value, immanent but latent from the origins of capitalism, is now issuing contradictions that can no longer be "fixed" by technical, organizational, or imperial restructuring. The ongoing closure of frontiers limits the capacity of capital and states to attenuate the rising costs of production and the geometrically rising volume of waste from the global determination of profitability. If capitalism is an "economy of unpaid costs,"[188] the bills are coming due. And if only that were the crux of the problem! As we have seen, capitalism is also a *system of unpaid work*, reliant on mobilizing human ingenuity in service to appropriating an ever-rising stream of unpaid work/energy. With negative-value, we are tracing much more than socio-ecological externalities, although these externalities are indeed part of the problem. The combination of depletion and unpredictability—co-producing rising costs of production—is the hallmark of the ongoing transition from "surplus" to "negative" value. The core processes of capital accumulation are now generating increasingly direct and immediate barriers to the expanded reproduction of capital. These contradictions *within capital*, arising from negative-value, are today encouraging an unprecedented shift towards a radical ontological politics *beyond capital*. Such politics have found dramatic expression in movements for "food sovereignty," which maintains that sustainability, democracy, and cultural determination are inseparable when it comes to food. Because such politics pose an alternative, relational holism to the fragmented political and economic vistas of the bourgeoisie, they threaten to destabilize crucial points of agreement in the modern world-system: What is Food? What is Nature? What is Valuable?

---

188   K. William Kapp, *The Social Costs of Private Enterprise* (New York: Schocken Books, 1950).

The Rise of Negative-Value

The new politics of food justice movements can be understood as a response to the exhaustion of capitalism's agricultural revolution model. We have surveyed the exhaustion of the neoliberal model in relation to biotechnology. There has been no reversal of yield deceleration,[189] no net gain in food security.[190] "Dispossession" has registered so strikingly in radical discourse precisely because neoliberalism's agrarian transformations redistributed power and wealth from poor to rich without a productivity revolution.[191] This agro-ecological stagnation tells us something important about *capitalist* technological dynamism today. Absent the identification and appropriation of significant new streams of unpaid work/energy, technology is unable to deliver significant advances in labor productivity. Here the long Green Revolution mirrors the system-wide deceleration of labor productivity growth since the 1970s.[192]

But the situation is more explosive than a resource- and nutrient-depletion model suggests. On the one hand, the usual agro-capitalist technical fixes—or *attempted* fixes—are undermining whatever possibilities might remain for a new round of world accumulation. These movements reinforce extant tendencies towards nutrient- and resource-depletion: nature as "tap." On the other hand, the ongoing closure of the "waste frontier"—whose leading expression is climate change—is activating a new set of limits, swirling around nature as "sink."

This contradiction—between nature-as-tap and nature-as-sink—is issuing limits of a new sort: the limits of *negative-value*.[193] Negative-value can be understood as the accumulation of limits to capital in the web of life that are direct barriers to the restoration of the Four Cheaps: food, labor-power, energy, and raw materials. As we've seen, the food/labor nexus is especially important. Historically, the accumulation of negative-value assumed a latent or potential form. It is now activated through late capitalism's marriage of productivism, global trade and transport, and toxification. The contradictions are immediate, direct, and deepening in the early twenty-first century.

The accumulation of negative-value is therefore an immanent contradiction

---

189   Gurian-Sherman, *Failure to Yield* (2009).

190   UNCTAD [United Nations Commission on Trade and Development], *Wake Up Before It's Too Late* (New York: United Nations, 2013).

191   Harvey, *The New Imperialism* (2003); Moore, "The End of the Road?" (2010).

192   G. Balakrishnan, "Speculations on the Stationary State," *New Left Review* II, no. 59 (2009): 5–26; Gordon, "Is US Economic Growth Over?" (2012).

193   In this, Foster comes close conceptually—without altering his model of capitalism theoretically—to the present argument: "The accumulation of capital is at the same time accumulation of catastrophe, not only for a majority of the world's people, *but living species generally*" (J.B. Foster, "Capitalism and the Accumulation of Catastrophe," *Monthly Review* 63, no. 7 [2011]: 16, emphasis added).

of the production of surplus value in the circuit of capital. It should not be confused with a broader set of so-called "environmental" contradictions arising from the development of historical capitalism, largely because negative-value transcends the boundaries of the human and extra-human. Here the distinction between capital (as self-expanding value) and capitalism (as historical system) is key. Negative-value, from this perspective, is bound up with, but not reducible to, the externalization of costs and the social movements—environmentalism above all—that have developed in response to this externalization since the 1970s.

Understanding the capital relation as co-produced in and through the web of life entails a conceptualization of capital's internal crises as co-produced: the rising organic composition of capital, broadly conceived, entails the rising capitalized composition of global nature. The two are distinct expressions for a singular, uneven, historical process. If the former generates a tendency towards a declining rate of profit, the latter not only reinforces the former (as capital bears a rising share of reproduction costs for human and extra-human natures), but also generates a new set of problems. These problems, as I will try to make clear, combine the old and the new: in part, resource depletion and rising costs of production, yes. [194] But in part—and a rising part at that!—a destabilization of the conditions of biospheric stability and biological health that have obtained for centuries, even millennia.

Negative-value, then, is a means to situate three problems in a unified frame: 1) the ongoing, and impending, non-linear shifts of the biosphere and its biological systems; 2) the rising costs of production; and 3) the ongoing overaccumulation of capital. These three moments represent a bundle of contradictions within capital that provide fertile ground for a new radical politics that challenges capitalism on ontological grounds: questioning the practical viability, yes, of capitalist markets and production, but more fundamentally, the ontology of value and nature in the modern world-system.

Nature-As-Tap, Nature-As-Sink: Negative-Value's Combined and Uneven Development

The "normal" course of capitalist technological dynamism is not only failing to resolve the energy, nutrient, and resource problems it faces. These problems are getting worse; and they are getting worse out of all proportion to any linear expectation. Why? Because there is a cumulative dimension to primary production. The long era of high "rewards" with minimal "effort" and low environmental

---

194   Cf. Ponting, *A Green History of the World* (1991); J. O'Connor, *Natural Causes* (New York: Guilford Press, 1998).

impact is yielding to a non-linear curve of declining rewards and rising effort, implicating dramatically greater environmental changes.[195] Contrast an Oklahoma cricket pump in the 1930s with offshore drilling in the Gulf of Mexico today. The world-historical arc of the long Green Revolution reveals a similar process: more and more herbicides and fertilizers are necessary to produce each increment of (decelerating) productivity growth.

The cumulative and cyclical dimensions of nature-as-tap—taking the world-historical form of scientific, extractive, labor, and agricultural revolutions—are now meeting up with the cumulative dimension of nature-as-sink. Every great movement of appropriating new streams of unpaid work/energy implies a disproportionately larger volume of waste. That disproportionality has grown over time. The dimension of waste is therefore a crucial relation missing—to this point—from our simplified model of accumulation and crisis. Value and waste are dialectically bound, in a cumulatively disproportionate relation. Agriculture, however, was relatively immune from this contradiction until fairly late in the game. Not until the advent of the long Green Revolution did agriculture assume a vanguard role in toxification—flooding soils, water, and air with the effluents of petro-farming. Urbanization, mining, and industry had been generating a rising volume of wastes since the sixteenth century, when contemporaries observed poisoned streams and befouled air amid the mining boomtowns of central Europe.[196] The globalization of the Green Revolution through American-led developmentalism—and then neoliberal restructuring—changed that. Agriculture has now moved to the pole position in the race to pollute the earth—in part because of its energy- and chemical-intensity, but also because its role in land clearance removes forests which would otherwise lock up carbon.[197]

Capitalism's double squeeze on taps and sinks has been recognized—especially in relation to climate change—but I think its epochal implications are underappreciated. I would spotlight two aspects of this double squeeze. One is that capitalism's wastes are now overflowing the sinks, and spilling over onto the ledgers of capital. Climate change, once again, is our most expressive instance of this phenomenon. Hence, the connection between biospheric "state shifts" and accumulation crisis is more intimate than usually recognized. But I think there is another, deeper, historical-geographical problem that has not (yet) been sufficiently considered: the *temporality* of nature-as-tap differs significantly from the temporality of nature-as-sink. New primary production regimes, until now,

---

195   Davidson, et al., "The Effort Factor" (2014).

196   Nef, *Conquest of the Material World* (1964).

197   T. Herzog, "World Greenhouse Gas Emissions in 2005" (WRI Working Paper, (1964). Washington, D.C.: World Resources Institute, July 2009). Accessed July 4, 2014, www.papierenkarton.nl/uploads/world_greenhouse_gas_emissions_2005.pdf.

could develop much faster than did waste-induced costs. Outrunning these contradictions was possible because there were geographical frontiers—not just continents, but bodily, subterranean, and atmospheric spaces—from which "free gifts" could be extracted, and into which "free garbage" could be deposited.

There is, then, a fantastically non-linear dynamic at play. Capitalist technological advance not only produces a tendency for industrial production to run ahead of its raw materials supply—Marx's "general law" of underproduction. It also produces *a general law of overpollution*: the tendency to enclose and fill up waste frontiers faster than it can locate new ones. Thus the non-linear slope of the waste accumulation curve over the *longue durée*, with a series of sharp upticks after 1945, 1975, and 2008. As "resource quality"—a wretched term—declines, it is not only more costly to extract work/energy, *it becomes more toxic*. Thus the transition from placer to cyanide gold mining, or the rising share of strip mining in world coal production.[198] The result today is a world in which every nook and cranny bears the impress of capital's toxification: from heavy metals in Arctic glaciers and children's blood, to the plastic "garbage patches" in the Atlantic and Pacific Oceans, to rising atmospheric concentrations of CO_2.[199]

This unsavory convergence—of nature-as-tap and nature-as-sink—is rapidly undermining the possibility for "normal" capitalism to survive, over the medium run of the next 20–30 years. The contradictions of capitalism have always been escapable, until now, because there were escape hatches: peasantries to be proletarianized, new oil fields to exploit, new forests to convert to cash-crop agriculture. These processes continue, albeit under progressively more ruthless conditions. What merits our attention today—and what many Greens, unduly focused on what capitalism *does to* nature (the degradation question) rather than how nature *works for* capitalism (the work/energy question), have overlooked—is how capital is throwing up limits of an entirely new character.

Two major streams of negative-value can be identified immediately. (These are far from the only ones, and we focus on the explicitly biospheric and

---

198   Davidson, et al., "The Effort Factor" (2014).

199   S.M. Singh, et al., "Atmospheric Deposition Studies of Heavy Metals in Arctic by Comparative Analysis of Lichens and Cryoconite," *Environmental Monitoring and Assessment* 185, no. 2 (2013): 1367–1376; L. Pawłowski, "How Heavy Metals Affect Sustainable Development," *Rocznik Ochrona Środowiska* 13, no. 2 (2011): 51–64; C. Moore, "Trashed: Across the Pacific Ocean, Plastics, Plastics, Everywhere," *Natural History* 112, no. 9 (2003): 46–51; R.A. Lovett, "Huge Garbage Patch Found in Atlantic Too," *National Geographic News*, March 2, 2010. Accessed July 29, 2014, news. nationalgeographic.com/news/2010/03/100302-new-ocean-trash-garbage-patch; G.P. Peters, et al., "Rapid Growth in CO_2 Emissions After the 2008–2009 Global Financial Crisis," *Nature Climate Change* 2, no. 1 (2012): 2–4.

biological moments as particularly expressive of the problem, not as the boundaries of the process.[200]) One is climate change. Together, world agriculture and forestry (including land clearance) contributes between one-quarter and one-third of greenhouse gas emissions—rivaling or exceeding industry or energy.[201] On the one hand, climate change is reinforcing tendencies—such as aquifer depletion—already in motion before the 1990s. On the other hand, climate change is creating new problems: suppressing the yield of the "big four" cereals (rice, wheat, maize, and soy), changing precipitation patterns, and suppressing labor productivity during the increasingly hot summer months when most planting and harvesting occurs.[202] Yield suppression is already occurring.

---

200   A fuller analysis of negative-value would move beyond the immediately geobiological emphasis that I have presented, and unpack, for instance, the role of financialization in food commodity markets and in shaping global supply chains, from grain trading to supermarkets, which have the consequence of squeezing both producers and customers in the "corporate food regime." See respectively, Kaufman, *Bet the Farm*; S. Ryan Isakson, "Food and finance: the financial transformation of agro-food supply chains," *The Journal of Peasant Studies* 41, no. 5 (2014): 749–75; Philip McMichael, "The land grab and corporate food regime restructuring," *Journal of Peasant Studies*, 39, nos. 3–4 (2012): 681–701. The financialization of agro-food relations (including the recent "land grab"), moreover, signals a new stage in the fetishization of food at the very moment when the relations of power and production in the global food system have become more clear than ever before (see esp. J. Clapp, "Financialization, distance and global food politics," *The Journal of Peasant Studies* 41, no. 5 [2014]: 797–814). Such a line of investigation would reveal finance and farming as co-producing not only food and capital, but climate, power, and much more.

201   Intergovernmental Panel on Climate Change, *Climate Change 2007: Synthesis Report* (Geneva: Intergovernmental Panel on Climate Change, 2007), 36, www.ipcc.ch/pdf/assessment-report/ar4/syr/ar4_syr.pdf, accessed July 26, 2014; idem., "Summary for Policymakers," in *Climate Change 2014: Mitigation of Climate Change* (Geneva: Intergovernmental Panel on Climate Change, 2014), http://www.ipcc.ch/pdf/assessment-report/ar5/wg3/ipcc_wg3_ar5_summary-for-policymakers.pdf. Accessed January 20, 2015.

202   S. Peng, et al., "Rice yields decline with higher night temperature from global warming," *Proceedings of the National Academic of Science*, 101, no. 27 (2004): 9971–9975; C.E.P. Cerri, et al., "Tropical agriculture and global warming: impacts and mitigation options," *Scientia Agricola* 64, no. 1 (2007): 83–99; D.B. Lobell and C.B. Field, "Global scale climate–crop yield relationships and the impacts of recent warming," *Environmental Research Letters* 2, no. 1 (2007): 014002; Christopher J. Kucharik, and Shawn P. Serbin, "Impacts of recent climate change on Wisconsin corn and soybean yield trends," *Environmental Research Letters*, 3, no. 3 (2008): 034003; A.J. Challinor, et al., "A meta-analysis of crop yield under climate change and adaptation," *Nature Climate Change*, 4, no. 4 (2014): 287–91; J. Zivin and M. Neidell, *Temperature and the Allocation of Time*, Working Paper, 15717. National Bureau of Economic Research, Washington, DC., 2010; Kate Gordon, ed., *Risky Business: The Economic Risks of Climate Change in the*

Between 1980 and 2008, global "maize and wheat production declined by 3.8 percent and 5.5 percent, respectively, compared to a counterfactual without climate trends."[203] By 2035, agriculture will bear one-third, and by 2060 two-thirds, of the global costs issuing from climate change.[204] Here is negative-value at work: the production of direct barriers to capital's Cheap Nature model, mediated through the climate-induced erosion of agricultural productivity.

While no simple causal line can be drawn between climate change and particular events, the link between global warming, drought frequency and global aridity is well established.[205] One therefore reads with some concern about American maize production moving towards *more*—not less—drought sensitivity.[206] The American Midwest is responsible for one-third of world maize output and half of world exports:[207] any serious drought in the American agricultural heartlands is a world-historical event. By January 2014, "nearly all of California," the country's leading agricultural state, "was in a state of extreme drought" and half of the U.S. suffered from drought by May, affecting "54 percent of the national wheat crop, 30 percent of the national corn area, 22 percent of soya beans, 32 percent of hay crops and 48 percent of cattle."[208] By the end of 2014, we learned that California's drought was the "most severe . . . in the last 1200 years."[209] While drought is not exceptional in itself, the trend since 2001 is towards "longer, more severe droughts," a movement with dire implications for

---

United States (New York: Risky Business Project, 2014); S. Asseng, et al., "Rising Temperatures Reduce Global Wheat Production," *Nature Climate Change* (2014), online first.

203   Lobell, et al., "Climate Trends and Global Crop Production since 1980" (2011).

204   H. Braconier, et al., "Policy Challenges for the Next 50 Years," *OECD Economic Policy Paper No. 9* (Paris: Organization for Economic Cooperation and Development, 2014).

205   A. Dai, "Drought Under Global Warming," *Climate Change* 2, no. 1 (2011): 45–65.

206   Lobell, et al., "Climate Trends and Global Crop Production" (2011).

207   D.R. Ort and S.P. Long, "Limits on Yields in the Corn Belt," *Science* 344, no. 6183 (2014): 484–5; NASA, "Drought Stressing California's Plantscape" (February 14, 2014). Accessed May 19, 2014, earthobservatory.nasa.gov/IOTD/view.php?id=83124.

208   Ort and Long, "Limits on Yields in the Corn Belt," *Science*. NASA, "Drought Stressing California's Plantscape" USDM [United States Drought Monitor], "U.S. Drought Monitor" (May 15, 2014). Accessed May 18, 2014. http://droughtmonitor.unl. edu/, S. Horne, "US Drought Could Halve Wheat Harvest in Oklahoma," *Farmer's Weekly* (May 12, 2014), www.fwi.co.uk/articles/12/05/2014/144492/us-drought-could-halve-wheat-harvest-in-oklahoma.htm.

209   D. Griffin, and K. J. Anchukaitis, "How unusual is the 2012–2014 California Drought?", *Geophysical Research Letters* 41, (2014): 9017.

yields[210]—and for rising costs of production. The bill for the 2014 drought comes to $1.5 billion for California agriculture alone.[211] Worse still, not only do rising temperatures suppress crop and labor productivity, but rising CO_2 concentrations alter the nutritional content of cereal crops in exactly the wrong direction: reducing protein, zinc, and iron content at a time when nutrient deficiencies *already* affect some three billion people.[212]

The Superweed Effect: Not Just Weeds . . .

A second stream of negative-value accumulation is more subtle, but just as problematic. This is the superweed effect: the tendency of extra-human natures to evolve more rapidly than the technological disciplines of capitalist agriculture. In essence, the superweed effect signifies the co-evolution of forms of work/energy that are hostile to capital accumulation, and whose hostility cannot be readily blunted by the usual strategies of the "taming cycle."

The superweed *effect* is at once creative and destructive. It is *creative* insofar as weeds have evolved to survive the RoundUp Ready herbicides (glyphosates) that are fundamental to genetically modified soy and other crops.[213] And, as if to move from the frying pan to the fire, rising CO_2 concentrations strongly favor invasive weeds, above and beyond rising temperature.[214] The superweeds' resistance is now calling forth a new effort by agro-biotech firms to introduce 2,4-D-resistant soybeans in the U.S., Brazil, Argentina, and South Africa. Perhaps best known as the key ingredient in the "Agent Orange" of the Vietnam War, 2,4-D is a known carcinogen and endocrine-disruptor. If successful, this newest round of GMOs would mark a "rerun of the 1990s' introduction of

---

210   P. Bump, "What's Exceptional about the Current Drought—And What Isn't," *Washington Post* (May 17, 2014), washingtonpost.com; W. Schlenker and M.J. Roberts, "Nonlinear Temperature Effects Indicate Severe Damages to U.S. Crop Yields Under Climate Change," *Proceedings of the National Academy of Sciences* 106, no. 37 (2009): 15594–8.

211   R. Howitt, et al., "Economic Analysis of the 2014 Drought for California Agriculture" (Center for Watershed Sciences, University of California-Davis, 2014). Accessed July 17, 2014, watershed.ucdavis.edu/files/content/news/Economic_Impact_of_the_2014_California_Water_Drought.pdf .

212   S. Myers, et al., "Increasing CO_2 Threatens Human Nutrition," *Nature* (online first, 2014); S. Keats and S. Wiggins, *Non-Staple Foods and Micro-Nutrient Status* (London: Overseas Development Institute, 2010).

213   N. Gilbert, "A Hard Look at GM Crops," *Nature* 497 (2013): 24–6.

214   L.H. Ziska, "Evaluation of the Growth Response of Six Invasive Species to Past, Present and Future Atmospheric Carbon Dioxide," *Journal of Experimental Botany* 54 (2003): 395–404.

Roundup Ready (glyphosate-resistant) crops, *only this time the herbicides in question are much more toxic.*"[215] Nor is this concern merely speculative. *Already,* 2,4-D applications in the U.S. have grown apace with glyphosate (e.g., RoundUp Ready) use—the former rising 90 percent between 2000 and 2012.[216]

Nor is the superweed effect limited to weeds. Antibiotic resistance, fueled by the meat-industrial complex and abetted by the Western medical model, has developed to such an extent that it threatens "to set medicine back a century."[217] For the World Health Organization, antibiotic resistance is an "impending public health crisis"[218]—although one wonders just how impending it really is. As with superweeds, "superbugs" have flourished in an era of warming climate, reinforcing the contradictions of antibiotic promiscuity.[219] Rising costs of "social" reproduction in this sphere are already evident. Antibiotic resistance in the U.S. *alone* is responsible for $21–35 billion in additional costs, eight million additional hospital days, and a net drag on GDP growth between .4 and 1.6 percent annually.[220] So far, the marginal benefit has favored the meat-industrial complex, for which antibiotic promiscuity facilitates about $2 billion in extra profits annually.[221] How long the trade-off can be sustained—even within a capitalist logic—is not clear. Fully three-quarters of "all emerging infectious diseases now originate in animals or animal products."[222] The combination of antibiotic resistance, climate change, and global flows of human and extra-human nature points towards disease as a significant nexus of negative-value in coming decades.

The superweed effect's creativity is matched by a less obvious, but portentous, movement of destruction. In this, the plight of our honeybees and the mysterious "colony collapse disorder" is instructive. A herald of our times, nobody really understands colony collapse—it is an unpredictable, unruly, unknown vector of a crisis that everybody sees but no one (not yet, not fully) really

---

215   GRAIN, "2,4-D Soy Waging War on Peasants," *GRAIN Report* (2014).

216   Food and Water Watch, *Superweeds* (2013).

217   "Antibiotic Resistance: The Drugs Don't Work," *Economist* (May 3, 2014).

218   WHO, *Antimicrobial Resistance* (Paris: World Health Organization, 2014).

219   WHO, *Climate Change and Human Health* (Paris: World Health Organization, 2003); S. Altizer, et al., "Climate Change and Infectious Diseases," *Science* 341, no. 6145 (2013): 514–19; T.P. van Boeckel, et al., "Global Antibiotic Consumption 2000 to 2010," *The Lancet Infectious Diseases* (July 10, 2014, early online publication).

220   G. Dantas and M.O.A. Sommer, "How to Fight Back Against Antibiotic Resistance," *American Scientist* 102 (2014): 42–51; WHO, *Antimicrobial Resistance* (Geneva: World Health Organization, 2014).

221   Pimentel, et al., "Food Production and the Energy Crisis," (1973), 270.

222   L. Reynolds and D. Nierenberg, "Disease and Drought Curb Meat Production and Consumption," in *Vital Signs 20*, ed. the WorldWatch Institute (Washington, D.C.: Island Press, 2013), 51.

understands.[223] While some species, like our superweeds, adapt by evolving quickly in the face of new pesticides, for others, the immediate options are more constrained. Collapse is as much a revolt against capitalist imperatives as surviving the toxic onslaught. If the proximate cause of colony collapse disorder is not yet clear, its socio-ecological roots are not hard to pinpoint. As Kosek explains capitalist beekeeping has

> radically altered the structure and behavior of the hive . . .[towards] *a fully industrialized hive modeled on the modern factory*. The bee's range has also been radically altered, from a radius of two miles to the migratory geography of the modern bee, who travels thousands of miles of on the back of semi-trucks and is fed on corn syrup and soy protein supplements in order to pollinate single crops for eight weeks at a time . . . This mobility in turn allowed for the rise of the industrial geography of beekeeping, in which 80 percent of the hives in the US are now trucked around the country, serving the mono-crop blooms of large scale industrial agriculture. Without this service, a large portion of contemporary agriculture would simply not be biologically or economically possible. [224]

Today the industrialization of honeybee production is approaching a tipping point. Bee colony loss rates increased from an average of 10 to 15 percent in the second half of the twentieth century to 20–30 percent (often on the high end) since 2006.[225] This is no small matter given that we rely, directly and indirectly, on animal (especially bee) pollination for one-third of the food we eat.[226] Some $19 billion in American, and $200 billion in world, agricultural output depends on this pollination.[227] Although pollination costs are a small part of farm costs,

---

223   R. Jacobsen, *Fruitless Fall* (New York: Bloomsbury, 2010).

224   J. Kosek, "The Natures of the Beast," in *Global Political Ecology*, ed. R. Peet, et al. (London: Routledge, 2011), 245.

225   The White House, "The Economic Challenge Posed by Declining Pollinator Populations," (2014). Accessed July 14, 2014, www.whitehouse.gov/the-press-office/2014/06/20/fact-sheet-economic-challenge-posed-declining-pollinator-populations; B. Plumer, "Honeybee Deaths Went Down Last Winter," *Vox* (May 15, 2014). Accessed July 13, 2014, www.vox.com/2014/5/15/5720232/good-news-honeybee-deaths-are-finally-declining.

226   C.A. Kearns, et al., "Endangered Mutualisms: The Conservation of Plant-Pollinator Interactions," *Annual Review of Ecology and Systematics* 29 (1998): 83–112.

227   A. Fairbrother, et al., "Risks of Neonicotinoid Insecticides to Honeybees," *Environmental Toxicology and Chemistry* 33, no. 4 (2014): 719–31; S. Ingber, "As Honeybees Die Off, First Inventory of Wild Bees Is Under Way," *National Geographic* [online] (July 11, 2014). Accessed July 14, 2014, news.nationalgeographic.com/news/2014/07/140711-wild-bees-north-america-honeybees-science.

the trend is not encouraging: hive costs have tripled over the past decade.[228] Nor is the recent experience of southwest China encouraging—where *hand*-pollination is common and "where wild bees have been eradicated by excessive pesticide use and habitat" removal.[229]

Among the culprits is the deployment of neonicotinoid insecticides, introduced in the mid-1990s. And while the evidence indicting neonicotinoids for colony collapse disorder is mounting,[230] it seems clear that the problem is animated by the logic of capitalist beekeeping over the past century, one immanent in the agricultural revolution model that is now faltering. In the heartland of the long Green Revolution, the American Midwest, some 45 percent of bee species have been wiped out[231]—a story sadly replicated across the globe's toxic landscapes of cash-crop cultivation.[232]

For colony collapse disorder is, say, a canary in a coalmine.

Towards a Socialist World-Ecology?

Agricultural biotechnology, as we know, has sought to extend the Cheap Food model. The optimistic estimates anticipate a one-third *decline* in the rate of output growth—from 1.5 percent to 1 percent annually—over the next decade.[233] Thus, agro-biotech has failed to reproduce modernity's agricultural revolution model—without which modernity as we know it does not exist. At best, agro-biotech has provided short-run gains to farmers, who quickly see those gains disappear, leaving them with increasingly heavy debt burdens and herbicide-dependency.[234] Very high agricultural productivity may, however, be possible with alternative farming practices premised on agro-ecology, permaculture, and

228   J. Marcotty, "Nature's Dying Migrant Worker," *Star-Tribune* (July 6, 2014). Accessed July 14, 2014, www.startribune.com/local/264929101.html.

229   D. Goulson, "Decline of Bees Forces China's Apple Farmers to Pollinate by Hand," *China Dialogue* (October 2, 2012). Accessed July 18, 2014, www.chinadialogue.net/article/show/single/en/5193.

230   V. Doublet, et al., "Bees under Stress: Sublethal doses of a neonicotinoid pesticide and pathogens interact to elevate honey bee mortality across the life cycle," *Environmental Microbiology*, online (2014); R.J. Gill and N.E. Raine (2014), "Chronic impairment of bumblebee natural foraging behaviour induced by sublethal pesticide exposure," *Functional Ecology*, 28, no. 6 (2014): 1459–71.

231   L.A. Burkle, et al., "Plant-pollinator interactions over 120 years," *Science*, 339, no. 6127 (2013): 1611–15.

232   Jacobsen, *Fruitless Fall.*

233   OECD/FAO, *Agricultural Outlook 2014–2023* (Paris: OECD Publishing, 2014).

234   Gurian-Sherman, *Failure to Yield* (2009); A. Kumbamu, *Grounding Global Seeds* (PhD dissertation, Department of Sociology, University of Alberta, 2010).

other non-capitalist agronomies. The spectacular, if episodic, success of the System of Rice Intensification[235] capable of producing more than 20 tons of rice on a hectare of land[236]—is highly suggestive of such an alternate path.

This alternative path can, of course, only be followed through class struggle—but a class struggle understood as a contest over the configuration of the *oikeios*. This is class struggle as the relation of production and reproduction, of power and wealth in the web of life. In this respect, the barriers to a new agricultural revolution are not limited to biophysical natures as such; they are also co-produced through the class struggle, itself co-produced through nature.

It is much easier to celebrate the class struggle than to analyze it. We can say with some confidence that food—not just land—has become a central site of the world class struggle in a way that is entirely unprecedented, and unthinkable even three decades ago. To be sure, the struggle over food is more than a class struggle, and many forms of food justice appear quite modest: calls for supporting organic agriculture, local farmer's markets, Transition Towns, and so forth. But if neoliberal subjectivities persist—sometimes subtly and at others rudely embracing individualizing- and market-dynamics—we appear to be witnessing an important shift since the mid-2000s. This is the movement, unevenly cultural and political, towards "food justice": the popular face of food sovereignty in the Global North.[237] As neoliberalism's macabre ontological shift in the definition of food has rolled out—shifting from the Green Revolution's caloric metric to the "edible foodlike substances" that now line our supermarket shelves[238]—it seems to have made food, and by extension nature, much more fundamental to the Old Left questions of *liberté, égalité, fraternité* than ever before. The class struggle of the twenty-first century will turn, in no small measure, upon how one answers the questions: What is food? What is nature? What is valuable?

Even on the basis of its strongest historical justification—the forces of production—capitalism now stumbles. For the alternative suggested by the System of Rice Intensification—taken in both literal and metaphorical senses of the

---

235 N. Uphoff, "Agroecological Implications of the System of Rice Intensification (SRI) in Madagascar," *Environment, Development and Sustainability* 1, nos. 3–4 (1999): 297–313.

236 J. Vidal, "Miracle Grow: Indian Rice Farmer Uses Controversial Method for Record Crop," *Guardian* (May 12, 2014). Accessed May 28, 2014, www.theguardian. com/global-development/2014/may/13/miracle-grow-indian-rice-farmer-sri-system-rice-intensification-record-crop.

237 See A.H. Alkon and J. Agyeman, eds., *Cultivating Food Justice* (Cambridge, MA: MIT Press, 2011); A.H. Alkon and T.M. Mares, "Food Sovereignty in US Food Movements," *Agriculture and Human Values* 28 (2012): 347–59; H. Friedmann, "Food Sovereignty in the Golden Horseshoe Region of Ontario," in *Food Sovereignty in Canada*, ed. H. Wittman, et al. (Halifax: Fernwood, 2011), 168–89.

238 M. Pollan, *In Defense of Food* (New York: Penguin, 2008).

concept—cannot be generalized except through a new imagining of food, nature, and value. It is in this sense that the agro-ecological alternative is a path that points to way out of capitalism and towards a socialist world-ecology.[239] This alternative can only be realized—*can only be organized in the present*—through a class struggle that redefines what is valuable (and what is not) in the civilization we wish to build.

What would a socialist valuation of humans and the rest of nature look like? This can only be answered through practical activity and reflexive theorization. But provisional answers, taken as guiding threads, can be offered. In my view, the elements of a socialist world-ecology are all around us. And though these elements are not limited to food, food politics today offers some of the most hopeful glimpses of the future many of us wish to see. In the United States,

> organic, urban, community-assisted and guerrilla agriculture are still small parts of the picture, but effective ones—a revolt against what transnational corporate food and capitalism generally produce. This revolt is taking place in the vast open space of Detroit, in the inner-city farms of West Oakland, in the victory gardens and public-housing of Alemany Farm in San Francisco, in Growing Power in Milwaukee and many other places around the country. These are blows against alienation, poor health, hunger and other woes fought with shovels and seeds, not guns. At its best, tending one's garden leads to tending one's community and policy, and ultimately becomes a way of entering the public sphere rather than withdrawing from it.[240]

Even allowing for some measure of exaggeration in this statement—it is clear, for instance, that state power will be needed, in the U.S. and elsewhere, to re-orient agriculture towards democratic and sustainable practices[241]—food and agriculture has become a decisive battleground of the world class struggle. It is no longer largely a struggle of peasant against landlords. Food security, safety, and sustainability have become central questions in the everyday lives of the world proletariat, from Beijing to Boston.[242]

---

239   E. Holt-Gime´nez and M.A. Altieri, "Agroecology, Food Sovereignty, and the New Green Revolution," *Agroecology and Sustainable Food Systems* 37, no. 1 (2013): 90–102.

240   R. Solnit, "The Revolution Has Already Occurred," *The Nation* (June 27, 2008).

241   And yet it is far from clear what such a deployment of state power would look like. The role of the state, as Bernstein notes, is the "elephant in the room": not just for food sovereignty but red-green politics more broadly (H. Bernstein, "Food Sovereignty via the 'Peasant Way,'" *Journal of Peasant Studies* [2014]: 1–33).

242   H-M. Lam, et al., "Food Supply and Food Safety Issues in China," *The Lancet* 381 (2013): 2044–2053.

Of course such developments in the North are still modest in world perspective. In this respect, the rise of La Vía Campesina signals an important development in the world history of food.[243] For Vía Campesina, representing some 200 million people, challenges the very heart of capitalist productivism in agriculture through its articulation of food sovereignty. Food sovereignty, at its best, asserts a revolutionary ontology of food—food as biospheric, as democratic, as cultural . . . *all at the same time.*[244] Each moment is implied in the others, "sustainability" unthinkable except through democratic and egalitarian praxis. In this vision, food sovereignty becomes the

> right of peoples to healthy and culturally appropriate food produced through ecologically sound and sustainable methods, and their right to define their own food and agriculture systems. It puts the aspirations and needs of those who produce, distribute and consume food at the heart of food systems and policies rather than the demands of markets and corporations. It defends the interests and inclusion of the next generation. It offers a strategy to resist and dismantle the current corporate trade and food regime, and directions for food, farming, pastoral and fisheries systems determined by local producers and users. Food sovereignty prioritizes local and national economies and markets and empowers peasant and family farmer-driven agriculture, artisanal fishing, pastoralist-led grazing, and food production, distribution and consumption based on environmental, social and economic sustainability. Food sovereignty promotes transparent trade that guarantees just incomes to all peoples as well as the rights of consumers to control their food and nutrition. It ensures that the rights to use and manage lands, territories, waters, seeds, livestock and biodiversity are in the hands of those of us who produce food. Food sovereignty implies new social relations free of oppression and inequality between men and women, peoples, racial groups, social and economic classes and generations.[245]

But, if class struggle is always present, it frequently takes "structural" forms. Capitalism's agricultural revolution model *is* about class; it is about capital; and it is about a capitalist project to make nature external, controllable, and cheap. Power, capital, and nature form an organic whole.

---

243   We must be careful to analyze closely Via Campesina's class divisions, which cannot be collapsed into a global peasantry (Bernstein, "Food Sovereignty".).

244   McMichael, *Development and Social Change* (2012); H.K. Wittman, et al., eds., *Food Sovereignty* (Halifax, NS: Fernwood, 2010); Akram-Lodhi, "How to Build Food Sovereignty" (2013).

245   Nyéléni Forum for Food Sovereignty, "Nyéléni Declaration on Food Sovereignty," *Journal of Peasant Studies* (2009 [2007 orig.]): 673–6.

Conclusion

Capitalist agriculture today is headed towards an epochal transition: from contributing to capital accumulation by reducing the costs of labor-power, to undermining even the middle-run conditions necessary for renewed accumulation. This is signaled by the rise of negative-value. At the point of production, the superweed effect shows our future in the present: more energy- and chemical-intensive strategies to discipline agro-ecologies as these evolve into forms of work/energy hostile to the law of Cheap Nature. At the scale of the biosphere, the energy-intensive character of capitalist agriculture now feeds a spiral of global warming that increasingly limits capitalism as a whole.

Global warming poses a fundamental threat not only to humanity, but, more immediately and directly, to capitalism itself. This inverts the usual line of radical critique, which overstates the resilience of capitalism in the face of these changes—an overstatement that derives from a view of capitalism as a social system that acts upon nature, rather than a world-ecology that develops through the web of life. The condition for maintaining negative-value in its latent state was the possibility for moving entropy out of commodity production. Today, such latent negative-value can no longer be moved out, as biospheric changes penetrate global re/production relations with unusual power and salience. Global warming will, in the coming two decades, so thoroughly mobilize until-now latent negative-value—fed by capitalist agriculture and in turn undermining the Cheap Food model—that it is difficult to see how capitalist agriculture can survive.

This is not only because of its internal contradictions (within the circuit of capital) but also because of the new ontological challenge to capitalism's valuation project itself (within capitalist civilization). Negative-value is destabilizing surplus value, and in doing so it is making possible new, emancipatory and egalitarian vistas. Negative-value, as it congeals from here forward, is a barrier to capital as such; its encouragement of a new ontological politics carries forth the possibility of alternative valuations of food, nature, and everything else. It is these alternative valuations that will be pivotal to translating today's negative-value into alternative—and transformative—ethico-political valuations. In revealing capitalism's value-relations as the "value of nothing,"[246] the new contradictions and new movements, together, call into question the value of everything. The end of Cheap Food may well be the end of modernity, and the start of something much better.

---

246   Patel, *The Value of Nothing* (2009).

The End of Cheap Nature?: The World-Ecological Limit of Capital Is Capital Itself

We need now to go further, along paths hitherto little explored, to see the successive synchronous patterns of historical social systems within the ecological whole that is the earth. Wallerstein, 1980

Does capitalism today face the end of Cheap Nature? Of course, nature in a holistic sense is never cheap. *Cheap Nature* is the invention of a civilization premised on dualism. For five centuries, that dualism proved extraordinarily functional. Natures were appropriated. Capital was accumulated. Wastes were dumped overboard. That logic—and the strategies premised on it—has now reached the end of its particular road. Another course will have to be charted.

I have argued three propositions, in turn ontological, methodological, and historical-analytical. First, ecology as *oikeios* stands as a signifier of the whole and not the parts. If there is something resembling a fundamental ontological relation, it is between humans and the rest of nature—the *oikeios*. No domain of human experience is independent of it. World-ecology, as a framework for unifying the production of nature, the pursuit of power, and the accumulation of capital, offers a way of re-reading the diversity of modern human experience as unavoidably, irreducibly, socio-ecological. The upshot is that nature is a *historical* relation. But too little attention has been given to "incorporating" nature into the mode and method of analysis. There has been too little investigation into how bundles of human and extra-human relations constitute modernity's historical natures, and how patterns of power and capital are producers *and* products of those natures. The conventional wisdom says that modernity makes environmental history. But is not a more relational proposition more tenable: modernity *as* environmental history?

Methodologically, once we acknowledge that the old containers (Nature/Society) need to be radically refashioned, a different reading of capitalism's history is possible. We can begin to read modernity's world-historical patterns—soil exhaustion and deforestation, unemployment and financial crashes—through successive historical natures. Some of these expressions operate at ground level; others at the scales of accumulation. Many more processes work in between. Many do not appear to be socio-ecological at all—financialization, national identities, the prison-industrial complex. And this is precisely the point. A perspective that begins by *narrowing* the field of vision may not be the most fruitful choice in an era when an elusive logic of financial calculability rules the roost of global capitalism, shaping, as never before, the structures of everyday life—*including* the "everyday lives" of birds and bees and bugs, alongside human beings.

The alternative is a part-whole approach through which *concrete totalities* emerge. This approach "says to keep moving out by successive determinations, bringing successive parts—themselves abstract processes—in continuous juxtaposition and in this way form the whole which you need for interpreting and explaining . . . historical change."[1] For example, one may take the concept of a singular social metabolism, as we saw in Chapter Three, as a historically concrete relation that emerges through the "continuous juxtaposition" of various parts (e.g., episodes of resource exhaustion and urbanization), stabilized provisionally in "successive determinations" over the *longue durée*. Deforestation and resource depletion become historical facts only through such concrete movements, taken as movements of the whole. In other words, *historical* nature merits incorporation into the emergence of successive world capitalisms, in the spirit of McMichael's contention that "*neither* whole *nor* parts are permanent categories or units of analysis."[2]

If historical nature and historical capitalism form a dialectical unity, our thinking about capital undergoes a meaningful shift. We begin to see that the logic of capital owes its success as much to the extension of appropriation as it does to the capitalization of production—this, the dialectic of productivity and plunder. Capital's necessary balance between capitalization and appropriation—its inflection point ever-shifting—is important to acknowledge if we are to move beyond the incantation of "ecological" crisis as *external*, somehow, eventually, converging with *internal* "economic" crisis. For the claim of externality asserts the very question that merits investigation: the adaptability and evolution of the relation between humans and the rest of nature in the modern world. My view is therefore one that extends to the *oikeios* Arrighi's emphasis on capitalism's essential flexibility: "One of the major problems of the left, but also on the right, is to think there is only one kind of capitalism that reproduces itself historically; whereas capitalism has transformed itself substantively—particularly on a global basis—in unexpected ways."[3]

Can we not say the same thing about historical natures in the modern

---

1   Hopkins, "World-Systems Analysis" (1982), 147.

2   P. McMichael, "Incorporating Comparison Within a World-Historical Perspective," *American Sociological Review* 55, no. 2 (1990): 386.

3   Arrighi, "The Winding Paths of Capital" (2009): 92.

world-system? (Our historical-analytical proposition.) The nature produced through early capitalism and its scientific revolution was not the same nature produced through American-led monopoly capitalism and the scientific management revolution. And the historical nature of the post-World War II golden age differed from the nature produced through neoliberalism and its project to create "life as surplus."[4] Here is a way to engage with both the popular and scholarly debates over socio-ecological limits. But without invoking neo-Malthusian scarcity. To be perfectly clear: There *are* limits. But how do we identify, narrate, and explain the emergence of these limits, historically and in the present conjuncture?

I have done my best to offer a way to answer to these questions. I am convinced—and I hope the reader will be persuaded, at least in part—that the dualisms that have framed the conventional approach to modernity's limits will not suffice. These dualisms are, indeed, part of the problem. This hardly means that we need to give up making distinctions; only that we need a better, more dialectical, more historical, more relational way of making these distinctions. Just as "capital" and "labor" move relationally through value relations in Marx's critique of capitalism, humans and the rest of nature move relationally through the *oikeios*. That relation that cannot be reduced to the interactions of Nature/Society. Through the *oikeios*, we may begin to see the evolving and punctuated developments of class structures, modes of production, and the *technics* of civilizations as environment-making processes. This does not displace our manifold ways of discerning coherence and difference in world history, but rather grounds those ways in the making and unmaking of successive historical natures. In this, our understanding of class, race, gender, the state, culture (and so much more) has been limited by the either/or bias of Cartesian dualism, driving our interpretations of historical change into a Hobson's choice of social reductionism or environmental determinism. Both claims are true. Both are also false.

A more "radically honest" approach, as Raymond Williams might say, recognizes the partial truths—and falsehoods—of both. An effective alternative, moreover, goes beyond saying that Society and Nature matter equally. The categories themselves are fragmented; they preconceptualize reality before it can be studied. If we begin instead with a guiding thread of the double internality—that human organizations internalize and are internalized by the web of life—then we may identify the dominant "bundles" of human and extra-human nature in successive historical systems. The bundles reflect the choices of civilizations in deciding what is—and what is not—valuable. If the Marxist language of a "law of value" seems antiquated today—and there may be a better way to phrase it—all civilizations nevertheless choose to value some relations over others. In

---

4   Cooper, *Life as Surplus* (Seattle: University of Washington Press, 2008).

feudalism, this was land productivity organized through the parcellized sovereignty of feudal lords; in capitalism, it is labor productivity organized through the exploitation of labor-power and the appropriation of Cheap Nature. A sustainable and socialist law of value would privilege the healthy, equitable, and democratic relations of reproduction for *all* nature. Laws of value are therefore important politically, but also help us to discern and to analyze the relevant bundles of human and extra-human nature in historical change. This premise may facilitate a new means of making distinctions without succumbing to the symbolic violence of dualism.

It may also help us to learn more about how capitalism has overcome its recurrent crises historically. At every turn, crisis-resolution has turned on reconfiguring the *oikeios*, and the dialectic of appropriation and capitalization in their qualitative and quantitative dimensions. Such restructuring bundles not only the human and the extra-human, but also the material and the symbolic. The cyclical restructuring of capitalism has unfolded through the premise and project of Cheap Nature—understood as a praxis of external Nature.

The likely demise of Cheap Nature today therefore signals the exhaustion of a civilizational model, punctuated by the rise of negative-value. Capitalism will give way to another model—or models—over the next century. Hence the centrality of the new ontological politics—of food sovereignty, climate justice, de-growth, and cognate movements. Whether or not the exhaustion of the Cheap Nature model leads to something better, or something worse, remains to be seen. But the politics of fear and catastrophism that have permeated Green politics will not produce the clarity necessary to face the challenges ahead. It is in such periods of civilizational crisis—an epochal crisis of capitalism as world-ecology—that such intellectual clarity is most needed, and most influential. In such moments, ideas, too, become material forces.

Perhaps the greatest need for clarity turns on the nature of civilizational limits. At best, the commonplace assertion of Nature as external limit describes a very general tendency. Such assertions cannot explain how capitalism has co-produced limits of its own making through the *oikeios*. Why? Because the dualist conception of limits stops our investigations of capitalism's double internality before they can begin. It prevents us from seeing how human organization emerges and reproduces through environment-making, a process in which a multi-layered nature continually asserts itself, flowing inside and outside the eminently *natural* bodies and relations of humans. Dualism appears to highlight the role of environmental change. But this is a mirage. Because dualism cannot admit social relations as relations of the *oikeios*, it radically understates the centrality of environment-making to human history. The widespread cognitive habit and conceptual practice of referring to "the" environment as an object, rather than a relation governed by the double internality of humanity-in-nature, hides from view the relations—through the *oikeios*—that have enabled, and now increasingly constrain in capitalism today.

THE RISE AND ONGOING DEMISE OF VALUE

Capitalism has exhausted the historical relation that enabled it to appropriate the work of nature with such extraordinary and unprecedented power. The limits to growth faced by capital today are real enough: they are "limits" co-produced through capitalism. The world-ecological limit of capital is capital itself.

What we are seeing today is the "end" of Cheap Nature as a civilizational strategy. It was born, as we have seen, during the long sixteenth century. An ingenious civilizational project has been at the core of this strategy, to construct nature as external to human activity, and thence to mobilize the work of uncommodified human and extra-human natures in service to advancing labor productivity within commodity production. The revolutionary shift in the scale, scope, and speed of landscape and biological transformations in the three centuries after 1450—stretching from Poland to Brazil, from the North Atlantic's cod fisheries to Southeast Asia's spice islands—may be understood in this light. Such transformations were the epoch-making expressions of a new law of value that reconfigured uncommodified human and extra-human natures (slaves, forests, soils) in servitude to labor productivity and the commodity.

This new law of value was quite peculiar. Never before had any civilization negotiated this transition from land productivity to labor productivity as its metric of wealth. This strange metric—value—oriented the whole of west-central Europe towards an equally strange conquest of space. Marx called this strange conquest the "annihilation of space by time," and across the long sixteenth century we can see a new form of time—abstract time—taking shape. While all civilizations in some sense are built to expand across varied topographies—they "pulse"[5]—none represented these topographies as external and progressively abstracted in the ways that dominated the life of a civilization. External nature—Nature with a capital 'N'—was at the heart of early capitalism's geographical praxis. It has remained so ever since.

The early modern transition from land productivity, in manifold "tributary" relations, to labor productivity, in manifold "commodity" relations, emerged through a powerful bundle of processes co-produced by human and extra-human natures. The story of these processes is the subject of voluminous historiographies: of the environment, the economy, territorial states and empires, science and ideas of nature, culture, and much, much more. I have drawn on these

---

5   C. Chase-Dunn and T.D. Hall, *Rise and Demise* (Boulder: Westview, 1997).

historiographies—and many other literatures as well—as best I can, with an eye to showing how one might go about connecting the relations of power and re/ production within a "unified field": the sort of field that is ruled out by dualistic habits of thought and its allied institutional structures. I do not pretend that the models and narratives on offer exhaust the possibilities for elaborating a unified theory—and holistic narrative—of capitalist development. But the approach, pivoting on the *oikeios*, gives us a relational rather than substantialist pivot: a clear alternative to conventional dualisms as well as to network eclecticism.

Capitalism, as project and process, unfolds in and through the *oikeios*: the creative, generative, and multi-layered relation of species and environment. In this, human organization becomes not only a producer but also a product of environmental change, wrapped up in patterns of environment-making. This is the double internality of historical change.

To be sure, humans are distinctive in forming historically specific notions of our place in the web of life. This is the history of ideas of nature, which are in fact ideas of everything that humans do.[6] We are among the planet's more effective "ecosystem engineers"; and even so, our civilizations are made and unmade by the environment-making activities of life. (Does anyone today doubt that disease and climate make history every bit as much as any empire or class or market?) To take this position is to immediately abandon the notion of civilization (or capitalism) *and* environment, and instead re-focus on the idea of civiliza- tions-*in*-nature, on capitalism as environment-making process. These processes include factories no less than forests, homes no less than mines, financial centers no less than farms, cities no less than countrysides.

If environment-making is always co-produced, revealing the adaptability of human organization in its double role as producer and product, the question of nature is still a vexing one. I have tried to break the ice of the frozen history of nature "in general." Nature is general—as noumenon—is always there. But for those committed the histories of humanity-in-nature, it will not do. It will not do any more than "production in general" helps one come to grips with neolib- eral restructuring, flexible accumulation, and the globalization of production. Only a conception of *historical nature* will suffice. In this sense, historical nature operates in a double register, as the field upon which capitalism unfolds—a field whose bounds are subject to revision—and as object. This latter is historical nature as Nature: as resource zone and rubbish bin, as zone of production and reproduction. To engage the problem of *historical natures*—in their manifold layers of time and space—is to depart from the wistful philosophizing that goes with saying humans are a part of nature, and to begin to develop workable analytics. These will allow us to interpret historical change as actively

---

6   Glacken, *Traces on the Rhodian Shore* (1967).

co-produced by humans and the rest of nature. This transition from holistic philosophy to relational history is the core of the world-ecology argument. Crucially, this line of reasoning takes historical nature—as matrix (process) and as object (project)—as something that must be explained through capitalism's world-praxis. For Nature could not be made "cheap" until it was rendered external. Yes, the distinction between human and extra-human natures has a long history that stretches back to Greco-Roman antiquity.[7] But never before had Nature as external object become an organizing principle for a civilization.

Capitalism's basic problem is that capital's demand for Cheap Natures tends to rise faster than its capacity to secure them. The costs of production rise, and accumulation falters. This was recognized by Marx long ago, not only in his "general law" of the "overproduction" of machinery and the "underproduction" of raw materials, but also in his perceptive observations that the bourgeoisie tends to accumulate capital by exhausting "labour-power, in the same way as a greedy farmer snatches more produce from the soil by robbing it of its fertility."[8] The solution? Move to the frontier, so much the better if such frontiers were colonies: thus the salience of Irish workers, Caribbean sugar, Mississippi cotton in Marx's day. For this reason, capital finds itself continually dependent on capitalist power and bourgeois knowledge to locate Natures whose wealth can be mapped, reshaped, and appropriated cheaply.

Is the exhaustion of the historical natures created through neoliberal capitalism a cyclical phenomenon—such as we saw at the end of the late eighteenth century, or during the long 1970s—or is it the end of Cheap Nature? Are we now living through a developmental crisis, one whose contradictions can be fixed through renewed capitalization, rationalization, and dispossession? Or is it, rather, an epochal crisis, one that will compel fundamentally new relations of wealth, power, and nature in the century ahead?

This line of questioning has been marginal in today's proliferating literature on economic and ecological crisis. This may explain some measure of the profound undertheorization of "ecological crisis," and the reluctance of critical scholars to explain nature as constitutive of capital accumulation.

THE LIMITS TO CAPITAL

What would such an explanation—one premised on the co-production of capitalism by humans and the rest of nature—look like? This book has offered one way to answer the question.

---

7   Ibid.
8   Marx, *Capital*, Vol. I (1977), 376.

My argument has focused on two big issues swirling about nature, capital, and limits today. One is historical. The other is conceptual. In the first instance, we must ask whether the peculiar train of events since 2003, when the latest commodity boom began, represents a cyclical or cumulative "end" of the Four Cheaps? (Food, labor-power, energy, and raw materials.) Capitalism since the early nineteenth century has been remarkably adept at overcoming the actual (but temporary) and averting potential (but threatening) bottlenecks relating to the rising price of the Big Four inputs. This capacity to overcome and avert such bottlenecks can be seen in successive epoch-making agricultural revolutions, expansively reproducing the Cheap Food/Labor nexus. England's late eighteenth-century agricultural stagnation and food price woes were resolved through the American farmer's marriage of mechanization and fertile frontiers after 1840. The productivity stagnation of early twentieth-century capitalist agriculture in Western Europe and North America was resolved through successive "Green" revolutions, manifested in the postwar globalization of the hybridized, chemicalized, and mechanized American farm model. From this perspective, we might reasonably call the post-2008 conjuncture as a developmental crisis, one that can be resolved through renewed rounds of commodification, especially, but not only, in agriculture. *However*, as we have seen, the latest wave of capitalist agricultural revolution—agro-biotechnology—has yet to arrest the productivity slowdown. It is therefore also possible that capitalism has entered an era of epochal crisis.

Developmental and epochal crises give expression to the maturing contradictions inscribed in those regimes of value, power, and nature that govern capitalism over the *longue durée*. In place of the converging crises model,[9] we may instead view our era's turbulence as a singular crisis—of capitalism as a way of organizing nature—with manifold expressions. Food and climate, finance and energy represent not multiple, but manifold, forms of crisis emanating from a singular civilizational project: the law of value as a law of Cheap Nature.

This directs our attention to how capitalism goes about forming and re-forming its specific configurations of wealth, power, and nature: not as three independent boxes, but as mutually relational moments in the cumulative and cyclical development of the modern world-system. To pursue this line of inquiry brings us squarely onto the terrain of capitalism's law of value. For it is the emergence, development, and cyclical restructuring of capital, power, and nature that are conditioned decisively by capitalism's value relations.

We might think about value relations in two major ways. The first is value as method. This approach reconstructs historical capitalism through "the

---

9   Cf. Foster, "The Epochal Crisis" (2013).

production and reproduction of real life" as "distinctions within . . . the organic whole."[10] This permits a world-ecological recasting of "nature" and "society" in favor of the contradictory unity: "the production and reproduction of real life." It is a unity that cuts across and destabilizes any *a priori* boundary between human activity and the rest of nature; the "reproduction of real life" includes the extra-human entwined with the human at every step. Taking the production and reproduction of life as our guiding thread allows us to dissolve the divide between the economic and the ecological, in favor of definite historical configurations of human and extra-human natures. Once freed from the fetish of "the economy," we can focus on the relations of power and (re)production that make possible the endless reproduction of value in its double existence: as abstract social nature and abstract social labor.

This latter is socially necessary labor-time. While all species "work" in some fashion, only humans create and labor under socially necessary labor-time. Only humans, and only *some* humans at that. The law of value—not the theory of value, but its actual historical operation—is anthropocentric in a very specific sense. Only human labor-power directly produces value. A tree, or a horse, or a geological vent cannot be paid. And yet, commodified labor-power cannot produce anything without the unpaid work of the horse or the tree. Socially necessary *unpaid* work is the pedestal of socially necessary labor-time.

Unlike the horse or the tree, unpaid human work could be paid. But capitalists do not like to pay their bills, and for good reason. To fully commodify the reproduction of labor-power would do away with the unpaid work that allows accumulation to proceed at acceptable rates of profit. Marxists will sometimes characterize capitalism as a system in which "the bulk of society's work is done by propertyless labourers who are obliged to sell their labour-power."[11] But this is exactly what cannot occur! If the bulk of the work carried out within capitalism were ever to be monetized, the costs of labor-power would soar. Capital accumulation as we have known it would be impossible.

None of this suggests that wage-labor is epiphenomenal. Quite the contrary! Rather, proletarianization may be more adequately understood as a "connective historical process" fundamental to the capitalist world-ecology.[12] In this light, the law of value is not centered on the rise of the modern proletariat as such, but on the uneven globalization of wage-work dialectically joined to the "generalization of its conditions of reproduction."[13] Value, as abstract social labor, works

---

10   F. Engels, "Engels to J. Bloch in Berlin, London, September 21, 1890," *New International* 1, no. 3 (1934): 81–5; Marx, *Grundrisse* (1973), 99–100.

11   E.M. Wood, *The Origin of Capitalism* (London: Verso, 2002), 2.

12   P. McMichael, "Slavery in Capitalism," *Theory and Society* 20, no. 3 (1991): 343.

13   Ibid.

through, not in spite of, its partiality. Life-activity outside commodity production, but articulated with it, is socially necessary unpaid work. Strictly speaking, it cannot be quantified in the same fashion as commodified labor-power because the condition of quantifiable abstract social labor is an even greater mass of unquantifiable work. Unpaid work can—and often is—measured (as in "ecosystem services"); but it cannot be valued.

What capital strives to achieve is the reduction of necessary labor-time. This reduction is intrinsic to capital's existence: hence capitalism's emphasis on labor productivity over land productivity, and capital's mobilization of Cheap Natures in order to make this emphasis possible. The acceleration of landscape change and the emergence of a tentative but tenacious regime of abstract social labor were two sides of the rise of capitalism in the sixteenth century. Abstract social labor could only take shape on the basis of a new, sharply accelerated, relation to the unpaid work of Cheap Nature.

In the conventional narrative, rising labor productivity is a story of technological advance and organizational innovation in industrial production. This is true enough. But is it the whole story? New machinery and organization at the point of production can only advance labor productivity—reducing necessary labor-time over the long run—through new technologies of power that reduce the value-composition of the Big Four inputs. The Four Cheaps could be restored only partly through innovations within established zones of commodity production; historically, they also depended on new strategies of appropriation, on new commodity frontiers. Here we find a systemic connection between the accumulation of capital and the rise of capitalist power in making possible a civilization cohered by the law of value. In order to reduce necessary labor-time, capital sets in motion—and struggles to create, through varied combinations of coercion, consent, and rationalization—a civilization that aims to maximize the unpaid "work" of life outside the circuit of capital, but within reach of capitalist power.

The reduction of socially necessary labor-time through commodification is what I have been calling capitalization; the maximization of unpaid work in service to capitalization, is what I have called appropriation. There is some overlap, to be sure. Where the Cartesian frame presumes separation of humanity and nature, the world-ecology argument presumes a dialectical unity that proceeds from the distinctiveness of humans (among many other species) within the web of life. So our focus is directed towards the ways that capitalization and appropriation work together as patterns and rules of reproducing value and power in the web of life. This gives us a way to identify and to explain patterns of environment-making across the *longue durée* of historical capitalism.

ACCUMULATION CRISES, OR CAPITALISM AS FRONTIER

These patterns of environment-making have turned upon a new kind of geographical expansion. For capitalism is impossible to understand as a closed system; the endless accumulation of capital is the endless internalization of nature. Capitalism is defined by frontier movement. The conceit of early modern cartographic revolutions was to conceive of the earth as abstract space rather than as concrete geographies. The latter, abolished in theory, would continually reassert themselves, as geographical particularities (climates, soils, topographies, diseases) entered into dynamic tension with bourgeois fantasies of abstract space. The great advantage of mapping the world as a grid, and nature as an external object, was that one could appropriate the work of nature in a fashion profoundly efficient for capital accumulation. The very dynamism of capitalist production is unthinkable in the absence of frontier appropriations that allowed more and more materials to flow through a given unit of abstract labor-time: value's self-expanding character depends on an exponential rise in the material volume of production, but without a corresponding rise in the abstract labor implied in such production. This incessant reduction of labor-time can occur only to the extent that the Four Cheaps can be secured through appropriation. This requires the continual enlargement of the geographical arenas for such appropriations. Thus are capital and capitalist power joined in the co-production of Cheap Natures.

For this reason, frontiers are much more central to the expanded reproduction of capital and capitalist power than commonly recognized. When Harvey opines that capitalism, confronting the end of frontiers, might "actively manufacture" such frontiers, he reflects the common sense of the contemporary radical critique. But this is a profound mis-reading.[14] The processes of privatization and finance-led dispossession, insofar as they operate within the domain of capitalized relations, cannot revive accumulation; indeed, these processes worked in the neoliberal era because they were bound to the release of minimally commodified labor-power, food, energy, and raw materials into the circuits of capital.

Depeasantization, the reorientation of peasant agriculture towards the world market, the extraction of abundant energy and mineral wealth—these great movements of modern world history have been frontier movements, some more obvious than others. These movements of appropriation have enlarged the reserve army of labor; expanded food supplies to the world proletariat; directed abundant energy flows to, and boosted labor productivity within, commodity production; and channeled gigantic volumes of raw materials into industrial

---

14 Harvey, *The New Imperialism* (2003), 131.

production. Put simply, the Great Frontier that opened the capitalist epoch did so by making Nature's free gifts—and human natures' too—more or less cheaply available to those with capital and power.

The Great Frontier was inside as well as outside. Frontier appropriations occurred not only on capitalism's outer edges, but also on the "vertical" axis of socio-ecological reproduction, within the heartlands of commodification. Not just colonies, then, but also women's unpaid work became subject to (partial) commodification. Although the horizontal and vertical moments of these frontier appropriations unfolded in distinct geographical zones with specific socio-ecological inflections, they were unified through their relation to the accumulation process. Commodity frontiers worked in both heartlands and hinterlands by appropriating and transferring unpaid work from zones of appropriation, centering on relations of reproduction, and towards zones of commodification. In the heartlands, the appropriation of women's unpaid work was central to the Cheap reproduction of labor-power; in the hinterlands, the appropriation of extra-human natures (forests, soils, mineral veins) was often primary. The secret of the law of value is in this epochal synthesis: of the exploitation of labor-power and the appropriation of the unpaid work/energy. The regime of abstract social labor—premised on socially necessary labor-time—emerged historically, and restructured cumulatively, through the formation of regimes of abstract social nature which made legible new zones of appropriation.

This abstract social nature—a systemic family of processes aimed at rationalizing, simplifying, standardizing, and otherwise mapping the world as external object—is directly constitutive of Cheap Nature. From the sixteenth century, the cascading and converging processes of commodification, capital accumulation, and symbolic innovation constituted a virtuous circle of modern world development. I do not propose a revision of Marx's law of value in a strict sense: the substance of capital is abstract social labor. I *do* propose that we take value relations as a methodological premise focused on the trinity of capital/power/nature and the dialectic of capitalization and appropriation.

From this perspective, value relations are grounded historically in successive configurations of abstract labor and abstract nature. Those configurations are historical natures. Each historical nature, co-produced by the law of value, enables the renewed exploitation of labor-power and the renewed appropriation of life-activity as unpaid work. The appropriation of unpaid work must outstrip the exploitation of labor-power, else the Four Cheaps cannot return, and neither can capitalist prosperity. Abstract social nature names those processes that extend, through new forms of symbolic praxis and knowledge formation, the frontiers of accumulation.

Value is therefore not an economic form with systemic consequences. It is, rather, a systemic relation with a pivotal "economic" expression (abstract social labor). One cannot think about the accumulation of capital without abstract social labor and the struggle to reduce socially necessary labor-time. By the same measure, one cannot think about the accumulation of capital without the symbolic praxis of abstract social nature, allowing for the appropriation of unpaid work on a scale that dwarfs the exploitation of labor-power. Unifying these two moments calls for a mode of inquiry that unifies the circuit of capital and the appropriation of life: a world-ecological framework for interpreting the history of capitalism and value's fluctuating gravities of nature, power, and capital.

The rise of capitalism launched a new way of organizing nature, mobilizing for the first time a metric of wealth premised on labor productivity rather than land productivity. This was the originary moment of today's fast-fading Cheap Nature. This strange law of value, taking shape out of the vast frontier appropriations and productive innovations of the sixteenth century, allowed for capitalism's unusual dynamism: appropriating the whole of nature within its grasp to advance the rate of exploitation. From the 1450s, there commenced a succession of movements of productivity and plunder. These joined the vast appropriation of nature's free gifts with extraordinary technical innovations in production and transport. At a time when Green Thought still confuses the Industrial Revolution with the origins of ecological crisis, this deeper historicization permits an analysis of the *relations* that have proven so dynamic for capitalism. (Indeed, the Industrial Revolution may be taken as a shorthand for the organizational revolution that "fixed" early capitalism's contradictions.)

This transition from land to labor productivity during the early modern era explains much of the revolutionary pace of early modern landscape transformation.[15] The soils and forests of northeastern Brazil, Scandinavia, and Poland were appropriated (and exhausted) in the long seventeenth century; human nature too was freely appropriated (and exhausted), as New World sugar frontiers and African slaving frontiers moved in tandem. Far from being abolished after the eighteenth century, the great waves of accumulation in the long nineteenth and twentieth centuries were equally dependent on appropriation, this time of vast subterranean coal and oil frontiers. These frontiers have always been pivotal to the new "tools of empire" and metropolitan productive capacities that destabilized (and appropriated the labor of) peasant formations from South Asia to southern Italy. In light of this history, we may well ask: Is capitalism today

---

15   Moore, "Ecology and the Rise of Capitalism" (2007); "Madeira, Sugar, and the Conquest of Nature in the 'First' Sixteenth Century, Part I," (2009); "'Amsterdam Is Standing on Norway' Part I"; "'Amsterdam Is Standing on Norway' Part II" (2010); "Madeira, Sugar, and the Conquest of Nature in the 'First' Sixteenth Century, Part II" (2010); "This Lofty Mountain of Silver Could Conquer the Whole World" (2010).

capable of appropriating nature's free gifts on a scale sufficient to launch a new phase of accumulation, or are we witnessing the exhaustion of the productivity and plunder dialectic that has underwritten capital accumulation since the sixteenth century?

Each wave of capitalism depended on great frontier movements, the agrarian counterpart to the spatial and productive "fixes" of capital accumulation in the metropoles. Together these movements of appropriation and capitalization constituted world-ecological revolutions through which new opportunities for peak appropriation were realized, and capital accumulation maximized. These revolutions—and the organizational structures they implied—encompassed innovations in industry and finance no less than in agriculture and resource extraction. These innovations at first liberated accumulation, only to fetter it over time, as the great windfalls of frontier expansion gradually—sometimes rapidly—disappeared: newly proletarianized workers began to organize, farming regions became exhausted, coal seams were mined out. The tendential result has been a lurching movement towards a rising value composition of capital and a declining ecological surplus.

Capitalism's Cheap Nature strategy has aimed at appropriating the biological capacities and geological distributions of the earth in an effort to reduce the value composition of production, thereby checking the tendency towards a falling rate of profit. As opportunities for accumulation by appropriation contract, we would expect to see a profound shift from spatial to temporal fixes, moving from the appropriation of space to the colonization of time. Is this not the greatest strength of neoliberal financialization? By the early twenty-first century, the end of Cheap Nature was in sight. More violence, more biopower, and more guns restored the Four Cheaps for two decades after 1983. But the bloom was off the rose by the turn of the new millennium. Appropriation was faltering. Rising costs of production and extraction in agriculture, energy, and mining began. The price movement was made official by 2003, with the onset of a seemingly endless commodity boom. Labor-power seemed cheap, but here too the Cheap Labor strategy showed signs of wear. Nor did the rising capitalized composition of nature stop there. Appropriation has not only faltered in all the old ways; it now carries forth a new stench of unfathomable toxification: hydro-fracked aquifers, mountaintop removals, the overnight devastation of the Gulf of Mexico.

The problem today is one of capitalism exhausting its *longue durée* ecological regime. That process of getting extra-human natures—and humans too—to work for very low outlays of money and energy is the history of capitalism's great commodity frontiers, and with it, of capitalism's long waves of accumulation. The appropriation of frontier land and labor has been the indispensable condition for great waves of capital accumulation, from Dutch hegemony in the seventeenth century to the rise of neoliberalism in the 1970s and 1980s. The crucial "work" of these commodity frontiers has been unpaid; on that basis, the Cheap Nature strategy has renewed the Four Cheaps.

With frontiers fast closing, that strategy is failing in a double sense. On the one hand, new streams of unpaid work are materializing slowly, if at all. On the other hand, the accumulation of waste and toxification now threatens the unpaid work that *is* being done: this is the transition from surplus-value to nega-tive-value. Climate change is the greatest example here. But it is not the only one. It is increasingly certain that global warming constitutes an insuperable barrier to any new capitalist agricultural revolution—and with it, any return of Cheap Food. From this perspective, the greatest problem of the twenty-first century may well not be one of resource "taps" at all. The end of cheap garbage may loom larger than the end of cheap resources. The shift towards financialization, and the deepening capitalization in the sphere of reproduction, has been a powerful way of postponing the inevitable blowback. It has allowed capitalism to survive. But for how much longer?

Abel, Wilhelm, 129
abstract social labor: and capital accumulation, 305; and frontier, 222; and geographical expansion, 221; and value, 195, 205
abstract social nature: and appropriation of unpaid work, 206; and capital accumulation, 196, 201; and Cheap Nature, 304; emergence of, 203; and labor productivity, 202; and metric system, 203–4; production of, 208; and rise of capitalism, 208–19; and value relations, 206
abstraction, and Netherlands, 210
accumulation. *See* capital accumulation
agency, 36–7
agriculture: alternative farming, 288–92; and capitalism, 242; and cheap food, 68; and class struggle, 247, 288–91; and climate change, 67, 275, 282–4, 307; and crisis, 244; cropland expansion, 254n65, 264;
     crops: cereal, 59, 128n32, 186, 248–50, 254, 256, 259n97, 266, 282, 284; corn, 85, 114, 135, 249–51, 283; maize, 104; soy, 111, 149, 207, 266, 269, 271–3, 282, 284, 286; sugar, 9, 59, 68, 71–2, 99, 107, 111, 144, 146–7, 149, 182–3, 186, 188–9, 212, 231, 245, 254, 273, 299, 306; wheat, 47, 51, 71–2, 128n32, 129, 136, 242, 248–51, 256, 259, 266, 282–3;
     and debt, 258–64; and developmental crisis (1700s), 127–30; and exhaustion, 165; export expansion, 258–60; externalities of, 253; factory farming, 232;
     family farms, 104, 107, 114, 144, 153, 243, 250, 289; disappearance of, 252, 259, 264
fertilizer, 104, 107, 245, 250–2, 254, 255, 266, 275, 279; and feudalism, 126; and fossil fuel, 104; genetically modified (GMO), 207, 270–4, 284–5; global South as world farm, 161;
     industrial, 58, 99–100, 245, 262–4; and capitalization, 114, 146; and ecological surplus, 97–8, 100; and energy use, 252, 254; epochal transition of, 291; and honeybees, 286–7; and industrialization, 247–8; meat-industrial complex, 200, 232–3, 265, 285; and proletarianization, 241–2; and unpaid work, 143–4;
     and labor productivity, 242; and neoliberalism, 243, 258; and oil, 252–3;
     and pesticides, 99, 207, 250–3, 273, 286–7; Agent Orange, 285; DDT, 253; RoundUp Ready, 271, 273–4, 284–5;
     revolution of, 72, 128, 136, 183, 243–4; debt regime, 258–64; in England, 244–6; exhaustion of, 277; Green Revolution, 249–55; in United States, 246–9;
     soil fertility, 107; superweeds, 99, 121, 207, 271–6, 284–6, 291; and toxification, 253, 280; vegetable gardens, 223; and water, 254; and world market, 263–4. *See also* biotechnology; food
Anthropocene, 25, 169–73; argument, 171, 175–6, 179–80, 187; or Capitalocene, 77, 173; and dualism, 171–2, 179; an easy story, 170; periodization of, 169n1
antiobiotic resistance, 285
appropriation, 70; and capitalization, 137, 146, 149, 152, 154–5, 196, 221–2, 221–3, 294, 302; and commodification, 200, 208, 217; and costs, 145–6; definition of, 17; dualism bypassed by, 55, 100; and energy revolution, 135; and exploitation, 54, 95, 102–3, 111, 195, 216, 304; forms of, 146–7; and frontier, 73, 119, 144–5, 148; and innovation, 56–7; neoliberalism as contraction of, 154; peak, 105–7, 137, 139–40, 147–8, 155, 306; and time, 146, 158; and toxification, 307; and unpaid work, 17, 29, 54, 64, 95, 97, 101–2, 119, 141, 149–50, 175, 221, 255, 305; and value, 16, 29, 54, 61
Araghi, Farshad, 241
arithmetic. *See* equivalence; Green Arithmetic; quantitative reasoning
Arrighi, Giovanni, 26, 158, 165, 243; on capital accumulation, 158–63; on capitalism, 119, 294; on financialization, 103. *See also* organizational revolution
atmosphere, as waste dump, 101

Baffes, John, 269
binary. *See* dualism
biosphere, 43–4
biotechnology, 99, 256, 266, 270–4, 277, 284, 287–8, 300. *See also* agriculture; innovation
Birch, Charles, *The Liberation of Life*, 23
Bois, Guy, 126–7
botany, 212–13; Kew Gardens, 62, 117, 213
boundary maintenance, 17–18
Bourdieu, Pierre, 178
Braudel, Fernand, 74, 117, 199, 244
Brenner, Robert, 257
Bunker, Stephen G., 180
Burkett, Paul, *Marx and Nature*, 83–4

capital: "blood into capital" (Marx), 14, 221; and capitalism, 278; and control, 274–5; and life, 65; limits to, 30, 111, 161–2, 164–5, 278, 281, 297
capital accumulation: and abstract social labor, 305; and abstract social nature, 196, 201; Arrighi on, 158–63; and capitalization, 111; and Cheap Nature, 85, 103, 118–19, 191, 195; and crisis, 91, 141–2; and dualism, 2, 19; and ecological surplus, 144, 157; and Four Cheaps, 103, 118–19; and frontier, 115, 147, 208, 307; and historical nature, 151, 161, 196; and internalization, 101, 303; and modernity, 95; and proletarianization, 221, 301–2; revolt against, 207–8; and space, 160–1, 191; and time, 160; as transformation of Earth, 195; and unpaid work, 96, 98, 208, 301; and value, 54
capitalism: and agriculture, 242; and capital, 278; and climate change, 276, 291; collapse of, 86; contradictions of, 281; and crisis, 77, 80, 91; and double internality, 18; and dualism, 40, 69, 76, 100, 208; as ecological regime, 158; and ecological surplus, 118; and economics, 206–7, 218; emergence of, 126; and environment-making, 179; and exhaustion, 228, 306–7; and flexibility, 66, 73; flexibility of, 30, 66, 73, 86, 117, 160, 163, 229–30, 294; and fossil fuel, 198; and frontier, 63, 101, 107, 149, 303; and innovation, 16; and internalization, 101; and labor productivity, 71; limits of, 109, 123;

and nature, 2, 13, 18–19, 26–7, 30, 39, 59, 78, 86–7, 104, 112, 125, 193, 199, 255, 305; in/finite demands/resources, 112–13;
and nature-in-general, 116; phases of, 73, 113, 117–19, 126–7, 164, 211; as planetary system, 137; and reproduction, 230;
rise of, 182; and abstract social nature, 208–19;
and technology, 156; and time, 97, 116, 190, 231; transformations from, 183–90; transition to, 59–60; and true costs, 145; Two Century model, 92, 175, 181–2; "undermines soil and worker," 26, 228; and unpaid work, 54, 64, 69, 302; and value, 51–2, 68, 100; and web of life, 43, 60, 123, 174, 179; and world-ecology, 3–4, 8n15, 13–14, 45, 86
capitalization: and appropriation, 137, 146, 149, 152, 154–5, 196, 221–2, 221–3, 294, 302; and ecological surplus, 164; and exhaustion, 117, 123; and historical nature, 153, 294; and industrial agriculture, 114, 146; and labor productivity, 217;
of nature, 97, 99, 106, 111–14, 117, 141, 143–4, 156–7, 252; corrosiveness of, 114–15; explanation of, 114; and world-ecological revolutions, 113, 117, 153, 155, 164;
and underproduction, 114; and unpaid work, 114, 118
Capitalocene, 77, 173
Capra, Fritjof, *The Web of Life*, 3
Cartesian thought. *See* Descartes; dualism
cartography. *See* mapping
cereal, 59, 128n32, 186, 248–50, 254, 256, 259n97, 266, 282, 284
change, 34, 299; and crisis, 79; and dualism, 41; and environment-making, 82, 174; and language, 78; unsavory undercurrent to literature on, 196
Cheap Energy, 85, 92, 99, 104–6, 108–9, 111, 132–3, 143, 146, 154, 158, 252, 254, 266–7, 270; and economy, 109. *See also* energy
Cheap Food, 54, 68, 72–3, 78, 87, 92, 103, 106–7, 131–2, 153, 173, 241–4, 246–7, 249–50, 255–8, 265–71, 287, 291–2, 300, 307; and agricultural revolution, 128; and debt regime, 261–3; definition

of, 241; end of, 265–70; and Green Revolution, 250; and modernity, 241, 292; and proletarianization, 147. *See also* agriculture; food

Cheap Labor, 236–40

Cheap Money, 53n5, 107

Cheap Nature: and abstract social nature, 304; and appropriation, 17, 29; and capital accumulation, 85, 103, 118–19, 191, 195; conditions of, 54; and dualism, 293; exhaustion of, 16, 108–9, 112–13, 237, 241, 296–7, 299, 306; and frontier, 87, 155; and industrial production, 93; and industrial revolutions, 111; and innovation, 226; and labor productivity, 62, 192; and landscape transformation, 217; and law of value, 14; origins of, 63; and peak appropriation, 147; and pesticides, 207; production of, 53, 64; and space-time, 61–2. *See also* nature

civilization: collapse of, 86; and internalization, 101; and *oikeios*, 123; and value, 174

Clark, Gregory, 134

class formation, and primitive accumulation, 98

class struggle, 55, 207, 238; and agriculture, 247, 288–91; and time, 234

classification, 152, 213

climate change, 29–30, 34, 36–8, 85, 169, 173, 280–1; and agriculture, 67, 275, 282–4, 307; and capitalism, 276, 291; and crisis, 79; and *oikeios*, 38

clocks, 189, 229, 233–5

coal, 44, 54, 66, 71, 85, 87, 92, 102, 106, 128, 131–2, 134–7, 145, 147–9, 151, 155–6, 163, 170, 172–3, 176–7, 179–80, 187, 198, 227, 281, 306

Cobb, John B., *The Liberation of Life*, 23

collapse, 86–7

Columbian Exchange, 42, 187, 278

commodification, 95, 192, 207; and appropriation, 200, 208, 217; and food, 228

commodity boom, 27, 237–8, 250, 257, 267–70, 300, 306; and neoliberalism, 241

consumer revolution, 143

correspondence project, 207, 235

costs: of antibiotic resistance, 285; and appropriation, 145–6; of energy, 104, 107–9, 113, 148–9, 268–9, 276, 281;

externalization of, 101, 161–2, 253, 278; of pollution, 228; of production, 120, 268–9, 273–5, 277, 282–3, 299, 306; true, and capitalism, 145

cotton, 135, 155

crisis: and agriculture, 244; and capital accumulation, 91, 141–2; and capitalism, 77, 80, 91; and change, 79; and clarity, 296; and climate change, 79; conceptualization of, 169, 173; converging crises, 2, 40; developmental, 124–5, 164, 299–300; and agriculture (1700s), 127–30; and world ecological revolutions, 141

ecological, 27, 30, 41, 80, 125, 127, 135, 150, 175n21, 177, 179, 294, 299, 305; epochal, 27, 125–7, 182, 299; and exhaustion, 159, 162, 226–7; and nature, 127; and neoliberalism, 165, 237–8, 241, 270; as opportunity, 85; and overaccumulation, 226–7; and overproduction, 137; and perception, 3; signal, 1, 226, 237–8, 241, 270; singular, 300; world-ecological, 177, 179

Crosby, Alfred W., 42

cultural fix, 200–1

DDT, 253

debt, 258–64

Deepwater Horizon, 149

Deere, John, 247

deforestation, 182, 184–5, 261, 294

depletion, 105–6, 109, 278; and exhaustion, 225; and scarcity, 109

Descartes, René, 19–20, 63, 171

dialectics, and object, 75

disease, 285

DNA, 212

double internality, 1, 5, 13, 48, 77, 201, 276, 295–6; and capitalism, 18; as internalization, 78–9

drought, 275, 283–4

dualism: and Anthropocene, 171–2, 179; appropriation transcends, 55, 100; and capital accumulation, 2, 19; and capitalism, 40, 69, 76, 100, 208; and change, 41; and Cheap Nature, 293; critique of, 28; and Descartes, 19–20; and environmental history, 40; and Green Thought, 22, 39, 176, 225; Hegel on, 1; and history, 123n21, 296; and industrialization, 176; and language, 5,

134; and limits, 295; and metabolism, 75–8, 80–1, 84, 225; Nature/Society, 1–2, 4, 6–7, 9, 13–23, 25, 27, 29, 33; and *oikeios*, 12; and periodization, 175; rejected despite vocabulary, 33–5; and relations, 298; and scientific revolution, 19; as substance over relations, 7, 19, 52, 106, 119, 124, 178, 195; and value, 52, 86; and web of life, 30; and work, 230

Earth: capital accumulation as transformation of, 195; as resource supply center, 212; toxification of, 281

ecological crisis, 27, 30, 41, 80, 125, 127, 136, 150, 175*n*21, 177, 179, 294, 299, 305

ecological regime, capitalism as, 158

ecological surplus, 95–8, 100, 113, 137, 139; and capital accumulation, 144, 157; and capitalism, 118; and capitalization, 164; decline of, 97, 107, 226–9, 235, 237; and fossil fuel, 145; and Four Cheaps, 96, 141; future of, 165; and Green Revolution, 254; and innovation, 96; and unpaid work, 106, 117; and world-ecological revolutions, 149

ecology, and value, 83–4

economic downturn (1974–1975), 257, 260

economics, and capitalism, 206–7, 218

economy: and Cheap Energy, 109; debt and agriculture, 258–64; and environment, 2, 294; Great Boom, exhaustion of, 85; and reproduction, 301; and value, 305

ecosystem services, 64

energy: and agriculture, 252, 254; consumption increase, 58; cost increase, 104, 107–9, 113, 148–9, 268–9, 276, 281; Deepwater Horizon explosion, 149; and entropy, 97; EROCI, 96, 106–8; EROI, 95–6, 106; fracking, 149, 228, 307; and labor productivity, 104, 147–8; quantification of, 106; revolution of modernity, 131–6; and toxification, 281. *See also* Cheap Energy; coal; oil

Engels, Friedrich, 36

entropy, 97

environment: and economy, 2, 294; as external, 208–9; as factory, 232, 298; and Green Thought, 34, 39

environment-making, 11–12, 21, 45, 79; and Anthropocene, 172; and capitalism,

179, 219; and change, 82, 174; and dualism, 296; and geographical expansion, 303; and humanity, 298; and reproduction, 127

environmental history, 11–12, 39–40, 42, 57; and dualism, 40; and modernity, 293

environmental movements, 228

epistemic rift, 76, 78, 86

equivalence, 206–7

exhaustion, 68, 120–4; and agriculture, 165, 249, 277; and capitalism, 228, 306–7; and capitalization, 117, 123; of Cheap Nature, 16, 108–9, 112–13, 237, 241, 296–7, 299; and crisis, 159, 162, 226–7; and depletion, 225; and financialization, 227, 307; of frontier, 165; of Great Boom, 85; and innovation, 115; and *oikeios*, 123; and relations, 124, 162; and resource depletion, 157; and underproduction, 121; and unpaid work, 68, 225; of workers, 224–5, 228, 235. *See also* costs; deforestation; depletion; limits

exploitation, 15, 68, 70; and appropriation, 54, 95, 102–3, 111, 195, 216, 304; and frontier, 192; and value, 16, 54; and wage-work, 64

externalities, 101; of agriculture, 253; nature as, 2, 17, 19, 30, 47, 61–2, 77, 86, 181, 192, 213, 218, 294, 296–7, 299

extraction, 120–2

feminism, 52–3, 64, 232. *See also* gender; women

fertilizer, 104, 107, 245, 250–2, 254, 256, 266, 276, 279. *See also* pesticides

feudalism, 125–7, 146, 202, 233–4, 296

financialization, 103–5, 148–9, 269; and exhaustion, 227, 307; and food, 270; and profit, falling rate of, 159; and time, 306; and world ecological revolution, 161–2

flexibility, 30, 66, 73, 86, 117, 160, 163, 229–30, 294

food: cheap, 73, 103–4; and class struggle, 288–91; and commodification, 228; convenience eating, 231; "edible foodlike substances," 289; and energy, 252; expenditures, 252, 257; and financialization, 270; and honeybees, 286–7; and Nature/Society dualism, 47; and oil, 252; prices, 128–31, 136, 250, 255–6, 258, 264–5, 267, 269; and productivity revolution, 72; self-sufficiency declining, 262; sovereignty, 290, 296; transformation of diets, 186; and women, 231. *See also* agriculture; Cheap Food

food justice movement, 277, 288

Fordism, 15, 23, 96, 102, 154

fossil fuel: and agriculture, 104; and capitalism, 198; and ecological surplus, 145; fetishism of, 177; and unpaid work, 152. *See also* oil

Foster, John Bellamy, 80–4, 86; *Marx's Ecology*, 84

Foucault, Michel, 57, 216

Four Cheaps, 17, 53–4, 62–3, 67, 73, 96, 101–3, 111–12, 114–15, 117–8, 124, 141, 150–1, 155, 164, 175, 191, 201, 208, 241, 268, 270, 278, 300, 302; and abstract social nature, 208; and capital accumulation, 103, 118–19; and crisis of exhaustion, 226–7; and ecological surplus, 96, 141; erosion of, 241, 300, 305; and frontier, 115; and limits, 101

fracking, 149, 228, 307

frontier: and abstract social labor, 222; and appropriation, 73, 119, 144–5, 148; and capital accumulation, 115, 147, 208, 307; and capitalism, 63, 101, 107, 149, 303; and Cheap Nature, 87, 155; closure of, 238–9, 276, 306–7; constitution of, 195; and consumption, 175; and control, 274–5; exhaustion of, 227; and exploitation, 192; Great Frontier, 84–5, 87, 304; exhaustion of, 165; and labor productivity, 190 and industrial agriculture, 248; Marx on, 60, 66; and raw material, 304; and unpaid work, 63, 66; and violence, 157; waste, 84, 101, 278, 280; and women, 239–40

gender, 134, 199, 216. *See also* feminism; women

geographical expansion, 12, 54, 58, 61, 63, 66, 68, 83, 95–6, 98, 102, 107, 126, 138–9, 144, 155, 157–9, 161, 182, 186, 208, 221, 226, 244, 252–4, 280, 303–4; and abstract social nature, 221; and environment-making, 303

geology, 44, 179–80

global warming. *See* climate change

God-trick, 62, 86

Gould, Stephen Jay, 181

Gowan, Peter, 262

Green Arithmetic, 2, 22, 25, 33–5, 41, 82, 170, 172, 181; and crisis, 80; geometry, 214; limits of quantification, 106; and Marx, 80

Green Revolution (agriculture), 249–55, 266; accomplishments of, 250; and ecological surplus, 254; and energy use, 253–4; and toxification, 253, 280

Green Thought, 3, 6–7, 9, 19, 24, 170–1, 175; defining feature of, 5–6; and dualism, 22, 39, 176, 225; emergence of, 34; and environment, 34, 39; on industrial revolution, 177, 305; and language, 33–5; and metabolism, 75; and nature-in-general, 19; and *oikeios*, 9

Gurian-Sherman, Doug, 271

Haraway, Donna, 23, 35n6

Harvey, David, 158, 160, 164; on frontier, 303; "The Nature of Environment," 23; on spatial fix, 163

health, 226, 253, 273, 279, 285; mental, 225

Hegel, G.W.F.: on dualism, 1; on value, 52

hegemonies, world, 162–3, 244

historical nature, 12, 19, 29, 112, 116–17, 150, 198–9, 295, 298–9, 305; and capital accumulation, 151, 161, 196; and capitalization, 153, 294; and neoliberalism, 164

history: and double internality, 5; and dualism, 123n21, 296

Hochschild, Arlie, 237, 239

holism, 4, 9, 24, 178, 209, 277

honeybees, 284–5

Hribal, Jason, 65

humanity: and environment-making, 298; and nature, 5–6, 21–2, 26–7, 49, 171–3, 176, 182, 211; -in-nature, 1, 3–6, 12–13, 22–4, 28, 34–5, 42, 49, 75–8, 81–2, 165, 170, 180, 192, 195, 197, 297–8;

and nature and civilizational collapse, 86; dualism rejected despite vocabulary, 33–5

and *oikeios*, 46; as species-environment relation, 11; and substantialism, 178; and web of life, 12, 78; and world-ecology, 82

industrial agriculture. *See* agriculture, industrial

industrial revolution, 102, 155, 173, 245; and Cheap Nature, 111; Green Thought on, 177, 305; and periodization, 175; and quantitative reasoning, 181; second, 138; and unpaid work, 227

industrialization: and dualism, 176; and Four Cheaps, 227; and industrial agriculture, 247–8; and modernity, 176–7; and nature, 180; two moments of, 187

information technology, 227, 238

innovation, 15–16, 54, 70–1, 91, 96, 115, 118, 121, 132, 136, 138, 142–3, 150–2, 155–6, 158–61, 163–5, 188, 213, 217, 226, 243, 246, 248, 302, 305–6; and appropriation, 56–7;
     and capitalism, 16; rise of, 208–19
     and Cheap Nature, 226; clocks, 189, 229, 233–5; and ecological surplus, 96; and exhaustion, 115; and extraction, 121; mapping, 17, 20, 62, 67, 70–3, 79, 86, 98, 106, 118, 131, 150–2, 155, 192, 196–7, 201–6, 209, 212, 214–15, 217–19, 218, 222, 299, 303–4; metric system, 203–4; and modernity, 197; organizational revolution, 159–64, 243, 305; railroads, 59, 71, 103, 134–7, 153, 226, 246; Renaissance perspective, 70, 214, 235;
     scientific revolutions, 9, 17–19, 21, 36, 56, 62, 73, 94, 96, 101, 113, 118, 125, 150, 152, 154, 197, 201–2, 295; and capitalism, rise of, 208–9, 211, 213; and dualism, 19; and nature, 211
     steamships, 134–7, 153, 246; and unpaid work, 155; and value, 191, 305. See also geographical expansion

internalization, 78–9, 101, 144, 276; and capital accumulation, 101, 303

Kew Gardens, 62, 117, 211

knowledge: and capitalism, 205; and classification, 152, 213; and mapping, 210; production of, 18, 20, 25, 196–7, 218

Kosek, Jake, 286

Kosík, Karel, 75

labor-power: and nature, 230; reproduction of, 221–30; and unpaid work, 230. See also Cheap Labor

labor productivity: advancement of, 16, 120, 122, 188–90; and agricultural

revolution, 248–9, 251; and agriculture, 242; and capitalism, 71; and capitalization, 217; and Cheap Energy, 104; and Cheap Nature, 62, 192; definition of, 15; and energy, 104, 134, 147–8; land productivity succeeded by, 51, 58–9, 107, 129, 173, 189, 202, 216, 219, 233–4, 296–7, 302, 305; and nature, 140; origins of, 234; and profit, falling, 154–5; and time, 231; and unpaid work, 71, 102. See also Cheap Labor

land productivity, labor productivity succeeds, 51, 58–9, 107, 129, 173, 189, 202, 216, 219, 233–4, 296–7, 302, 305

landscape, transformation of, 9, 57, 59–60, 62, 67, 146, 173–4, 179, 182, 186–7, 189, 191, 213, 217, 235, 287, 297, 302, 305

language, 4–5; and change, 78; distinctions, 22; and dualism, 5, 134; dualism rejected despite vocabulary, 33–5; and Green Thought, 33–5, 39; vocabulary, 23

Lefebvre, Henri, 10

life: and capital, 65; patenting of, 212; reproduction of, 301; and value, 100

limits, 60, 80, 84, 86–7; to capital, 30, 111, 161–2, 164–5, 278, 281, 297; of capitalism, 109, 123; and dualism, 295; eco-historical, 164–5; and Four Cheaps, 101; to growth, 86, 101, 109, 123, 127, 164, 297; and nature, 296; of quantification, 106; and web of life, 123

Linnaeus, 152, 213

Lohmann, Larry, 38n13

machines, 150–1, 177

Malm, Andreas, 177

Malthus, 92

mapping, 17, 20, 62, 67, 70–3, 79, 86, 98, 106, 118, 131, 150–2, 155, 192, 196–7, 201–6, 209, 212, 214–15, 217–19, 218, 222, 299, 303–4; and capital accumulation, 303; and knowledge, 210. See also frontier; geographical expansion; landscape; space

Marx, Karl: "annihilation of space by time," 10, 61, 153, 231–3, 297; on appropriation, 17; "blood and dirt," 246; "blood into capital," 14, 221; Capital, 224; on capital accumulation, 91; ecological thought of, 80–2; on frontier, 60, 66; on humanity and nature, 21–2; on labor,

221, 223; on language, 4; on limits, 162; on manufacturing, 189; on metabolism, 45, 75; "modes of life," 36, 64; on nature as external, 46; and primitive accumulation, 98, 224; on profit, falling, 141–3; on relations, 22, 25–6, 44, 145, 295; on scarcity, 92–3; on soil fertility, 107, 219; on technology, 150–1; on underproduction, 93, 97, 120, 137, 280, 299; on value, 51–2, 57–8, 60–1, 63, 65, 70, 83, 143, 195, 205–6, 304; on working day, 66–8, 146, 195, 222, 224, 230. *See also* soil

McMichael, Philip, 294

meat-industrial complex, 200, 232–3, 265, 285

meat packing, 232–3, 265, 284

Meillassoux, Claude, 221

mental health, 225

Mercator, Gerardus, 215

metabolism, 45, 80; and dualism, 75–8, 80–1, 84, 225; Marx on, 45, 75; metabolic rift, 75–7, 81–4; metabolic shift, 15, 76, 83–4; singular, 83, 86, 294; and value, 81; and work, 230

metric system, 201–2

Mitchell, Timothy, 205, 211

modernity: and boom of economic prosperity, 85; and boundary maintenance, 17–18; and capital accumulation, 95; and Cheap Food, 241, 292; and collapse, 87; and dualism, 295; energy revolution of, 132–6; and environmental history, 293; and industrialization, 176–7; and innovation, 197; origins of, 169, 172–3, 175; violence of, and dualism, 4

Monsanto, RoundUp Ready, 271, 273–4, 284–5

Mumford, Lewis, 176–7

nature, 85–6; and capitalism, 2, 13, 18–19, 26–7, 30, 39, 59, 78, 86–7, 104, 112, 125, 193, 199, 255, 305; in/finite demands/resources, 112–13; capitalization of, 97, 99, 106, 111–14, 117, 141, 143–4, 156–7, 252; corrosiveness of, 114–15; explanation for, 114; and world-ecological revolutions, 113, 117, 153, 164; and crisis, 127; definition of, 12; as external, 2, 17, 19, 30, 33, 46–7, 61–2, 77, 86, 181, 192, 213, 218, 294, 296–7;

299; -in-general, 19, 29, 44, 115–16, 151, 298; as God-trick, 62, 86; and humanity, 5–6, 21–2, 26–7, 49, 171–2, 171–3, 176, 182, 211; and civilizational collapse, 86; dualism rejected despite vocabulary, 33–5; and industrialization, 180; and labor, 140, 230; and limits, 296; as matrix, 197; and *oikeios*, 48; production of, 79; and scientific revolutions, 211; and time, 154; and unpaid work, 62; and value, 56, 191. *See also* Cheap Nature; historical nature

Nature/Society, 1–2, 4, 6–7, 9, 13–23, 25, 27, 29, 33, 39, 43, 47–8, 84, 180, 196–7, 201, 232; and metabolism, 75–8, 80; and modernity, 4

neoliberalism: and agriculture, 243, 258; and Cheap Labor, 236; and commodity boom, 241; as contraction of appropriation, 154; and crisis, 165, 237–8, 241, 270; and debt regime, 258–64; and historical nature, 164; and scientific revolutions, 211–12. *See also* financialization

Netherlands, and abstraction, 210

Nixon, Richard, 257

object, 18, 21, 23, 27–8, 33–4, 36, 75–6, 100, 112, 116, 198–9, 205–9, 296, 299, 303–4; and dialectics, 75

oikeios, 35–6, 41–2, 44–6, 49; and civilization, 123; and climate change, 38; definition of, 4, 8–10; and dualism, 12; and exhaustion, 123; and Green Thought, 9; and humanity, 46; as limit of capitalism, 109; and nature, 48

oil, 36, 54, 66, 71, 85, 87, 96, 102, 104–9, 127, 138, 147, 151, 154, 156, 163, 226–7, 236, 257, 264, 268–9, 281, 306; and agriculture, 252–3; Deepwater Horizon explosion, 149; exploration and production, 108; and food, 252; fracking, 149, 228, 307; price vs. production cost, 107; production costs of, 148–9; shale, 107–8, 144; and unpaid work, 71. *See also* energy

organizational revolution, 159–64, 243, 305

overaccumulation crisis, 226–7

overproduction, 299; and crisis, 137; transition to, 137; and underproduction, 136, 138

Parenti, Christian, 38*n*13
peak appropriation, 105–7, 137, 139–40, 147–8, 155, 306; and Cheap Nature, 147; and quantification, 106; and relations, 140; and unpaid work, 139
perception, and crisis, 3
Perelman, Michael, 93
periodization, 113, 117–19, 173; or Anthropocene, 169*n*1; and dualism, 175
perspective, 70; Renaissance, 70, 211, 235
pesticides, 99, 207, 250–3, 273, 286–7; Agent Orange, 285; and Cheap Nature, 207; DDT, 253; RoundUp Ready, 271, 273–4, 284–5
Pickles, John, 214
pollution, 228. *See also* toxification
Pomeranz, Kenneth, 245–6
power, and production, 176–7
primitive accumulation, 9, 19, 27, 48, 62, 67, 71*n*62, 73, 95, 98, 103, 129, 134–5, 150, 152, 179, 197, 203, 217–18, 224, 246; and class formation, 98
printing press, 188
privatization, 303
production: costs of, 120, 268–9, 273–5, 276, 282–3, 299, 304; and power, 176–7
profit: falling rate of, 141–3, 236, 255; and financialization, 159; and labor productivity, 154–5
proletarianization, 99, 133; and capital accumulation, 221, 301–2; and Cheap Food, 147; and industrial agriculture, 241–2; and neoliberalism, 237; and surplus value, 222; and unpaid work, 223

quantitative reasoning, 106, 181, 213–14

railroads, 59, 71, 103, 134–7, 153, 226, 246
raw materials, 131–3, 155, 158, 163, 257, 262, 268, 303–4; and frontier, 304
relations, 5, 7–8, 11, 13, 45–7, 173, 176, 179–80; and dualism, 298; and exhaustion, 124, 162; Marx on, 22, 25–6, 36, 44, 145, 295; and peak appropriation, 140; and substance, 7, 19, 52, 106, 119, 124, 178, 195; value-, 21, 28, 44, 52, 54–7, 63, 65, 68–9, 71, 73, 81, 83, 85–6, 92, 94, 100, 102, 116, 137, 150, 174, 191, 195, 201, 205–6, 217, 219, 225, 292, 295, 301, 304
Renaissance perspective, 70, 214, 235

reproduction: and capitalism, 230; and environment-making, 127; of labor-power, 221–30; of life, 301; and unpaid work, 226, 228
resources, 197–8; depletion, 157
revolt, 207–8
RoundUp Ready, 271, 273–4, 284–5

Sayer, Derek, 21
scarcity, 92–3, 105; and depletion, 109
scientific revolutions, 9, 17–19, 21, 36, 56, 62, 73, 94, 96, 101, 113, 118, 125, 150, 152, 154, 197, 201–2, 295; and capitalism, rise of, 208–9, 211, 213; and dualism, 19; and nature, 211; and neoliberalism, 211–12
Scott, James C., 218
Seccombe, Wally, 229–30
shale oil, 107–8, 144
slave trade, 9, 70, 147, 183, 215, 224, 306; standard slave, 215
soil, 26, 48, 51, 59, 63, 68, 70–1, 104, 106–7, 111, 152–3, 157, 174, 219, 224–5, 228, 245, 247, 249, 263, 293, 299, 305
soy, 111, 149, 205, 268, 270–3, 282, 284, 285
space, 10–11; annihilation of, by time, 10, 61, 153, 231–3, 297; and appropriation, 146, 158; and capital accumulation, 160–1, 191; and capitalism, 190; and capitalization, 114, 116; and Cheap Nature, 61–2; homogeneity of, 56–7; and metric system, 203; production of, 59; spatial fix, 163; -time compression, 233; transformation of, 214; and value, 192, 297. *See also* frontier; geographical expansion; landscape; mapping
spatial fix, 208, 306
steamships, 134–7, 153, 246
substance, and relations, 7, 19, 52, 106, 119, 124, 178, 195
sugar, 9, 59, 68, 71–2, 99, 107, 111, 144, 146–7, 149, 182–3, 186, 188–9, 212, 231, 245, 254, 273, 299, 306
superweeds, 99, 121, 207, 271–6, 284–6, 291
surplus capital, 113
surplus value, 15–16; and proletarianization, 222
sustainability, 296
symbolic power, 205

taxonomy, 152, 213
Taylorism, 187, 202

technics, 59, 70, 71, 100, 148, 150–1, 156, 187, 190–1, 204, 215, 222, 234–5, 293; Mumford on, 176–7

technology: and capitalism, 156; information technology, 227, 238; Marx on, 150–1. *See also* innovation

Theophrastus, 8, 35, 41

Third World, 260–1

Thompson, E.P., 231

time, 231–5; as annihilation of space, 10, 61, 153, 231–3, 297; and appropriation, 146, 158; and capital accumulation, 160; and capitalism, 97, 116, 190, 231; and capitalization, 114, 116; and Cheap Nature, 61–2; and class struggle, 234; and clocks, 189, 229, 233–5; and financialization, 306; homogeneity of, 56–7; is money, 234; and nature, 154; -space compression, 233; standardization of, 234; Taylorism, 187, 202; turnover, 232; and value, 192. *See also* periodization

toxification, 48, 52, 98, 149, 228, 253, 261, 273–6, 278, 280–1, 285–7, 307; and agriculture, 253, 280; and appropriation, 307; and energy, 281; pollution, 228

underproduction, 91–4, 97, 104; and capitalization, 114; and crisis, 91–2; and exhaustion, 121; and financialization, 105; Marx on, 93, 97, 120, 137, 280, 299; and overaccumulation, 91; and overproduction, 136, 138; and wage-work, 92

unpaid work: and appropriation, 17, 29, 54, 64, 95, 97, 101–2, 119, 141, 149–50, 175, 221, 255, 305; and capital accumulation, 96, 98, 208, 301; and capitalism, 54, 64, 69, 302; and capitalization, 114, 118; and ecological surplus, 106, 117; and exhaustion, 68, 225; and fossil fuel, 152; and frontier, 63, 66; and industrial agriculture, 143–4; and industrial revolution, 227; and innovation, 155; and labor-power, 230; and labor productivity, 71, 102; and nature, 62; and negative-value, 277; and oil, 71; and peak appropriation, 139; and proletarianization, 223; quantity of, 64; and reproduction, 226, 228; and value, 54, 64–5, 100, 102; and wage-work, 99, 102, 216; and waste,

280; and women, 65, 133, 219, 223, 229–30, 239–40, 304

value, 13, 73–4; and abstract social nature, 206; and space, 297; and appropriation, 16, 29, 54, 61; and capitalism, 51–2, 100; and civilization, 174; and dualism, 52, 86; and ecology, 83–4; and economy, 305; and exploitation, 16; and innovation, 191, 305;
law of, 14, 51–8, 66–8, 70, 191–2, 208, 295–7, 300–2, 304–5; and capitalism, rise of, 208–9, 213, 216, 218–19; planetary influence, 137; and turnover time, 232
and life, 100; Marx on, 51–2, 57–8, 60–1, 63, 65, 70, 83, 143, 195, 205–6; and metabolism, 81; and nature, 56, 191; negative-, 275–9, 281, 284–5, 291–2, 296, 307; and revolutions, 191; significance of, 204–5; and space, 192, 297; substance of, 53, 65–7, 195; substance vs. relations of, 195; and sustainability, 296; and unpaid work, 54, 64–5, 100, 102; use-, 63, 149–50; and waste, 280; vs. wealth, 52, 57; and web of life, 191. *See also* surplus value

value relations, 21, 28, 44, 52, 54–7, 63, 65, 68–9, 71, 73, 81, 83, 85–6, 92, 94, 100, 102, 116, 137, 150, 174, 191, 195, 201, 205–6, 217, 219, 225, 292, 295, 301, 304

Via Campesina, 289

Volcker, Paul, 260

von Tunzelmann, G.N., 133

wage-work, 16; and exploitation, 64; nature sacrificed for, 87; and underproduction, 92; and unpaid work, 99, 102, 216

Wallerstein, Immanuel, 26, 293

waste, 84, 101, 276, 278, 280, 307

water, 254

web of life, 3, 6; and capitalism, 43, 60, 123, 174, 179; and civilization, 44; and dualism, 30; and humanity, 12, 78; and limits, 123; and value, 191

Webb, Walter Prescott, 84–5

Weiner, Douglas R., 40

wheat, 47, 51, 71–2, 128n32, 129, 136, 242, 248–51, 256, 259, 266, 282–3

White, Richard, *The Organic Machine*, 14–15

Williams, Raymond, 123, 293

women, 52, 54; and food, 231; and unpaid work, 65, 133, 219, 223, 229–30, 239–40, 304. *See also* feminism; gender
work/energy, 14–15, 29
workers, exhaustion of, 224–5, 228, 235
working day, Marx on, 66–8, 146, 195, 222, 224
world-ecological revolutions: and capitalization of nature, 113, 117, 153, 155, 164; and developmental crises, 141; and ecological surplus, 149; and

financialization, 161–2; functions of, 151; and use-value, 150
world-ecology, 179, 293, 299; and capitalism, 3–4, 8n15, 13–14, 45, 86; phases of, 118
challenge of, 48; core of, 28; distinctiveness of, 42; and humanity, 82; socialist, 289
world hegemony, 163–4, 244
world market, and agriculture, 263–4
Worster, Donald, 33
Wright, Melissa, 229